RACE, EMPIF
WORLD WA

M000250466

This volume brings together an international cast of scholars from a variety of disciplines to examine the racial and colonial aspects of the First World War and show how issues of race and empire shaped its literature and culture. The global nature of the First World War is fast becoming the focus of intense enquiry. This book analyses European discourses about colonial participation and recovers the war experience of different racial, ethnic and national groups, including the Chinese, Vietnamese, Indians, Maori, West Africans and Jamaicans. It also investigates testimonial and literary writings – from war diaries and nursing memoirs to Irish, New Zealand and African American literature – and analyses processes of memory and commemoration in the former colonies and dominions. Drawing upon archival, oral, literary and visual material, the book provides a compelling account of the conflict's reverberations in Europe and its empires, and reclaims the multiracial dimensions of war memory.

SANTANU DAS is Reader in English at King's College London, and is the author of *Touch and Intimacy in First World War Literature* (2005).

RACE, EMPIRE AND FIRST WORLD WAR WRITING

EDITED BY

SANTANU DAS

Queen Mary, University of London

CAMBRIDGE
UNIVERSITY PRESS

32 Avenue of the Americas, New York NY 10013-2473, USA

Cambridge University Press is part of the University of Cambridge.

It furthers the University's mission by disseminating knowledge in the pursuit of
education, learning, and research at the highest international levels of excellence.

www.cambridge.org
Information on this title: www.cambridge.org/9781107664494

© Cambridge University Press 2011

First published 2011
3rd printing 2012
First paperback edition 2013

A catalog record for this publication is available from the British Library.

Library of Congress Cataloging in Publication data
Race, empire and First World War writing / edited by Santanu Das.
   p. cm.
ISBN 978-0-521-50984-8 (hardback)
1. World War, 1914–1918 – Social aspects.   2. World War, 1914–1918 – Historiography.
3. Europe – Armed Forces – Colonial forces – History – 20th century.   4. Europe –
Colonies – Race relations – History – 20th century.   5. Europe – Colonies – History –
20th century.   6. Imperialism.   7. Indigenous peoples.   I. Das, Santanu.   II. Title.
D639.A7.R34 2011
940.3´1–dc22   2010046884

ISBN 978-0-521-50984-8 Hardback
ISBN 978-1-107-66449-4 Paperback

Contents

Illustrations

Acknowledgements

I would like to thank, above all, the contributors for all their hard work and enthusiasm for this volume, and for dealing with various queries with meticulous care, speed and good humour. I am grateful to the readers of Cambridge University Press for their thoughtful and warm engagement with the project. These readers – whom I now know to have been Sarah Cole, Kate McLoughlin, Vincent Sherry and Jay Winter – were open-handed with their knowledge and expertise. John Horne, George Morton-Jack, Heather Jones, Jennifer Keene and Hugh Stevens read the Introduction during a busy part of the term, and their insightful comments helped to push my thoughts forward. For their encouragement and support at various points, I would like to thank Michèle Barrett, Gillian Beer, Julia Boffey, Margaret Higonnet, Keith Jeffery and Jon Stallworthy. I am grateful to the British Academy for offering me a post-doctoral fellowship during which the project germinated, and to my department, the School of English and Drama, Queen Mary, University of London. I would also like to thank Hugh Stevens for his support throughout the project, and to my editors at Cambridge University Press, Ray Ryan and Maartje Scheltens, for their enthusiasm and efficiency. Pat Harper has been a wonderfully efficient and attentive copy-editor. Many thanks to Mike Leach for compiling the index. Every effort has been made to trace and contact the copyright holders of the material used in this volume. The cover image has been reproduced courtesy of Brett Butterworth.

Contributors

PAUL J. BAILEY is Professor of Modern Chinese History at the University of Durham. His publications include *Gender and Education in China* (2007), *China in the Twentieth Century* (2001), *Postwar Japan* (1996), and *Reform the People* (1990). He is currently completing a socio-cultural history of Chinese contract labour in First World War France, to be entitled 'The Sino-French Connection: Chinese Indentured Labour in World War I France and the Chinese Francophile "Lobby"'.

MICHÈLE BARRETT is Professor of Modern Literary and Cultural Theory at Queen Mary, University of London, where she is currently Head of the School of English and Drama. She is the author of many books and papers including, on the First World War, *Casualty Figures: How Five Men Survived the First World War* (2008) and 'Subalterns at War: Colonial Forces and the Politics of the Imperial War Graves Commission' in *Interventions* (2007).

SANTANU DAS is Senior Lecturer in English at King's College London, and has held research fellowships at St John's College, Cambridge and at the British Academy, London. He is the author of *Touch and Intimacy in First World War Literature* (2006) and he is currently editing the *Cambridge Companion to the Poetry of the First World War*. In 2009 he was awarded a Philip Leverhulme Prize, and he is working towards a monograph on India, empire and the First World War.

DOMINIEK DENDOOVEN is a historian and assistant curator at In Flanders Fields Museum, Ypres, where he curated the exhibition 'Man–Culture–War: Multicultural Aspects of the First World War' in 2008. He is the editor (with Piet Chielens) of *World War I: Five Continents in Flanders* (2008) and is the author of a number of books related to the First World War. He is currently working on a doctoral thesis at the University of Antwerp on the relationship between the local population and non-white soldiers behind the Ypres front in 1914–18.

ALISON S. FELL is Senior Lecturer in French at the University of Leeds. She is the editor of *Les Femmes face à la guerre / Francophone Women Facing War* (2009) and co-editor of *The Women's Movement in Wartime: International Perspectives 1914–1919* (2007). She is currently carrying out research for a forthcoming book on women, feminism and the legacy of the First World War in France and Britain.

KIMLOAN HILL did her doctorate work in Southeast Asian History and has been a lecturer on Vietnamese language and culture at the University of California, San Diego since 1999. Her book *Coolie into Rebels – Impact of World War I on French Indochina* is forthcoming. She is currently working on her memoir.

KEITH JEFFERY is Professor of British History at Queen's University Belfast. He is the author or editor of fourteen books, including *Ireland and the Great War* (2000), *Field Marshal Sir Henry Wilson: A Political Soldier* (2006) and *The GPO and the Easter Rising* (2006). His official history *MI6: The History of the Secret Intelligence Service* was published in 2010.

HEATHER JONES is Lecturer in International History at the London School of Economics and Political Science. Her most recent publications include *Untold War: New Perspectives in First World War Studies* (2008) co-edited with Jennifer O'Brien and Christoph Schmidt-Supprian. Her book *Violence against Prisoners of War in the First World War: Britain, France and Germany, 1914–1920* is due to be published by Cambridge University Press in 2011.

CHRISTIAN KOLLER is Senior Lecturer in Modern History at Bangor University and Privatdozent at the University of Zurich. He is the author of *'Von Wilden aller Rassen niedergemetzelt': Die Diskussion um die Verwendung von Kolonialtruppen in Europa zwischen Rassismus, Kolonial- und Militärpolitik (1914–1930)* (2001), *Fremdherrschaft: Ein politischer Kampfbegriff im Zeitalter des Nationalismus* (2005), *Streikkultur: Performanzen und Diskurse des Arbeitskampfes im schweizerisch-österreichischen Vergleich (1860–1950)* (2009) and *Rassismus* (2009).

JOE LUNN is Professor of African and Modern European History at the University of Michigan-Dearborn. He is the author of *Memoirs of the Maelstrom: A Senegalese Oral History of the First World War* (1999) which was awarded the Alf Heggoy Prize by the French Colonial Historical Society, as well as numerous articles. He is presently working on 'African

Voices from the Great War: An Anthology of Senegalese Soldiers' Life Histories', which will further explore the impact of the First World War on the lives of West African veterans and the transmission of Senegalese collective memory of the wartime sacrifices across several generations.

MICHELLE MOYD is Assistant Professor of African History at Indiana University in Bloomington, Indiana. She received her doctorate in History from Cornell University in 2008. She has contributed essays to *Uncovered Fields: Perspectives in First World War Studies* (2004) edited by Jenny Macleod and Pierre Purseigle and to *The Maji Maji War as Local Event and National Legacy* edited by James Giblin and Jamie Monson (forthcoming). She is currently working on her first book, which explores the social and cultural history of how African soldiers acted as agents of the colonial state in German East Africa.

JOCK PHILLIPS is the General Editor of *Te Ara*, the Online Encyclopedia of New Zealand in the Ministry for Culture and Heritage. He took up this position after thirteen years as New Zealand's Chief Historian. He has taught American and New Zealand History at Victoria University of Wellington, where he founded and was the first Director of the Stout Research Centre for New Zealand Studies. He has written or edited twelve books on New Zealand history, of which the best-known is *A Man's Country?: The Image of the Pakeha Male – A History* (1987).

CHRISTOPHER PUGSLEY is a Senior Lecturer in the Department of War Studies, RMA Sandhurst. A former New Zealand Army officer, his many books include *On the Fringe of Hell: New Zealanders and Military Discipline in the First World War* (1991), *Gallipoli: The New Zealand Story* (1998), and *The Anzac Experience: New Zealand, Australia and Empire in the First World War* (2001). He is a research fellow at the New Zealand Studies Centre, Birkbeck College and UCL, Senior Associate Fellow, Department of History, Canterbury University, and Fellow of the Royal Historical Society.

RICHARD SMITH teaches in the Department of Media and Communications, Goldsmiths University of London. He specialises in the race and gender implications of military service, and is currently researching imperial propaganda in the West Indies during the First World War, paramilitary activity among West Indian veterans, and cinematic representations of colonial troops. His book *Jamaican Volunteers in the First World War* (2004) has recently been reissued.

PETER STANLEY is Director of the Centre for Historical Research at the National Museum of Australia. From 1980 to 2007, he worked at the Australian War Memorial, where he was Principal Historian. He has published widely on Australian and British military, social and medical history. His most recent book is *Bad Characters: Sex, Crime, Mutiny, Murder and the Australian Imperial Force* (2010), his twenty-second.

MARK WHALAN is Senior Lecturer in American Literature and Culture at the University of Exeter. He is the author of *The Great War and the Culture of the New Negro* (2008) and *American Culture in the 1910s* (2010). He is currently working on a new project on American fiction and the First World War.

Introduction

Santanu Das

On the rainy night of 2/3 March 1915, Jemadar Mir Mast, an Indian soldier serving in the 58th Vaughan's Rifles (Bareilly Brigade) at Neuve Chapelle, deserted and quietly crossed over to the German side with a group of fellow Pathans. Mir Mast was an enterprising man. It is believed that he became part of a *jihad* mission from Germany, and Anglo-Indian myth has it that the Kaiser decorated him with the Iron Cross.[1] Because of the exceptional nature of the event, his trench notebook is now housed in the National Archives in Delhi, contained in a hitherto sealed envelope marked 'His Majesty's Office'.[2] It is a curious document. Along with a hand-drawn trench map, some casual jottings and numbers, it comprises a long list of words, first in Urdu and then in English. The words range from the functional ('haversack', 'blanket', 'please') to the warmly human ('hungry', 'nephew', 'honeymoon') to the robustly earthy ('testacles' [*sic*], 'brests' [*sic*]) (Figure 1). This tantalising and hitherto unknown 'diary' (as referred to in the National Archives catalogue) – a rare, if not the only surviving, example of a trench notebook by an Indian soldier of the First World War – raises a number of broad questions. What do we know about the daily lived war experience of these men from the former colonies and from different racial and ethnic groups? How were they perceived by the white soldiers and civilians and what was the degree of contact between them within and outside the war zone? Is Mir Mast to be remembered as an imperial deserter, a transnational *jihadist* or, with hindsight, as an anti-colonial nationalist – and what do these categories tell us about the nature of war memory, and its relation to subsequent historical events or shifts in political consciousness? These questions, among others – in various national, racial and socio-cultural contexts – lie at the heart of this book.

The volume examines the racial and colonial aspects of the war of 1914–18. The wider aim is to embed the experience and memory of the First World War in a more multiracial and international framework. The contours of the 'Great War and modern memory' start to look different if,

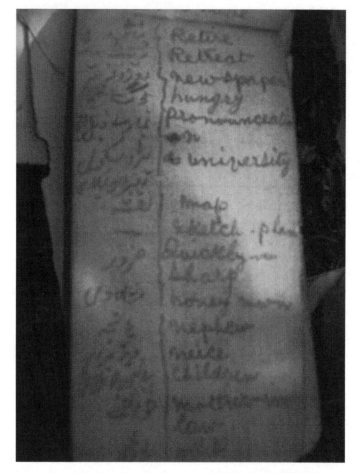

1. A page from the trench notebook of Jemadar Mir Mast

instead of the writings of an ordinary European soldier, let alone a Wilfred Owen or an Erich Maria Remarque, we take the memories of an Indian sepoy, a Chinese worker or an African *askari*. There has been a steadily growing interest within the academy, particularly in recent years, in the colonial and African American experiences of the conflict.[3] But in spite of important work being done on such aspects, the social and cultural history of the war continues to maintain a neat symmetry to the war itself: the non-European aspects, like the non-European sites of battle, remain 'sideshows'. While there has been some excellent work on the experience of individual racial groups or the contribution of the former colonies, a need has increasingly been felt to think through some of these issues in a comparative and cross-disciplinary framework.

The impulses behind the present collection of essays are both recuperative and analytical. The volume seeks variously to recover and analyse the war experience of the combatants and non-combatants from the former colonies and dominions, as well as of particular ethnic and racial groups from outside the colonial empires, such as the Chinese and the African Americans. At the same time, it also examines the different discourses – pan-European, national, racial or socio-cultural – surrounding their participation, moments of interracial contact, processes of post-war memory and literary representations. Given the wide range of the subject and sources, the essays are methodologically heterogeneous, but they are united by certain common themes and concerns. In this Introduction, I briefly indicate the scale and the intensity of the conflict for some of the various groups involved before going on to discuss particular issues arising out of this volume: the nature of the source materials and the challenges such material poses to scholars working in the field, the ways in which 'race' and 'empire' have been explored here and the variants of their relationship, and points of contiguity and difference among the histories the individual chapters examine.

In 1906, in a fictional narrative, the German writer F. H. Grautoff warned that 'a war in Europe ... must necessarily set the whole world ablaze'.[4] This was no Eurocentric boast. In 1914, Great Britain and France controlled the two largest colonial empires, and they would draw on them extensively during the war for both human and material resources. At the time, as Hew Strachan notes, 'war for Europe meant war for the world'; the whole of Africa, except Ethiopia and Liberia, was under European rule, and the first shot fired by a soldier in British service was in Togoland in Africa.[5] India, along with other parts of the British empire including the (white) dominions, entered the war on 4 August 1914, and on the same day the French war minister Messimy ordered the transport of ten West African battalions to France. On 7 August, French and British troops invaded German Togoland, and by 25 August they had destroyed the German wireless station at Kamina. Before the month was out, Japan had started making preparations for the capture of Tsingtao, and on 30 August New Zealand occupied Samoa. Over the next four years, fighting would take place in Europe, Africa and the Middle East, with brief excursions into Central Asia and the Far East. The litany of place names often becomes the marker of the 'world' nature of the First World War. Place names and battlefields remain sites of great importance and emotion, but as various social and cultural histories of the 1914–18 conflict have shown, the war can no longer be reduced to just battles.

The global reverberations of what at the time Germany alone, among the European nations, called the '*world* war' (Weltkrieg) become apparent as we substitute people, processes and effects of the war for places and events. Even a narrow view of 'numbers' and their movements across countries and continents suggests the scale of international upheaval. Among the various colonies of the British empire, India contributed the largest number of men, with approximately 1.4 million recruited during the war up to December 1919.[6] The dominions – including Canada, South Africa, Australia, New Zealand and Newfoundland – contributed a further 1.3 million men.[7] New Zealand's mobilisation of more than 100,000 men may seem relatively small compared to India's, but in proportionate terms New Zealand made one of largest contributions in the British empire, with 5 per cent of its men aged 15–49 killed.[8] In addition to the 90,000 *troupes indigènes* already under arms when the war started, France recruited between 1914 and 1918 nearly 500,000 colonial troops including 166,000 West Africans, 46,000 Madagascans, 50,000 Indochinese, 140,000 Algerians, 47,000 Tunisians and 24,300 Moroccans.[9] Most of these French colonial troops served in Europe. However, the majority of the Africans served as labourers or carriers in Africa. In total, over 2 million Africans were involved in the conflict as soldiers or labourers; 10 per cent of them died, and among the labourers serving in Africa, the death rates may have been as high as 20 per cent.[10] On the other hand, nearly 140,000 Chinese contract labourers were hired by the British and French governments, forming a substantial part of the immigrant labour force working in France during the war.[11] With the entry of the United States into the war, nearly 400,000 African American troops were inducted into the US forces, of whom 200,000 served in Europe.[12] Even by conservative estimates, the total number of non-white men, combatants and non-combatants, mobilised into the European and American armies during the First World War comes to well over four million, though not all of them saw active service.[13]

In a grotesque reversal of Joseph Conrad's novelistic vision, hundreds of thousands of non-white men were voyaging to the heart of whiteness, as it were, to witness 'The horror! The horror!' of Western warfare. 'This is not war. It is the ending of the world,' wrote a wounded Indian sepoy from England.[14] The war also resulted in an unprecedented range of interracial and cross-cultural encounters, experiences and intimacies. There were vast movements of men outside Europe: among others, more than half a million

Indians were sent to Mesopotamia, over a million African labourers, particularly carriers, were recruited from different parts of Africa for the East African campaign, and there was the famous expedition of the Australians and New Zealanders to Gallipoli in April 1915. For the different dominions, colonies and racial groups around the globe, the war experience was profoundly transformative at different levels: from Australia coming to 'know itself' as a nation, as Charles Bean noted, during the war to remote towns such as Invercargill at the southernmost tip of New Zealand or small villages in India and Africa opening up to the wider world.[15] What are often considered sideshows in the grand European narrative of the war were momentous events with enduring consequences for the local communities. Nor, for many of these groups, did the war – at the basic, physical level – end with the Armistice. For two weeks after the guns fell silent on the Western Front, the wily German commander General Paul von Lettow-Vorbeck carried on his campaign in East Africa. In Europe, Chinese labourers started clearing up the battlefields of the Western Front, and French African troops stationed in the Ruhr region till early 1921 became the target of vicious racist propaganda. The German sociologist Max Weber had complained about 'an army of niggers, Ghurkhas and all the barbarians of the world'.[16] This volume is about them, as well as their brethren from Ireland and the dominions, including Maori, Aboriginal Australians and the First Nations Canadians.[17]

The essays are heterogeneous in method. Some of the chapters recover the war experiences of marginalised racial groups through fresh material, some are more discursively developed examinations of the war experience within European, national or racial contexts, some are critical readings of the literary records of these experiences or analyses of post-war memory. This methodological diversity – encouraged by the nature of the subject – is something the volume wishes to highlight as an important dimension of collaborative, cross-disciplinary scholarship. The plurality becomes particularly important in an area where the archives are often more than ordinarily silent, where the range of sources is complex and sometimes beyond the limits of traditional historical enquiry, and where the structures of knowledge and levels of existing scholarship vary widely. The authors here are drawn from different disciplines – history, colonial studies, literary criticism, sociology and modern languages. Scholars who have already written on the war experience of particular countries or racial groups revisit the topic from fresh perspectives.

The book is divided into three parts. While a drive towards the historical recovery of the war experiences of non-white communities in Europe, as

well as in Mesopotamia and East Africa, characterises the essays in Part I
('Voices and experiences') of the volume, the essays in Part II ('Perceptions
and proximities') document and analyse the different sites and contexts of
interracial proximity or contact. The essays in Part III ('Nationalism,
memory and literature') – dealing with predominantly English-speaking
former colonies, dominions or racial groups (such as African Americans)
whose war experiences are relatively better-documented – engage with
processes of remembrance and literary representation, and their relation
to national, racial or cultural identity. These chapters address the construction of war memory and its shifting nature, as when imperial war service
accretes with time layers of nationalist meaning, like the 'Anzac legend'
(discussed in Chapter 11 by Peter Stanley), or when the rhetoric of the war is
appropriated for the fight for racial equality, as with the African American
writers of the Harlem Renaissance (as examined in Chapter 15 by Mark
Whalan).

In recent years, two parallel events have been taking place in the
European theatre of the Great War and public remembrance: we are
witnessing the demise of the last handful of European war veterans; at the
same time, the colonial non-white participants are slowly being wheeled in
from the shadowy chambers of modern memory. The opening of the
Memorial Gates at Hyde Park Corner in London in 2002 to commemorate
the services of the Indian subcontinent, Africa and the Caribbean to the two
world wars, the increased space devoted to the South African Native Labour
Corps in the museum for South African troops in Delville Wood in France,
or the exhibition 'Man–Culture–War: Multicultural Aspects of the First
World War' (2008) at In Flanders Fields Museum, Ypres are striking
examples.[18] Within the academy, there has been a swell of interest in the
transnational or global aspects of the conflict: two classic examples are the
two-volume *Capital Cities at War: Paris, London, Berlin, 1914–1919* (1999
and 2007) edited by Jay Winter and Jean Louis Roberts, and Hew
Strachan's *The First World War: To Arms* (2001).[19] If some of the earliest
accounts to highlight the colonial contributions were celebratory imperial
histories,[20] in recent years scholars such as Charles Balesi, Myron
Echenberg, Richard Fogarty, David Killingray, John Morrow, Marc
Michel, David Omissi, Melvin Page and Tyler Stovall – and including
many of the contributors to the present volume – have pioneered research
into the colonial and racial dimensions of the conflict.[21] While such works
have illuminated fresh areas of experience, these colonial histories are often
so complex and intricate that they become specialised and independent
spheres of scholarship. *Race, Empire and First World War Writing* at once

demonstrates the kinds of work that are being done in the field and intends to open up a space for discussion and dialogue. While most of the essays focus on particular groups or countries, the volume collectively explores patterns of similarity and difference across them.

In 2003, Gail Braybon noted that 'more words have been written about the British war poets than about all the non-white troops put together'.[22] Eurocentrism is, however, only one part of the problem; the fact remains that the war poets have written more words about the conflict than all the non-white troops put together. As Paul J. Bailey notes in Chapter 1 of this volume, '"An Army of Workers": Chinese indentured labour in First World War France', 'how are we to capture the voices of the workers themselves given the paucity of written records?'[23] Often recruited from non-literate or semi literate backgrounds, these men have not left behind the letters, poems and memoirs that form the cornerstone of European war memory. Bakary Diallo's *Force Bonté* (1926) is the only published memoir by a tirailleur sénégalais, just as Rihana Karkeek's *Home Sweet Home* (2003) is the only published diary so far about the Maori war experience; Mulk Raj Anand's *Across the Black Waters* (1939) is the only Indian 'Great War novel'. An important source is the substantial collection of censored letters of the colonial troops and workers, and reports of the postal censors, but they are a particular kind of evidence and raise particular problems. Increasingly, a need is being felt to go beyond the official archives. In African history, scholars such as Charles Balesi and Joe Lunn have made extensive use of oral interviews of war veterans. Similarly, South Asian scholars have started to draw on a wider base of material, including prisoner-of-war camp journals and the voice-recordings of over two thousand POWs in Germany done by the Prussian Ethnographic Commission.[24] Essays in the present volume address a variety of sources – personal testimonies including letters, diaries, and freshly unearthed (and translated) memoirs, government archives, contemporary publications, literature, songs, interviews, photographs, film and public memorials. There is an impulse in the volume towards the recovery of the individual voices, the intimate accounts, which have so far been marginalised or silenced in public and official accounts, but different kinds of evidence are read alongside each other, wherever possible.

The essays collected here fall broadly within the sphere of social and cultural history and literary criticism, and in different ways, they all underline the need for greater specificity and nuance. While the focus is on questions of colonialism and race, the chapters explore how these two factors operate in conjunction with issues such as gender, class, cultural identity, nationality, religion and military rank. Non-white troops and non-combatants faced racism in a variety of situations but such experiences need to be contextualised. There are some pan-European affinities but also distinct differences. The institutional racism of the British army – its refusal to promote the colonial soldiers beyond a certain rank or its politics of segregation (as with the South African Native Labour Corps in France or the Indian wounded in the Brighton Pavilion, England) – was different from the working-class racism faced by the Chinese workers in France in 1917. Moreover, European attitudes to the different races varied and there were many instances of individual kindness. Many of the colonial and African American troops spoke very warmly of their French hosts. Class, not race, argues Heather Jones in Chapter 9, 'Imperial captivities: colonial prisoners of war in Germany and the Ottoman empire, 1914–1918', was the scandal in Mesopotamia. Religion and place too played a part. Michèle Barrett in her Afterword ('Death and the afterlife – Britain's colonies and dominions') uncovers evidence from the archives of the Imperial War Graves Commission about its decision that West Indians – 'Negroes in West Indian Regiments' – were to be 'commemorated individually when buried in East Africa' for they were 'Christians' while for the native Africans, a policy of 'no individual commemoration' was to be followed.

The two terms in the book's title – 'empire' and 'race' (in the twentieth-century sense of 'colour', as explained more fully in the next section) – frequently overlap but they are by no means coterminous. The essays discuss the experiences of both non-white and white subjects of the empire to see how colonial war experience and memory differ across the colour line. At the same time, the volume draws in two other racial groups – the Chinese workers and African American troops – to examine how racial politics works outside the framework of colonial structures. While the issue of race connects the Chinese and the African Americans to the colonial non-white troops, how does their political status affect European attitudes towards them (interestingly, Chinese contract workers were referred to as 'colonial' or 'exotic' workers, as opposed to the term 'immigrant workers' used for non-French European workers) and indeed their war experience? The experience of these two groups alerts us against any neat conflation of the terms 'race' and 'empire' in spite of their frequent overlap. During the First World War, political status and nationality intersected with race to create a range of experiences. The experience of being colonised (like Indians or the Vietnamese) was substantially different from being a subjugated race within a self-governing dominion (like Aboriginal Australians) or within an independent nation (like African Americans). These widely varying axes on which non-white identities were forged in relation to the First World War created a range of similarities and differences in war experiences and post-war memory.

Given the magnitude of the subject, this volume neither is nor pretends to be comprehensive in any way; gaps are inevitable.[25] Instead, the fifteen chapters deal with a selected range of subjects and seek to create a platform for dialogue. In spite of the diversity in material and treatment, there are certain deep continuities and overlaps; narratives intersect. Recovery of wartime voices and experiences in Part I necessarily includes some investigation of the interracial perceptions developed in Part II, while both are carried forward in fresh contexts in discussions of post-war memory in Part III. In Chapter 1, Paul J. Bailey's examination of the Chinese war experience includes, alongside the workers' voices, the way they are represented, a point taken up by Dominiek Dendooven in Chapter 7, on 'Living apart together: Belgian civilians and non-white troops and workers in wartime Flanders' in Part II. Santanu Das's exploration of the Indian experience in Mesopotamia through Bengali letters and memoirs in Chapter 3, 'Indians at home, Mesopotamia and France, 1914–1918: towards an intimate history', similarly intersects with Heather Jones's account of the European discourses surrounding Mesopotamia in Chapter 9. The idea of radicalisation of soldiers and workers, implicit in different chapters in Part I of the volume, is developed by Richard Smith in Chapter 14 ('"Heaven grant you strength to fight the battle for your race": nationalism, Pan-Africanism and the First World War in Jamaican memory') and Mark Whalan in Chapter 15 ('Not only war: the First World War and African American literature'), both in Part III. Similarly, the theme of interracial contact is carried forward to Part III through Peter Stanley's investigation in Chapter 11 of Australian war experience in Gallipoli, Ceylon and Africa ('"He was black, he was a White man, and a dinkum Aussie": race and empire in revisiting the Anzac legend'). Racial discrimination and hierarchy, a recurring theme in the essays, is developed in a comparative context by Michèle Barrett in the Afterword through an exploration of the official commemoration of Indian, African and Canadian men. Her investigation of the archival records of the Imperial War Graves Commission shows that, in spite of proclamations of complete equality, its commemorative practices varied significantly. Such differences were made not just between the 'white' dominions and the 'coloured' colonies but involved intricate distinctions between the different colonies and racial groups, in conjunction with factors such as rank, location and religion.

EMPIRE, RACE, COLOUR

The way in which the two terms in the book's title – 'empire' and 'race' – have been explored needs some explanation. If imperial rivalry was one of the causes of the conflict, the war led to the dissolution of empires: not only of the aspiring German empire, but of the older, vaster and multi-ethnic empires of Austro-Hungary, Russia and the Ottomans. Ethnic tension and conflict within wartime Europe, including the Armenian genocide in wartime Turkey, are big and complex areas which need separate studies and are beyond the framework of this volume.[26] In this collection, the focus is on the colonial empires of Great Britain, France, and Germany as well as on other racial groups, such as the Chinese and the African Americans. The term 'race' (as explained below) is used in its twentieth-century meaning to denote differences in skin colour while acknowledging its continuing complexity and fluidity (to denote ethnicity) during the war.

According to one native South African labourer, the most remarkable part of his war experience was 'to see the different kinds of human races from all parts of the world'.[27] This racial diversity on European soil was largely the result of French and British decisions to employ colonial non-white troops against Germany on the Western Front. For France, the war was the testing ground for General Mangin's theory of 'La force noire': the creation of a large reserve of African troops to counter France's demographic imbalance vis-à-vis Germany and use them for its own defence.[28] While France, with its assimilationist model, deployed these troops in Europe, a similar decision for Great Britain caused more soul-searching. The British had regularly used colonial troops for imperial defence but not in Europe or against other white races. Indian troops were not allowed to fight in the Boer War in South Africa (1899–1902). If a 'coloured' man was trained to raise arms against another European, what guarantee was there, so the thinking went, that he would not one day attack his own white master? However, after the heavy casualties suffered by the British Expeditionary Force in August 1914, two Indian divisions were diverted to France. Among the colonial non-white troops of the British empire, only Indians were allowed to fight in Europe.[29]

Conceptions of race were important to the European imagination in the nineteenth century. Race was not exclusively associated with skin colour and remained a notoriously difficult concept to define. In the eighteenth century, racial difference had often been defined in terms of physical characteristics, environment, languages and behaviour, but by the 1850s 'scientific' evolutionary concepts were being developed.[30] In Great Britain, the Scottish ethnologist Robert Knox in *The Races of Man* (1850) constructed a global racial hierarchy, with the white races (though subdivided) at the top and the 'dark races' at the bottom because of 'a physical and, consequently a psychological, inferiority'. The 'type' of the 'negro' was placed in the lowest evolutionary category, termed as 'foetal':

What signify these dark races to us? Who cares particularly for the Negro, or the Hottentot or the Kaffir? These latter have proved a very troublesome race, and the sooner they are put out of the way the better . . . No one seems much to care for them. Their ultimate expulsion from all lands which the fair races can colonise seems almost certain.[31]

Knox's ideas, though influential, were not universally accepted. Moreover, scholars such as Daniel Pick have pointed out that ideas about race around this time cannot be reduced to 'West versus the rest'.[32] Throughout the nineteenth century, race remained a fluid term, used interchangeably with ethnicity and even nationality. Knox himself divided the Europeans into different 'races', creating internal hierarchies; J. Deniker in *The Races of Men: An Outline of Anthropology and Ethnology* (1900) divided Europeans into six principal and four secondary races. By the end of the Victorian age, ethnographers had devised such a bewildering variety of racial classifications that the German racial scientist Ludwig Gumplowicz concluded that 'everything is higgledly-piggledly'.[33] Moreover, race was sometimes conflated with class: bourgeois representations of the working classes at times adopted a discourse of race.[34]

In *The Meaning of Race* (1996), Kenan Malik has argued that it is in the early years of the twentieth century, with the increasing democratisation of society and the expansion in imperialism, that racial discourse began to focus 'more exclusively upon black and white, West and the Third World'.[35] This was mirrored in the enactment of a series of discriminatory immigration policies based on colour in Canada, South Africa and parts of Australia. During the war years, various forms of intra-European racism continued, for example the racism towards the Russians even among the Allies. In addition, Germans were often viewed as a different 'race': they were regarded as a throwback to some 'Tartar stock' charged with the 'instincts . . . of some pre-Asiatic horde' and, in one instance, referred to as the 'Zulus of Europe'.[36] Yet, as the last phrase suggests, overriding the various intra-European 'racial' classification and prejudices there was a stronger axis of colour, of racial difference as one of skin colour. It was the deployment not of Jews, Russians or the Irish – who had been the victims of intra-European racism – but of the 'coloured races' in Europe that caused outrage in Germany and consternation in various parts of the British empire. The *Times History of the World* wrote: 'The instinct which made us such sticklers for propriety in all our dealings made us more reluctant than other nations would feel to employ coloured troops against a white enemy.'[37] Similarly in France, as Tyler Stovall has powerfully argued, with the massive immigration of workers from Morocco, China and Indochina to its fields and factories, 'concepts of racial difference, based on skin-colour became a significant factor in French working-class life for the first time'.[38] Colour largely determined the life of the combatant and non-combatant in Europe: from the rate of promotion and wages within the army to living conditions, mobility and social interaction. Therefore, while acknowledging the fluidity of the term 'race' to sometimes mean ethnicity during the period, it is in its twentieth-century sense of colour that the concept has been explored in this volume.

Racial categorisation, in the context of war, assumes one of its most insidious forms in the theory of the 'martial races'.[39] Both England and France divided their subject people into 'warlike' and 'non-warlike' races, into *races guerrières* and *races non-guerrières*. From the late nineteenth century, the martial race theory formed the backbone of the military recruiting system in British India. A combination of Victorian social Darwinism and indigenous caste hierarchy, this theory emphasised that some 'races' from Nepal and the North Indian provinces – particularly Punjab – were inherently more 'manly' and warlike than men from other parts of India.[40] Raciology was similarly integral to Mangin's vision of 'la force noire'. West Africans, to him, were 'natural warriors', 'primitives . . . whose young blood flows so ardently, as if avid to be shed'.[41] Until the First World War, the Tirailleurs sénégalais (who were drawn from different tribes in French West and Central Africa) was largely a mercenary army, supplemented by partial conscription through the Conscription Law of 1912. But the First World War – particularly in its final year – altered this. Faced with the French government's demand for a levy of 50,000 soldiers from French West Africa, colonial administrators in the region put pressure on African chieftains who in turn mounted ruthless 'recruitment' campaigns, involving different forms of violence. Whole communities were traumatised: men fled to the bush or neighbouring neutral areas or even mounted armed resistance.[42] With the protest resignation of Joost van Vollenhoven as governor-general, Blaise Diagne became Senegal's first African deputy and was phenomenally successful in recruiting people: in the final year, he managed to net in some 63,000 recruits. Traces of the

'European war' in the villages of Africa survive even today, as in the following Chinyanja marching song:

> Helter-skelter! Helter-skelter!
> Helter skelter! Helter-skelter!
> What have you done, Sir?
> Germany has completely finished off our young men,
> Germany has completely finished off our young men.[43]

Race played an important and often fraught role in the 'white' dominions as well, particularly in relation to the war and post-war memory. It was in the dominions (except, to a lesser degree, in New Zealand) that the racial dimensions of the war service were most often marginalised or even actively edited out of official memory, as these societies, once colonial, became national; the notion of the blood sacrifice of the white soldiers on the Western Front or at Gallipoli sought to confirm this. It is often forgotten that, in spite of the opposition of the British government to arming the 'coloured' people in the dominions, the armies of Australia and Canada were not 'all-white'. Around 4,000 Canadian Aborigines served with the Canadian Expeditionary Force, including the Olympic athlete Alexander Decoteau, while some 400 or 500 Aborigines served in the Australian Imperial Force.[44] As Peter Stanley notes in Chapter 11 with reference to the consolidation of the Anzac legend, the imperial and racial dimensions of the war experience were written out, and the Australians behaved or came across as the colonisers. His story of 'Mick King', a gallant Aborigine in the Australian Imperial Force, provides insights into the fostering of 'whiteness' as a racial and national identity during the war. After Mick King was blown up by a shell at Ypres in 1917, his bereaved comrade Henry Raine, writing his epitaph years later, noted: 'although he was black, he was a White man, and a dinkum Aussie'.

VOICES AND EXPERIENCES

The essays in the first part of the volume share a commitment towards recovering and examining marginalised histories of non-white combatants and non-combatants through fresh material, archival, published and oral. In view of some of the recuperative work done in recent years, particularly with regard to African and Indian troops, it is possible to explore such histories with a more critical and informed perspective than hitherto: to move beyond the stereotypes of the simple 'izzat'-driven sepoy or the 'loyal *askari*' to investigate in greater detail these combatants' motives and actions, their emotional worlds, and to nuance generalised statements to particular contexts.

Among the various racial groups in France, one of the most fascinating but least-known stories is that of the approximately 140,000 Chinese workers who were hired by the British and French governments. The mobilisation and extensive use of labour in different theatres of battle remain underresearched areas. There has been important work on the use of carrier corps in sub-Saharan Africa, where men were reduced to 'beasts of burden' and suffered very high casualty rates, often from disease and malnutrition; within Europe, the stories of the South African Native Labour Corps and the Maori Pioneer Battalion have received attention in recent years.[45] But the story of the Chinese labour force has been equally ignored in Chinese and European history, as well as in studies on the First World War. In Chapter 1 '"An army of workers": Chinese indentured labour in First World War France', Bailey recovers their buried experience. To understand such experience more fully, he locates it within the official and the Chinese Francophile discourses surrounding the war service, and then contrasts European representations of these workers with their lived reality, culled from a range of sources, including documents freshly translated from Chinese. Father Van Walleghem, whose diary Dominiek Dendooven examines in Part II of the volume, could easily have met and written about some of the people whose lives Bailey recovers.

On the other hand, one of the most visible groups on the Western Front was the Indian sepoys. Starting with the responses to the war within India, my essay 'Indians at home, Mesopotamia and France, 1914–1918: towards an intimate history' (Chapter 3) seeks to recover Indians' varied experiences as well as certain structures of feeling resulting from the conjunction of race, colonialism and the war through a dialogue between archival, testimonial and literary material. Two newly unearthed accounts – the only records so far of the Indian captivity experience in Mesopotamia – help to move the focus beyond Europe into this shadowy world. Close engagement with these accounts, along with the diaries of an aristocrat and the sepoys' censored letters, reveals the diversity of experience and complexity of feeling, leading one to question the construction of a monolithic 'Indian war experience'.

Wartime recruitment is a recurring theme in many of the chapters. While there was a substantial amount of forced recruitment, particularly in Africa, the essays also suggest that a large number of colonial recruits did volunteer for war service, at least in the early stages of the conflict. Prestige, masculinity, social aspiration, a sense of adventure, naivety about the nature of war, or a combination of influence and coercion by local chieftains: all these were important factors. Motives of course varied between the various groups but, as several chapters (2, 3, 5, 14) suggest, financial reward was a major incentive. Moreover, for many, coming to Europe for the first time was an overwhelming experience, as the following letter from an Indian sepoy illustrates:

On the voyage to Europe, I saw on land and sea such wonderful things as I had never even dreamed of, and when I reached Europe itself even stranger things came into view. The Europe that I speak of is that Europe which all people are longing to see. It is the 'first Golden Age' in which all knowledge and beauty and wealth are found.[46]

Even while some of the censored letters hint at a sense of plebeian wonder, it is important, as I note in Chapter 3, to view the sepoys as alert, if circumscribed, agents rather than wholly passive receptacles of Western civilisation. What happens once the initial sense of wonder fades away? Many letters also suggest the formation of transcultural and even transnational identities.

Romance and sex were often areas in which these transcultural relations were most intimately formed. The war upset the traditional colonial relation between race and gender. Instead of white imperialists having access to local women, France now had a huge population of non-white men among its own female population. As John Horne has closely argued, the number of marriages between French women and foreign men increased substantially in the war years; moreover, in cities like Marseilles, prostitution boomed.[47] Lal Baz, an Indian sepoy in France, wrote to his brother in the Frontier Constabulary, India: 'Do not resort to harlots and do not gamble.'[48] The Indochinese men, as Kimloan Hill demonstrates in Chapter 2 'Sacrifices, sex, race: Vietnamese experiences in the First World War', seem to have ignored both instructions. Through censored letters and governmental records, she opens up the world of the Indochinese soldiers and workers, testifying at once to the trauma of the war and the pleasures of European life. Intimacy between French women and the colonial workers could lead to resentment and violence not only from the local French men but, as Hill shows, from other racial communities, such as the Senegalese. Several essays in fact touch upon the theme of racial tension and violence. Conflict and rioting over perceived wrongs seem to have marked the experience of the Chinese workers in France, whether with the North Africans over food rations, or with the French at Le Creusot in November 1916 (Bailey) or with the New Zealanders around Christmas 1917 (Dendooven). Potential zones of contact thus could at times degenerate into actual zones of conflict. The essays of Das and Hill address the experience of two groups for whom race and colonialism overlapped and who served as both combatants and non-combatants.

The last two essays in Part I – Michelle Moyd's Chapter 4, 'We don't want to die for nothing': *askari* at war in German East Africa, 1914–1918' and Joe Lunn's Chapter 5, 'France's legacy to Demba Mboup? A Senegalese griot and his descendants remember his military service during the First World War' – seek to recover the African war experience from either side of the political divide. Moyd's chapter is a discursive examination of the *askari* war experience in German East Africa; Lunn, on the other hand, recovers through oral interviews the life story of a West African war veteran.

According to Moyd, the world of the German *askari* in East Africa cannot be explained away solely in terms of an 'organic loyalty' to the Schutztruppe commander General Paul von Lettow-Vorbeck but has to be understood through a frame of multiple, shifting opportunities available and a more historicised context. Consider, for example, the rather extreme case of Kazibule Dabi, a German *askari*, who was captured by the British:

They said that we should become soldiers … We asked them how much they would pay us if we enlisted. They said one pound, one shilling, and fourpence [a month]. We told them that we would not accept that. We told them that when we were on the German side we used to receive three pounds and ten shillings. We refused and there was great talk about it. When they saw that we were not willing to give way, they decided not to give us food … As a result we ended up by enlisting.[49]

Dabi is no string puppet or uncomprehending, inarticulate creature: he thinks, compares, and tries to negotiate, even though his freedom is brutally curtailed. By placing the *askari* in their social, economic and cultural contexts, Moyd highlights their complex desires and loyalties. Joe Lunn, on the other hand, closely focuses on the life of Demba Mboup, a Senegalese griot, from enlistment through his wounding and invalidation to a retrospective assessment of the significance of his war service – the third full life story of a West African veteran of the First World War. Lunn's use of oral interviews helps to illuminate an area of experience about which very little is known, and his detailed narrative brings out the emotional, humane dimension of the recuperative project.

A number of the chapters address the theme of agency, however limited, in a variety of contexts: from strikes organised by Chinese workers in protest against their reduced bread rations (Chapter 1) to *askari* women deciding to march with their men in violation of Paul von Lettow-Vorbeck's command

(Chapter 4), to members of the British West India Regiment rebelling at Taranto in December 1918 against discriminatory rates of pay and the menial nature of their work (Chapter 14). Similarly, protest could take culturally specific forms, from a Chinese worker refusing to cut his *queue* to Indian sepoys refusing to eat horsemeat during the siege of Kut in Mesopotamia.

Is there any relationship between war service and the subsequent rise in nationalist or racial consciousness in former parts of the empire? As different chapters suggest, aspirations towards equality often shaped the national, racial or ethnic discourses surrounding war service among various groups and colonies. This was powerfully expressed in a 1915 article in the Jamaican journal *Grenada Federalist*:

As Coloured people we will be fighting for something more, something inestimable to ourselves. We will be fighting to prove to Great Britain that we are not so vastly inferior to the white. We will be fighting to prove that we are no longer merely subjects but citizens – citizens of a world empire whose watch-word should be Liberty, Equality and Brotherhood.[50]

In some of the colonies, there was also a conscious degree of political calculation: parties such as the Indian National Congress supported the war in the hope of greater political autonomy as a reward. However, for many of these colonies, the post-war period was deeply disillusioning. But did the war experience radicalise the soldiers and workers who actually served? While it is not always possible to draw a direct trajectory between war experience and anti-colonial resistance, several essays indicate that the war significantly raised the levels of self-confidence and political, national or racial awareness among different groups.[51] Some of these issues return in the final part of the volume in the context of West Indian and African American memories of the war and the evolution of a Pan-African consciousness.

PERCEPTIONS AND PROXIMITIES

The mobilisation of troops and workers from different parts of the world created an immense range of transnational movements and interracial encounters. During the war years, on French soil alone – in its trenches, fields and factories – there were over one million non-white men mobilised by France, Britain and the United States.[52] How were these men perceived and represented by the European troops and civilians? Does physical proximity among different races suggest contact, or does it reinforce racial prejudice? Moreover, what were the nature and range of encounters outside Europe?

On the topic of wartime interracial encounter within Europe, there has been some important work in recent years, based on the collections of censored letters.[53] The actual context and environment often played a key role in determining the nature of the relationship: the interaction of a colonial worker and a French woman in a factory, for example, was very different from a fleeting encounter between a colonial soldier and a French sex worker. Part II of the volume explores interracial perceptions and proximities through a number of sites or spaces – the battlefield (the Western Front), the prisoner-of-war camp (in Germany and Mesopotamia), the hospital, and a small provincial town in Belgium. These site-specific studies help us to capture and nuance the racial 'undertones of war': were these relationships irreversibly entrenched in, or did they at times challenge, existing racial hierarchies?

The image of the non-white soldier was a particularly charged one in wartime Europe: racialism, exoticism, fear and anxiety were combined.[54] The relations of France and of Britain with their respective colonial troops were very different, often involving further distinctions between different racial groups. At the same time, some stereotypes were pan-European. Colonial troops were depicted, at best, as gallant, courageous, loyal, ferocious, but they were said to lack the qualities of the European master: qualities of leadership, stoicism, decision making; moreover, their sexual appetites were said to be voracious, their battlefield practices savage. A French cartoon portrayed with elegant symmetry the competing discourses of racial and nationalist prejudice: it shows a barefoot tirailleur sénégalais with knife in mouth pitted against a German soldier with a saw-tooth bayonet. The cartoon asks, 'Who's the savage?'[55]

The real-life nature of these encounters is here discussed by Christian Koller in Chapter 6, 'Representing Otherness: African, Indian, and European soldiers' letters and memoirs'. Investigating a range of material – German propaganda, Allied representations, as well as accounts by Indian and African soldiers – Koller conducts a two-way dialogue: a comparison among German, French and English representations of the colonial troops as well as these soldiers' accounts of their experience in Europe. His examination of German propaganda letters shows a pitch of racist hysteria that looks forward to the discourse about 'the black shame on the Rhine' in 1919. According to Jones in Chapter 9, 'the atrocity image' of the colonial soldier 'created a safe space for articulating thoughts about fear, wartime violence, killing and atrocity which could not be expressed with regard to one's combat actions'. Similar fears may have underpinned the Allied narratives of racial savagery, such as the story of European soldiers' ears being chopped off, that Dendooven, Koller and Jones encounter in different contexts and find attributed to different racial groups. How were the non-white soldiers and workers perceived in France? Belgium and France, being at the centre of the war zone in the west, experienced the highest number of such encounters. Did the French assimilationist model of colonisation equip them better to handle these interracial proximities? The African veterans, when interviewed, emphasised that 'blacks were highly esteemed there; there was no question of race'.[56] The enthusiastic accounts of the African Americans – 'They treat us so good that the only time I ever know I'm colored is when I look in the glass'[57] – have fostered the myth of a 'colour-blind' France, but it has been challenged in recent years. First, French attitudes to different racial groups differed significantly. Moreover, colonial soldiers were viewed as saviours but colonial workers, as Tyler Stovall points out, were often 'seen not only as competitors for French jobs and French women, but also as a substitute labour force that allowed the government to send more French men to battle'.[58] However, the Belgian responses have up until now remained largely unknown. In Chapter 7, 'Living apart together: Belgian civilians and non-white troops and workers in wartime Flanders', Dendooven illuminates this area by focusing on a particular region in West Flanders – Westhoek – and examining a range of local Flemish material, including both interviews and the extraordinary diary of Father Van Walleghem. What come across are carefully nuanced perceptions and a range of conflicted feelings about the various racial groups. While revisiting the story of the Chinese workers, Dendooven's essay also introduces a theme that is developed by Alison Fell in Chapter 8, 'Nursing the Other: the representation of colonial troops in French and British First World War nursing memoirs': the world of the female nurses who looked after these men.

How did European women view the colonial troops? In her memoir *Des inconnus chez moi* (1920), Lucie Cousturier recalls the initial local responses to the African soldiers:

In April and May 1916, we credited our future friends with many acts of horror. All the peasants joined in. There is no crime they were not accused of . . . drunkenness, theft, rape and . . . causing epidemics. 'What is to become of us?' moaned the farmers' wives . . . We will not dare let our young daughters walk the paths among those savages. We will not dare go out alone ourselves to cut the grass or gather wood . . . 'Just think of it ! If we were to be taken by these gorillas!'[59]

Such anxieties intensified in the intimate, enclosed spaces of the hospital as thousands of young women, often from sheltered backgrounds, nursed the injured colonial troops. But the anxiety was often laced by a strong, almost erotic, curiosity: the focus on the physical features of the 'beautiful Goumier' noted by Dendooven in the diary of De Launoy in Chapter 7 is echoed in Fell's examination of the lingering gaze on a 'particularly muscular' Moroccan soldier in the writing of Emmanuel Colombel, who set up a Red Cross hospital at Arras. In her chapter, Fell focuses on the representation of the non-white body in both British and French nursing memoirs by middle-class women. These women draw upon the existing imperial, often racist, discourses of otherness to understand and represent the 'coloured' body but a closer investigation of some of the memoirs, Fell argues, shows such attitudes being challenged and altered under the pressure of actual encounters. The essays by Dendooven and Fell share a common impulse: focusing closely on individual responses, they open up an affective space where perceptions shift and exoticism and racism coexist with *caritas* and sympathy. While both essays show that the 'zones of contact' are underwritten by racial prejudices, they also indicate such hierarchies being challenged, pointing to the irreducibility of human experience.

Racism cannot be restricted, however, to the white/non-white divide. In the Indian war novel *Across the Black Waters* (1939), the sepoys see an African soldier and exclaim 'habshis' (a derogatory term for 'black'), emboldened by their 'superior brown skin': 'They are surely savages, are they not?' they ask.[60] In his exploration of the Anzac legend in Chapter 11, Stanley discusses a similar case of a West Indian soldier addressing an Australian Aborigine as 'an Australian nigger'.[61] Some of the most complex encounters between different racial groups took place in the mixed prisoner-of-war camps where the different kinds of identities – racial, national, religious and class – constantly reinforced and contradicted each other. In his memoir *In Kut and Captivity, with the Sixth Indian Division* (1919), Major Sandes recalls his 'shock' not only at how the Turks made the Muslim (beef-eating) Indian officers eat at the same table as the British officers but that, at breakfast, they served the Muslim officers first.[62] In Chapter 9, 'Imperial captivities: colonial prisoners of war in Germany and the Ottoman empire, 1914–1918', Heather Jones argues how Ottoman captivity involved a 'complex inversion of representations and power hierarchies'. Did the British soldiers view the Indians as fellow sufferers and allies or as the racial/colonial Other, or both at once? How did the Germans view their Turkish allies in relation to their white and non-white prisoners, and why did the 'racialised' discourse differ so much between the British, the Germans and the Ottomans? Jones's comparative investigation of these discourses in the war camps in

Germany and Mesopotamia complements the chapters by Koller and Das and opens up possibilities for transnational site-specific comparisons.

A new interracial dynamic is opened up by Christopher Pugsley in Chapter 10 ('Images of Te Hokowhitu A Tu in the First World War'), the final essay in this part of the volume. For the dominion troops, the racialised subject was not always the colonial Other or the enemy. Attitudes towards the participation of the indigenous people varied in the dominions, from General Botha's racist opposition in South Africa to the contemporary celebration of the Maori participation by New Zealand as an essential part of its fighting effort. Pugsley, who documented Maori participation in *Te Hokowhitu A Tu: The Maori Pioneer Battalion in the First World War* (2006), focuses here on their representations in cinema, a medium that was developing during the war. Through film footage and archival records, he investigates at once the Pakeha (white New Zealander) perception of Maori and their exoticisation on camera in France and Gallipoli in order to highlight the country's distinctive war contribution. If most of the chapters explore racial perception along the colonial axis, these images, trying to emphasise the young nation's racial integration, raise instead questions about the relationship between nationality, race relations and war service.

MEMORY, NATIONALISM AND LITERATURE

One of the most powerful areas of interest in recent years has been the subject of memory. '*Lieux de mémoire* exist because there are no longer *milieux de mémoire*, settings in which memory is a real part of everyday experience,' claims the French historian Pierre Nora, the main force behind the influential seven-volume *Les lieux de mémoire* (1984–92).[63] The public attention surrounding the death of Lazare Ponticelli, the last French combatant, in 2008, or of Harry Patch, 'the last British Tommy', in 2009 not only dramatised the relationship between the 'end of directly conveyed lived experience' and the 'increased demand for remembrance', but also underlined the connections between national identity, cultural memory and the First World War.[64] In such a context, one wonders what the European responses would have been if the last veteran were a tirailleur sénégalais or a Chinese worker. But, more important, how is the war remembered in the former dominions and colonies, and what differing uses is war service put to among the various racial and national groups? The essays in Part III explore these issues, often with reference to literary representations.

The work of Jay Winter on the European cultural memory of the First World War – particularly *Sites of Memory, Sites of Mourning* (1996) and

*Remembering War: The Great War and Historical Memory in the 20th
Century* (2006) – has been seminal to what he has called the 'memory
boom' in war studies.[65] Engaging with Nora's ideas, Winter notes:

One way to adapt the notion of *lieux de mémoire* in postcolonial scholarship is to
insist upon the hybrid character of colonial and postcolonial sites of memory. Each
and every one is a palimpsest, an overwritten text, with patterns emerging that
varied from the intention of the authors. Here I would like to use the word
'palimpsest' as something that is reused or altered but still bears visible traces of
its earlier form.[66]

The concept of the 'palimpsest' is richly suggestive. As Peter Stanley and
Jock Phillips explore, with reference to Australia and New Zealand respectively, the memory of the war is rewritten in a variety of contexts –
nationalism, official intervention or subsequent wars – but 'traces of its
earlier form' remain. Many of the chapters in this section excavate these
'traces' through a dialogue between archival, historical and literary material. At the same time, the essays also explore the national aspirations and
anxieties behind these accretions. In addition to such subsequent accretions, different, even contradictory, traces can be written at the same time:
war memory can be a patchwork too. For example, in a small private
archive in Chandernagore, India, one comes across the photograph of a
young man, his blood-stained broken glasses and a label that identifies
him as 'Dr. J. N. Sen, MD, MRCS, Private, West Yorkshire Regiment . . .
he was the first Bengalee, a citizen of Chandernagore, killed in 1914–1918
War'.[67] Now, was Dr Sen, a member of the elite Indian Medical Services,
fighting as a British imperial subject, or as a Bengali (a member of the
'non-martial' races) or as a resident of Chandernagore, which was a French
colony, or as all three?

   The nature of war memory differs substantially across the different parts
of the former empires. While in the former dominions such as Canada,
Australia and New Zealand, war service is often made the ground of
national identity, in countries such as India, Pakistan or Bangladesh the
subsequent nationalist struggle throws its shadow over imperial war participation. One further difference between war memory in the dominions and
the colonies is that the latter often do not have institutions comparable to
the Australian War Memorial (Canberra) or the Alexander Turnbull
Library (Wellington), nor is popular consciousness embedded in 'sites of
memory' such as war poems, exhibitions and memorials. Moreover, the
colonial home front remains one of the weakest links in the cultural history
of the war. Whilst work has been done on civilian responses in the

dominions, such as Joy Damousi's *The Labour of Love: Mourning, Memory and Wartime Bereavement in Australia* (1999) or the Canadian writer David Macfarlane's *The Danger Tree: Memory, War and the Search for a Family's Past* (1991), we know very little about wartime mourning in the villages of Asia or Africa.[68] Yet, often in these places, there remains a rich, subcutaneous layer of memory, not so much in official 'sites' but in acts of 'collective remembrance',[69] such as folksongs, stories and family histories.

Most of the essays in Part III examine the overwritten space between war experience and immediate post-war memory on one hand, and how this memory gets codified or accretes layers of meaning over time on the other. A good example is the Anzac myth in Australia. Peter Stanley in Chapter 11, "He was black, he was a White man, and a dinkum Aussie': race and empire in revisiting the Anzac legend', traces the extraordinary journey of 'Anzac' from an acronym to 'an idea, an ideal'. He illuminates a whole web of racial and imperial relationships from issues surrounding Aboriginal contribution to aspects of the Australian experience in Ceylon and West Africa which have largely been expunged from the Anzac legend and its celebratory rhetoric. The relation between the public and the private is also the theme for Jock Phillips's exploration of war memory in New Zealand in Chapter 12, 'The quiet Western Front: the First World War and New Zealand memory'. Here, as Phillips shows, a tradition of largely antiwar and anti-British 'digger' sentiments, surviving in private letters, memories and conversations, was buried or superseded by a government-driven culture of triumphant memorials, drawing on imperial and classical iconography. Traces of dissent remained in the form of the important antiwar novels of the 1930s, such Archibald Baxter's autobiographical *We Shall Not Cease* (1939) which went largely unnoticed. Antiwar literature and sentiment, central to British war memory – one of the main planks of Paul Fussell's argument in *The Great War and Modern Memory* (1975) – was not till the 1980s the dominant force in New Zealand.

One of the most fraught negotiations of war memory in recent years has been over the case of Ireland: long a source of division, war service has been re-examined in light of the Irish Troubles and turned into a platform for negotiation.[70] If nationalist rumblings were heard across the empire in 1914–1918, it was in Ireland that they were loudest, with the Easter Rising erupting in 1916. It is often assumed that in the post-war years, the Dublin GPO replaced the Somme in the nationalist iconography and the memory of the eleven rebels executed by the British supplanted that of the thousands of war dead. Not immediately or wholly, however, argues Keith Jeffery, whose *Ireland and the Great War* (2000) has played an important role in

debates about Irish war memory. In Chapter 13, '"Writing out of opinions":
Irish experience and the theatre of the First World War', he demonstrates
through a focus on Sean O'Casey's *The Silver Tassie* (1928) and Patrick
MacGill's *Suspense* (1930) that the so-called 'national amnesia' about nationalist (or rather 'non-unionist', as Jeffery puts it) Ireland's involvement in the
war was neither total nor immediate. If in current literary memory – as in
Frank McGuinness's play *Observe the Sons of Ulster Marching Towards the
Somme* (1985) – war service is often configured as an exclusively Protestant,
unionist affair, Jeffery analyses a more complex historical reality. Though
the focus is on Ireland, the chapter addresses certain issues underlying the
final part of this volume: the complex and multi-layered nature of memory
of the war, as well as the relationship between historical experience and
literary narrative.

A similarly fraught relation between imperial loyalty and nationalist aspiration underpinned war support in many of the colonies. An obvious parallel
to Ireland was India. At once echoing, and marking his difference from the
Irish nationalists, Mahatma Gandhi wrote: 'I thought that England's need
should not be turned into our opportunity.'[71] And yet, as with Irish non-
unionist volunteers, there was a strong expectation among Indians that war
service would lead to greater political autonomy. It is this terrain caught
between imperial zeal and a burgeoning nationalist/racial aspiration that
Richard Smith explores in relation to another colony: the West Indies. If
Smith recovered the war experiences in *Jamaican Volunteers in the First World
War* (2004), here he examines, in Chapter 14 ('"Heaven grant you strength to
fight the battle for your race": nationalism, Pan-Africanism and the First
World War'), the competing discourses surrounding such service and the
politics of war memory and commemoration in a postcolonial context.

What is particularly striking in the post-war discourses in Jamaica, as
Smith shows, is the evolution from an original agenda of imperial citizenship to a Pan-African consciousness. A key figure in this transformation was
Marcus Garvey. His move from Jamaica to the United States, and the
establishment of the Universal Negro Improvement Association (UNIA) in
1917 in Harlem, New York, partly signalled the shift. At a mass meeting in
Brooklyn in January 1919, Garvey declared:

Our sacrifices, as made in the cause of other people, are many . . . it is time that we
should prepare to sacrifice now for ourselves . . . Africa will be a bloody battlefield in
the years to come.[72]

Here we find a powerful appropriation of First World War vocabulary in
the fight against racism which, as Mark Whalan notes in the penultimate

essay (Chapter 15, 'Not only war: the First World War and African American literature'), characterises the representation of the war by the African American writers of the Harlem Renaissance. As for the colonial troops, war participation was for African Americans a momentous experience. In *The American Negro in the World War* (1919), Emmett Scott notes that service in the war had imbued the African American with 'a keener sense of his rights and privileges as a citizen of the US'.[73] Some of the most powerful expressions of this sentiment are to be found in the realm of literature. Concentrating on two novels – Jessie Fauset's *There Is Confusion* (1924) and Victor Daly's *Not Only War* (1932) – Whalan shows how these writers seize upon the war as the site for political change. For these writers, war trauma is not an interruption but a continuation of peacetime victimhood; no-man's-land is not the shot-riddled space evoked by Owen or Remarque but a zone of liberation where racial segregation does not operate. The increased political consciousness of the non-white soldiers and workers and the consequences of their war service – a theme implicit in many of the chapters in this volume – find some of their most complex explorations in the literature of the Harlem Renaissance.

In her introduction to *Evidence, History and the Great War* (2003), Gail Braybon noted that the future of First World War studies lies 'in collaboration and comparison': 'A more modest approach about the war in general would also be useful, together with an acknowledgement of how much there is still to find out'.[74] This is particularly true in relation to the colonial and racial aspects of the war where the scope and magnitude of the experience and its after-effects are almost inversely proportional to the attention that has been paid to them. Much work remains to be done. The fifteen chapters and the Afterword, through their selective focus, seek to suggest the richness of the subject, encourage dialogue and to make the memory of the war more multiracial and international.

NOTES

1 'India' is used here to refer to undivided British India which would today include India, Pakistan, Bangladesh and Sri Lanka. Mir Mast's desertion was an exceptional event and attracted wide notice. It is mentioned in the letters of E. B. Howell in December 1915, when he refers to Mir Mast and 'the German mission to Kabul', *Censor of Indian Mails 1914–1918*, l/MIL/5/828, Part I FF.1–202, 62–3 (India Office Library, British Library, London). In the Political Archive of the Foreign Office in Berlin, a document mentions 'Mirmatshah Sipahi' among the Afridi deserters interned in the POW camp at Sennelager and then includes 'Mirmast Sipahi' among the list of people who went to Constantinople

(Politisches Archiv des Auswärtigen Amtes, Berlin, April, 1915, R 21082–1, 13, f. 6). (I am grateful to Heike Liebau for pointing me to this reference.) Mir Mast's brother Mir Dast, also serving with the British army in the war, was awarded the Victoria Cross for his gallant actions in April 1915 and is commemorated in the Indian War Memorial in Hyde Park, London.

2 'Jemadar Mir Mast's diary', National Archives of India, Delhi, Foreign and Political, War B (Secret), February 1916, 32–4. I came upon the sealed envelope in the National Archives, Delhi in November 2006, and am grateful to the staff for allowing me to break the seal and read the fragile diary.

3 'Colonial troops and non-combatants' in this Introduction refer to the non-white troops and non-combatants of the British and French empires. In recent years, works on the contribution of the colonies and of particular racial groups have steadily grown in volume and they are mentioned under individual chapters. Also see Marc Michel, *L'Appel à L'Afrique, contributions et réactions à l'effort de guerre en AOF 1914–1918* (Paris: Publications de la Sorbonne, 1982); Myron Echenberg, *Colonial Conscripts: The Tirailleurs Sénégalais in French West Africa, 1857–1960* (London: James Curry, 1991); Melvin Page (ed.), *Africa and the First World War* (Basingstoke: Macmillan, 1987); David Omissi, *The Sepoy and the Raj: The Indian Army, 1860–1940* (London: Macmillan, 1994); David Killingray and David Omissi (eds.), *Guardians of Empire: The Armed Forces of the Colonial Powers c.1700–1964* (Manchester University Press, 1999); Chris Pugsley, *Te Hokowhitu a Tu: The Maori Pioneer Battalion in the First World War* (Reed: Auckland, 1995); Richard Smith, *Jamaican Volunteers in the First World War: Race, Masculinity and the Development of National Consciousness* (Manchester University Press, 2004); Joe Lunn, *Memoirs of the Maelstrom: A Senegalese Oral History of the First World War* (Portsmouth, NH: Heinemann, 1999); Christian Koller, *'Von Wilden aller Rassen niedergemetzelt'. Die Diskussion um die Verwendung von Kolonialtruppen in Europa zwischen Rassismus, Kolonial- und Militärpolitik (1914–1930)* (Stuttgart: Franz Steiner, 2001); Richard S. Fogarty, *Race and Empire in France: Colonial Subjects in the French Army, 1914–1918* (Baltimore, MD: Johns Hopkins University Press, 2008); George Robb, *British Culture and the First World War* (London: Palgrave, 2002), particularly the chapter on 'Nation, Race and Empire' (5–31). For the African American contribution, see Arthur E. Barbeau and Florette Henri, *The Unknown Soldiers: African-American Troops in World War I* (1974; New York: Da Capo Press, 1996); Mark Whalan, *The Great War and the Culture of the New Negro* (Gainesville: University Press of Florida, 2008). Also see Heike Liebau, Katrin Bromber, Katharina Lange, Dyala Hamzah and Ravi Ahuja (eds.), *The World in World Wars: Experiences and Perspectives from Africa and Asia* (Leiden and Baston: Brill, 2010). This volume was published when the present collection was already in the press and hence could not be engaged with in the Introduction or any of the chapters.

4 F. H. Grautoff, *Der Zusammenbruch der alten Welt*, quoted in Hew Strachan, *The First World War* (London: Viking, 2003), 69–70.

5 Strachan, *The First World War*, 69 (particularly see the chapter 'Global War', 67–95). For a powerfully detailed account of the opening years of the conflict, see Strachan, *The First World War: To Arms* (Oxford University Press, 2001).

6 According to *Statistics of the Military Effort of the British Empire during the Great War, 1914–1918* (London: His Majesty's Stationery Office, 1920), the total number of Indian ranks (combatants and non-combatants) recruited during the war and up to 31st December 1919 was 1,440,437; in addition, there was an estimated 239,561 men in the British Indian army in 1914 (777).

7 It is difficult to be precise about the numbers: estimates vary according to the sources and time frames used. The above figures are from *Statistics of the Military Effort*, 756, which lists the contributions of the British empire in terms of manpower between 4 August 1914 and 11 November 1918 as follows: 'British Isles 5,704,416, Canada 628,964, Australia 412,953, New Zealand 128,525, South Africa 136,070, India 1,440,437, Other Colonies ('Coloured troops from South Africa, West Indies & c') 134,837' (756). These are usually considered to be reliable, if approximate, figures: contributors of the following chapters consult and cite other sources as well.

8 Jay Winter, *The Great War and the British People* (London: Macmillan, 1986), 75.

9 As with troops from the British empire, the estimates vary. The figures cited are from Richard Fogarty, *Race and War in France*, 27. They are close to the figures given by Jacques Frémeaux according to whom a total of 545,240 *indigènes* were mobilised into the French army, of whom 437,653 came to Europe (*Les colonies dans la Grande Guerre: Combats et épreuves des peuples d'outre-mer* (Paris: Soteca, Editions 14–18, 2006, 63)). Also see Marc Michel, *L'Appel à L'Afrique*, 404. A helpful break-up of the different contingents of colonial troops and labourers mobilised into the European armies is provided in Christian Koller, '*Von Wilden aller Rassen niedergemetzelt*', 89–96.

10 Strachan, *The First World War* (2003), 67.

11 For an investigation into immigrant labourers in wartime France and their ethnic composition, see John Horne, 'Immigrant Workers in France during World War I', *French Historical Studies*, 14/1, 1985, 57–88.

12 Emmett Scott, *Scott's Official History of the American Negro in the World War* (Washington, DC, 1919), 458.

13 The term 'non-white' is admittedly problematic, defining people by what they are not, rather than what they are. But it is used here in an attempt to encompass people from the wide variety of racial and ethnic backgrounds from different parts of Asia, Africa and America who were pressed into service, as combatants and non-combatants, by the European and American armies during the First World War. The figure of over 4 million is arrived at easily by adding up the 1.4 million Indians, 2 million Africans, 400,000 African Americans, 100,000 Indochinese and 140,000 Chinese labourers, mentioned above. To this should be added, among other groups, the numbers of Maori, Aboriginal Australians, First Nations Canadians, West Indians and Amerindians. Not all of them saw active service though.

14 Letter originally in Urdu from England, 29 January 1915, *Censor of Indian Mails, 1914–1918*, L/MIL/5/828, Part 2, FF 203–408, 233, India Office Library, British Library, London.

15 Charles Bean (ed.), *The Official History of Australia in the War of 1914–1918*, 12
    vols., (Sydney: Angus and Robertson, 1921–43), vol. VI, 1,095; also see Kathryn
    Hunter, 'Sleep on dear Ernie, your battles are o'er': A Glimpse of a Mourning
    Community, Invercargill, New Zealand, 1914–1925', *War in History*, vol. 14 no. 1
    (2007), 36–62. According to Melville Page, 'the participation of the Malawians
    in the East African campaign drew them inexorably into a wider world . . . into a
    modern world system' (*The Chiwaya War: Malawians and the First World War*,
    (Oxford: Westview Press, 2000), 215).

16 Quoted in Christian Koller, 'Military Colonialism', in Dominiek Dendooven
    and Piet Chielens (eds.), *World War I: Five Continents in Flanders* (Ypres:
    Lanoo, 2006), 19.

17 For work on the contributions of these groups, see Pugsley, *Te Hokowhitu a Tu*;
    Desmond Ball (ed.) *Aborigines in the Defence of Australia* (Sydney: Australian
    National University Press, 1991); L. James Dempsey, *Warriors of the King:
    Prairie Indians in World War I* (Regina: Canadian Plains Research Centre,
    1999).

18 The exhibition also resulted in the lavishly illustrated and fascinating book
    World War I: Five Continents in Flanders.

19 John Horne's compendious edited volume *The Companion to World War I*
    (Malden and Oxford: Wiley-Blackwell, 2010) was published too late to be
    considered in the writing of this Introduction, or any of the essays in this book.

20 Examples would include Charles Lucas, *The Empire at War* (Oxford University
    Press, 1921) and Albert Sarraut, *La mise en valeur des colonies françaises* (Paris,
    1923).

21 See note 3.

22 Gail Braybon (ed.), *Evidence, History and the Great War: Historians and the
    Impact of 1914–18* (New York and Oxford: Berghahn Books, 2003), 28.

23 See Paul J. Bailey, Chapter 1 in this volume, 40.

24 See Joe Lunn, 'Remembering the Tirailleurs sénégalais and the Great War: Oral
    History as Methodology of Inclusion in French Colonial Studies', *French
    Colonial History* 10 (2009), 125–49. The audio recordings of POWs in
    Germany are now held by Lautarchiv of the Humboldt-University of Berlin.
    For research on audio recordings in German POW camps, see Jurgen
    Mahrenholz, 'Ethnographic Audio Recordings', and Britta Lange,
    '(Coloured) Prisoners of War', in Dendooven and Chielens (eds.), *Five
    Continents in Flanders*, and Phillip Scheffner's documentary *The Half-Moon
    Files* (2007). Also see Liebau *et al.* (eds.), *The World in World Wars*, and Ravi
    Ahuja, Heike Liebau and Franziska Roy (eds.), *'When the War Began, We Heard
    of Several Kings': South Asian Prisoners in World War I Germany* (Delhi: Social
    Science, forthcoming).

25 Given its focus on colonialism, this volume does not address the Jewish
    experience of 1914–18. This is an important area, but a separate study is needed
    to address the complexity of the subject. Existing works include George Mosse,
    Towards the Final Solution: A History of European Racism (New York: Howard
    Fertig, 1978); Mosse, *The Jews and the German War Experience 1914–1918*

(London: Leo Baeck Memorial Lecture, 1977); Leon Poliakov, *The History of Antisemitism: Suicidal Europe 1870–1933* (4 vols.) vol. iv trans. George Klin (Oxford University Press, 1985).

26 See Donald Bloxham, *The Great Game of Genocide: Imperialism, Nationalism and the Destruction of the Ottoman Armenians* (Oxford University Press, 2005); Jay Winter (ed.), *America and the Armenian Genocide of 1915* (Cambridge University Press, 2008); Aksakal Mustafa, *The Ottoman Road to War in 1914* (Cambridge University Press, 2009). Also see Panikos Panayi, *Minorities in Wartime: National and Racial Groupings in Europe, North America and Australia during the Two Wars* (Oxford: Berg, 1993).

27 'Letter from an African in France', *The Church Abroad*, 15 (1917), 122, quoted in Page, *Africa and the First World War*, 2.

28 Charles Mangin's arguments are set forth in *La Force Noir* (1910). Also see Charles John Balesi, *From Adversaries to Comrades-In-Arms: West Africans and the French Military 1885–1918* (Waltham, MA: African Studies Association, 1979), 57–78; Fogarty, *Race and Empire in France*, 15–54.

29 As already noted, the phrase 'colonial troops' is used in the Introduction to refer to colonial non-white troops.

30 For nineteenth-century writings on race, see Robert Knox, *The Races of Man* (London: Henry Renshaw, 1862), John Beddoes, *The Races of Britain* (London: Trubner and Company, 1885) and J. Deniker, *The Races of Men: An Outline of Anthropology and Ethnography* (London: Walter Scott, 1900). There is a substantial amount of good work on race. For works relevant to the present topic, see George Mosse, *Toward the Final Solution*; Daniel Pick, *Faces of Degeneration: A European Disorder 1848–1918* (Cambridge University Press, 1993); Kenan Malik, *The Meaning of Race* (London: Palgrave, 1996). Also see Peter Robb (ed.), *The Concept Of Race in South Asia* (Delhi: Oxford University Press, 1997); Richard Ned Lebow, *White Britain and Black Ireland: The Influence of Stereotype on Colonial Policy* (Philadelphia: Institute for the Study of Human Issues, 1976).

31 Knox, *The Races of Man*, 224, 268, 314.

32 Pick, *Faces of Degeneration*, 38–9.

33 Quoted in Malik, *Meaning of Race*, 120.

34 Pick, *Faces of Degeneration*, 41. At the same time, one can argue that cutting across the conflation of race with ethnicity and class, a sense of the 'immeasurable gulf' between the 'white' and 'dark' races remained even in the Victorian times.

35 Malik, *Meaning of Race*, 117.

36 J. H. Morgan, *German Atrocities: An Official Investigation* (London: T. Fisher Unwin, 1916) 52–3, 114–15; quoted in Albert Marrin, *The Church of England in the First World War* (Durham, NC: Duke University Press, 1974), 92.

37 *The Times History of the War*, vol. i (London: The Times, 1914), 155.

38 Tyler Stovall, 'The Color Line behind the Lines: Racial Violence in France during the Great War', *American Historical Review*, vol. 103, no. 3 (June 1998), 740. A different dynamic was, however, at work with African American troops.

39 See Heather Streets, *Martial Races: The Military, Race and Masculinity in British Imperial Culture, 1857–1914* (Manchester University Press, 2005); Fogarty, *Race and War in France*, 96–132.

40 For army recruitment according to the 'martial race' theory, see Omissi, *The Sepoy and the Raj*, 1–46; also see Tai Yong Tan, *The Garrison State: The Military, Government and Society in Colonial Punjab 1849–1947* (New Delhi: Manohar, 2005).

41 Mangin, *La Force Noir*, 258, quoted in Joe Lunn, '"Les Races Guerrieres": Racial Preconceptions in the French Military about West African Soldiers during the First World War', *Journal of Contemporary History*, vol. 34. no. 4 (October 1999), 523 (517–36).

42 See Echenberg, *Colonial Conscripts*, 42–6; Fogarty, *Race and War in France*, 24–54.

43 *Communication for New Loyalties: African Soldiers' Song*, quoted in Page, *Africa and the First World War*, 15.

44 See Dominiek Dendooven, 'The British Dominions and Colonies' in *World War I: Five Continents in Flanders*, 96; Duncan Campbell Scott, 'Canadian Indians and the Great War', in *Canada in the Great World War: Guarding the Channel Ports* by 'Various Authorities' (Toronto: United Publishers of Canada Limited, 1919), vol. III, 285–328. Also see Calvin Ruck, *The Black Battalion 1916–1920: Canada's Best Kept Military Secret* (Halifax: Nimbus Publishing Limited,1987).

45 David Killingray, 'The War in Africa', in Strachan (ed.), *The Oxford Illustrated History of the First World War* (Oxford University Press, 1998), 98. Also see David Killingray and James Matthews, 'Beasts of Burden: British West African Carriers in the First World War', *Canadian Journal of African Studies*, vol.13, No.1/2 (1979), 7–23; Geoffrey Hodges, *The Carrier Corps: Military Labour in the East African Campaign of 1914 to 1918* (New York: Greenwood Press, 1986). Albert Grundling, 'The Impact of the First World War on South African Blacks', *War and Society*, 3, 1 (May, 1985); Pugsley, *Te Hokowhitu a Tu*.

46 Letter from an unnamed sepoy, Brighton Pavilion Hospital, 14 January 1916, *Censor of Indian Mails*, 1914–1918, L/MIL/5/828, Part I, FF.1–202, 112, India Office Library.

47 John Horne, 'Immigrant Workers in France during World War I', *French Historical Studies*, vol. 14 no. 1 (Spring 1985), 80; 57–88. Tyler Stovall has worked extensively in this area: see 'Love, Labor and Race: Colonial Men and White Women in France During the Great War', in Stovall and Georges Van Den Abbeele (eds.), *French Civilisation and Its Discontents* (Lanham: Lexington, 2002).

48 Omissi (ed.), *Indian Voices*, 99.

49 Quoted in Page, *The Chiwaya War*, 32.

50 The *Grenada Federalist* (27 October 1915), quoted in Glenford Howe, *Race, War and Nationalism: A Social History of West Indians in the First World War* (Kingston: James Currey, 2002), 17.

51 See James K. Matthews, 'World War I and the Rise of African Nationalism: Nigerian Veterans as Catalysts of Change', *Journal of Modern African Studies*, 20, 3 (1982), 493–502.

52 Stovall, 'Love, Labour, Race', 297. Though the wounded Indian soldiers were nursed in hospitals in England, it was largely the white dominion troops who were more welcome to, and indeed did visit, the imperial centre.

53 Omissi (ed.), *Indian Voices*; Stovall, 'Love, Labour and Race', 297–321; Horne, in 'Immigrant Workers in France' (57–88), focuses on a particular economic class and gives an illuminating account of different racial and national groups.

54 See Martin Gregory, 'The Influence of Racial Attitudes on British Policy towards India in the First World War', *Journal of Imperial and Commonwealth History* 14 (1986), 91–113; Gregory, 'German and French Perceptions of the French North and West African contingents, 1910–1918', *Militärgeschichtliche Mitteilungen* 56 (1997), 31–68.

55 See Dendooven and Chielens (eds.), *World War I*, 197.

56 Balesi, *From Adversaries to Comrades-in-Arms*, 117.

57 Cited in W. Allison Sweeney, *History of the American Negro in the Great War* (Chicago, 1919), 195.

58 Tyler Stovall, 'The Color Line behind the Lines: Racial Violence in France during the Great War', *American Historical Review*, vol. 103, no. 3 (June 1998), 766 (737–69).

59 Lucie Cousturier, *Des inconnus chez moi* (1920; Paris: L'Harmattan, 2001), 8–9. Cousturier records how, with time, such dread changes to one of warm greeting. I am grateful to Alison S. Fell for her translation.

60 Mulk Raj Anand, *Across the Black Waters* (1939; Delhi: Orient Paperbacks, 1980), 93–4.

61 See Peter Stanley, Chapter 11 in this volume, 225.

62 Major F. W. C. Sandes, *In Kut and Captivity, with the Sixth Indian Division* (London: John Murray, 1919), 285, 287.

63 Pierre Nora, 'General Introduction: Between Memory and History', in *Realms of Memory: Rethinking the French Past*, ed. Lawrence D. Kritzman, trans. Arthur Goldhammer, 3 vols. (New York: Columbia University Press, 1996–8), vol. 1, 1. This is the English translation of the original seven-volume *Les lieux de mémoire* (Paris, 1984–92) edited by Pierre Nora.

64 See, for example, Peter Parker, *The Last Veteran: Harry Patch and the Legacy of War* (London: Fourth Estate, 2009).

65 In *Sites of Memory*, Winter famously took issue with Paul Fussell's thesis in *The Great War and Modern Memory* (Oxford University Press, 1975) that the war ushered in the modern 'ironic consciousness'; Winter instead convincingly goes on to show the continuation of more traditional forms of mourning. Also see Dan Todman, *The Great War: Myth and Memory* (London: Hambledon and London, 2005). Winter's other works include: Winter and Emmanuel Sivan (eds.), *War and Remembrance in the Twentieth Century* (Cambridge University Press, 2000); Winter and Antoine Prost, *The Great War in History: Debates and Controversies* (Cambridge University Press, 2005).

66 Jay Winter, 'Palimpsests', in Indra Sengupta (ed.), *Memory, History and Colonialism* (London: German Historical Institute, 2009), 167 (167–73).

67 Dr J. N. Sen, 'Papers', Dupleix House, Chandernagore, West Bengal.

68 An encouraging example of this kind of work is Melvin Page's *The Chiwaya War* which explores the war's social and emotional impact on Malawi, then Nyasaland.

69 See Winter and Sivan, *War and Remembrance in the Twentieth Century*, 6–10.

70 See Keith Jeffery, *Ireland and the Great War* (Cambridge University Press, 2000); also see Adrian Gregory and Senia Paseta (eds.), *Ireland and the Great War* (Manchester University Press, 2002)

71 M. K. Gandhi, *An Autobiography or, The Story of My Experiments with Truth*, trans. Mahadev Desai, (Harmondsworth: Penguin, 1982), 317.

72 Marcus Garvey, *West Indian* (Grenada), 28 February 1919. See Richard Smith, Chapter 14 in this volume, 275.

73 Scott, *The Official History of the American Negro*, 458.

74 Braybon, *Evidence, History and the Great War*, 8.

PART I

Voices and experiences

CHAPTER I

'An army of workers': Chinese indentured labour in First World War France

Paul J. Bailey

In the autumn of 1919, as the victorious allies gathered in France for the Versailles Peace Conference to draw up the post-World War One settlement, they were joined by the little-noticed delegation from China. Having formally declared war on Germany in August 1917, China had earned the right to attend the conference – its presence symbolising, in effect, the first time in the modern era that the Western powers had acquiesced in China's membership of the international community.[1] While his colleagues busied themselves preparing their negotiating positions, a member of the Chinese delegation – a legal counsellor employed by the Ministry of Internal Affairs – composed the words of a stirring song to commemorate the contribution China had made to the war:

> Since leaving our motherland
> we have crossed seas and mountains.
> Whether metal, stone, earth or wood, we can work it,
> the devastation of war we can repair.
> We, the children of sacred China whose fate lies with heaven,
> esteem the farmer and favour the artisan, but never resort to force.
> Marching, marching, ever marching.
> All within the four seas are brothers.
> We are an army of workers devoting ourselves to labour
> in order to build peace for you, humanity.[2]

The 'army of workers' referred to by the Chinese counsellor were the nearly 140,000 Chinese contract labourers (mainly from the northern provinces of Shandong and Hebei) recruited by the British and French governments between 1916 and 1918 to make up for labour shortages in France, as well as to release British dockworkers in French ports for military duty.

During their sojourn in France these Chinese labourers, most of whom were not repatriated until 1919–20, were involved in a wide variety of war-related work both behind the lines (transportation, armaments and munitions production, machinery maintenance, and aerodrome construction) and

at the front (road repairs, digging trenches, burying war dead). Those recruited
by the British government (organised into labour battalions under the general
name of the Chinese Labour Corps) constituted a significant proportion of the
total amount of overseas manpower used by Britain in France during the war
(totalling nearly 96,000, Chinese workers represented nearly fifty per cent of
the total number of overseas labour that included 48,000 Indians, 21,000 black
South Africans, 15,000 Egyptians, and 8,000 West Indians). France recruited
more widely from its colonies (78,000 from Algeria, 49,000 from Vietnam,
35,500 from Morocco, and 18,000 from Tunisia), but still relied upon a
relatively large number of Chinese workers (approximately 37,000) to carry
out vital war work.[3] They were fitters, for example, in locomotive and tank
workshops, power and pumping stations and heavy plants. Much of the port
construction work was carried out by Chinese labour, while in some ports,
such as Dieppe, virtually all the cranes were operated by Chinese workers.

The song's representation of the Chinese workers as the confident and
proud benefactors of world peace, however, contrasted sharply with the
attitudes expressed in a poem that had appeared one year earlier in the
memoir of the British commander of a Chinese labour battalion. Entitled
'The Happy Labourer', the poem emphasised the childlike naivety of the
Chinese worker and the opportunity *given* by the 'white man' to add
meaning to his *pointless and blank life* by becoming involved in the war:

> In the Middle Kingdom he was born,
> frail life, left alone, forlorn.
> Among the millet, rape and rice
> he seemed unworthy at half price.
> Uglier than the dust he seemed,
> love was not his, dead or dreamed. [...]
> Until one day the Great White came
> and gave his pattern mind an aim,
> and sent him packing overseas
> with a hundred thousand more Chinese,
> and landed him in warring France
> to do his bit and take his chance.
> With pick and shovel, pole and spade,
> The happy labourer, born not made,
> bears his burden and does his bit –
> with nimble limb and nimble wit,
> side by side with Tommy he toils
> all unaware for immortal spoils.[4]

These contrasting representations of Chinese workers were echoed in the
very terms used to designate them. In Chinese documents of the time, the

contract workers recruited by Britain and France were referred to as *huagong* (overseas Chinese worker), a term that was meant to differentiate them from indentured workers ('coolies') of the past, who had contemptuously been referred to as *zhuzai* ('swine') by Chinese officials – reflecting a long tradition of official condemnation of, and scorn for, all those who in one way or the other emigrated from China to improve their livelihoods. Chinese workers recruited by France, however, were unceremoniously categorised together with conscript workers from France's colonies and placed under the administrative supervision of the Service d'organisation des travailleurs coloniaux (Colonial Labour Service).[5] Those recruited by Britain, moreover, continued to be referred to as 'coolies' in the English version of the written contract (French-language documents, by way of contrast, used either the more neutral terms of *travailleurs chinois* and *main-d'oeuvre chinois* or the more orientalist *main-d'oeuvre exotique*).

   While attention has always been paid by both Western and Chinese historians to the May Fourth Movement, large-scale student and worker protests in 1919 against the Allied decision at Versailles to allow Japan to retain control (acquired in 1914) of the former German leasehold territory of Jiaozhou in northern China rather than returning it to Chinese sover-eignty – protests that conventionally have been viewed as signifying the beginnings of a mass nationalism in China – the story of Chinese contract workers seems to have disappeared down a historical black hole or, at best, has been relegated to a brief reference or footnote in general histories of modern China.[6] Conventional Eurocentric approaches to the First World War have also largely overlooked the story of the Chinese labourers, a lacuna that persists in English- and French-language scholarship on First World War labour mobilisation.[7] Chinese-language scholarship on the subject has likewise been sparse, producing to date only one monograph.[8] There are two reasons for this. First, while in 1922 T. Z. Tyau, a lawyer and technical adviser to the Chinese delegation at the League of Nations Assembly, fulsomely praised the 'honourable' role played by Chinese workers in the recent world war and claimed that the admiration and gratitude expressed by both publics and governments in Britain and France meant that the 'world may be almost said to be lying at the Chinese labourer's feet',[9] post-1949 Chinese Communist historiography especially has considered the recruitment of Chinese workers in the First World War as simply a minor and shameful episode in a much longer history of Western exploitation of China and hence not worthy of in-depth study. Second, the episode has always been overshadowed by the greater attention paid to the over 1,000 Chinese work-study students who went to France in the period immediately after the First World War (especially as such students included the future Chinese Communist Party leaders Zhou Enlai and Deng Xiaoping).

CHINESE SUPPORT FOR THE RECRUITMENT

Although the recruitment of Chinese contract workers during the First World War should certainly be viewed as an episode in a much longer history of overseas Chinese labour migration that dates from the nineteenth century, it is important to note that the First World War recruitment was very different from the unregulated and illegal 'coolie' trade of the nineteenth century, when up to 500,000 Chinese indentured workers were recruited principally to work on sugar plantations in Peru, Cuba, British Guiana and the Caribbean.[10] The trade was illegal because the reigning Qing dynasty in China had officially proscribed emigration in 1712. The ban reflected a long-held assumption that overseas migrants were potential troublemakers who might participate in rebellion on their return or engage in piracy along China's coastal regions. Such an official ban, however, did not deter foreign agencies based in China's treaty ports – where they enjoyed immunity from Chinese jurisdiction because of the privilege of extraterritoriality granted to all foreigners in China – from recruiting Chinese indentured labour (often forcibly or through deception) from the mid 1840s to 1873 (when the trade was formally ended). The appalling conditions and treatment suffered by these labourers gradually convinced the dynasty that strict official supervision of recruitment practices and conditions had to be implemented, although the 'coolies' were by no means mere passive victims of the trade. In 1857, for example, the *Anaïs*, a French-registered ship carrying Chinese indentured labourers to Cuba, was discovered wrecked off the coast near Macao in southern China. Apparently, the 'coolies' had mutinied, killing all officers and seamen on board, and had tried to steer the ship back to the coast. After running aground near Macao, according to official French sources, the 'coolies' all dispersed and returned to their homes.[11]

In 1866, in response to the British and French demand in 1860 that the ban on emigration be lifted, the Qing government drafted regulations on the recruitment of Chinese indentured labour; these regulations would have limited the term of indenture to five years and guaranteed free passage home after expiry of the contract.[12] They were to serve as the basis for both the recruitment of Chinese labour to work in the gold mines of the Transvaal in South Africa in 1904–6[13] and, especially, for war-related work in France during the First World War. By this time, in fact, it was accepted by both British and French recruiters that, first, in order to guarantee transparency, the text of the indenture had to be published openly in the Chinese press and had to specify duration, wage rates and the number of working hours. Second, indentured labourers should be given the right to free medical assistance and paid passage home after the contracts had expired; and thirdly, that Chinese inspectors were to be present at embarkation ports and in France to oversee the workers' welfare.

Two important Chinese constituencies actively supported the recruitment of Chinese labour during the First World War. The first comprised government and official elites in Beijing, who responded enthusiastically to the initial French request for Chinese labour in 1915 in order to enhance China's standing at a future peace conference (on three occasions between 1914 and 1917, the Chinese government actually proposed China's *military* participation in the war – a prospect rejected outright by the American and British governments for logistical and financial reasons, as well as from a general lack of faith in the fighting potential of the Chinese soldier, although the French government continued to support the idea until March 1918).[14] The second constituency was a group of Chinese Francophile intellectuals and educators who, since the turn of the twentieth century, had been promoting Sino-French cultural relations and the importance of overseas study in France. The most prominent member of this group was Li Shizeng (1881–1973), son of a Qing court official who had studied in France during 1902–7 (at the École pratique d'agriculture in Montargis and the Pasteur Institute in Paris).[15] Li became a fervent admirer of French culture (including French anarchist thought), and often contrasted the 'worthy' ideals of the French secular republic ('freedom', 'creativity', 'pacifism') with the apparently more 'brutal' ideals of German 'autocracy, utilitarianism, and militarism'.[16]

Li and other members of the Chinese Francophile lobby welcomed the prospect of France's recruitment of Chinese labour in 1916 as part of their larger cultural and social agenda. Li confidently predicted that enormous benefits would accrue to China, as the Chinese labourers would form the vanguard of an educated workforce contributing to the diffusion of industrial skills and reform of society on their return. During their time in France, Li predicted, Chinese workers would become truly 'civilised', divesting themselves of their 'backward' and 'unseemly' habits and customs.[17] He joined with prominent French intellectuals such as Alphonse Aulard in establishing the Sino-French Education Association in 1916 as an umbrella organisation to promote cultural relations as well as to organise part-time education for the soon-to-be-arriving Chinese workers.

ATTITUDES TOWARDS THE CHINESE WORKERS

As early as May 1916, the first contract for recruitment of Chinese labour had been signed by representatives of the French government in Beijing and a private Chinese company (in effect, a front for the Chinese government itself since China was still officially neutral at this time); the first group of Chinese workers (totalling nearly 1,700) arrived in France in August 1916. The first contingent of Chinese workers recruited by Britain (totalling 1,000) arrived in Plymouth in April 1917 before being transported to France. Whereas those recruited by Britain had three-year contracts (to be paid one franc a day) and were billeted in camps along France's western coast to replace British dock and transport workers, those recruited by France had five-year contracts (to be paid 2.5 francs a day, although more skilled workers such as machinists were paid between five and eight francs a day). They were more widely dispersed throughout the country in smaller camps near rural settlements, working in government munition plants as well as in privately owned metallurgical, chemical and construction firms. However, after August 1917, when China formally declared war on Germany, Chinese workers were also expected to work near the front lines, exhuming and burying the war dead as well as repairing trench dugouts and keeping machine-gun emplacements in order. The large majority of these Chinese workers were from poor peasant families in northern China (in particular the province of Shandong, the birthplace of Confucius), although a Chinese employee of the YMCA in France at the time later recalled that included among the ranks of this 'army' of Chinese labour were a small number of impoverished students and holders of the traditional lower-level civil service degree, unemployed minor officials, and demobilised soldiers.[18] Early contingents were transported via the Suez Canal and the Mediterranean or the Cape of Good Hope; many of the later contingents – in order to avoid possible German submarine attack – were conveyed to Europe via the Pacific, then overland by train across Canada, before finally being shipped across the Atlantic to England.[19] Gu Xingqing, a Chinese interpreter who accompanied one group of 3,000 workers in 1917, later remembered that while the group was being transported across Canada, British troops were stationed in every carriage to ensure that no Chinese worker absconded and 'disappeared' amongst the Chinese emigrant community already in Canada. The whole journey lasted nearly three months.[20]

How were Chinese workers perceived by their British and French employers, and how are we to capture the voices of the workers themselves given the paucity of written records? Only a few scattered oral testimonies have been recorded, and they contain only frustratingly thin details. Thus the 86-year-old Cong Shugui (from Weihai in Shandong province) remembered in 1988 that he and other Chinese workers were present at the Third Battle of Ypres in 1917 repairing trenches and carrying the wounded to safety; he also mentioned that since most of his compatriots had never seen a plane before, they would often recklessly come out of their dugouts to marvel at the German planes overhead with the result that many were killed.[21] Another former First World War worker, Yan Zhensheng, remembered (in the 1990s) the role played by British missionaries operating in Shandong province in publicising and encouraging the recruitment, and that the primary motive for him and others from his village in signing up was to 'make a lot of money' *(fale dacai)*.[22] Zhang Bangyong, a student at the time who signed up to be an interpreter for the Chinese Labour Corps, remembered in the 1960s that some of the Chinese workers still wore *queues* – the Manchu hairstyle for men that had been formally proscribed after the overthrow of the Manchu Qing dynasty in 1911. One worker in particular (who was adept in martial skills) refused the order of a British recruiting officer in Weihai to cut off his *queue* (the officer apparently backed down when the worker threatened to return home), and again refused to obey such an order when he arrived in France; it was only when Zhang himself convinced the worker that the *queue* was *not* a venerable Chinese tradition that he finally cut it off.[23]

Nevertheless, an indirect insight into what Chinese workers thought, how they viewed their surroundings, and how they responded to perceived mistreatment or poor working conditions can be gained from a reading of the Chinese-language journals published in France by the Chinese Francophile 'lobby', as well as the reports of French employers complaining about the attitudes and behaviour of Chinese contract workers. Such a reading highlights the ways in which the workers confounded the stereotypical and condescending views their hosts had of them. A prevailing view at the time of the recruitment, for example, was that the Chinese workers were 'docile', 'malleable' and 'childlike' – well illustrated by a 1917 report in *The Times*. It noted that, as a result of the recruitment, it was normal that the Picardy landscape in France might include 'a squad of Chinamen in blue or terracotta blouses and flat hats, hauling logs or loading trucks, always with that inscrutable smile of the Far East upon their smooth, yellow faces':

The Chink, like the Kaffir, has to be kept under ward when he is not working. He gives little trouble if rightly managed, gambles a good deal, but does not get drunk or commit violence and is docile and obedient.[24]

One year later, as the Chinese workers recruited by Britain were about to be repatriated, an article in the *North China Herald*, an English-language newspaper managed by British residents in Shanghai, informed its readers:

Not a man will return [i.e. to China] the same as he came out . . . After all, they are only great big boys, and whatever their age may be, they are none of them older than ten years in character . . . very amenable, easily managed with kindness and firmness, and loyal to the core if treated with consideration . . . They bear nothing but dislike for anyone who is afraid of them. A dog is the same.[25]

However, significantly imbricated in such condescending attitudes was always an underlying fear of 'loss of face' on the part of French and British authorities vis-à-vis the Chinese contract workers – a concern that revealed more about French and British feelings of insecurity than anything else. Instructions from the Service d'organisation des travailleurs coloniaux sent to potential French employers of Chinese labour in September 1916 clearly demonstrated this French obsession with 'face':[26]

The Chinese have considerable self-pride (*amour-propre*), and it is therefore appropriate to treat them with kindness, and give them a reward, however minimal, every time they try to do something well. An act of brutality will bring the opposite of what is intended, since anyone giving in to anger will lose all credibility in their eyes . . . It is imperative that employers, foremen, etc., realise that in the view of the Chinese, to give in to an external manifestation of anger is proof of an inability to control oneself *and thus (in the eyes of the Chinese) to remain a barbarian*. [emphasis mine].[27]

A 1919 report in *La revue de Paris* on a Chinese labour camp near Rouen likewise condemned the general demeanour of the Chinese workers because they 'retained towards us [i.e. the French] their condescending and arrogant superiority'.[28]

A similar paranoia underpinned instructions from General HQ for officers of the British-managed Chinese Labour Corps in October 1917. These instructions insisted that barracks housing the Chinese workers should not be located in close proximity to camps accommodating white personnel; furthermore, Chinese workers were not to be allowed to work in locations 'where they could judge or criticise the same class of work performed by white men'.[29] Further instructions in 1918 stressed the need for careful management of the Chinese workforce because the Chinese 'coolie' could 'drive a hard bargain, and is an artist at loafing and a splendid bluffer'. Any mismanagement, it declared, would 'induce them [i.e. the Chinese] *to regard our brains as inferior to their own* [emphasis mine]'.[30] Significantly, a British missionary referred in 1920 to the apparent Chinese proclivity for dressing up in foreign garments and caricaturing the 'funny' foreigner.[31]

A condescending approach towards the Chinese workers also character-ised the views of Li Shizeng and other members of the Chinese Francophile lobby, for whom the First World War recruitment of Chinese labour was a heaven-sent opportunity to 'correct' the character deficiencies of the Chinese worker; for example, Li believed that since the French were both diligent and proficient at 'accumulating money' (*zhuji*), they would be appropriate role models for the 'irresponsible' and 'spendthrift' Chinese worker. In 1916, Li Shizeng opened a Chinese workers' school in Paris (with financial help from the French government) to provide instruction in French, Chinese and science.[32] Cai Yuanpei, another prominent member of the Francophile lobby (and the first Minister of Education of the newly established Chinese Republic in 1912) who was shortly to be appointed Chancellor of Beijing University, compiled a series of lectures for the school that drew attention to Chinese people's 'backward' habits (such as unclean-liness, cursing in public, and superstitious beliefs) and recommended the adoption of 'civilised' Western ways such as politeness, a sense of decorum (which included standing up for women on public transport), a love of animals, and concern for public welfare.[33] Li Shizeng prescribed a detailed set of behavioural rules for Chinese workers in 1917 designed to make them more 'civilised'; such rules included to wipe shoes before entering a build-ing, not to open a window in the morning if still dressed in nightclothes, always to knock and wait for a reply before entering a room, not to spit or shout in public, and not to pick a fight if pushed or shoved in a crowd.[34] The Chinese Minister to France at this time likewise evinced a concern with protecting China's reputation, insisting that Chinese workers in France had to be seen as frugal and industrious in order to avoid ridicule and scorn from their hosts.[35]

CHINESE WORKERS' VOICES

These representations notwithstanding, it is clear from a reading of con-temporary Chinese-language journals and the reports of French employers that another reality existed. Chinese workers exercised considerable initia-tive in deciding what their interests were and in responding to or protesting against perceived breaches in their contracts, the dangerous nature of their work, and the harsh treatment to which they were at times exposed. The 700 Chinese workers in Toulouse, for example, organised spare-time classes for themselves (sometimes asking for help from Chinese members of the

YMCA in France).[36] After 1918–19, when an increasing number of Chinese work-study students began arriving in France,[37] workers would often set up their own spare-time school and then invite students to help with the teaching, as did four hundred Chinese workers employed in a factory in Fargniers (Picardy).[38] Literacy was perceived by workers as especially beneficial because it would enable them to avoid reliance on the more educated Chinese interpreters to read their letters from home for them (not all interpreters were infallible, since one unfortunate in Caen was severely assaulted by an irate Chinese worker after the interpreter had apparently got the gist of a letter wrong!).[39] Literacy in French was also prized by the Chinese workers as it would enable them to avoid unfortunate misunderstandings such as befell one of their number in Le Creusot (Burgundy) in January 1918. Not realising the significance of the bread ration ticket that he had been given, the worker did not take it when he visited a local bakery; when he was refused bread, he expressed his bewilderment and frustration by smashing up the premises.[40] The workers' study endeavours could be impressive. Of the 930 Chinese workers employed at a match factory in Vonges (Côte d'Or in eastern France), for example, 20 per cent were attending spare-time classes and lectures by March 1919; a further 50 per cent were studying in their spare time, and 30 per cent were reading (on a regular basis) copies of the *Huagong zazhi* (Chinese Workers' Magazine), a Chinese-language journal published in France by Li Shizeng and other members of the Francophile lobby.[41]

Chinese workers also organised 'self-governing associations' (*zizhi hui*) of their own; these were mutual help organisations that aimed to oversee members' behaviour and encourage the elimination of 'bad habits' such as drinking, fighting, frequenting prostitutes, and gambling (the latter could have drastic consequences: one worker in Le Creusot, for example, committed suicide after he lost more than 1,000 francs in a gambling spree).[42] Members of such associations could be fined, and it was impressed upon them that it was their *patriotic duty* to save money and study.[43] At the end of 1919, a General Association of Chinese Workers in France (*liufa huagong gonghui*) was established with similar aims; by 1920, it had a membership of 1,500, according to the Paris Prefect of Police.[44]

In addition to their active pursuit of literacy and self-improvement, many Chinese workers in France clearly began to think of themselves as belonging to a wider constituency than simply their lineage, village or province – a development that can be seen as the beginnings of a concrete manifestation of a burgeoning national consciousness that transcended more narrow loyalties. In October 1919, for example, Chinese factory workers in Capdenac (southern France) got together to embroider a flag commemorating 'national day' (10 October 1911, when a military mutiny in central China had presaged the overthrow of the Qing monarchy and the establishment of a republic).[45] More remarkably, hundreds of Chinese workers responded to the news that floods had engulfed the northern province of Hebei in 1918 by contributing some of their hard-earned wages to famine relief. The 500 workers in Le Creusot donated 557 francs, the 550 in Suresnes (west of Paris) donated 1,643 francs, and the 1,000 in Vonges contributed over 2,000 francs. Even the small group of Chinese workers in Boulogne (35 in all) gave nearly 700 francs.[46] Such an emerging national consciousness could also be especially sensitive to any perceived slight. Gu Xingqing remembers that after the war, the British army in Belgium organised an international athletics meeting; although nearly 6,000 Chinese workers turned up to participate in the competition, they withdrew when they noticed that no Chinese flag was being displayed.[47]

Contemporary reports by French officials and employers of Chinese labour also indicate that Chinese workers were not the 'docile' and 'obedient' workforce (if 'handled properly'!) they were assumed to be. Their protests against perceived injustices took a variety of forms. In some cases they would resort to flight, such as those at a munitions plant in St Louis de Rhône (near Arles); when refused overtime pay in March 1918, they simply upped sticks and set off for Marseilles by foot (they apparently did not get very far since they were arrested by local police just outside the town).[48] Others, such as the 200 in Caen, went on strike in response to the reduction of bread rations in May 1918; an insistence that they be given 'proper food' (and the threat of strike action) compelled French employers to abandon their ploy of substituting horse-meat for beef or other meat.[49] At dockyards such as Saint-Nazaire, Chinese workers simply refused to unload coal because they considered such a task unsafe (and 'dirty') and not part of the contract – much to the fury of French dockyard managers and local officials, who frequently condemned the Chinese workers as 'lazy troublemakers' and demanded that they be replaced by more 'amenable' workers. The 150 Chinese workers at Saint-Nazaire were eventually transferred in February 1918 to Nantes, where they were employed in unloading goods such as cereals (which they regarded as acceptable).[50] Strikes also took place amongst Chinese working on the railroads, for example, on the Paris–Orleans line at Perigueux in February 1917, when over 100 protested over pay (in July 1917 two striking Chinese workers actually attempted to derail a train at St.Barthelemy-le-Plain in south-central France).[51]

In other cases, disputes could lead to physical violence. One such serious incident occurred in Le Creusot in November 1916. A group of French workers became infuriated when a Chinese worker refused to help them pull a baggage cart and, in the scuffle that ensued, they gravely wounded this Chinese man. On learning this, his compatriots from a nearby camp came out in force to avenge him. One of the French workers was beaten up while the others took refuge in a local café, which was literally placed under siege by the angry Chinese workers (totalling about two hundred according to official reports); following the demise of one of them, shot dead by the café owner, the Chinese workers proceeded to demolish the café. Only police intervention and the arrest of the café owner on a charge of homicide (he was later released) brought an end to the violence.[52] In March 1918, French soldiers fired on protesting Chinese workers in Rouen who had attacked a police station in which a French soldier thought to be one of the assailants of a Chinese worker earlier in the day had taken refuge.[53]

In two incidents the previous year, Chinese workers had been killed by armed police or troops. At a chemical plant in Saint-Fons (near Lyon) in July, striking Chinese workers attacked with sticks and stones both the manager and soldiers posted outside the camp; the soldiers fired on them and two workers were killed.[54] Two months later, five hundred Chinese workers in Firminy (Loire region) refused to work because of the dangers posed by enemy bombardments. When the police were called in to preserve order, they were met by a hail of bricks; although those police units that were armed began firing in the air, the Chinese workers were apparently not intimidated in any way. The police thereupon fired directly at them, killing one and seriously wounding six.[55] At the steelworks in St-Etienne, according to a secret telegram sent by the Interior Ministry to the War Ministry on 17 July 1917, 'agitation' amongst the 1,000 or so Chinese workers was considered sufficiently dangerous for the local police chief to be warned that the number of armed troops on the site was insufficient and they ran the risk of being 'massacred' in case of an attack.[56] Chinese workers at times were also involved in physical clashes with other colonial workers when sufficiently angered over a perceived wrong. In April 1918, for example, fights broke out between Chinese and North African workers in Marseilles, apparently because the latter were thought to have stolen the Chinese workers' food rations. Not long afterwards, separate barracks were built for the two groups of workers.[57] According to Li Jun, a Chinese inspector posted in France to oversee the welfare of the Chinese workers, the French authorities may have also feared that conscripted Vietnamese workers from their colony of Indochina could be susceptible to the subversive 'nationalist' influence of Chinese workers and thus ensured they were clearly segregated.[58]

Dissatisfaction with the 'unruly' Chinese workers had reached such a pitch by 1918 that a Ministry of War report declared that the recruitment had been a failure since nearly 3,000 of them had turned out to be 'undesirables' whose behaviour had 'destabilised the functioning of national industries' with riots, mutinies, fights, strikes and refusal to work.[59] At the end of the war, meetings were held by representatives of the ministries of War and Justice as well as local army commands to discuss complaints sent in by local communities (especially from the Somme region and the Pas de Calais) concerning Chinese workers in their midst. Such complaints referred to the Chinese committing crimes 'of all sorts', to the extent that locals no longer felt safe and were contemplating moving away unless the Chinese workers were withdrawn. The municipal administration of Lille in northern France demanded that Chinese workers in the region be immediately with-drawn because of vociferous complaints from locals.[60] The military prison in Noyelles (at the mouth of the Somme), where one of the largest camps for British-recruited Chinese workers was located, drew up a list of crimes committed by 38 of them; they included 'offering violence to a senior officer', 'resisting authority', 'possession of firearms', and 'firing at a patrol of British soldiers with intent to murder'.[61] The French official and popular suspicion and condemnation of the indentured Chinese workers contrasted with the grandiose Gallic rhetoric during the early years of the twentieth century amongst French diplomats and intellectuals which insisted China and France enjoyed a unique relationship of mutual respect and admiration because both cultures had much in common; thus France, in their view, was considerably more appreciative of Chinese culture than the other Western powers.[62]

CONCLUSION

Not surprisingly, and despite the pride expressed by T. Z. Tyau after the war at the contribution of his compatriots to the Allied cause (referred to at the beginning of this chapter), the entire episode soon faded from the official and public view. In 1925, the General Association of Chinese Workers petitioned the French government to erect a commemorative monument to the Chinese workers, to establish a national cemetery for those who had died in France, either from illness or enemy attack (totalling nearly 2,000), and to help finance the repatriation of those who were still living in France (according to a 1925 report by the French Interior Ministry, there were still 3,000 Chinese workers in the country).[63] The petition was politely, but firmly, rebuffed.[64] As late as 1934, fifty unemployed Chinese workers in Paris took part in a demonstration organised by the Association of Chinese Volunteers in the First World War (Association amicale des engagés volontaires chinois de la grande guerre) calling for free repatriation.[65] In recent years, however, the story of the indentured Chinese labourers has gained new prominence, primarily as part of a wider agenda amongst French official circles to celebrate the contemporary Chinese ethnic community in France. Thus in November 1988 a plaque was officially unveiled in Paris (near the Gare de Lyon) to commemorate (finally!) the contribution of Chinese workers to the Allied war effort. During the ceremony, the Minister of Communications and Transport (representing President Mitterrand) bestowed Légion d'honneur medals on two former Chinese workers, Lu Huchen and Zeng Guangpei. At the turn of the twenty-first century the mayor's office in Noyelles-sur-Mer produced a visitors' pamphlet providing information on the Chinese Cemetery (in which nearly 900 Chinese workers are buried) and commemorating the role of the Chinese workers stationed in the town.[66] The condescending tone that had greeted the Chinese workers in 1916–17, however, has not entirely dissipated. A contributor to the Noyelles pamphlet notes:

An Lung-hsin, Chai Nai-lai and Chaing Hsiao, among many others here [in the Chinese Cemetery] are taking their last slumber in the soil of Picardy. Holidaymakers who pass by here should stop a while and spare a thought of gratitude for these children of the Far East who offered themselves for the defence of French territory, and who died in a war of which they doubtless had no comprehension at all.[67]

The story of Chinese indentured labour in First World War France deserves more than simply being appropriated for public relations campaigns to celebrate ethnic diversity or to promote tourism in contemporary France. It represented a significant turning point in the history of Chinese overseas labour migration that had begun in the nineteenth century. Furthermore, the active and enthusiastic support for the recruitment by both official and intellectual elites in China (both having their own wider political, social and cultural agenda) suggests that Sino-French interaction at this time should be seen as more of a two-way process than the conventional view of China at this time as merely the passive recipient of Western semi-colonialism. Finally, the experiences and actions of the Chinese workers themselves constitute an important and significant aspect of China's twentieth-century labour history.

NOTES

1 Zhang Yongjin, *China in the International System 1918–1920* (London: Macmillan, 1991), 5.

2 *La Politique de Pékin,* no. 8 (22 February 1920), gives the text in Chinese and French. I have translated directly from the Chinese. All translations from Chinese sources are mine.

3 G. Cross, *Immigrant Workers in Industrial France* (Philadelphia: Temple University Press, 1983), 35–6; J. Horne, 'Immigrant Workers in France During World War One', *French Historical Studies* 14.1 (Spring 1985), 59; M. Summerskill, *China at the Western Front* (London: Michael Summerskill, 1982), 163.

4 D. Klein, *With the Chinks* (London: John Lane, 1918), xi. The book is a summary of Klein's diary covering the training period in China during late 1917 and early 1918 before he accompanied the labour battalion to France.

5 In its first report, the Service d'organisation des travailleurs coloniaux in January 1917 gave a figure of 80,879 'colonial workers' currently in France that included 5,982 Chinese. Archives Nationales, Paris F^{14} 11334, 'Conférence interministèrielle de la main d'oeuvre' (meeting of 3 March 1917).

6 For example, Chow Tse-tsung, *The May Fourth Movement* (Cambridge, MA: Harvard University Press, 1960), 37–40; J. Spence, *The Search for Modern China* (New York: W. W. Norton, 1999), 286–7.

7 For example, J. Horne, *Labour at War* (Oxford: Clarendon Press, 1991); J. Horne (ed.), *State, Society and Mobilisation in Europe During the First World War* (Cambridge University Press, 1997). Examples of brief summaries in French-language scholarship are Live Yu-sion, 'Les travailleurs chinois et l'effort de la grande guerre', *Hommes et Migrations,* no. 1,148 (November 1991), 12–14; and Live Yu-sion, *Chinois de France* (Paris: Mémoire Collective, 1994), 9–12.

8 Chen Sanjing, *Huagong yu Ouzhan* (Chinese Workers and the European War) (Taibei: Zhongyang yanjiuyuan jindaishi yanjiusuo, 1986). Recently, however, the Modern History Research Institute at the Academia Sinica in Taiwan has published a volume of archival materials from the Chinese Foreign Ministry specifically dealing with the recruitment of Chinese labour in 1916–18. See *Ouzhan huagong shiliao* (Historical Materials on Chinese Workers in the European War) (Taibei: Zhongyang yanjiuyuan jindaishi yanjiusuo, 1997).

9 T. Z. (Min-Ch'ien) Tyau, *China Awakened* (New York: Macmillan, 1922), 225–6.

10 D. Northrup, *Indentured Labour in the Age of Imperialism 1834–1920* (Cambridge University Press, 1995), 25, 37, 38, 61; L. Pan (ed.), *The Encyclopedia of the Chinese Overseas* (Cambridge, MA: Harvard University Press, 2006), 98–9, 248–50, 254, 356–7.

11 Centre d'archives d'outre-mer, Aix-en-Provence 'Fonds ministériels/généralités', Carton 126/Dossier 1097.

12 Yen Ching-hwang, *Coolies and Mandarins* (Singapore University Press, 1985), 32–71, 102–11.

13 On early-twentieth-century Chinese labour in South Africa, see P. Richardson, *Chinese Mine Labour in the Transvaal* (London: Macmillan, 1982); and Li Anshan, *Feizhou huaqiao huaren shi* (A History of Overseas Chinese in Africa) (Beijing: Zhongguo huaqiao chubanshe, 2000), 106–16, 121–5.

14 'Fonds Clemenceau', 6N 130 ('Rapports des attachés militaires'), Archives du service historique de l'armée de terre, Château de Vincennes, Paris. See also M. Chi, *China Diplomacy 1914–1918* (Cambridge, MA: East Asian Research Center, Harvard University, 1970), 20, 72, 129–30. A French military plan in the spring of 1918 proposed that a Chinese expeditionary force (comprising 1,543 officers and 44,900 men) be sent to the Western Front.

15 For more information on Li, see P. Bailey, *Reform the People* (Edinburgh University Press, 1990), 227–36; P. Bailey, 'The Sino-French Connection', in D. Goodman (ed.), *China and the West* (Manchester University Press, 1990), 74–8; and his 'Voltaire and Confucius: French Attitudes Towards China in the Early Twentieth Century', *History of European Ideas* 14.6 (1992), 817–37.

16 Bailey, *Reform the People*, 228.

17 In his contribution to *Lü'ou jiaoyu yundong* (The Educational Movement in Europe) (Tours: n.p., 1916), 82–3. See also *Li Shizeng xiansheng wenji* (Collected Writings of Li Shizeng) (Taibei: Zhongyang weiyuanhui dangshi weiyuanhui, 1980), 1: 220–5.

18 *Jiaoyu yu minzhong* (Education and the Masses), 2.7 (March 1931), 3.

19 In February 1917, for example, the troopship *Athos* was torpedoed in the Mediterranean, resulting in the death of 540 Chinese workers.

20 Gu Xingqing, *Ouzhou gongzuo huiyilu* (A Recollection of Experiences in the European War) (Changsha: n.p., 1938), 4–16.

21 Cong Lingzi, 'Bilishi zhanchangshang de Weihai huagong' (A Chinese Worker from Weihai at the Battlefront in Belgium). I am grateful to the director of the Weihai Archives Bureau, who kindly provided me with this document while I was doing research there in September 2000. If the birth dates given for Cong are correct, he would have been just fifteen years old at the time. The paucity of memoirs and testimonies can be explained by the fact that for most of the post-1949 period, Chinese official and academic authorities simply did not believe that the story of Chinese indentured labour in the First World War was worthy of commemoration.

22 Yan Zhensheng, 'Wo dang huagong de jingli' (My Experiences as a Chinese Overseas Worker), *Shandong wenshi jicui* (Jinan: Shandong renmin chubanshe, 1993), 281–90. Yan, however, provides very little substantial information on his experience in France other than to note the harsh discipline imposed by the British on the Chinese workers at Noyelles (western France), one of the largest camps for the arriving workers.

23 Zhang Bangyong, 'Huagong canjia diyici shijie dazhan de pianduan huiyi' (Fragments of Memories concerning my Participation in the First World War as an Overseas Chinese Worker), *Wenshi ziliao xuanji*, no. 38 (September 1963), 1–22.

24 'An Army of Labour', *The Times* (27 December 1917).

25 Cited in Summerskill, *China on the Western Front*, 132.

26 A character trait that has ironically always been attributed to the Chinese by Western sociologists.

27 Archives du service historique de l'armée de terre, 'Fonds Clemenceau' 6N 149 ('Mission de recrutement des ouvriers chinois').

28 A. Dupuoy, 'Un Camp de Chinois', *La revue de Paris* (November–December 1919), 161–2. An obsession with a potential loss of face was also evident in French official censorship reports on the correspondence sent by Vietnamese workers to their relatives back home in Vietnam.

29 PRO (Public Record Office) Archives, London, WO 107/37 ('Correspondence, Quartermaster General Papers').

30 *Ibid.*

31 E. Thompson, 'The Chinese Labour Corps, and the Effect of Its Sojourn here as a Possible Help to Missionaries', *East and West: A Quarterly Review for the Study of Missionary Problems* (October 1920), 316.

32 Intriguingly, however, a memo from the French Foreign Ministry in April 1916 expressed unease about the school, warning that it might make potential socialists out of the workers and encourage them to demand equal pay with French workers. Archives du ministère des affaires étrangères, Paris, E-22-15, E-110-2.

33 *Cai Yuanpei xiansheng quanji* (Collected Works of Cai Yuanpei) (Taibei: Commercial Press, 1968), 202–5, 210–20.

34 *Huagong zazhi* (Chinese Workers' Magazine), no. 2 (25 January 1917), no. 3 (10 February 1917).

35 *Dongfang zazhi* (Eastern Miscellany), 14.7 (1917), *neiwai shibao* ['domestic and foreign news'], 172.

36 *Lü'ou zazhi* (Journal For Chinese Students in Europe), no. 24 (1 October 1917).

37 On the Chinese work-study students in France after the First World War and their interaction with Chinese workers there, see P. Bailey, 'The Chinese Work-Study Movement in France', *China Quarterly*, no. 115 (September 1988), 441–61.

38 *Lü'ou zhoukan* (weekly journal for Chinese students in Europe), no. 8 (3 January 1920).

39 *Huagong zazhi*, no. 29 (25 December 1918).

40 *Huagong zazhi*, no. 17 (10 January 1918).

41 *Jiaoyu gongbao* (Bulletin of Education), no. 4 (April 1919), *jizai* (record of events), 22–5.

42 *Huagong zazhi* no. 5 (10 April 1917).

43 'Xucai yu aiguo' (Saving Money and Patriotism), *Huagong xunkan* (Chinese Workers' Fortnightly) (15 February 1921).

44 Archives du ministère de l'intérieur, F[7] 12900.

45 *Dongfang zazhi* 15.6 (1919), 54–60.

46 *Huagong zazhi*, no. 18 (25 January 1918); no. 20 (25 March 1918); no. 21 (25 April, 1918); no. 22 (25 May 1918); no. 24 (25 July 1918).

47 Gu Xingqing, *Ouzhan gongzuo huiyilu*, 50–1.

48 Archives du service historique de l'armée de terre, Fonds Clemenceau, 6N 149 ('Mission de recrutement des ouvriers chinois').

49 Archives du service historique de l'armée de terre, Fonds Clemenceau, 6N 149 ('Travailleurs coloniaux'). See also Chen Sanjing, *Huagong yu Ouzhan*, 117–18.

50 Archives nationales, F[14]1131 ('Main-d'oeuvre exotique').

51 Archives nationales, BB[18]2589, 'Crimes d'ouvriers chinois travaillant à Perigueux, sur les chantiers au chemin de fer Paris-Orleans, à Roupéroux et à la pouderie de Saint-Fons (1914–1918)'.

52 Archives nationales, BB[18]2588, 'Rixe au Creusot entre les ouvriers chinois et des ouvriers français, et entre les ouvriers chinois et les surveillants de même nationalité (1916–1917)'.

53 Archives nationales, F[14]1131 ('Main-d'oeuvre exotique').

54 Archives nationales, BB[18]2589, 'Crimes d'ouvriers chinois travaillant à Perigueux'.

55 Archives nationales: BB[18]2596, 'Rebellion d'ouvriers chinois à Dunkerque (1917)'.

56 Archives du service historique de l'armée de terre, Fonds Clemenceau, 6N 149 ('Mission de recrutement des ouvriers chinois').

57 *Ibid.*

58 See Li Jun's report to the Chinese Foreign Ministry on 10 June 1918 in *Ouzhan huagong shiliao*, 381.

59 Archives du service historique de l'armée de terre, Fonds Clemenceau, 6N 111 ('Faits divers').

60 Archives du service historique de l'armée de terre: 7N 2289 ('Affaires britanniques/travailleurs chinois'). At one such meeting on 18 October, 1919 it was decided that the Chinese should 'disappear as soon as possible'.

61 PRO, FO 228/2895 ('Chinese Labour Corps').

62 On this, see Bailey, 'Voltaire and Confucius', 819–21.

63 Archives du ministère de l'intérieur, Paris, F[7]1348, 'Chinois résidant en France 1914–1927'.

64 Archives du ministère des affaires étrangères, Paris, E-544-1, 'Chinois en France 1922–1929'.

65 Archives du ministère de l'intérieur, F[7]13518, 'Les étrangers en France'. The association had been founded in 1931.

66 Commune de Noyelles, *Cimetière chinois de nolette* (Noyelles-sur-Mer, 2001).

67 Interestingly, a 1980s report on the Noyelles Chinese Cemetery in the Chinese official communist newspaper, *Renmin ribao* (People's Daily), noted with great pride that 168 people had signed the visitors' guest book between June and November 1986, expressing gratitude for the contribution of Chinese workers to the Allied victory and apparently claiming that the French people would never forget them. Such sentiments, the report concluded, were ample proof that people all over the world were 'linked in their hearts'. 'Wang ling jie: diaohua gongmu' (Festival to Commemorate the Dead: Paying Condolences at the Chinese Cemetery), *Renmin ribao* (5 April 1987).

CHAPTER 2

Sacrifices, sex, race: Vietnamese experiences in the First World War

Kimloan Hill

With the mobilisation of its able-bodied men during the First World War, France turned to neighbouring countries and the colonies, including Indochina, for manpower.[1] Between 1915 and 1919, 48,922 Vietnamese soldiers and 48,254 Vietnamese workers were recruited to serve in France.[2] Some recruits were sent to Africa, the Balkans and the Middle East, but the great majority went to France. They were sent to battlefields, factories, hospitals, construction sites, commercial businesses, and agricultural regions to work as soldiers, military labourers, factory workers and farmers.[3] The Vietnamese experience of the First World War has not attracted much attention, apart from occasional discussion in histories of Vietnam, where it has been the source of some debate. Nguyen Ai Quoc (or Ho Chi Minh as he was later known) wrote in 1925 that all the recruits were conscripted, leading a number of historians to claim that the recruiting campaign, while ostensibly voluntary, was in fact based on conscription.[4] However, fresh archival evidence and greater socio-historical contextualisation suggest, as I argue, that most recruits in fact did volunteer to serve for a variety of reasons: their desire to escape from their world of economic hardship, to see France, or to achieve some freedom from traditional social and moral codes.

This chapter aims to recover the experiential reality of the lives of the Vietnamese men in France during the First World War and its consequences for the colonial enterprise in Vietnam. Starting with a discussion of the recruitment process and the traumatic voyage overseas, I examine the men's varied experiences in France, from the trauma of war to the pleasures of sex and gambling to instances of racial tension and violence. I conclude by briefly considering the post-war activities of some of these men, and how their radicalisation by their war experiences affected their attitude to both traditional Vietnamese society and their colonial masters. I have drawn on a varied body of material: presidential, ministerial and other official documents, contemporary newspaper articles, diaries and memoirs, as well as extracts from personal letters deposited in archives in France and Vietnam.[5] Two bodies of work have been particularly important to my thinking and analysis of the Vietnamese war experience: Anthony Reid's method of 'total history' with its stress on traditional practices and socio-economic factors for a more nuanced understanding of an 'event', and Harry Benda's work on peasants' lives and movements in Southeast Asia.[6]

GOING AWAY: RECRUITMENT, VOLUNTEERING AND THE VOYAGE TO FRANCE

In the decade before the outbreak of the First World War, Indochina experienced extreme economic distress, especially in Tonkin and Annam, where floods and drought triggered famine and rebellions among the peasantry and the imperial army. Floods occurred annually in Tonkin between 1902 and 1918, those in 1913 and 1915 being the most serious. In 1915, 365,000 hectares, or 25 per cent, of the cultivable land in Tonkin were submerged under 20 feet of water.[7] On the other hand, from 1899 to 1916 Annam suffered a long period of intense drought, triggering robberies, lootings, murders, and even mutinies by soldiers in the imperial army.[8] Given these contexts of natural disasters, and the resulting economic crisis for the local people, already living amidst poverty, it is not surprising to find that nearly 90 per cent of all Indochinese who took part in the war came from Tonkin and Annam; most of them were peasants for whom money was a major incentive.[9]

There was a certain degree of war excitement and enthusiasm as well. Ho Chi Minh, known as Nguyen Tat Thanh at the time, was living and working in London. He went to a recruiting centre to sign up but, failing to meet the 'requirements' because he was a member of a French colony, he sailed the next day to France, presumably to join the French army as a volunteer.[10] François Bertrand Can, a naturalised French citizen in Cochinchina, remembered the support for France: 'We held our heads high in indignation; our tongues uttered trains of words, speaking only of retaliation.'[11] Although France did not recruit indigenous soldiers and workers from Indochina until December 1915, some wrote to the French resident superior in Tonkin in early 1915 offering to volunteer.[12] Once the recruitment began, others – peasants, native district chiefs and judges, soldiers in the royal army such as Nguyen Van Ba, and students – offered to serve as soldiers, workers, interpreters, inspectors or monitors in workers' and soldiers' camps. Members of the royal families were also found among the volunteers; even prisoners offered to serve as labourers with the hope that their sentences would be commuted.[13] Such evidence goes against the thesis of forced mass conscription. There were some isolated incidents where individuals were coerced into joining up,[14] but they cannot be turned into a general narrative of mass conscription and French exploitation.

Even some women volunteered. In early 1916, a group of women wrote to the governor of Indochina volunteering to work in the health service or in factories 'by the side of our French sisters'.[15] Reports from Pierre Guesde and a M. Lamarre, inspectors of Indochinese worker camps in France, suggest that there were female Indochinese workers in workers' camps, and that workers in Limoges were given days off to visit their parents and relatives in Bergerac, Angoulême, and Périgueux.[16] The fact that workers visited their parents, and not just their fathers, supports the view that women, as well as men, were recruited to work in France.

The recruitment campaign in Vietnam began on 17 December 1915, after France had already started to mobilise its own men and after the performance of some 4,000 skilled Vietnamese workers, hired earlier on a one-year basis in France, was deemed satisfactory. The Vietnamese royal court at Hue issued an edict offering 200 francs to each indigenous volunteer who passed the physical examination.[17] All volunteers signed a contract to serve during the period of hostilities and for six months after the ceasefire.[18] *Yet thi*, or public announcements, promised bonuses, family allowances, pensions, mandarin titles, posthumous honours, and an exemption from the body tax – a big relief for a peasant family. Recruits had to be eighteen years of age or older. The recruitment campaign included pictures of Vietnamese soldiers posing with Allied soldiers, *ban dong minh*, or with French officers and soldiers, *ban tong chinh* and of smartly dressed military workers posing proudly with their French supervisors.[19] All these seemed to promise prosperity, social status, and racial equality – something many Vietnamese, especially the peasants, would have craved intensely.

Each active soldier and each reservist received a 50-franc bonus or an amount equal to two months' salary, whichever was greater, for signing up for the military campaign in France.[20] Each new recruit, however, received a 200-franc bonus and the family of each soldier received a 3-piastre monthly allowance. Warrant officers were paid 1.89 francs per day, sergeants 1.65 francs, corporals and privates first class 0.75 francs, and privates second class 0.60 francs. If a soldier died in the line of duty, his family received 120 francs as immediate compensation plus a pension.[21] On the other hand, there were five types of workers: skilled, unskilled, health, clerical and administrative, and interpreters; the base pay for all of them was 0.75 francs per day, increasing with seniority.

For most of the soldiers and workers from Vietnam, the voyage to France was the first lesson in disillusionment. The voyage took about six weeks, during which the recruits endured extreme heat, unsanitary living conditions, poor food, and attacks by German submarines. Several people, including François Bertrand Can and Nguyen Van Ba, described the food on board as 'disgusting'.[22] The captains' logs of the *Amiral Latouche Tréville* and *Meinam* recorded stormy weather, rough seas, and deaths among the Vietnamese recruits.[23] The *Pei Ho* carried about 2,500 military and labour recruits, who cooked their meals next to latrines and slept among the livestock. While the ship was crossing the Indian Ocean there was an outbreak of cholera on board. At its height, between 17 and 19 May 1916, an average of four people died each day, and there were even some cases of suicide. When the ship reached the Suez Canal, the passengers were evacuated and treated at a British hospital. By the time the surviving recruits continued their journey on 18 June, 104 of their countrymen had died. The voyage lasted for three and a half months, instead of the usual thirty days.[24] Records of such traumatic experience have largely gone unnoticed in discussions of the Vietnamese war experience. Yet they are central to an understanding of the widespread anxiety and disillusionment among the recruits as they reached the shores of France.

SACRIFICE AND DISCONTENT

In France, the soldiers formed nineteen colonial infantry battalions: four combat battalions and fifteen labour battalions.[25] Most of the labour battalions were deployed along the Western Front, digging and guarding trenches, transporting ammunition, and patrolling no-man's-land. The combat battalions participated in battle at the Somme, Verdun, Aisne, Chemin-des-Dames, Vosges, Reims and elsewhere. What were the experiences and emotions of these men as they encountered modern industrial warfare for the first time? Intimate descriptions of trench life such as we find in European war diaries and memoirs are few, but in their memoirs and letters François Bertrand Can and Nguyen Van Ba provide insights into Vietnamese experience in the trenches.

Can arrived at Marseilles on 5 May 1915. Initially assigned to the 23rd Colonial Regiment to train young volunteers, he was finally sent to the front at Champagne on 29 September 1915. On the early morning of 2 October, his battalion formed part of an offensive, and Can recalled:

The troops were definitely entering into hell . . . with flaming sky, shrieking sounds of the new howitzer shells, thundering explosions, and earthquake-like effects on the ground.

Shells and the artillery raged all night like rain. Today [3 October] began with a preparation for more attacks; [but] like yesterday we had nothing to eat and our stomachs screamed for food.[26]

Can lost his left forearm in a German grenade explosion and was awarded the Croix de Guerre with palm leaf, France's highest military honour, before being discharged from the army.[27]

If Can's account captures his battle experience, Corporal Nguyen Van Ba's memoir gives insights into the daily life of a military labourer just behind the front line. After arriving in France in September 1917, Nguyen Van Ba was attached to Battalion no. 2 and sent to the Northern Front in the Rennes sector. There, he repaired roads and railroads, transported munitions, poison gas cylinders and artillery shells, and cut rocks and stones. He noted that there was not a single day when German shells did not fall on his work site, and that although the French army had 'thousands and thousands of men, horses, canons, trucks, and flying machines', it could not stop the 'German pirates'.[28] In May 1918, Ba was injured when a shell exploded in his bunker, killing thirty men in his company.[29]

Extracts from letters, copied out by the postal censors, reflect the traumatic experience of trench warfare for these men. Vietnamese soldiers suffered their heaviest casualties in 1917. One soldier wrote: 'Since April, of the 330 [Vietnamese] soldiers [in my battalion], 250 were killed. Only twelve of those whom I had known since I left Indochina are still alive.'[30] According to Corporal Chan, 'the bodies [of the Vietnamese] were stacked in heaps like herrings in a jar'.[31] Newly enlisted and inexperienced soldiers were often the first casualties. Some soldiers surrendered, crossing over to the German side and giving themselves up even before 'they fired a shot at the enemy'.[32] Some praised the Germans as being more 'powerful' because 'for every German prisoner we took, the Germans took ten Frenchmen'.[33] Sergeant Binh in Battalion no. 6 asked: 'For what end are we separated from our parents and our children? I am not very happy here – bad food and no rest!' He went on to advise his parents: 'Tell village elders not to recruit young men and send them here [to die].'[34] The letters suggest that there was not only widespread dejection in the Vietnamese camp in 1917 but also a great deal of regret among soldiers about their decision to volunteer.

The experiences of the workers were different. Upon arriving in France, skilled workers with prearranged contracts went directly to work. The rest took a professional aptitude test before being placed in factories and commercial and military establishments throughout France. However, the living conditions varied widely. Vietnamese workers employed at a naval arsenal in Toulon enjoyed facilities similar to those enjoyed by French sailors: heated rooms, hot and cold showers, and a choice of Asian or European food. 'Their material condition left nothing to desire.'[35] Workers at Camp Bassen, on the other hand, lived in dirty barracks, with 225 men crammed into buildings designed for 175. They had to walk 1.5 miles to get their meals which comprised 'scraps and bones'.[36] Only 200 pairs of leggings and 600 pairs of boots were available for 2,400 men. Toward the end of the war, men wore 'tattered clothes ... even patches had holes'.[37]

Working hours varied in different regions and according to the type of job. Workers at Camp Bergerac worked for eight hours a day, while workers in naval bases worked for nine hours.[38] Complaints about long working hours became common among workers as the war dragged on: 'There has been no rest, not even a Sunday off. If we are tired, we just take liberty to rest at home. However, for each day we were absent without permission, we were thrown in jail for 15 days and [the colonial government in Indochina] cut off the monthly allowance to our families.'[39] Such grievances were compounded by shortages of food. Do Van Diem complained that the only food he ate in two weeks 'was one loaf of bread'; others complained that they were 'famished'.[40] As the war progressed and such resentments increased, Vietnamese workers staged a series of strikes and protests, copying the methods used by French workers. In December 1917, military workers in the École d'Aviation in Chartres refused to go to work because their workplace was not heated; in January 1918, the men in Tarbes refused to eat because their meals were not cooked properly; in April 1918, 150 agricultural workers at Bordeaux went on strike to demand an extra day off work each month.[41] It is in these staged protests and increasing awareness of their rights as workers, modelled on their French working-class counterparts, that these Vietnamese workers had their first dose of political radicalisation, something that became very important in the post-war years.

MONEY, LOVE AND SEX

The Vietnamese recruits had one common goal when they volunteered to serve in France: to earn money. The majority seem to have achieved that goal. Inspector Lamarre reported in May 1918 that twenty-two groups of agricultural workers in Bordeaux saved 965,000 francs – of which 794,068 francs were remitted to their families in Indochina. He also reported that workers in Toulouse remitted 292,000 francs to Indochina and saved 96,000 francs in national defence bonds. An official report published on 24 May 1918 stated that 36,715 Indochinese workers saved a total of 5,943,933 francs in the form of remittances, bonds, and family allowances.[42]

Some workers, however, spent their money on gambling and prostitutes. Gambling was a popular pastime in workers' camps, and the reports reveal an intricate web of social interaction as well as changing attitudes to money. A Vietnamese worker complained that his countrymen 'gambled as if every day were *Tet* [the Vietnamese New Year].'[43] In Marseilles, card games were held every night and attracted even Chinese and Arab workers. Some players lost as much as 7,500 francs in a single night.[44] Mao, a worker at Salin de Giraud, wrote that he lost 1,000 francs one night and won it back the next.[45] For Tran Ngoc Yen at Camp Bergerac, winning 2,000 francs in one card game gave him a much-cherished sense of independence: 'I have all the money in the world, I kowtow to no one.'[46] On the other hand, Luong lost not only all his money but also his belongings in a card game during a big party held for 1,200 workers in the workers' headquarters in Marseilles.[47] After losing his money to a Senegalese, Yen in Saint-Raphael stabbed the man and took his money back. He boasted that he had committed a similar offence before but escaped arrest because he was 'protected by some sergeants in the Workers' Headquarters.'[48]

If gambling provided an outlet from the pressures of war, so did eros. Photographs of nude women were commonly included in letters to Indochina, only to be confiscated by the postal censorship bureau. The presence of large numbers of foreign soldiers and workers increased the demand for prostitutes; similarly, the war displaced many women for whom prostitution offered the only means of support. The number of brothels increased rapidly, especially near the military and foreign worker camps.[49] One official remarked that French women often chased the Vietnamese because they had money.[50] Sergeant Tam wrote that 'pleasure from sex is better than pleasure from opium'.[51] A number of his compatriots boasted that they had concubines. Having *nam the bay thiep* [five wives and seven concubines] was a sign of a man's wealth and social power.[52] To impress his relatives in Indochina, one man sent a picture showing him lying in bed while his French 'concubine' caressed him.[53] Not surprisingly, frequenting brothels led to the spread of venereal diseases. A few months after a brothel opened near the explosives factory in Angoulême, where more than 2,500 Vietnamese worked, fifteen of them had contracted venereal diseases. In Bordeaux at certain periods, seven out of ten Vietnamese agricultural workers were infected with syphilis or gonorrhea.[54]

Along with such casual sexual encounters, there were also more enduring relationships. Vietnamese men and French women interacted not only in brothels but also in workplaces. These liaisons could result in serious relationships and sometimes even in marriage. As the number of Vietnamese–French couples increased, the French authorities took harsh measures to deter Vietnamese men from getting involved with French women, instructing the French supervisors and local mayors to report such liaisons. If a Vietnamese–French couple was found out, the Vietnamese man would be punished or transferred to a different location. Such measures did not always work, however. After Nam Tran was transferred to Marseilles to break up his relationship with his French 'mistress', she found him and brought their child to Marseilles to live with him.[55] Although the French authorities tried to deter Vietnamese–French marriages, when both partners were serious they could file for permission to marry; before they could be married, however, the man had to undergo a background check and be certified to be single.

Franco-Vietnamese liaisons also violated traditional customs and familial practices in Indochina, where marriages were arranged and required parental consent. Knowing that his parents would not approve of his marriage to an eighteen-year-old French girl, Nguyen Van Dat married her before informing them. Corporal Nguyen Van Trung told his mother to cancel the marriage she had arranged for him because he had already 'converted to Catholicism and married a French girl'.[56] Records show that by the end of the war, 250 Vietnamese–French couples were officially married and 1,363 couples were living together without the approval of the French authorities or parental consent.[57]

Love and intimacy led to these marriages, but for many Vietnamese men such a marriage was also a statement of their coming of age. These men showed that, despite their status as colonial subjects living in France, they were no different from Frenchmen living in Indochina: marrying local women, and frequenting local brothels and cabarets. Such behaviour also indicated that they no longer felt constrained by Vietnamese customs. Thus, there was a shift in their consciousness, a transformation of their attitude towards both the French and the established order in Indochina.

RACE AND CONFLICT

The liaisons between Vietnamese men and French women could cause tension and conflict between the Vietnamese and men from other races, especially Frenchmen who viewed them as competitors not only for women but also for jobs. One French soldier lamented: 'Are we fighting so that the Chinese, the Arabs and the Spaniards can marry our wives and our daughters and share our France, for which sooner or later we will get ourselves killed at the front?'[58]

To vent their frustration, Frenchmen sometimes harassed, insulted, and assaulted foreign workers and there were occasional instances of murder as well.[59] At Versailles, Vietnamese workers were ridiculed by the French because of their black-dyed teeth, the way they took showers, and the way they dressed, leading to violence between the two groups.[60] In the army, such hostility was no less intense. According to J. Bosc, a monitor of the living and working conditions of the Indochinese, French soldiers and officers in the infantry regiment in the Meuse region inflicted serious injuries on their Vietnamese soldiers on more than one occasion. A Vietnamese was brutally beaten up and murdered on 31 May 1917, and there was a similar case the following month. French soldiers had accused the victims of being cowards for not fighting on the front line.[61] Vietnamese men seen visiting or going out with French women were also attacked. Cang Xuong wrote that one day after visiting Renée, a female co-worker, he was chased and attacked by a group of [French] 'hoodlums'. Outnumbered, he 'submitted to their blows and punches' while running towards his compound.[62]

Competition for women between Vietnamese and African men similarly fuelled racial tensions and even murder, as in October 1918. The Senegalese 119th Battalion and 483 Vietnamese military labourers in the Engineering Service were deployed to build a road linking Morlaàs with Pau. The Senegalese resented the Vietnamese because the latter had more money and better food, and were favoured by the local people and by women at a nearby brothel. On the evening of 27 October 1918, after leaving a night-club, three Vietnamese men were attacked by a Senegalese who lay in wait for them. One was injured while the other two escaped unharmed. Later, the Vietnamese retaliated by shooting a Senegalese soldier who happened to walk by their barracks. In a counter-attack, some members of the Senegalese battalion ignited gunpowder barrels to cause explosions; others armed themselves with rifles and bayonets stolen from the munitions depot and attacked the Vietnamese while they were asleep in their barracks. The incident ended only when the Senegalese ran out of ammunition and the French riot police arrived. Sixteen Vietnamese were killed, eighteen were seriously injured, and many more suffered less serious wounds. Fearing that the Vietnamese would seek revenge, the military authorities divided them into small units and reassigned them to different parts of France. Only one Senegalese was tried and convicted.[63] Such an outcome did not instil in the Vietnamese men much faith in the French justice system; instead it created an intense awareness of racial and national marginalisation. Such consciousness of racial injustice would become increasingly politicised through the propaganda of the French Communist Party in the post-war years and would contribute to the gradual change in attitude of these men towards the French *colons*.

POST-WAR DEVELOPMENTS

What happened to these soldiers and workers once the war was over? By the end of the war, 1,797 soldiers and 1,548 workers, representing about 3.5 per cent of the Vietnamese men who went to France, had died.[64] After the signing of the Armistice, several thousand were transferred to reconstruction projects or other non-combatant duties in France and occupied territories, but a large number were repatriated.[65] About 2,900 gained permission to stay in France to work, study or marry. Students had their education paid for by the colonial government on condition that after graduating they would return to Indochina and work in modern industries such as the paper mills and cement, glass and rubber factories.[66]

It is not known if Nguyen Tat Thanh, the future Ho Chi Minh, fought in the war. However, he emerged in 1919 as Nguyen Ai Quoc and submitted a petition ('Revendications du Peuple Annamite') to the leaders of the Allied Forces in Versailles demanding human rights and political rights for the Vietnamese people. Nguyen Ai Quoc had become a popular figure among Vietnamese soldiers in France since the end of the war. Political tracts under his name were distributed among Vietnamese soldiers in France, advocating independence for Indochina. These soldiers believed that he had received the mantle of revolutionary leadership from the renowned Phan Chu Trinh, who had been living in exile in Paris since 1911.[67] Such fame did not help Nguyen Ai Quoc to find stable employment. To earn a living he worked as a part-time photographic retoucher, a waiter, a painter, a distributor of communist revolutionary pamphlets to Vietnamese and Malagasy workers, and a contributor of short articles to anti-colonial publications such as *L'Humanité* and *Les Opprimés*.[68] He lived in poverty until the 1920s when he found his niche in the French Communist Party, opposing French colonialism and promoting independence for Indochina. In 1925, he founded the Vietnamese Revolutionary Youth Movement or Thanh Nien, the proto-Vietnamese Communist party. In February 1930 he abolished the Thanh Nien and established the Vietnamese Communist Party.

Before returning to Vietnam to lead the communist revolutionary move-ment and overthrow the French colonial regime in 1954, he adopted the name Ho Chi Minh.[69]

The majority of the volunteers returned to Indochina. After a brief exposure to the communist movement in Paris, some like Ton Duc Thang returned to Vietnam with a communist agenda. During the war, Ton had been employed either as a military supervisor or as an interpreter at a naval arsenal base in Toulon.[70] He claimed to have joined French sailors in raising the red Soviet flag during the Black Sea Mutiny in 1919.[71] He returned to Indochina in 1920 and worked as a mechanic. In 1927 he organised a workers' union in Sai-Gon and joined the Thanh Nien. In 1930, when Nguyen Ai Quoc founded the Vietnamese Communist Party, he joined the party; subsequently he rose to the highest offices, becoming the first vice president (1960–9) of the Democratic Republic of Vietnam (DRV), formerly North Vietnam. When Ho Chi Minh died, he became the second president of the DRV (1969–75), and he was the first president of the current Socialist Republic of Vietnam (1975–80).[72]

For most returnees, however, the options were more varied. Though affected and transformed by their experiences in France, most did not have such a well-defined political career. Instead, they engaged themselves in different kinds of work, including developing new land provided by the colonial government, working in modern industries, or re-enlisting in the colonial army.[73] Some, like Nguyen Van Ba, returned to their villages and worked to modernise the countryside: building roads, reconstructing dykes, and teaching new farming techniques. Not all succeeded, however. Many could not find the kind of jobs and wages they had had in France because Indochina was not wholly industrialised and modernised and still had plenty of cheap labour. Veterans who had been peasants before the war now could not bring themselves to compete with their peers for low-paying manual jobs. Employers preferred peasants to 'specialists who could do only piece-work but could not deliver a complete product',[74] and suggested that 'industrial workers are not useful in Indochina. It would be best that they be kept in France.'[75]

The returnees' sense of alienation was compounded by what was often perceived in local villages as their haughtiness and sense of entitlement. In Thanh Hoa, most of the 10,000 returnees refused to work as labourers and farmers and demanded regular compensation for their service in France, including an annual provision of clothing from the local government – benefits bestowed only on royal officials. Moreover, as the returnees side-stepped village authorities to deal directly with French administrators, the villagers felt that they were 'arrogant' and 'boastful,' and even a source of 'embarrassment'.[76] Facing rejection from both the French and their own people, some resorted to alcohol and violence and a few even committed suicide.[77]

It was a decade after the war that the long-term effects of the war experience on these men and their varying degrees of social and political radicalisation in France started to become evident. In the 1930s, when the Great Depression hit Indochina, disenchanted First World War veterans rose up under the leadership of communist agents. In May 1929 the returnees were participants in a workers' strike in Hanoi and raised the communist red flag. In 1930, seventeen First World War veterans were mutineers in the soldiers' revolt at Yen Bay. Another 1,500 took part in five labour demonstrations in May 1930; about 5,000 were leading strikers at Vinh and Ben Thuy in May 1931.[78] No doubt these veterans had reconnected with one another; their experience in France had given them confidence, and raised their political awareness. Drawing upon their wartime experience of organising protests, learnt from their French counterparts, they now planned revolts and labour demonstrations against the colonial government and businesses. Under the leadership of their former comrades such as Nguyen Ai Quoc and Ton Duc Thang, they formed a formidable political and revolutionary force that was the precursor of the communist-led nationalist movement of 1945–54, which would end the French domination in Indochina.

In conclusion, the First World War was a turning point in the history of French Indochina. The men who went to France were transformed, and in many cases radicalised, in varying degrees by their experiences. From poor and ignorant subjects of the French colonial empire, they became professional soldiers and workers, and more confident and politically conscious subjects. They no longer felt inferior to the French or their native leaders. While some of these veterans were able to take advantage of the available opportunities in the post-war period, many felt betrayed both by their own society and by France and its failure to look after them.[79] These disillusioned and bitter veterans formed a large class of men who were receptive to the arguments of those who challenged the status quo – namely, the Communist Party – and took their anger to the streets. Tran Van Giau, a high-ranking member of the Vietnamese Communist Party and its historian, noted that 'a number of the returnees from France' under the guidance and leadership of the Communist Party had been directly involved in agitating, organising, and leading the pro-labour and anti-French movements in the 1920s.[80] By recruiting men from Indochina, France had

inadvertently set in train events that would eventually contribute to the loss of its Indochinese colonies.

NOTES

1 Jean-Jacques Becker, *The Great War and the French People*, trans. Arnold Pomerans (Dover, NH: Berg, 1985), 3–6.
2 Albert Sarraut, *La Mise en Valeur des Colonies Françaises* (Paris: Payot, 1923), 42–3. These numbers are the official figures from the Ministry of the Colonies. Records at the Military Archives for the Service Historique de l'Armée de Terre (henceforth SHAT) in Paris note that 'nearly 100,000 men – 48,981 workers, 43,430 soldiers – were sent to France'. See file SHAT 10 H 18, *Historique des Tirailleurs Tonkinois*. Scholars often round up the figures to 100,000, as in Paul Isoart, *Le Phénomène National Vietnamien* (Paris: Librairie Générale de Droit, 1961), 235.
3 Sarraut, *La Mise en Valeur des Colonies*, 42–3; Exposition Coloniale Internationale de Paris, *Les Armées Françaises d'Outre Mer – Les Contingents Coloniaux du Soleil et de la Gloire* (Paris: Imprimerie Nationale, 1931), 74.
4 Nguyen Ai Quoc, *Le Procès de la Colonization Française* (Hanoi: Édition en Langues Étrangères, 1962), 9–22. Also see Virginia Thompson, *French Indochina* (New York: Macmillan Company, 1937), 90, 480; Joseph Buttinger, *A Dragon Embattled*, vol. 1 (London: Pall Mall Press, 1967), 96, 490; Martin J. Murray, *The Development of Capitalism in Colonial Indochina 1870–1940* (Berkeley: University of California Press, 1980), 217.
5 I note that the Vietnamese Latinised script, *quoc ngu*, was not officially adopted until 1917; I have not consulted records written in *chu nom* or *chu nho* (Chinese scripts).
6 Anthony Reid, *Southeast Asia in the Age of Commerce, 1450–1680* (New Haven, CT: Yale University Press, 1988), xiv–xv; Harry Benda, 'Peasant Movements in Colonial Southeast Asia', in *Continuity and Change in Southeast Asia: Collected Journal Articles of Harry J. Benda* (New Haven, CT: Yale University Press, 1972), 223–5. Also see Samuel L. Popkin, *The Rational Peasant: The Political Economy of Rural Society in Vietnam* (Berkeley: University of California Press, 1979), 4, 88.
7 Pierre Gourou, *The Peasants of the Tonkin Delta: A Study of Human Geography*, trans. Richard Miller (New Haven, CT: Human Relations Area Files, (1936) 1955), 80–1, 90–1; 'La Lutte contre les inondations' in *La Ville*, March 1916.
8 James C. Scott, *The Moral Economy of the Peasants: Rebellion and Subsistence in Southeast Asia* (New Haven, CT: Yale University Press, 1976), 127–8. Nouveau Fonds 226 (henceforth NF), 'Rapport sur la situation politique de l'Annam' by the governor general of Indochina, 12 April 1916. This collection is deposited at the French national Centre des Archives d'Outre Mer (hereafter CAOM) in Aix-en-Provence and at SHAT.
9 9 PA 13 (Papiers de l'Albert Sarraut; henceforth PA). Memo from the governor of Cochinchina and the resident superiors of Tonkin, Annam, and Cambodia

regarding the total number of soldiers and workers in France during the First World War, 2 June 1918. This collection of papers of the former Minister of the Colonies, Albert Sarraut, is deposited at CAOM.

10 William J. Duiker, *Ho Chi Minh, A Life* (New York: Hyperion, 2000), 53–4; Tran Ngoc Danh, *Tieu Su Ho Chu Tich* [A Biography of President Ho] (Paris: Chi Hoi Lien Viet Tai Phap, 1949) 25–8.

11 François Bertrand Can with George Gurrwell, *Carnet de Route d'un Petit Massouin Cochinchinois. Impressions et Souvenirs de la Grande Guerre* (Saigon: Imprimerie Albert Portail, 1916), 1–9.

12 RST 21374, Letter from Trinh Huy Kon, 15 February 1916. RST is an acronym for Résidence Supérieure au Tonkin (or North Vietnam). These records are deposited at the Vietnamese national archives Cuc Luu Tru I in Ha Noi and at CAOM.

13 See Jean Marquet, *Lettres d'Annamites – Lettres de Guerre, Lettres de Paix* (Hanoi: Edition du Fleuve Rouge, 1929). This is a collection of letters from a volunteer soldier, Nguyen Van Ba, between 1917 and 1929; see also Christopher Giebel, 'Ton Duc Thang and the Imagined Ancestries of Vietnamese Communism' (PhD dissertation, Cornell University, 1996), 30–1; 3 SLOTFOM 2, 1 SLOTFOM 4, 10 SLOTFOM 5; 10 SLOTFOM 6, 'Liste nominative des gens de la famille royale d'Annam dans des bataillons Indochinois', 1919. SLOTFOM is an acronym for Service de Liaison avec les Originaires des Territoires de la France d'Outre Mer. The acronym is used to refer to the boxes which are deposited at CAOM and SHAT.

14 See Kimloan Hill, 'A Westward Journey, An Enlightened Path – Vietnamese *Linh Tho* in France, 1915–1930 (PhD dissertation, University of Oregon, 2001).

15 RST 73172; the letter was signed by a group of 'Annamite' women, 23 March 1916.

16 RST 73172, Report from Pierre Guesde, 31 December 1917; 10 SLOTFOM 4, Report No. 109 by Lamarre, 10 April 1918.

17 *Journal Officiel de l'Indochine Française*, 29 March, 1 July, and 22 November 1915, 26 January and 2 February 1916; Emmanuel Bouhier, 'Les troupes coloniales d'Indochine en 1914–1918' in Claude Carlier and Guy Pedroncini (eds.), *Les Troupes Coloniales dans la Grande Guerre* (Paris: Economica, 1997), 69–81.

18 Amiraux 1893–1934, Presidential decree, signed by President R. Poincaré, 21 August 1916. The term 'Amiraux' refers to boxes deposited at CAOM which contain communications between the Ministry of the Colonies in France and the office of the Governor General of Indochina in Ha Noi; 10 SLOTFOM 5, Letter from the Minister of the Colonies, 1919.

19 RST 73172, public announcement and posters, 20 January 1916.

20 Soldiers and workers were hired on a daily rate but the bonuses were based on the total wage they would receive each month.

21 1 SLOTFOM 1, 'Action de l'autorité militaire – Rapport sur le recrutement indigène demandé à l'Indochine d'Août à Décembre 1915'.

22 Can, *Carnet de Route d'un Petit Massouin Cochinchinois*, 1–10; Marquet, *Lettres d'Annamites*, 11–15.

23 SHAT 26 N 874, *Journal de Marche et d'Operation du 13ᵉ Bataillon Tirailleurs Indochinois*, 21 January 1916 – 5 June 1919.
24 *Ibid.*
25 Exposition Coloniale Internationale de Paris, *Les Armées Françaises d'Outre Mer*, 72–97.
26 Can, *Carnet de Route d'un Petit Massouin Cochinchinois*, 35, 37.
27 *Ibid.*, 39–45.
28 Marquet, *Lettres d'Annamites*, 33–4: Nguyen Van Ba's letter of January 1918, informing his family in Indochina of his arrival in France and his life on the front line.
29 *Ibid.*, 40.
30 NF 227, letter from Thanh in Battalion no. 7, November 1917.
31 NF 227, Postal Censor Report, November 1917.
32 *Ibid.*
33 *Ibid.*
34 1 SLOTFOM 8, Postal Censor Reports, December 1916.
35 'Le Groupement des travailleurs Indochinois employés à l'arsenal de Toulon', in *Le Courrier d'Haiphong*, 28 March 1917.
36 10 SLOTFOM 3, Report by Inspector Lamarre, 18 December 1917.
37 10 SLOTFOM 3, Report by Inspector Lamarre, 15 January 1918; 10 SLOTFOM 5, Report by Inspector Tri Phu Vinh, February 1918.
38 10 SLOTFOM 3, Report by Lamarre on Indochinese workers in the 12th and 18th regions, 3 June 1917.
39 3 SLOTFOM 93, Postal Censor Report, July 1918.
40 1 SLOTFOM 8, 3 SLOTFOM 93, Postal Censor Reports, March, May and July 1918.
41 10 SLOTFOM 3, NF 246; 10 SLOTFOM 3, Reports by Lamarre, 24 February, 30 April 1918; NF 227, Postal Censor Report, March 1918.
42 NF 249, Report by Inspector Lamarre, 1st Semester 1918. NF 226, 249, 3 SLOTFOM 93, Reports from Inspector Lamarre in 1917, 1918.
43 1 SLOTFOM 8, Postal Censor Report, November 1917.
44 *Ibid.*
45 *Ibid.*
46 *Ibid.*
47 NF 227, Postal Censor Report, January 1918.
48 NF 227, Postal Censor Reports, September 1918
49 Alan Corbin, *Women for Hire: Prostitution and Sexuality in France after 1850*, trans. Alan Sheridan (London: Harvard University Press, 1990), 334–6.
50 10 SLOTFOM 4, quote from a report by Inspector Lamarre regarding the 'Annamite' workers at Tarbes, 20 May 1918.
51 1 SLOTFOM 8, Postal Censor Report, March 1917.
52 Phan Van Thiet, *Phu Nu Viet Nam Truoc Phap Luat* [Vietnamese Women and the Law] (Saigon: Tu Sach Pho Thong, 1955), 39–45.
53 1 SLOTFOM 8, Postal Censor Report, March 1917.

54 10 SLOTFOM 3, Report No. 100 by Inspector Lamarre, 24 October 1917 and 19 March 1918. Venereal diseases were also widespread among soldiers in the Allied forces. For problems among Americans see Gary Mead, *The Doughboys: America and the First World War* (Woodstock, NY: Overlook Press, Peter Mayer, 2000), 112–14, 202–5.

55 1 SLOTFOM 8, Postal Censor Report, February 1918.

56 1 SLOTFOM 8, Postal Censor Report, March 1917; 190 SLOTFOM 5, Postal Censor Report, December 1918.

57 10 SLOTFOM 5, Postal Censor Report, December 1918.

58 Roger Magraw, quote from Le Havre's Police Report, May 1917, in *A History of the French Working Class*, vol. 11 (Cambridge, MA: Blackwell, 1992), 152.

59 10 SLOTFOM 5, NF 248, Report by Inspector Pech in Toulouse, 14 February 1918

60 10 SLOTFOM 5, Report by Inspector Dupuy, September 1917; report by Tri Phu Vinh, 14 January 1918.

61 10 SLOTFOM 5, Report by J. Bosc, 15 July 1917. The report also cited reports from the commander in Frère-en-Tardenois on 9 June 1917, the commander general of the army in Champagne on 14 June 1917, and the commander of Battalion no. 16 on 20 June 1917. No specific date was given to the murder in June 1917.

62 SHAT 7 N 997, Postal Censor Report, August 1917.

63 10 SLOTFOM 5, reports by Inspectors Tri Phu Vinh and Paul Chassaing and Colonel Briand on 6, 7, and 14 November 1918 and official memorandum from the office of the Ministry of War on 13 February 1919.

64 10 SLOTFOM 4, Notes in file, 1918.

65 SHAT 7 N 2030, Memo from the commander of the 15th region to the minister of war, 11 January 1919.

66 1 SLOTFOM 4, report from the Workers Management office, 1932; *Chronique d'Haiphong*, 11 October 1919.

67 1 SLOTFOM 8, Postal Censor Report, May 1919; 1 SLOTFOM 4, Memo from the inspector general of the Indochinese troops, 1 and 28 December 1920.

68 1 SLOTFOM 8, Dispatch by the Ministry of War on 3 July 1919 to the president of the Council of War and the minister of the colonies; SPCE (Service de Protection du Corps Expéditionnaire Française en Indochine) 365. Reports by Sûreté agent Desire, 19 June 1922.

69 3 SLOTFOM 2, Sûreté report, 12 March 1920; report by agent Desire, 19 June 1922; Tran Ngoc Danh, *Tieu Su Ho Chu Tich*, 37–49; Huynh Kim Khanh, *Vietnamese Communism 1925–1945* (Ithaca, NY: Cornell University Press, 1982), 57–67; Duiker, *Ho Chi Minh*, 248. According to Duiker, in the 1940s Nguyen Ai Quoc posed as a Chinese journalist and adopted the name Ho Chi Minh to keep his identity secret.

70 Giebel, 'Ton Duc Thang', 38–9. Ton's uniform in a picture showing him with other Vietnamese workers at the Toulon naval arsenal, suggests that he was working either as an interpreter or as a supervisor of workers.

71 *Ibid.*, 15–47. Giebel cites various conflicting accounts in Ton's biography and historical evidence to question the authenticity of Ton's claim.

72 *Ibid.*, 1–5.

73 10 SLOTFOM 4, Notes in file, 1918; 9 PA 13, R. Helgé, 'Problème de Demain', in *Le Courrier d'Haiphong*, 9 May 1917.

74 9 PA 13, R. Helgé, 'Problème de Demain', in *Le Courrier d'Haiphong*, 9 May 1917.

75 9 PA 13, 'Les Ouvriers Indigènes en France', in *Le Courrier d'Haiphong*, 13 October 1918.

76 RST 73172, report to the resident superior in Tonkin, 3 July 1922; RST 73172, report by the provincial governor of Kien An, 5 July 1922.

77 RST 73172, report from the Council to the Government in June 1921; 9 PA 13, Albert Chevalier, 'Un État d'esprit nouveau', in *L'Opinion*, 8 November 1918.

78 3 SLOTFOM 22, reports by the resident superior of Tonkin on 'Mentality of WWI returnees', 17 March and 20 April 1930; 3 SLOTFOM 7, Report to the Ministry of the Colonies, 21 August 1933; *L'Humanité*, 18 March 1930.

79 5 SLOTFOM 36, Tran Xuan Mai 'La Voix d'Annamite', in *La Paria*, September-October 1919.

80 Tran Van Giau, *Giai Cap Cong Nhan Tu Dang Cong San Thanh Lap Den Cach Mang Thanh Cong* [The Working Class from the Establishment of the Vietnamese Communist Party to a Successful Revolution] (Hanoi: Nha Xuat Ban Su Hoc, 1962), 317, 369.

CHAPTER 3

Indians at home, Mesopotamia and France, 1914–1918: towards an intimate history

Santanu Das

At the heart of Delhi stands the India Gate, a majestic 42-metre-high colonial arch, dedicated to the 'dead of the Indian armies who fell honoured in France and Flanders, Mesopotamia and Persia, East Africa, Gallipoli and Elsewhere in the Near and the Far East in the 1914–1918 war' and to those killed in the North-West Frontier operations and the Afghan War of 1919.[1] India made the largest contribution to the First World War in terms of manpower of any of the colonies or dominions of the British empire. According to government records of the time, the total number of Indian ranks recruited during the war up to 31 December 1919 was 877,068 combatants and 563,369 non-combatants, making a total of 1,440,437; in addition, there were an estimated 239,561 men in the British Indian army in 1914.[2] Yet in metropolitan middle-class memory in India (except in the Punjab), there is often a strange gap about the Indian experience of the First World War. Coming largely from the semiliterate, peasant-warrior classes of northern India, these men and their stories have been doubly marginalised: they have mostly been ignored in Indian nationalist-elitist historiography as well as in the modern European memory of the First World War.

Memory also exists privately, stubbornly. In the village of Lehri in north Pakistan, a simple plaque commemorates the number though not the names of the 391 men from the village who went to the war. Opening the diary of Private Charles Stinson, 1st Australian Light Horse Brigade, in the Australian War Memorial, one comes across a page where an Indian soldier had signed his name, Pakhar Singh, in Urdu, Gurmukhi and English (Figure 2). From an old shellac recording, now housed in the Lautarchiv of the Humboldt University in Berlin, rasps the desolate voice of Mall Singh, a prisoner of war, referring to himself in the third person: 'Germany captured this man. He wishes to return to India.'[3] A search through the memorabilia of my extended family in Kolkata revealed the war mementoes of Captain

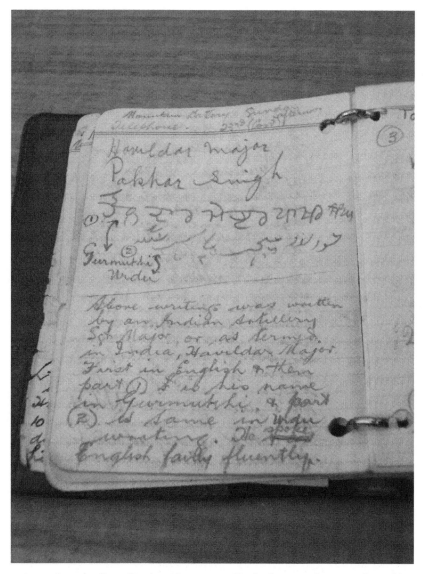

2. A page from the diary of an Australian private, Charles Stinson, where an Indian soldier had signed his name in English, Urdu and Gurmukhi

Dr Manindranath Das, including his uniform, a Military Cross, and a certificate commending his 'gallant and distinguished services' signed by Winston Churchill. Das was one of several distinguished Indian doctors who served with the Indian troops in Mesopotamia.

There has been sporadic interest in the military achievements of the Indian sepoys (from the Persian *sipahi* meaning 'soldier') in Europe, their experiences in France and Belgium, and the political and economic effects of the war in India.[4] In recent years, the substantial collection of censored extracts from Indian soldiers' letters has attracted notice, and an excellent selection titled *Indian Voices of the Great War: Soldiers' Letters, 1914–1918* (1999) was published by David Omissi who has done important work in this area. Another unusual plebian archive – a collection of some 2,677 sound recordings of around 250 languages and traditional music among prisoners of war in Germany made by the Royal Prussian Phonographic Commission between December 1915 and December 1918 – has surfaced, encouraging new lines of enquiry.[5] However, attention has habitually focused on the Indian sepoys in Europe. In comparison, very little is known about the emotional and literary responses to the war in India or about the Indian experiences in Mesopotamia where most of the Indian men served.[6]

This chapter seeks to explore an intimate history of the Indian experience of the First World War by at once recovering fresh voices, of both men and women, combatants and non-combatants, from India, Mesopotamia and France, and investigating the complex 'structures of feeling'[7] created by the overlapping histories of empire, race and the war. I draw on archival, oral and literary sources from Europe and India, as well as on personal testimonies, including a hitherto unknown and possibly the only existing Indian captivity memoir from Mesopotamia. As with European subjects, there were 'different wars' for the Indians too. Any monolithic notion of an 'Indian war experience' has to be nuanced to a number of factors, including issues of gender, class and caste, occupation and military rank, the province within India from which the participants came, and the theatre of war.

THE HOME FRONT: PRESTIGE, NATIONALISM, LAMENT

In August 1914, when the 'King-Emperor' sent his message asking for help to the 'Princes and People of My Indian Empire', the responses in India were largely enthusiastic.[8] The native princes, who still ruled one-third of India in various partnerships with the Raj, were overwhelmingly supportive. Extraordinary sums of money flowed in from the 700-odd native princes, from the Nizam of Hyderabad's offer of six million rupees for the maintenance of two cavalry units in France to the donation by the Thakur of Bagli of 'socks, shirts, mufflers, tobacco, cigarette, chocolates' for the Indian troops in East Africa, Mesopotamia and Egypt'.[9] More striking was the enthusiasm of the political bourgeoisie and the educated middle classes. The Indian National Congress of 1914, dominated by the political moderates, pledged their whole-hearted support to the Allies. Other parties and communities such as the All India Muslim League, Madras Provincial Congress, Hindus of Punjab and the Parsee community of Bombay concurred. Meetings were held in Calcutta, Bombay, Lahore and Allahabad. Addressing a big gathering in Madras, Dr Subramania Iyer claimed that to be allowed to serve as volunteers is an 'honour superior to that of a seat in the Executive Council and even in the Council of the Secretary of State'.[10] There was indeed a degree of political calculation, as is evident in the wartime writings of Annie Besant who founded the India Home Rule League in 1916: 'When the war is over, . . . we cannot doubt that the King-Emperor will, as reward for her glorious defence of the Empire, pin upon her breast the jewelled medal of Self-Government within the Empire.'[11] Mahatma Gandhi, who was in London in 1914 trying to raise an ambulance corps, demurred – 'it was more becoming and far-sighted not to press our demands while the war lasted'[12] – but it was widely felt that war service could later be used to press for 'responsible self-government'.

This political framework is often used to understand and explain war enthusiasm in India, but a closer investigation of wartime writings reveals a more complex and messy emotional response. The First World War catches the Indian middle-class consciousness at a fragile spot between a continuing, if increasingly qualified, loyalty to the Raj and a burgeoning nationalism.[13] Within colonial and postcolonial studies, scholars have powerfully drawn attention to the 'psychological damage' wrought by colonialism, showing how the imperial racist hierarchy is often internalised by the colonised, resulting in the corrosion of self-esteem and confidence.[14] Being constantly made to feel small before the allegedly 'superior' civilisation of Great Britain and with the fraught memories of the Sepoy Mutiny of 1857, Indian middle-class national discourse seized upon war service in Europe as an opportunity towards establishing racial equality and proving their courage and loyalty. This psychology is widely evident in the different writings collected in the compendious volume *All About the War: The Indian Review War Book*, edited by G. A. Nateson. A good example is the following wartime speech made at the Madras Provincial Conference in 1918 by the female nationalist leader and future president of the Indian National Congress Sarojini Naidu:

Let young Indians, who are ready to die for India and to wipe from her brow the brand of slavery, rush to join the standing army or, to be more correct, India's citizen army composed of cultured young men, of young men of traditions and ideals, men who burnt with the shame of slavery in their hearts, will prove a true redeemer of Indian people.[15]

Imperial war service here becomes a way of salvaging national prestige. Naidu was actively involved in the war efforts through the Lyceum club in London. An internationally celebrated 'poetess', she writes thus about the Indian soldiers in her poem 'The Gift of India':

> Gathered like pearls in their alien graves,
> Silent they sleep by the Persian waves.
> Scattered like shells on Egyptian sands
> They lie with pale brows and brave, broken hands.
> They are strewn like blossoms mown down by chance
> On the blood-brown meadows of Flanders and France.
>   . . .
> And you honour the deeds of the deathless ones,
> Remember the blood of thy martyred sons![16]

What would have been a rather forgettable English war lyric becomes distinctive when written by an Indian nationalist woman. The aestheticised vocabulary with its murmur of labials and sibilance resembles Georgian poetry, going back to Tennyson and Yeats, and reveals the intimate processes of colonial education upon the Bengali middle class. But the imperial framework is slyly offset by a nationalist aspiration: the emotive power of the poem is rooted in the war-bereaved consciousness of the mother who fuses, in this context, with the powerful, indigenous trope of 'Mother India' suffering under colonialism. Naidu's poem is not an aria for the death of the European bourgeois consciousness but rather a plea for the recognition of the Indian sepoys.

Yet how did the non-literate women in hundreds of villages in northern India, women whose fathers, sons or husbands actually went to the war, remember it? The highest rate of recruitment was in Punjab which had contributed by the time of the Armistice 360,000 recruits.[17] Among certain communities, such as the Jat Sikhs, the rate of recruitment varied between 30 and 50 per cent.[18] We confront the limits of official archival knowledge when we try to gauge the responses within these villages. What do survive, however, are folksongs about the war and recruitment – songs of lament and mourning from the women – pointing to a subcutaneous but powerful layer of memory. Consider the following Punjabi First World War folksong extracts recovered by the distinguished Punjabi poet Amarjit Chandan:

My husband, and his two brothers
All have gone to laam. [l'arme]
Hearing the news of the war
Leaves of trees got burnt.

Without you I feel lonely here.
Come and take me away to Basra.
I will spin the wheel the whole night.
. . .
War destroys towns and ports, it destroys huts
I shed tears, come and speak to me
All birds, all smiles have vanished
And the boats sunk
Graves devour our flesh and blood.[19]

According to Chandan, 'They [the women] hate war and the warmongers, whether the British or the Germans . . . There is nowhere any hint of martyrdom in these songs. They knew their men were mercenaries and not fighters in the Sikh or Rajput or *jihadi* tradition.'[20] Last year, I interviewed in Kolkata the Punjabi novelist Mohan Kahlon who mentioned how his two uncles – peasant-warriors from Punjab – perished in Mesopotamia, and his grandmother became deranged with grief; in the village, their house came to be branded as 'garod' (the asylum).[21] War trauma here spills into the furthest reaches of the empire. This is an idiom very different from Naidu's abstract rhetoric of 'martyrdom', showing how emotional resonances of the war were often fundamentally divisive across class lines, with memories of the poor village women refusing to fit the national discourses of enthusiasm or martyrdom.

HONOUR AND SLUR: THE WAR DIARIES OF THAKUR AMAR SINGH

In September and October 1914, the first two Indian divisions – renamed Lahore and Meerut – arrived at Marseilles to joyous cries of 'Vivent les Hindous'. They were put under the command of Lieutenant-General Sir James Willcocks and took part in some of the severest fighting, including the battle of Neuve Chapelle in which the Indian infantry formed half the attacking force.[22] A total of 132,496 Indians, including both combatants and non-combatants, were sent to France up to 31 October 1918; the majority of them served there between October 1914 and December 1915, when the infantry was withdrawn and sent to Mesopotamia.[23]

While the sepoys' censored letters have attracted attention, a different and unusual perspective is opened up through the diaries of the Rajput

aristocrat Thakur Amar Singh.[24] Trained at the Imperial Cadet Corps, the
36-year old Amar Singh was appointed aide-de-camp to General Brunker,
who commanded the 9th Sirhind Brigade which was part of the Lahore
Division. Amar Singh served intermittently in France from December 1914
to December 1915 and was near the war zone during the Indian exploits in
Festubert, Givenchy and Neuve Chapelle, though he did not take part in
the actual fighting. In January 1916, he joined his brigade in Mesopotamia.
Amar Singh's position was anomalous, one of enormous privilege but of
little power. His duties were restricted to the back of the front: he looked
after the transport, visited the sepoys in the trenches, went riding, and did
the occasional translation; most important, he kept a daily diary in English,
writing down everything he witnessed in exhaustive detail. The war years
are part of his diaries which stretch almost daily from 3 September 1898 to
the day of his death on 1 November 1942, running into eighty-nine volumes.

The war diaries are an extraordinary combination of description, observation, emotion, opinion and analysis. Records of key events such as the
battle of Givenchy (18–22 December 1914) or Neuve Chapelle (10–13 March
1915) are supplemented by more analytical accounts written shortly afterwards. If Merewether and Smith provide the official account of the battle of
Neuve Chapelle,[25] Amar Singh gives us an intimate history, from vivid
descriptions of bombardments to German gunsh 'mowing our men down'
to a poignant account of a 'cold, hungry, thirsty, wounded' German in no-
man's-land calling out to his comrades.[26] Amar Singh's meditation on the
'terrible' nature of war reminds one of European officer-writers but, unlike
theirs, his 'structures of feeling' are created not so much by war trauma as by
the complex conjunction of class, racial and colonial politics in wartime.

'Slur' is a recurrent word in the diaries; a constant oscillation between
aristocratic privilege and racial discrimination forms their emotional core.
Experiences of 'slight' range from the refusal of the English soldiers to salute
him (though he was a King's Commissioned Officer) to being teased for not
eating beef to being 'very rudely' asked to leave the room when important
military details were discussed. The personal and the racial are interlinked.
When Amar Singh suggested sending an all-Indian force to Egypt, General
Brunker had turned on him 'fiercely': 'you can't fight with native troops
only'. Singh criticises General Brunker's decision to mix British and Indian
troops, for 'the Indians must have felt it as a slur on them':[27]

The great trouble under which we have laboured is that whenever we fail in the
slightest degree anywhere people raise a hue and cry whereas if the British troops
fail under the same circumstances no one mentions it. The Indian troops had done
very well all along but when we had the reverse at Givenchy and Festubert there was

a hue and cry . . . Plainly the thing is that if there is a success it is due to the British element but if there is a reverse then it is all put down to the Indian troops. I do not know what is expected of the Indians.[28]

Amar Singh may occasionally have been too enthusiastic or defensive about the Indian performance but what comes across powerfully is his frustration and resentment at the racist ideology of the British army. According to General Willcocks, the Indian officer 'can *never* replace . . . the natural instincts of the white man'.[29] The uneven performance of the Indian Corps is understood not in terms of inadequate military training but instead attributed to the Indians' 'natural inferiority'.

The diaries capture the emotional pulse of Indian army life and its hierarchies as Singh moves between the worlds of the British military elite and a semiliterate sepoy community. Singh is generally very sympathetic towards the sepoys. After the first day of the battle of Neuve Chapelle, he describes how he saw wounded Sikh soldiers 'empty their magazines and throw all the ammunition in the ditch'; when he assures two Gurkha officers that they will be back in India in 'three or four months' time', they answer back: 'Jabtak kaun zinda rahega' ('as long as someone is alive').[30] Informed about the desertion of a group of Pathans, he notes that 'perhaps they had enough of fighting'; when told about the low levels of recruitment in India, he writes: 'He [the Indian] is perfectly safe at home and well protected . . . He cannot see why he should hazard his life.'[31] Singh's understanding of the conflict's mercenary nature for the Indian – rather than seeing it as propelled by *izzat*, or honour – is acute. Ironically, however, it is his 'education' in the imperial ideology as well as in Rajput aristocratic and masculine codes that prevents his sympathy from developing into a critique of the empire or into war protest. As with Naidu, imperial war service becomes a way of salvaging national prestige: 'The lives of a few thousand are nothing compared to the honour of a nation.'[32]

MEMORIES OF MESOPOTAMIA: CAPTAIN DR KALYAN
MUKHERJI AND SISIR SARBADHIKARI

The history of the war in Mesopotamia, like the war itself, has remained a sideshow. Major Carter's account of a convoy steamer bringing in the wounded from Ctesiphon, covered in their own faeces, has come to represent all that was horrific about the campaign, which was marked by mismanagement, starvation and brutality by the Turkish captors.[33] As mentioned earlier, Mesopotamia was India's main theatre of war. The largest number of

Indian men – some 588,717, including 7,812 officers, 287,753 other ranks and 293,152 non-combatants (often forming porter and labour corps) – served there.[34] A large number of Indians from the 6th Division were captured at Kut-el-Amara after General Charles Townshend's surrender on 29 April 1916, but the precise numbers are not known. According to one estimate, the number of Indians captured was around 10,440, including 204 officers, 6,988 rank and file and 3,248 followers.[35] However, with the exception of a few interviews, the sources for the Indian experience under siege or in captivity have been exclusively British. In such a context, the freshly unearthed letters of Captain Dr Kalyan Kumar Mukherji and the captivity memoir of Sisir Prasad Sarbadhikari, a medical orderly, are singularly valuable; they are also rare examples of educated, middle-class Indian voices of the war.

Captain Mukherji, a member of the Indian Medical Service, was appointed a military doctor to Indian Expeditionary Force D. He was in Mesopotamia from his arrival at Basra on 9 April 1915 till his death from high fever in 1917 and was posthumously awarded the Military Cross. A popular doctor, he was mentioned by Major Sandes in *In Kut and Captivity* (1919), as well as by Sarbadhikari. After his death, his eighty-year-old grandmother wrote his biography *Kalyan-Pradeep: The Life of Captain Kalyan Kumar Mukhopadhay, IMS* (1928), extracting his war letters in full. Sarbadhikari's memoir, on the other hand, has a tantalising textual history. It was based on his secret Mesopotamia diary, written in captivity, which was broken up into individual pages and hidden in his boots during the horrific march from Samarra via Mosul to the POW camp in Ras-el-Ain in July 1916. Later, the contents of the faded pages were copied into a new diary which was hidden underground and retrieved at Ras-el-Ain.[36] Both men were Bengalis from Kolkata, yet due to differences in rank their experiences varied significantly.

The letters of Captain Kalyan Mukherji are some of the finest in the grand pantheon of First World War letters. As part of the ambulance corps attached to the 6th Division and working just behind the firing line, he witnesses severe fighting at Nasiriyah (24 July 1915), Sunaiyat and Kut-al-Amara (26–28 September 1915). On 26 July 1915, two days after the battle of Nasiriyah, he writes to his mother: 'I had been working constantly, with hardly any time to breathe, from 6 o'clock in the morning till 1 p.m. Rivers of blood, red – everywhere – I was myself covered in blood . . . Why is there so much bloodshed?' As the Allied troops take over Kut, he writes on 28 October 1915: 'We have advanced quite a lot – why more? It is us, the victors, who are snatching away from the enemies everything they have; after all, the enemies have not yet done anything.'[37]

His powerful antiwar views are contained in several lengthy letters to his mother. Consider the following extract, written on 20 October 1915 from Aziziya, a couple of weeks after the battle of Kut-al-Amara:

England is the educator. The patriotism that the English have taught us all this time, the patriotism that all civilised nations have celebrated – that patriotism is responsible for this bloodshed. All patriotism – it means snatching away another's country. Therefore patriotism builds empires, kingdoms. To show patriotism, nationalism, by killing thousands and thousands of people and snatching away a bit of land, well, it's the English who have taught us this.

The youths of our country, seeing this, have started to practise this brutal form of nationalism. Therefore, killing a number of people, throwing bombs at an innocent overlord – they have started these horrific things. Shame on patriotism. As long as this narrowness does not end, bloodshed in the name of patriotism will not cease. Whether a man throws a bomb from the roof-top or whether fifty men start firing from a cannon-gun – the cause of this bloodshed, this madness is the same.[38]

The level of intellectual maturity and antiwar fervour places these letters alongside the pacifist missives of an Owen or a Sassoon. But they are essentially different. Mukherji's letters are not just a condemnation of violence or patriotism. The radicalism is twofold. A colonial subject, he exposes the intimate relationship between patriotism and imperialism. However his critique of imperialism, even as he acknowledges the deep educational influence of England upon the Indian bourgeoisie, cannot be equated with Indian nationalism. Through acute reasoning, he associates imperial aggression with its obverse – nationalist terrorism – which shook India just before the war. For Mukherji, imperialism, revolutionary nationalism and the European war are all implicated in the same vicious cycle of violence, a vision that reminds one of the anti-colonial and anti-nationalist views of the Indian poet and Nobel laureate Rabindranath Tagore.[39]

Sisir Sarbadhikari's *Abhi Le Baghdad* (1957) begins where Mukherji's letters end. While Mukherji's letters after the defeat at Ctesiphon (22–25 November 1915) dwindle to the occasional telegram, Sarbadhikari's 209-page memoir gives us a veritable sociology of life in Mesopotamia under siege and in captivity. Sarbadhikari volunteered for the Bengal Ambulance Corps as a stretcher-bearer and arrived at Basra on 15 July 1915.[40] He witnessed the battle of Ctesiphon, nursing the wounded just behind the firing line; during the siege of Kut, he worked first in a makeshift hospital in a date grove amidst regular shelling and was one of the first Indian orderlies to work in the British General Hospital at Kut. Above all, he survived the 500-mile march to Ras-el-Ain in July 1916. As a medical orderly who knew English and Turkish, Sarbadhikari worked for the next two and a half years in hospitals in Ras-el-Ain and Aleppo, and then in the German camp at Nisibin.

How does the experience of shared captivity reconfigure hierarchies between the British and the Indians – does it create new structures of feeling and intimacies? In *In Kut and Captivity* (1919), Major Sandes writes that on reaching Baghdad, 'our first business was naturally to get separate accommodation for the Indian officers': 'we explained also that Indian officers ... were always of inferior ranks to British officers'.[41] Even in captivity, the colonial, racist hierarchy is put forward as 'natural'. Sarbadhikari similarly records how, on the steamer voyage to Baghdad after the surrender at Kut, the British troops were provided with sleeping places in the lower deck while six hundred sepoys were crammed onto the exposed upper deck. During the journey, the British soldiers blamed and some even tried to physically attack the sepoys for the debacle at Kut. Sarbadhikari also notes the daily institutional racism:

The discrimination that is always practised between the whites and the coloured is highly insulting. The white soldier gets paid twice as much as the Indian sepoy. The uniform of the two is different – that of the whites is better ... In fact, whatever little provisions can be made are made for the Tommy. Even the ration is different – the Tommies take tea with sugar, we are given only molasses.[42]

Sarbadhikari does not speak of any close English 'friends'. The experience of colonial subjugation draws him instead towards other oppressed people at the general hospital in Aleppo (1916–17), such as the Armenian cleaner Maryam or the fifteen-year-old Armenian orphan Elias. He mentions the Armenian massacre and records the panic among the Armenian community. One of the most poignant moments in the memoir is his midnight farewell embrace with Elias as the latter escapes from Nisibin: Sarbadhikari gives him his warm coat.[43] On the other hand, Jumman, a north Indian sweeper, finds an Armenian orphan beside a well, names him Babulal, raises him like a son, and after the war manages to take him back to India.[44] What *Abhi Le Baghdad* evokes hauntingly is an affective community of the displaced and the derelict at the premises of the hospital at Aleppo.

The exact number of casualties among the Indian prisoners in Mesopotamia is unknown.[45] This has given rise to a general belief that the Indians were better treated than the British by the Turks: however, substantial evidence is still lacking. While Muslim prisoners received preferential treatment, it is not clear whether similar discrimination worked across racial lines as well. Sarbadhikari's account of the 48-day, 500-mile traumatic march from Samarra to Ras-el-Ain in July 1916 does not suggest any

favouritism towards Indians; of his thirteen friends held in captivity, six
died, that is, nearly half. This is a high mortality rate. Amar Singh records
meeting some exchanged Indian prisoners who resembled 'a bag of bones
and there was hardly any flesh on them'; Captain Mouseley records that 'out
of the night one heard the high Indian wail: 'Margaya, sahib, margaya'
['Dying, sahib, dying'].[46] Sarbadhikari escaped the plight of the Hindu
sepoys employed for construction work at Ras-el-Ain who resembled,
according to a British eyewitness account, 'animated skeletons hung
about with filthy rags'.[47] Sarbadhikari recalls instances of sadistic behaviour
from the Turkish and Arab guards in the hospital but in his memoir there is
a marked absence of the racialised discourse of fear and savagery around the
Turks that one finds in European narratives. In Sarbadhikari's account,
instances of brutality by the Turkish guards are offset by a shared intimacy
with the Turkish wounded in the hospital:

We used to talk about our country, about our joys and sorrows . . . One thing, they
always used to reiterate. What is your gain in this war? Why are we cutting each
other's throats? You live in Hindustan, we live in Turkey, we don't know each
other, we don't have any quarrel between us . . .
   There was one more thing noticeable amongst them – that was a common hatred
of the Germans . . . The main cause for discontent was that whatever was good in
this country, the Germans would have it first. The eggs would first go to the
German hospitals and leftovers – if any – would then go to the Turks. The same
happened with everything. We used to think that the same thing happens in our
country but our only solace is that we are at least a subjugated nation, whereas
Germany and Turkey are friends![48]

What brings captive and captor together here is a shared anti-European
sentiment, based on a history of economic exploitation and a sense that the
war was not theirs. Hierarchies of captor and captive are further reversed
when Sarbadhikari offers food and cigarettes to his Turkish captors whom
he describes as poor and dishevelled. These examples of contact, absent
in British memoirs, suggest occasional pockets of intimacy between
Indians and the Turks and resist the imposition of rigid grids on their
interactions.

SEPOY LETTERS: PALIMPSESTS, *IZZAT*
AND TRANSCULTURAL IDENTITIES

What do we know about the emotional world of the sepoys who formed the
majority of the men serving abroad? In spite of scattered archival records,
some interviews and the voice recordings of Indian POWs in Germany, the

most substantial source remains the sepoys' censored mail. Given the considerable attention the letters have already received, I shall turn to them briefly to make a few points.[49] These letters were often dictated by the sepoys and written down (and sometimes embellished) by a scribe and then translated and extracted by the censors; these extracts are what survive today. Indeed, they open up in extraordinarily rich detail the world of the sepoys – the shock of the first encounter with Europe, homesickness, war trauma, interracial romance – but at the same time they cannot be taken as the transparent envelope of sepoy experience.

Given their multiple sites of textuality, these letters are perhaps best read as palimpsests where underneath accretions by different agencies, traces of the sepoy's original intent remain. Often quoted, their narrative structures are seldom investigated. Consider the following letter from Saif Ali from France on 17 August 1915:

> The country is very fine, well-watered and fertile. The fields are very large, all gardens full of fruit trees. Every man's land yields him thousands of *maunds* of wheat ... The fruits are pears, apricots, grapes and fruits of many kinds. Even the dogs refuse them at this season. Several regiments could eat from one tree. The people are very well-mannered and well-to-do. The value of each house may be set down as several *lakhs* or *crores* of rupees. Each house is a sample of paradise.[50]

The sepoy here seems to be overwhelmed by the embarrassment of riches of the West, but we need to be equally alert to the narrative strategies. What we have here is not just the spontaneous overflow of powerful feelings but also the construction of 'wonder' for the anticipated reader. In the extract quoted above, the narrative proceeds from hyperbolic quantification through a litany of the names of fruits and estimates of property value to the mythical: 'a sample of paradise'. This final phrase recurs in other letters, suggesting it to be a scribal embellishment. Moreover, how does this 'wonder' evolve and change with time, and how is it measured against other kinds of experience, such as homesickness or transactions with the local population? Rather than reading the sepoy as a passive receptacle for overwhelming experiences of wonder or, later, of the trauma of industrial warfare, it is more productive to regard him as a thinking and alert, if circumscribed, agent who not only perceives but also negotiates Western culture as well as, on occasions, military, medical and social institutions.[51]

A recurring word in the letters is *izzat* – an Urdu word, roughly translated as 'honour', 'prestige' or 'reputation' – which is often understood by scholars as something organic and fundamental to the sepoy's identity.[52] However, what emerges from the letters is an exceptionally complex and fluid concept of *izzat* that takes on a variety of shades from national, tribal, regional and caste prestige to matters of family, sexual and personal honour. 'I am convinced that only in the army is any *izzat* to be acquired,' writes a sepoy from Rouen as late as September 1916 but for another sepoy, writing from the Kitchener hospital on 3 June 1915, *izzat* has already been severed from military service: 'There is abundance of everything but there is no honour (*izzat*). No black man has any *izzat*. Men wounded four or five times are sent back to the trenches'.[53] As Ravi Ahuja, who has perceptively investigated the concept in a recent essay, notes, 'with regard to the Indian combatants of the Great War, it appears that neither was martial valour the only (or necessarily most important) route nor was the Indian army the only (or necessarily most important) social sphere for the acquisition or defence of *izzat*'.[54] Moreover, statements in the letters such as '*izzat* is dearer even than life itself'[55] which have often been taken at face value need to be placed alongside other kinds of evidence, particularly the suspiciously high number of 'hand wounds' reported among the Indian sepoys in October 1914.[56] The rate of wounding dropped dramatically after five sepoys were shot that winter, but the rates increased again when new sepoys arrived from India in May 1915. Within the first few weeks of warfare, notions of *izzat* seem to have been renegotiated with the shock of industrial combat and the lived reality of the body.

At the same time, the thesis of the acquisition of transcultural identities by the sepoys also has to be pursued with caution. Letters show the deep impact of European social practices and thoughts on the sepoy's inner world: 'You ought to educate your girls as well as your boys and our posterity will be the better for it.'[57] But how far these ideas were followed through or implemented once the sepoy returned home, and their effects on Punjab's patriarchal structures and patterns of female education need more intensive investigation. In France, it was the realm of interpersonal relationships that was the most intimate zone of contact. Consider the following oft-quoted letter by a sepoy describing his 'French mother', a figure who became a recurrent trope in the letters:

The house in which I was billeted was the house of a well-to-do man, but the only occupant was the lady of the house, and she was advanced in years. Her three sons had gone to the war. One had been killed, another had been wounded and was in hospital, and the third was at that time in the trenches ... There are miles of difference between the women of India and the women of this country. During the whole three months I never once saw this old lady sitting idle, although she belonged to a high family. Indeed, during the whole three months, she ministered to me to such an extent that I cannot adequately describe her [kindness]. Of her own free will she washed my clothes, arranged my bed, polished my boots for three months ... When we had to leave the village this old lady wept on my shoulder.[58]

This is the rich and stirring realm of interpersonal contact: affection, maternity, bereavement, loneliness are all combined. It is not in the world of casual sex and romance but in these affective dyads between the young sepoys and the elderly, bereaved French women that some of the most fruitful Indo-European encounters took place. Yet what is often overlooked is that there is a complex dialectic between retrenchment and realignment of gender and racial roles. The role of the elderly woman caring for the young man fits neatly with the cultural assumptions of the anticipated reader. But if this is a reassertion of traditional Indian emotional values, the idea of an elderly white woman of 'high family' polishing shoes or washing 'my clothes' suggests at once a new awareness of the democratisation of labour and an inversion of racial hierarchies.

Whether in Mesopotamia or in France, an investigation of the emotional histories of the Indian combatants and non-combatants, as well as of their families back in India, shows not only the war's tumultuous effects but also its enmeshment in particularities of class, gender, local and regional identity, military rank and theatre of battle, among others. Such findings undercut the notion of any single or uniform 'Indian war experience'. Investigation of different kinds of evidence reveals complex structures of feeling that refuse to fit neat categories and suggests the powerful reconceptualisation of racial, colonial and cultural identities for these men. It is difficult to draw a direct trajectory between war experience and the rise of Indian nationalism – it is a different, though fascinating, story and more intensive research is needed in the field – but the war experience abroad did give these men fresh confidence and political awareness. As a Punjabi veteran of the First World War noted in 1972, 'when we saw various peoples and got their views, we started protesting against the inequalities and disparities which the British had created between the white and the black'.[59]

NOTES

1 Parts of this chapter were presented at the two conferences on South Asian experiences in the world wars organised by Ravi Ahuja, the first at Zentrum Moderner Orient in Berlin in 2007, and the second at the School of Oriental and African Studies in London in 2009. I would like to thank the participants of both conferences for the stimulating discussions, and Heather Jones and George Morton-Jack for carefully reading the chapter at short notice.

Initially known as the All India War Memorial, the Delhi Gate was designed by Edwin Lutyens and the foundation stone of the memorial was laid in 1921.

2 *Statistics of the Military Effort of the British Empire during the Great War, 1914–1920* (London: His Majesty's Stationery Office, 1920), 777; reproduced in *India's Contribution to the Great War* (Kolkata: Superintendent Government Printing, India, 1923), 79. Both note that between August 1914 and December 1919, India sent overseas 1,096,013 (Indian) men, comprising 621,224 soldiers, both officers and other ranks, and 474,789 non-combatants (*Statistics of the Military Effort*, 777; *India's Contribution*, 98).

3 Charles Stinson, 'Diary', Australian War Memorial, Canberra, PR84/066; Mall Singh's voice recording was done on 11 December 1916 by the Royal Prussian Phonographic Commission and is held by the Lautarchiv of the Humboldt-University in Berlin, PK 619.

4 One of the earliest military records is Lt Col. J. W. B. Merewether and Sir Frederick Smith, *The Indian Corps in France* (London: John Murray, 1918), which also lists the original composition of the Indian Corps in France (10–12). See also Dewitt Ellinwood and S. D. Pradhan (eds.), *India and World War I* (Delhi: Manohar, 1978); David Omissi, *The Sepoy and the Raj* (Basingstoke: Macmillan, 1994); Omissi (ed.), *Indian Voices of the Great War 1914–1918* (Basingstoke: Macmillan, 1999); Gordon Corrigan, *Sepoys in the Trenches: The Indian Corps on the Western Front 1914–1915* (Staplehurst: Spellmount, 1999); Susan VanKoski, 'Letters Home 1915–1916: Punjabi Soldiers Reflect on War and Life in Europe', *International Journal of Punjab Studies*, 2/1 (1995), 43–63; Rozina Visram, *Asians in Britain* (London: Pluto Press, 2002); Jeffery Greenhut, 'The Imperial Reserve: the Indian Corps on the Western Front, 1914–1915', *Journal of Imperial and Commonwealth History* 12 (1983), 54–73; Tai Yong Tan, *The Garrison State: the military, government and society in colonial Punjab 1849–1947* (New Delhi: Manohar, 2005); George Morton-Jack, 'The Indian Army on the Western Front, 1914–1915: A Portrait of Collaboration', *War in History*, 2006, 13: 329–62. See also Heike Liebau, Katrin Bromber, Katharina Lange, Dyala Hamzah and Ravi Ahuja (eds.), *The World in World Wars: Experiences, Perceptions and Perspectives from Africa and Asia* (Leiden and Boston: Brill, 2010). Though a couple of the chapters were heard or read in draft versions, this important volume was published while the present collection was in the press and hence could not be engaged with.

5 Jürgen Mahrenholz, Britta Lange and Phillip Scheffner brought the sound archives to wider attention through their work, including Scheffner's film *The Half-Moon Files* (2007). See also Ravi Ahuja, Heike Liebau and Franziska Roy (eds.), *'When the War Began, We Heard of Several Kings': South Asian Prisoners in World War I Germany* (Delhi: Social Science, forthcoming). I am grateful to Ravi Ahuja for letting me read his thoughtful article 'The Corrosiveness of Comparison: Reverberations of Indian Wartime Experiences in German Prison Camps (1915–1919)' ahead of publication in Liebau *et al.*, *The World in World Wars*, 131–66.

6 The very few articles on the Indian experience in Mesopotamia include Nikolas Gardner, 'Sepoys and the Siege of Kut-al-Amara, December 1915–April 1916', *War in History*, vol. 11, 3 (July 2004), 307–26, and Radhika Singha, 'Finding

8

86   SANTANU DAS

Labour from India for the War in Iraq', *Comparative Studies in Society and History* 49:2 (2007), 412–45.

7 See Raymond Williams, *Marxism and Literature* (Oxford University Press, 1977), 129–33; also see Santanu Das, *Touch and Intimacy in First World War Literature* (Cambridge University Press, 2005).

8 Quoted in *India and the War* (London: Hodder and Stoughton, 1915), 40–1. There were isolated revolutionary activities centred round the activities of the Ghadr party. See A. C. Bose, 'Indian Revolutionaries during the First World War', in Ellinwood and Pradhan, *India and World War I*, 109–26; F. C. Isemonger and J. Slattery, *Account of the Ghadr Conspiracy (1913–1915)* (Delhi: South Asia Books, 1998).

9 National Archives of India, Delhi (hereafter NOI), Foreign and Political, Internal B, April 1915 nos. 319–46; NOI, Foreign and Political, Internal B, April 1915 nos. 972–7.

10 Quoted in *India and the War* (Lahore: Khosla Brothers, n.d.), 34–5.

11 Annie Besant, 'India's Loyalty and England's Duty', in G. A. Nateson (ed.), *All About the War: The India Review War Book* (Madras, 1915?), 267.

12 M. K. Gandhi, *An Autobiography or, The Story of My Experiments with Truth*, trans. Mahadev Desai (Harmondsworth: Penguin, 1982), 317.

13 I have explored the responses of the political bourgeoisie more fully in 'Imperialism, Nationalism and the First World War in India', in Jennifer Keene and Michael Neiberg (eds.), *Finding Common Ground: New Directions in First World War Studies* (Leiden: Brill, 2010).

14 Ashis Nandy, *The Intimate Enemy: Loss and Recovery of the Self under Colonialism* (Delhi: Oxford University Press, 1983), 3.

15 Quoted in M. B. L. Bhargava, *India's Services in the War* (Allahabad: Standard Press, 1919), 208–9.

16 'The Gift of India' in Sarojini Naidu, *The Broken Wing: Songs of Love, Death and Destiny 1915–1916* (London: William Heinemann, 1917), 5–6. For a detailed exploration, see Santanu Das, ' "Indian Sister! . . . Send your husbands, brothers, sons": India, Women and the First World War', in Alison Fell and Ingrid Sharp (ed.), *The Women's Movement in Wartime: International Perspectives, 1914–1919* (London: Palgrave, 2007), 18–37

17 Omissi, *The Sepoy and the Raj*, 39

18 S. D. Pradhan, 'The Sikh Soldier in the First World War' in Ellinwood and Pradhan (eds.), *India and World War I (213–25)*, 217.

19 These extracts are quoted from Amarjit Chandan, 'How they Suffered: World War One and its Impact on Punjabis', http://apnaorg.com/articles/amarjit/wwi (accessed on 22 September 2009). They have been translated by Chandan and Amin Mughal. Chandan recited the song in Punjabi at the 2009 conference in London on 'South Asian Experiences of World Wars'.

20 *Ibid.*

21 Interview conducted with Mohan Kahlon in Kolkata, 20 December 2007.

22 See Corrigan, *Sepoys in the Trenches*, 146–72; for differing views of the military achievements and morale of the Indians Corps in France, see Greenhut, 'The Imperial Reserve', 54–73 and Morton-Jack, 'The Indian Army', 329–52.

23 *India's Contribution to the Great War*, 96.

24 Diaries of Major General Amar Singh, 1914 Jan-Dec (Microfilm R3540 Index 9), 1916 Jan-Dec, 1917 and Jan-Aug 24 (Microfilm R3541 Index 10), Nehru Memorial Museum and Library, Teen Murti House, New Delhi. I would like to acknowledge the help and courtesy of the Nehru Memorial Museum and Library and its staff in allowing me to read and photocopy parts of the diary. The original diaries are housed in the Kanota fort, Rajasthan; all references in the text are to the microfilm version of the diaries in the Nehru Museum, abbreviated as 'Singh Diaries'. The pages in the diary are not numbered. See Susanne Rudolph and Lloyd Rudolph's majestic edition of the diaries (1898 to 1905), *Reversing the Gaze: Amar Singh's Diary, A Colonial Subject's narrative of Imperial India* (Delhi: Oxford University Press, 2000), which was followed by DeWitt C. Ellinwood's illuminating biography *Between Two Worlds: A Rajput Officer in the Indian Army, 1905–1921* (Lanham: Hamilton, 2005).

25 See Lt Col. J. W. B. Merewether and Sir F. Smith, *The Indian Corps in France* (London: John Murray, 1918), 218–19.

26 Singh Diaries, 'A few notes about the severe fighting at Neuve Chapelle', Thursday, 8 April 1915, Boulogne.

27 Singh Diaries, 'Some notes about the severe handling we had at the fighting at Festuibert [*sic*] & Givenchy', Wednesday, 31 March 1915.

28 Singh Diaries, 'Some notes', Tuesday, 6 April 1915, Boulogne.

29 Willcocks to Hardinge, 30 December 1914, Hardinge 102/1/1153a, quoted in Greenhut, 'Imperial Reserve', 72.

30 Singh Diaries, 'A few notes about the severe fighting at Neuve Chapelle', Thursday, 8 April 1915; 'Some notes', Tuesday, 6 April 1915, Boulogne.

31 Singh Diaries, 'Some notes', Tuesday, 6 April 1915.

32 Singh Diaries, 'Some notes', Tuesday, 6 April 1915.

33 A. J. Barker, *The Neglected War: Mesopotamia 1914–1918* (London: Faber, 1967), 137; also see Paul K. Davis, *Ends and Means: The British Mesopotamian Campaign and Commission* (Madison: Associated University Presses, 1994).

34 *India's Contribution to the Great War*, 97.

35 The figures were published in the Turkish newspaper *Journal de Beyrouth* of 2 May 1916, and quoted in Major E. W. C. Sandes, *In Kut and Captivity, with the Sixth Indian Division* (London: John Murray, 1919), 261. These figures are also used by Barker, *The Neglected War*, 286, and are close to the figures cited in *Statistics of the Military Effort*, 330. The Table of Prisoners in the latter mentions a separate category for 'Indian Native Kut' but gives only the combined figure for 'Indian Native' (captured elsewhere on the Mesopotamia campaign) and 'Indian Native Kut' at 200 Indian officers, and 10,486 'other ranks' (330). See also Heather Jones's Chapter 9, 'Imperial captivities', in this volume, at page 178.

36 Mokkhada Devi, *Kalyan-Pradeep: The Life of Captain Kalyan Kumar Mukhopadhyay*, IMS. (Kolkata: privately printed, 1928). All official correspondence extracted at the end of the memoir refers to Kalyan Kumar as 'K. K. Mukherji' which is the surname used in the text (Mukherji is the Anglicised

version of Mukhopadhyay). See also Sisir Prasad Sarbadhikari, *Abhi Le Baghdad* (Kolkata: privately printed, 1957). Both these accounts are in Bengali; all translations are mine. I am very grateful to Sisir Sarbadhikari's daughter-in-law Mrs Romola Sarbadhikari for discussing his war experiences and the history of the diary with me in Kolkata in 2007. I would also like to thank Dr Kaushik Roy for sharing with me his copy of *Kalyan-Pradeep* in Kolkata in 2006.

37 Devi, *Kalyan-Pradeep*, 293, 336.
38 Letter dated 20 October 1915 in *ibid.*, 334.
39 Tagore's essays 'Nationalism in Japan', 'Nationalism in the West' and 'Nationalism in India' are collected in Rabindranath Tagore, *Nationalism* (New York: Macmillan, 1917).
40 The Bengal Ambulance Corps was masterminded by Dr. S. P. Sarbadhikari, a relative of Sisir Prasad Sarbadhikari, and did important medical work in Mesopotamia. See 'The Bengal Ambulance Corps', Confidential File 312/16, West Bengal State Archives, Kolkata.
41 Sandes, *In Kut and Captivity*, 285, 287.
42 Sarbadhikari, *Abhi Le Baghdad*, 188.
43 *Ibid.*, 178.
44 *Ibid.*, 175. Heather Jones has found a reference to a similar story of an Armenian child living with Indian prisoners of war in an English diary in the Imperial War Museum. See page 188 of this volume.
45 According to *Statistics of the Military Effort* (330), of the 10,686 Indians captured, 10 officers and 1,698 other ranks were reported dead and 1,324 men were untraced at the end of the war, totalling 3,032 men. But this figure may include Indian casualties from other phases of the Mesopotamian campaign, as well as the captives taken at Kut. According to Martin Gilbert, 9,300 Indian soldiers were captured at Kut, of whom 2,500 died *(The First World War*, London: HarperCollins, 1994), 248.
46 Singh Diaries, 'Notes about the sick and wounded', entry for Saturday, 20 May 1916, Maxim Mound; Mouseley, quoted in Ron Wilcox, *Battles on the Tigris: The Mesopotamia Campaign of the First World War* (Barnsley: Pen & Sword, 2006), 137
47 W. P. Long, *Other Ranks of Kut* (London: Williams and Norgate, 1938), 112.
48 Sarbadhikari, *Abhi Le Baghdad*, 158.
49 Among recent essays on the letters, see David Omissi, 'Europe Through Indian Eyes: Indian Soldiers Encounter England and France, 1914–1918', *English Historical Review* (2007) 122 (496), 371–96, and Claude Markovits, 'Indian Soldiers' Experiences during World War I', in *The World in World War*, 29–53. The second essay was published when the present volume was already in press and could not be engaged with here.
50 Military Department, *Censor of Indian Mails 1914–1918*, L/MIL/826, Part 2, India Office Library (abbreviated IOL), British Library, London.
51 See Ahuja, 'The Corrosiveness of Comparison', 131–66, for an investigation of the complexity of the negotiation through a focus on Indian prisoners of war in Germany.

52 For example, in the introduction to *Indian Voices*, David Omissi notes that *izzat* was 'even more important than mercenary motives ... Indian soldiers fought, above all, to gain or preserve *izzat* – their honour, standing, reputation or prestige' (*Indian Voices*, 12). However, he hints at a more complex notion of *izzat* in his exploration of the 'fighting spirit' in *Sepoy and the Raj*, 77–84.

53 Omissi, *Indian Voices*, 236; Censor of Indian Mails, 1914–1918, L/MIL/5/828, Part 2, FF203–408, 405.

54 Ahuja, 'The Corrosiveness of Comparison', 136.

55 Omissi, *Indian Voices*, 309.

56 Public Records Office, London, War Office, 154/14, 'Return Showing Court-Martial Convictions in Indian Corps from October 1914 to February 1915; PRO, WO, 256/4, Field Marshal Sir Douglas Haig, Western Front Diary IV, 5 May 1915. The hand wounds, widely alleged to have been self-inflicted, have to be considered, though their interpretation is a continuing point of debate. See Greenhut, 'The Imperial Reserve', 57, and Morton-Jack, 'The Indian Army', 340–1.

57 Omissi, *Indian Voices*, 258. The letter was written by a sepoy in France to his relative in Punjab.

58 Letter of Sher Bahadur Khan, France, 9 January 1916, *Censor of Indian Mails*, 1914–1918, L/MIL/5/828 Part I, FF.1–202, 112.

59 Interview with Lance-Naik Khela Singh conducted by Ellinwood and Pradhan, quoted in Pradhan, 'The Sikh Soldier', 224.

CHAPTER 4

'We don't want to die for nothing': askari at war in German East Africa, 1914–1918

Michelle Moyd

The First World War initially came to East Africa as a rumour. Mzee Ali, a senior *askari*,[1] recalled how he first heard in late 1914 of the 'great and terrible war' that would soon engulf German East Africa:

> From the talk around the campfires we knew this was to be no ordinary war. The sheer scale of it set it apart from any war we had known or been involved in . . . We knew from the gravity of the discussions that this war would come to our land and that only then would we fully comprehend its nature.[2]

German officers of the Schutztruppe commenced an 'intense' military training programme to whip the veteran soldiers back into shape after years of garrison life, and to train a new generation of recruits.[3] A seasoned veteran of East African warfare, Ali nevertheless felt great anxiety about this war's potential 'scale and horror' which 'had magnified out of all proportion in [the *askaris*'] minds'. Waiting to go into battle against Allied forces in East Africa in April 1915 and struggling to overcome his fear that he would mishandle his weapon in battle, he experienced agitation and sleeplessness. Finally, he pulled himself together: 'Breathing deeply to control my nervousness, I determined to put my faith and indeed my life in my training and in our officers.'[4] Relying on his officers and comrades renewed his resolve, and he found that he could sleep again, even while waiting for battle to commence.[5]

The tough training Ali underwent, first as a young slave-raider under his father's tutelage and later as an *askari* under German leadership, helped produce Ali's masculinity. Ali's father taught him the virtues of a successful caravan leader, namely the ability to project calmness, decisiveness and practical mastery of the basic skills of caravan life. When the Schutztruppe arrived in his homeland, Ali recalled German officers' 'harshness' and arrogance in asserting themselves as the new rulers, but he was also impressed with their intensity, technological mastery and discipline.[6] Ali experienced fear

90

many times during his service as an *askari*, but his years of experience in subordinating fear to faith in professional training, emotional toughness, and comradeship gave him the wherewithal to keep fighting.

Ali was one among the 14,000 *askari* recruited and conscripted by the German colonial administration for its East African campaign. But what were Ali and his fellow *askari* willing to fight and die for? Academic and popular authors have explained the *askari* willingness to fight in the East African campaign in terms of an organic 'loyalty' to their German officers, and especially to the Schutztruppe commander, General Paul von Lettow-Vorbeck.[7] *Askari* 'loyalty', detached from any sense of their particular histories, has sufficed to explain how they fought to the end of the bitter campaign. But as an explanation for the range of behaviours they exhibited in the First World War, 'loyalty' falls short. Each individual soldier's 'loyalty' depended on his ability to manage the difficulties of life at war, and it was not an inherent characteristic of the men who fought. It was a choice undertaken by some, but abandoned by many others under the stresses of war.[8] Past historical treatments of the war, in their uncritical repetition of German discourses on the loyal *askari*, have tended to obscure more substantive analysis of *askari* motivations to continue fighting, especially after the tide turned decisively against the Germans in East Africa in 1916.

Getting beyond the 'loyal *askari*' discourse requires temporarily directing our attention away from 1,200 *askari* who witnessed General Lettow-Vorbeck's surrender to the Allies at Abercorn, Northern Rhodesia, in November 1918.[9] What happened to the other estimated 11,000–12,000 soldiers not present at Abercorn? How do we explain the nearly 3,000 *askari* officially reported as 'deserters'? Or the 4,500 'missing' and 4,200 'captured'?[10] How did the relatively small number of soldiers at the surrender survive the war? Given the tremendous hardships of the campaign, and the very real potential of not surviving it, why did they stay with the force? What made it possible for them to continue fighting without compensation or even basic provisions? Between desertion at one end of the spectrum and remaining with the Schutztruppe until the surrender at the other, *askari* evaluated how best to survive the war, in part according to how they understood the East African campaign as a test of their officer-patrons' mettle as 'hard' men, leaders, patrons and professionals.

This essay examines the complex, shifting world of the *askari* at war in East Africa and recovers the particular economic, social and temporal contexts in which their war service in the Schutztruppe created meaning for them. It argues that the *askari* were willing to risk their lives in the First World War not out of some abstract loyalty to Germany, but because they understood themselves as professional soldiers and respectable men. It is true that the rank-and-file soldiers' respect for their officers was directly tied to individual officers' abilities to lead effectively and to show concern for their troops. But *askaris'* decisions about whether or not to stay with the Schutztruppe through to the end of the East African campaign stemmed from a range of factors and tough choices, including their desires to preserve their pre-war social status and identities. Closer examination reveals that their willingness to risk death in combat was not automatic, unlimited or uniform. It had little to do with nationalism or patriotism, but everything to do with their expectations of what the benefits of continued Schutztruppe membership would bring, including certain levels of care and compensation from the German officers. As one group of hungry, tired and angry *askari* put it to their commander before deserting the column he led in 1917, 'We don't want to die for nothing.'[11] But they *were* willing to fight for German officers who could, to their minds, realistically guarantee their status as men of means in the post-war period. On the other hand, *askari* were unwilling to fight for officers who they assessed as incapable of acting as strong patrons; moreover, conscripts, who began to comprise larger numbers of the Schutztruppe in late 1916, had little investment in the organisation.

Using German and British archival materials and published memoirs, this essay considers the everyday reality and the specific advantages or attractions for both the *askari* who decided to stay in the Schutztruppe and those who decided to desert (particularly the conscripts). The first two sections examine the various economic and social factors underpinning *askari* 'loyalty' – they included the degree to which *askari* felt that their officers met their responsibilities as patrons, the presence of household members, and the length of their service – while the final section investigates the equally complex reasons informing the decision of many to desert.

'SAFARI YA BWANA LETTOW': THE STRESSES OF WAR

The Allies and the Germans engaged over 100,000 colonial troops and thousands of porters and auxiliaries drawn from all over the continent and elsewhere to fight the East African campaign.[12] Lettow-Vorbeck's strategy from the outset of the war in Europe was to tie up as many Allied forces as possible in East Africa so that they could not fight in Europe. In 1914 and 1915, the Schutztruppe scored some significant victories against the British force, which tried to invade from British East Africa and from the Tanganyikan coastline.[13] The German East African economy functioned through 1915 at a sufficient level to sustain operations, fostering high morale among troops. Things began to go sour, however, when the Allies captured the German colonial capital of Dar es Salaam on 3 September 1916, and the new temporary capital at Tabora on 19 September 1916. Lettow-Vorbeck responded to these Allied successes by sending the majority of his forces south of the Rufiji River to prepare for a retreat into Portuguese East Africa. The Allies pursued and repeatedly tried to encircle the Schutztruppe, but failed to stop its momentum. Schutztruppe columns crossed into Portuguese East Africa in November 1917, and the Allied forces pursued. In summer 1918, the Schutztruppe crossed back into the former German East Africa, and in late October it turned back southwestward and crossed into Northern Rhodesia. The force finally surrendered there on 25 November 1918 after belatedly receiving notification of the German defeat in Europe.[14]

Once Lettow-Vorbeck shifted the campaign to the southern half of German East Africa in late 1916, conditions worsened considerably for all of the armies involved. When the First World War began in 1914, the region was still slowly recovering from the devastation wrought by the scorched earth tactics the Schutztruppe had used during the Maji Maji war of 1905–7.[15] Their actions during Maji Maji created famine conditions that resulted in abnormally low birth rates, labour shortages, and reduced crop yields in the region for several years afterwards. In 1913, regional drought exacerbated conditions of scarcity in an area ill-equipped to overcome them. Lettow-Vorbeck's decision to move his forces south of the Rufiji River in late 1916 meant that the region's inhabitants had to suffer through both the German and the Allied armies marching through their lands and requisitioning their food stores, livestock and anything else they wanted. Scarcity was the key issue that everybody in the southern reaches of German East Africa had to confront between late 1916 and November 1918.

African soldiers in the Schutztruppe referred to the latter half of the East African campaign as 'Safari ya bwana Lettow' or 'Mr Lettow's expedition'. German *askari* used this Kiswahili phrase to refer to 'the caravans, Lettow-Vorbeck's columns, which in the year 1918 cut through the wide steppes and forests of Africa in endless forced marches'.[16] The force that surrendered to the British in November 1918 was the remnant of an army which in different phases of the war had drawn on both conscription and voluntary enlistment. Approximately 1,200 *askari* surrendered at Abercorn on 25 November 1918. At their maximum strength in March 1916, Lettow-Vorbeck's army had numbered some 12,000 *askari*, supplemented by 2,000–3,000 irregulars.[17] Between late 1916 and November 1918, the combined effects of battlefield deaths, accidents, illness, capture by Allied forces and desertions dramatically reduced the Schutztruppe's numbers.

After 1916, the Schutztruppe had difficulties resupplying and compensating its troops, auxiliaries, and porters. The Allied blockade of the East African coast made resupply from the sea impossible. Nor could the Germans pay their soldiers' salaries, since their minting capabilities disappeared with the Allied seizure of Dar es Salaam and Tabora. *Askari* who had not been captured, killed or otherwise incapacitated by late 1916 experienced conditions of privation that made many of them consider the relative value of staying with or leaving the force amidst the stresses of a highly mobile campaign fought in a demanding environment. The *askari* and other members of the columns experienced prolonged periods of undernourishment, thirst and physical exhaustion. Such conditions increased their vulnerability to a wide range of diseases.[18] *Askari* who withstood the basic physical demands of the campaign still had to contend, of course, with the ever-present danger of confrontation with the Allies, whose troops had better supplies and equipment than the Schutztruppe.

These hardships produced a psychology of privation among Schutztruppe column members that caused the 'requisitioning' process, long a part of Schutztruppe expeditionary practice and East African warfare more generally, to be even more extortionate than usual. *Askari* and auxiliaries seized grain stores, produce, and livestock from any communities unfortunate enough to lie in the columns' paths.[19] Marine-Ingenieur Bockmann, a Schutztruppe company commander whose unit operated behind the Allied lines in the northern part of German East Africa in late 1917, described one instance in which he ordered his troops to 'requisition' thirty head of cattle from a Maasai community enclosure, or *kraal*, leaving the owners a receipt and instructing them to 'bring the receipt to Arusha at the war's end'. Bockman noted that '[u]nder all circumstances, I wanted to initiate a friendly relationship to the Maasai through gifts and good treatment'.[20] Notwithstanding Bockmann's stated good intentions, the Schutztruppe typically commandeered their provisions 'without any compensation to the owners', and their reputation for this sort of requisitioning preceded them wherever they went.[21]

Despite the ruthless requisitioning process *askari* undertook to feed themselves and their columns, they often could not find enough provisions to maintain minimal nutritional requirements. Officers feared that these shortfalls would lead to 'catastrophe', such as mass starvation or mutiny.[22] Bockmann described the disastrous toll that successive forced marches had taken on his column: 'The provisioning question was an exceptionally critical one. Consequently, a large part of the whites and coloureds were already so undernourished, that they could perform their duties only inadequately.'[23] This state of affairs forced Bockmann's superior to break the force into three smaller columns to be manoeuvred separately, and thus procure supplies more effectively than if they continued moving *en bloc*. After weeks of marching through the Maasai Steppe with its scarce food and water resources, Bockmann's unit was 'at the end of [its] strength'. He reported, 'Europeans, *askaris* and porters had thinned to skeletons, because they had not enjoyed any cereals in a long time.'[24] At other times, when meat and produce were scarce, cereals might be the only thing soldiers had to eat.

After crossing the Rovuma River into Portuguese East Africa, the Schutztruppe moved purposefully from fortress to fortress in search of supplies abandoned by the Portuguese forces fleeing the German advance.[25] In Portuguese East Africa, these fortresses, or *boma*s, were 'sited at distances of four to ten days' march from each other' and were connected by a series of narrow well-worn pathways.[26] The Portuguese force did little to defend the *boma*s – a state of affairs that Portugal's British allies found most irritating. General Northey wrote in his War Diary for January 1918:

In front of NGOMANO, VON LETTOW's troops were nearly out of food and ammunition: but since then they have got everything they want from the Portuguese: more arms, ammunition and machine-guns than they can use or carry: supplies, European and native, including medicines and quinine, which they badly needed, galore: and half-caste women to delight the Askari's heart.[27]

Although the press had reported that the *askari* were 'starving remnants who [would] be quickly rounded up', Northey felt that actually they were 'the fittest and best of the enemy troops, who have had both the will and the health to stick to their brave commander in spite of all hardships'.[28] Both German and British reports noted the ease with which the Portuguese troops gave up their *boma*s – a happy circumstance for the German *askari*, who of course benefited from the food, drink and other amenities they found at the abandoned Portuguese *boma*s.[29] For many soldiers, crossing into Portuguese territory held out the promise of plentiful food and wine stores, rest, and a new group of women to 'commandeer' for sex, camp work such as cooking and laundry, and, in some cases, either voluntary or involuntary incorporation into an *askari* household. Such abundant spoils of war convinced some *askari* to stay with the Schutztruppe, since taking their chances alone might lead them into worse circumstances.

Individual *askari* had far better chances of survival if they stayed with the columns. The core members of the columns were battle-tested and surprisingly well-armed soldiers with sound weaponry and requisitioning skills. Large numbers of porters in the columns meant that seizures from civilians could be transported and consumed over time rather than all at once. The

Schutztruppe also resupplied itself by taking stores from Allied units they forced to flee from their *boma*s, or defeated in skirmishes. But seizing goods through potentially deadly confrontation with dug-in Allied soldiers required concentrated force and coordination. Thus an individual *askari*'s chances of securing provisions that would last more than a day or two were directly tied to the logistical and military support the columns provided. Given the environment of scarcity, plus the animosity many people from the southern regions felt towards the Schutztruppe because of their actions during Maji Maji, and the dangers of striking out alone, many *askari* figured that staying with the columns maximised their chances for survival.

Veteran *askari* had far more experience in weathering such rough living than junior troops recruited or conscripted during the war. They had few reservations about taking what they needed as they moved from *boma* to *boma*, and younger soldiers quickly learned the value of seizing goods when opportunities arose to do so. Nonetheless, the constant state of uncertainty about when and where they would have their next meal or fresh water, coupled with the lack of basic equipment and supplies, only added to the anxieties and pressures of soldiering in East Africa.

RESPECTABILITY ON THE MARCH: MOBILE COMMUNITIES AT WAR

Many *askari* ameliorated the stresses of warfare by relying on household members, including wives, children, domestic servants and other dependants, to create mobile domesticity while on the march. *Askari* whose household members accompanied them were less likely to desert than unaccompanied troops, such as conscripts or younger recruits. Desertion cut them off from the relative safety of the columns, as well as the small comforts of domestic life these mobile communities recreated.[30] Moreover, those *askari* who deserted abrogated their responsibilities as heads of households, causing dire consequences for their dependants. Respectability was paramount for the *askari*, so moving without their families made little sense to them.[31]

Dependants of *askari* consistently asserted their place in the Schutztruppe way of war, creating difficulties for the officers who had to meet the columns' logistical requirements while avoiding exacerbation of already challenging provisioning problems. A reporter for the *Bulawayo Chronicle* gave a detailed description of Lettow-Vorbeck's surrender at Abercorn:

It was a most impressive spectacle. The long motley column, Europeans and Askari, all veterans of a hundred fights, the latter clothed with every kind of headgear, women who had stuck to their husbands through all of these years of hardships, carrying huge loads, some with children born during the campaign, carriers coming in singing in undisguised joy at the thought that their labours were ended at last. All combined to make a sight that was unique.[32]

This 'shabby cavalcade' numbered 4,500 people, including porters, women and children. Only 1,200 to 1,300 of these were *askari*.[33] Many British observers found the presence of women and children at the surrender remarkable. Sir Hugh Clifford, who commanded the Gold Coast Regiment in East Africa beginning in 1916, characterised them unfavourably as 'a commando of women under military escort, [which] was marched about the country' to serve the needs of both the *askari* and the Germans.[34]

Yet for the *askari* and their German officers and NCOs, such scenes confirmed the key role families played in the *askaris'* continued willingness to fight. Alongside the porters who moved the army's materiel, women, children, and other dependants served as the logistical backbone of the Schutztruppe,[35] carrying the *askaris'* personal equipment and supplies, gathering food, water and firewood, cooking, doing laundry and tending to the sick and wounded. *Askari* households also included '*askariboys*', who worked for the *askari* as servants. Some of them had volunteered to work for *askari*, but some had been 'forcibly carried off' in manpower levies or as spoils of war. Some of the *boys* learned the soldiering profession while on the march with their '*babas*', but their primary role was to work for the *askari* as gunboys and all-purpose servants.[36] The culture of privation the war generated meant there was no shortage of young men 'volunteering' to be *askariboys*, who were easily replaced if they fell ill or died.[37]

Members of *askari* households tied the *askari* to their cultural homelands and provided them with emotional and material support. They also signified an *askari's* social standing, since the bigger his household, the more status he exhibited. During the First World War, as in previous German colonial wars, *askari* household members became part of mobile communities at war, doing all necessary work once the columns stopped marching for the day. In this sense, they were indispensable to the Schutztruppe effort and to the *askaris'* combat effectiveness. They also helped the *askari* recreate some elements of garrison life while on the march.[38]

The presence of so many non-combatant column members benefited the *askari* but also necessitated a long 'train' of porters to transport provisions for the whole mobile community. In the autumn of 1917, in preparation for crossing into Portuguese East Africa, Lettow-Vorbeck decided to cut the force down 'to a tough fighting column of a maximum 2,000 rifles of which the European officers and men would not number more than 200'. He planned to leave behind several hundred Europeans and 600 *askari* just north of the border with Portuguese East Africa, to be 'picked up by the British'.[39] Lettow-Vorbeck planned to leave behind the women of the column as part of this group, but soon discovered that the women disagreed with his plan:

'This was awkward, but there was little I found I could do about it,' Lettow-Vorbeck said. 'In the conditions which we were facing, it was impossible to deny the troops the comforts to which they had accustomed themselves, and there is no doubt that they would sorely have missed their women, for more than obvious reasons. The women carried the loads. They also carried the children. It had not been unusual in the previous months for an askari to break off for a moment in the firing line to go to his *bibi* [Kiswahili: wife, woman] not more than a hundred yards behind to see how she was progressing in her delivery of their latest offspring [. . .] Most of the women insisted on accompanying their men-folk. When a woman did fall behind in a march, the askari would take up his child and march on with it on his shoulders.'[40]

Lettow-Vorbeck's observation highlights the degree to which fighting, family, and community were intertwined in this campaign.

Front and rear, front and home, soldier and civilian, family and camp follower were categories that overlapped and merged with each other in ways that reinforced *askari* visions of themselves as professionals. Their way of war was a non-negotiable part of their identity, and it caused their officers endless frustration. For example, on at least one occasion around January 1917, women accompanying Lettow-Vorbeck's force in the Rufiji region consumed their rations too quickly, and refused to go any further. Some even '[went] so far as to attack and beat the European who was in charge of the transport'.[41] To solve the problem, *askari* hunters were sent out to shoot game. *Askari* households were patrilineal, so women were expected to follow their husbands wherever they went. Many women living under colonialism found ways to negotiate these patriarchal structures to achieve relative economic independence for themselves, but the wartime context limited their options.[42] To maintain respectability as householders, *askari* could not afford to ignore women's complaints. Both *askari* and the Schutztruppe leadership recognised, in different ways, that failure to respond adequately to the women's demands might spell disaster for column order.

Askaris' tendencies to acquire more dependants while on the march meant that their household affairs featured prominently in the day-to-day management of the columns. At their camp in Nanungu in the north of Portuguese East Africa in autumn 1917, column commander Richard Wenig found himself embroiled in managing *askari* relationships not only with the women who had trekked with them from German East Africa, but also with a new population of local women. He referred to this period humorously as being 'under the sign of the women'. Knowing he could not control 'what happened in two hundred huts concealed by the night's darkness', he nonetheless insisted that 'marriage must be impeded because an expansion of the ladies' colony [*Damenkolonie*] with the expected arduous marches would be a great evil'.[43] Wenig's priorities as a Schutztruppe officer and his racist-paternalist world-view led him to try to limit column members' liaisons with local women. He, like many other Europeans, thought of his soldiers as overgrown children, in need of strong guidance. But his story about the events at Nanangu also suggests that *askari* and other column members built and rebuilt their households, asserted or reasserted their masculinity, and found comfort in domestic and sexual connections, however temporarily.

Schutztruppe conscription practices, initiated in late 1916 as German fortunes in the war deteriorated, also helped *askari* reassert their status in the Schutztruppe hierarchy. As troop numbers dwindled in late 1916, *askari* began rounding up 'all men and boys over the age of sixteen' from the villages they encountered while on the march. These young men were then 'immediately pressed into service as porters or *askaris*'.[44] Senior *askari* had no pity for the new conscripts, and instead ruthlessly upheld the military and social hierarchy of the Schutztruppe organisation. Senior *askari* positioned themselves as the new recruits' '*baba*s', disciplining them militarily but also in the same ways they disciplined their *askariboys*. In fact, senior *askari* probably saw little difference between those they conscripted and their gunboys, since they would all end up performing similar functions as the force shrank. Nonetheless, senior *askari* worked to reproduce the Schutztruppe social order by reinforcing obedience and deference to those of higher rank, even as the socio-economic order of German East Africa shifted around them. Senior *askari* opted to stay with the Schutztruppe because only active membership in the organisation allowed them to perform their version of respectability.

The case of the conscripts was different. The hierarchy of ranks helped the Schutztruppe function effectively under stress, but also made it a difficult place for conscripts. Their immediate status as clients, if not slaves, to the senior *askari* discouraged psychological investment in the new order of things. Conscripts had little stake in respecting senior *askari* because their own identities did not necessarily coincide with those of their new superiors, the senior *askari*. Before the war and in the first half of the campaign, recruits had joined the Schutztruppe voluntarily. By late 1916, membership in the Schutztruppe no longer appealed to young men for whom membership in the

colonial army had little concrete meaning, apart from hardship. The superficial training conscripts received during the war did not socialise them as
intensely as volunteer *askari* had been socialised in peacetime. First World
War conscripts experienced the harshness of Schutztruppe life on the march
without the benefits of having volunteered for service. Many desertions
likely came from this population of *askari*, who had a minimal stake in the
organisation. The Schutztruppe organisation bound veteran *askari* horizon-
tally and vertically, through their long-term comrades and officers. But the
conscripts likely felt no sense of being at 'home' with the Schutztruppe and so
felt less compulsion to stay with the force than the old veteran *askari* who
treated their conscripts quite badly.

DESERTION: A RESPONSE TO BROKEN CONTRACTS

Nearly 3,000 *askari* (of about 12,000) deserted the Schutztruppe during the
war.[45] Thus at least twice as many *askari* deserted as stayed to surrender at
Abercorn. Yet historiography on the First World War in East Africa has
inadequately addressed the reasons for such large numbers of desertions.
Schutztruppe officers – labouring under the illusions of their own loyalties
to the Kaiser – remarked on their soldiers' desertions with surprise, even as
they noted an obvious correlation between desertion rates and the often dire
provisioning problems the army experienced. Especially after the Allies began
achieving measured gains against the German force in late 1916, provisioning
for the German force became increasingly difficult.[46] Even Lettow-Vorbeck
admitted in his diary that 'there came a time that all hope was given up and
Askaris and Europeans were glad to be captured'.[47] Karl Vieweg, a platoon
leader operating in the Rufiji River region in mid-October 1916, reported that
eleven of his forty-three *askari* had deserted, and he remarked that similar
statistics applied to the other companies as well. According to Vieweg,
Europeans and 'coloureds' (including *askari*, porters and 'boys') received
meat only twice a week, and were given 500 grams of flour at the same time
as the meat distribution. If there was no meat to be distributed, they were
supposed to receive 750 grams of flour, although according to him, 'these
rations [were] hardly [ever] at full weight'. These rations were well below the
widely accepted colonial standard of one kilogram of starch per day for slaves,
day labourers and soldiers.[48] Grinding conditions of scarcity in the last two
years of fighting in East Africa severely threatened the Schutztruppe's ability to
wage war effectively, or even to subsist, at the most basic levels.

These conditions also undermined the *askaris*' householder and professional sensibilities. They fought under very harsh conditions with little

foreseeable prospect of recompense or relief, and unsurprisingly they abandoned the Schutztruppe at various points in the campaign. What is perhaps more surprising is that 1,200 *askari* remained till the surrender in November 1918. The *askari* who continued to fight for the Schutztruppe had received no pay since at least 1916. After 1916, Germany issued its colonial soldiers with credit vouchers to be redeemed at some future date. German officials also issued *askari* 'bush money' – worthless scraps of paper imprinted with self-made rubber stamps.[49] The *askari* were fully aware that this money was worthless in any commercial sense. One German officer reported that *askari* registered their anger at the Germans' inability to pay their salaries by throwing their pay books at the feet of a German NCO.[50] *Askari* deserted their units in response to their perceptions, usually accurate, that their needs were not being met, and thus that their core identities as respectable men were at stake. Weapons shortages, ragged uniforms, and lack of basic equipment also undermined their professional identities, since they were reliant on abandoned Allied supplies for their ability to continue fighting.[51]

Askari deserters risked punishment, capture and injury or death from exposure in the hopes that they would improve their circumstances by leaving the Schutztruppe behind. Rumours circulated among British officials that 'Von Lettow told Askaris that German East Africa would certainly be given back to Germany at [the] end of [the] war and that every deserter would then be hanged'. The telegram further noted that Lettow's alleged statement 'had great effect', and lamented that, 'We have been greatly handicapped in German East Africa by the fact that we cannot promise protection [to the *askari*] after the war.'[52] Certainly in the three decades of German colonial rule, in which public floggings and hangings occurred frequently as part of the punitive regime, *askari* likely took such rumours to heart.

Askari mobilised various survival strategies in the face of the contingent, changeable, and stressful environment. 'Survival' included overcoming the dangers of battle, starvation, thirst, or capture, and also continually positioning oneself to maintain status and privilege in the face of changing circumstances. By deserting the force, some *askari* expressed their discontent and disappointment with their German officers who, after 1916, appeared to have become weak. Especially in columns manoeuvring behind Allied lines, German officers had become incapable of providing their troops with even the most basic support required of them in their capacities as patrons. In September 1917, Marine-Ingenieur Bockmann, whose unit operated behind Allied lines in the northern part of German East Africa, had an exchange with some of his *askari* that laid bare their grievances in relation to the various privations they were experiencing in the wartime context.[53] Having sent

most of his available porters to pick up provisions that he had left at another
location, he ordered his *askari* to help with the daily incremental movement
of the materials needed for the camp:

And so it happened that the *askari* did not get the rest that I had promised them after
all. They began to grumble and every day there were disciplinary problems. Most
notably, the [senior] ranks, from whom I would have least expected it, stirred things
up. Now followed inane phrases like: 'We don't want to die for nothing [*burre*, i.e.
Kiswahili *bure* = free, for nothing, in vain]. The Europeans are terribly afraid of
being taken prisoner by the English because they will be put in chains and made to
carry rocks. The Germans have no more strength [*guwu*, i.e. Kiswahili *nguvu* =
hardness, strength], the English are now the rulers of the land. The German paper
money is good for nothing, they may as well have worked for nothing. [In the King's
African Rifles, or KAR] [t]he German *askari* would be promoted one service rank,
and would only have to perform duty at the *boma* [i.e., garrison duty].' My sol[54]
Majaliwa, an old soldier [who had served with Schutztruppe founder] Wißmann,
mentioned the matter to me and I gave the people a genuinely well-meaning speech.
The outcome was that the following night four *askari*, among them both of my
battle orderlies and a captured English *askari*, deserted with weapons.[55]

Schutztruppe officers usually avoided having their *askari* act as porters, since
the *askari* found such work insulting. Although *askari* and porters worked
and lived together while on the march, the *askaris'* responsibilities for guarding
against porter desertions and/or pilferage from the loads they carried ensured
that their relationship was a tense one. This particular feature of caravan
culture formed the specific context for the *askaris'* expression of discontent to
Bockmann. They described the Germans in terms of diminished masculinity,
a lack of *nguvu* that the British, on the other hand, seemed unequivocally
to possess. In German *askari* eyes, the KAR had more men, better uniforms,
abundant supplies, and it held out the possibility of enabling its soldiers to
live respectable lives after the war. Whether true or not, this assessment gave
some *askari* hope that changing sides would create new possibilities for them.
Desertion gave the *askari* a chance to connect or reconnect themselves to
other communities that could provide for their immediate needs, and potentially also to align themselves with the ascendant power broker in the region.
Bockmann's 'well-meaning speech' was not enough to restore the deserter
askaris' faith in his *nguvu*.

Weighing the diminishing benefits of staying with the force against the
privations they were suffering, *askari* did not simply forget that they were
professional soldiers. Indeed, it was precisely their own sense of what it
meant to be a professional that led them to desert in the hope of improving
their conditions, returning to their communities and families wherever they

might be, and recovering the elements of respectability that they had lost during the war. In the view of some *askari*, German officers had failed them as patrons. In a time of great privation and risk, some *askari* searched for new patrons, or turned to alternative social networks that could help them survive until new opportunities emerged.

The small force at Lettow-Vorbeck's disposal in November 1918 had survived an exhausting campaign, but its members faced a new set of white rulers and a changed political landscape. The British and Belgian victors took some time to sort out the future administration of Germany's former territory. Meanwhile, the *askari* underwent a brief period of internment, and then were released and left to reconstruct their lives on their own.[56] The soldiers had no work and no income. Their commander and ultimate patron General Lettow-Vorbeck finally secured their back pay for them in 1927, but between 1918 and 1927 they had no German support.[57] German *askari* do not seem to have joined the King's African Rifles or any other regional colonial militaries *en masse*. The East African campaign resulted in widespread, long-term suffering for African populations who lived through the war, particularly in the southern half of the colony.[58] While East Africans transitioned to a new colonial regime and tried to recover from the war's devastation, Germany began the process of adjusting to its defeat in the First World War, which included the loss of its overseas colonies. For interwar colonial activists, the *askari* became a valuable symbol of Germany's former military glories at home and abroad. They also symbolised Germany's vision of itself as a 'model coloniser' that deserved to get its colonies back. But the figure of the 'loyal *askari*' also covered up the terrible costs of the German colonial endeavour. Many East Africans who lived through the First World War remembered it as only the latest and most egregious example of German colonial abuse and violence, within a longer history that offered numerous examples from which to choose.

NOTES

For support while revising this essay, I would like to acknowledge the Institute for Historical Studies, University of Texas, Austin.

1 *Askari* is an Arabic and Kiswahili word for 'soldier' or 'police'. European colonial armies throughout eastern Africa used the term to refer to their African troops. The singular and plural forms of the word are the same, although some authors use '*askaris*' as the plural.

2 Bror Urme MacDonell, *Mzee Ali: The Biography of an African Slave-Raider Turned Askari and Scout* (Johannesburg: 30 Degrees South Publishers, 2006), 167, 168. MacDonell, a British colonial employee, recorded Mzee Ali's memories

of his time as a German *askari* in the late 1940s when they both worked as
colonial employees in Tanganyika. After many interventions in the manuscript,
the book was published as a 'biography,' despite being written in the first
person. I discuss the text as a historical source in Michelle Moyd, 'Becoming
Askari: African Soldiers and Everyday Colonialism in German East Africa,
1850–1918', PhD dissertation, Cornell University, Ithaca, NY, 2008, 117–20.

3 The Kaiserlichen Schutztruppe für Deutsch-Ostafrika was the full name of the
German colonial army in East Africa, composed of German officers and NCOs,
and African rank and file.

4 MacDonell, *Mzee Ali*, 169.

5 *Ibid.*

6 *Ibid.*, 84. Ali came from Unyamwezi, an area in the north-central steppe region
of present-day Tanzania (formerly German East Africa). The Germans arrived
at Tabora, the most important town in Unyamwezi, in 1891. *Mzee Ali* offers very
few specific dates as points of reference, but it is likely that Ali joined the
Schutztruppe sometime around 1895 when the Germans began recruiting
heavily in Unyamwezi.

7 See, for example, Brian Gardner, *German East: The Story of the First World War
in East Africa* (London: Cassell, 1963); Charles Miller, *Battle for the Bundu: the
First World War in East Africa* (London: Macdonald and Jane's, 1974); and
Leonard Mosley, *Duel for Kilimanjaro: An Account of the East African Campaign,
1914–18* (London: Weidenfeld and Nicolson, 1963). For German examples, see
Ludwig Deppe, *Mit Lettow-Vorbeck durch Afrika.* (Berlin: A. Scherl, 1919); and
Paul von Lettow-Vorbeck, *Meine Erinnerungen aus Ostafrika* (Leipzig: K. F.
Koehler, 1920), published in English as *My Reminiscences of East Africa*, trans-
lator unknown (London: Hurst and Blackett, n.d.).

8 Hew Strachan, *The First World War in Africa* (Oxford University Press), 103.

9 See, for example, Gardner, *German East*, 193; Miller, *Battle for the Bundu*, 326.

10 The official German history listed the total number of *askari* desertions as
2,847. Another 4,510 were reported missing, and 4,275 were reported captured.
Ludwig Boell, *Die Operationen in Ostafrika, Weltkrieg 1914–1918* (Hamburg:
W. Dachert, 1951), 424. Strachan uses these same figures in his recent reassess-
ment of the East African campaign (*The First World War in Africa*, 103).

11 Marine-Oberingenieur Bockmann, 'Berichte über Deutsch-Ostafrika',
Bundesarchiv-Militärarchiv, Freiburg, Germany, RM 8/368, 160.

12 David Killingray, 'The War in Africa' in Hew Strachan (ed.), *The Oxford
Illustrated History of the First World War* (Oxford and New York: Oxford
University Press, 1998), 93; and Strachan, *The First World War in Africa*, 93–184.

13 On the Tanga operation, see Ross Anderson, *The Battle of Tanga 1914* (Stroud:
Tempus, 2002).

14 On the operational and social history of the war, see Ross Anderson, *The
Forgotten Front: The East African Campaign 1914–1918* (Stroud, UK: Tempus,
2004); and Edward Paice, *Tip and Run: The Untold Tragedy of the Great War in
Africa* (London: Weidenfeld and Nicolson, 2007). Contemporary accounts of
the war include Deppe, *Mit Lettow-Vorbeck durch Afrika*; Lettow-Vorbeck,

Meine Erinnerungen aus Ostafrika; and Heinrich Schnee, *Deutsch-Ostafrika im Weltkriege: wie wir lebten und kämpften* (Leipzig: Quelle & Meyer, 1919).

15 See John Iliffe, *A Modern History of Tanganyika* (Cambridge University Press, 1979), 168–202 and Felicitas Becker and Jigal Beez (eds.), *Der Maji-Maji-Krieg in Deutsch-Ostafrika, 1905–1907* (Berlin: Links, 2005). The Schutztruppe's scorched-earth tactics during Maji Maji included the burning of villages and food stores, the seizure of livestock, and mass arrests and hangings for those considered ringleaders amongst the Maji Maji fighters. For estimates of the death toll during and after Maji Maji, see Ludger Wimmelbücker, 'Verbrannte Erde: Zu den Bevölkerungsverlusten als Folge des Maji-Maji-Krieges', in *Der Maji-Maji-Krieg in Deutsch-Ostafrika, 1905–1907*.

16 Richard Wenig, *Kriegs-Safari: Erlebnisse und Eindrücke auf den Zügen Lettow-Vorbecks durch das östliche Afrika* (Berlin: Scherl, 1920), 11.

17 *Ibid.*, 28, 134.

18 Karl Moesta, 'Die Einwirkungen des Krieges auf die Eingeborenenbevölkerung in Deutsch-Ostafrika', *Koloniale Rundschau*, 1–3 (1919), 5–25, *passim*; M. Taute, 'A German Account of the Medical Side of the War in East Africa, 1914–1918', *Tanganyika Notes and Records* 8 (1939), 1–20.

19 Iliffe, *A Modern History of Tanganyika*, 241. On famine in the Ugogo region during the war, see Gregory H. Maddox, 'Mtunya: Famine in Central Tanzania, 1917–20', *Journal of African History* 31, 2 (1990): 181–97.

20 Bockmann, 'Berichte über Deutsch-Ostafrika', 157. See also D. Malcolm, Rhodesia House, to H. F. Batterbee, Colonial Office, 3 June 1918, National Archives, Kew, London (NA-Kew), Colonial Office (CO) 691/20, 473–4 for a comment on Bockmann's harshness in requisitioning livestock from the Maasai.

21 MacDonell, *Mzee Ali*, 185, 209; Deppe, *Mit Lettow-Vorbeck durch Afrika*, 132.

22 Wenig, *Kriegs-Safari*, 61; Bockmann, 'Berichte über Deutsch-Ostafrika', 159.

23 Bockmann, 'Berichte über Deutsch-Ostafrika', 155–6.

24 *Ibid.*, 159.

25 Friedrich Wilhelm Mader, *Die rätselhafte Boma: Erzählung aus den Kämpfen der deutschen Schutztruppe in Ostafrika im Sommer 1918* (Berlin: Steiniger Verlag, 1942), *passim*; Heinrich Schnee, 'Meine Abenteuer in Deutsch-Ostafrika', Geheimes Staatsarchiv Preussischer Kulturbesitz, Berlin, Nachlass Schnee, Folder No. 17, 27, 40, 42, 52–3.

26 Wenig, *Kriegs-Safari*, 37.

27 General Sir Edward Northey, War Diary, January 1918, NA-Kew, London, Colonial Office 691/14, 120. Capitals in original text.

28 *Ibid.*

29 Mader, *Die rätselhafte Boma*, *passim*; Van Deventer to Colonial Office, June 1918, NA-Kew, London, Colonial Office 691/19, 135–6, 181–2, 185.

30 Nachlass Correck, diary entry for 5 July 1906, Bayerisches Hauptstaatsarchiv, Munich, HS 908. See also entries for 3 May 1906 and 4 May 1906.

31 Ascan Lutteroth, *Tunakwenda: Auf Kriegssafari in Deutsch-Ostafrika* (Hamburg: Verlag Broschek & Co., 1938), 156.

32 Charles Miller, *Battle for the Bundu: The First World War in East Africa* (London: Macdonald and Jane's, 1974), 326.

33 Gardner, *German East*, 193.

34 Hugh Clifford, *The Gold Coast Regiment in the East African Campaign* (1920; repr. Nashville: Battery Press, 1995), 76.

35 Allied armies operating in East Africa during the First World War do not seem to have included family members to the same extent as the Schutztruppe.

36 August Hauer, ' "Watoto", die Kleinsten der Lettow-Truppe' in Hans Zache (ed.), *Die deutschen Kolonien in Wort und Bild* (Augsburg: Bechtermünz, 2003), 460–3; Heinrich Fonck, *Deutsch-Ost-Afrika: Eine Schilderung deutschen Tropen nach 10 Wanderjahren* (Berlin: Vossische Buchhandlung, 1910), 65, 66–7.

37 Germans seemed to have adopted the term 'boy' from the British, appending *askari* to the term to highlight their distinct role.

38 Lutteroth, *Tunakwenda*, 158, 170–1, 174, 176, 177, 295–6; Walter Rehfeldt, *Bilder vom Kriege in Deutsch-Ostafrika nach Aquarellen* (Hamburg: Charles Fuchs, 1920), 6–14; Correck diary entries for 28 April 1906, 1 June 1906, and 1 July 1906, Bayerisches Hauptstaatsarchiv, Munich, Germany, Nachlass Correck, HS 908.

39 Mosley, *Duel for Kilimanjaro*, 177.

40 *Ibid.* Mosley conducted interviews with Lettow-Vorbeck, from which this excerpt is taken.

41 Lettow-Vorbeck, *My Reminiscences*, 177.

42 Dorothy Hodgson and Sheryl McCurdy, 'Wayward Wives, Misfit Mothers, and Disobedient Daughters: "Wicked" Women and the Reconfiguration of Gender in Africa', *Canadian Journal of African Studies* 30, 1 (1996): 1–9.

43 Wenig, *Kriegs-Safari*, 100.

44 MacDonell, *Mzee Ali*, 185.

45 See note 10.

46 Burkhard Vieweg, *Macho Porini – Die Augen im Busch: Kautschukpflanzer Karl Vieweg in Deutsch-Ostafrika; authentische Berichte 1910–1919* (Weikersheim: Margraf Verlag, 1996), 380.

47 Lettow-Vorbeck Diary, typescript, vol. 4, Jan 1917–Dec 1918, Imperial War Museum (IWM), London, no page numbers.

48 Vieweg, *Macho Porini*, 380–1. On food rations, see Joseph C. Miller, *Way of Death: Merchant Capitalism and the Angolan Slave Trade 1730–1830* (Madison: University of Wisconsin Press, 1988), 695–700.

49 Wenig, *Kriegs-Safari*, 74; Vieweg, *Macho Porini*, 409; Lutteroth, *Tunakwenda*, 168–70; G. G. Hajivayanis, A. C. Motowa, and J. Iliffe, 'The Politicians: Ali Ponda and Hassan Suleiman', in John Iliffe (ed.), *Modern Tanzanians: a Volume of Biographies* (Nairobi: East African Publishing House, 1973), 229.

50 Bockmann, 'Berichte über Deutsch-Ostafrika', 160.

51 MacDonnell, *Mzee Ali*, 205, 206, 211.

52 General Officer Commanding (GOC) in Chief, East Africa to War Office, 17 May 1918, NA-Kew, London, Colonial Office 691/19, 39. See also William. J. Maynard to Assistant Political Officer Shinyanga, 1 June 1918, NA-Kew, London, Colonial Office 691/15, 216.

53 Bockmann, 'Berichte über Deutsch-Ostafrika', 152.

54 *Sol* was the most senior Schutztruppe *askari* rank.

55 Bockmann, 'Berichte über Deutsch-Ostafrika', 160.

56 Van Deventer to War Office, 20 November 1918, NA-Kew, London, CO 691/19, 578–618.

57 See Lutteroth, *Tunakwenda*, 169; Sandra Maβ, *Weisse Helden, Schwarze Krieger: Zur Geschichte kolonialer Männlichkeit in Deutschland 1918–1964* (Cologne: Böhlau, 2006), 67.

58 Iliffe, *Modern History of Tanganyika*, 241.

CHAPTER 5

France's legacy to Demba Mboup? A Senegalese griot and his descendants remember his military service during the First World War

Joe Lunn

During the First World War, approximately 2 million subject peoples from Africa, Asia, and North America (including African Americans and Amerindians) were recruited to serve as soldiers in European and American armies.[1] Unlike their Western counterparts, who left over one thousand published memoirs and millions of letters, diaries, and other written accounts of their experiences, these men, who were usually drawn from pre-industrial and non-literate or semiliterate backgrounds, left precious few records of their wartime ordeal.[2] This essay seeks to redress this imbalance by introducing the oral history of a young Wolof griot, Demba Mboup (Figure 3), who was one of approximately 140,000 West Africans recruited into the French army to serve as combatants on the Western Front.[3] In a brief postscript, differing interpretations by his daughter and grandson about the significance of Mboup's wartime service are offered to illustrate how the meaning of the war for West Africans was transmitted and transmuted across multiple generations, and its shifting significance over time.

Mboup's life history is only the third published memoir by a West African veteran of the First World War.[4] Mboup's interview was one of 85 conducted in 1982–3 with Senegalese veterans or other witnesses of the First World War. Like Bernal Díaz's authoritative account *The Conquest of New Spain*, written in his mid seventies and with a preliminary note completed at the age of eighty-four, these African memoirs recorded in old age offer remarkable glimpses into their subjects' own youthful cross-cultural encounters.[5] Vivid recollections of their home leaving, their initial encounters with Europeans, and the mortal terror of combat were often seared into the witnesses' memories and recalled in later life in remarkable detail.[6] Only rarely and usually with cause – concealing pre-war enslavement or flight from French recruiters, for instance – were fundamental facts intentionally misrepresented.

3. Demba Mboup in later life, wearing his medal

As with all sources, it is appropriate to scrutinise the authenticity of such oral histories on a point-by-point basis; to dismiss them collectively because of the advanced age of the informants is insupportable.[7]

Methodologically, these 85 Senegalese interviews, including Mboup's, were conducted in accordance with the guidelines developed and institutionalised by oral historians during the past fifty years.[8] Informants were normally located through their regional Office des Anciens Combattants, and interviews were recorded in the respondent's primary language (in which they remembered the war) and then translated. Initial questions were very broad and open-ended; subsequent questions drew on the earlier responses of the informants. This technique enabled them to structure their individual accounts, varying widely in the character of their experiences and their interpretations of them, as they thought appropriate.[9]

The descendant of griots who served the *Damels* (rulers) of Kayor for more than 200 years, Mboup acquired French citizenship in 1915 (see below). Conscripted into the metropolitan French army, Mboup fought on the Western Front from 1916 to 1918 before being severely wounded ten days before the Armistice. After convalescing for over a year in a French hospital, he was decorated with the Médaille militaire, released from the army, and repatriated to Senegal as a *mutilé de guerre*. After the war, Mboup worked as a barrier guard on the Dakar–Niger railway and in the Hôpital principal in Dakar; he also remained active in local veterans' associations.

In addition to recounting his wartime experience, Mboup's memoir offers a unique vantage point on the changing tenor of colonial life. As a griot, Mboup was not only a trained oral historian and an especially articulate and keen observer of the unfolding of events: much of his social identity was rooted in the Wolof hierarchies of the past.[10] As a French citizen after 1915, however, Mboup was not only legally differentiated from millions of *sujets* bereft of political rights throughout Africa and the rest of the colonial world during this period, but his early acquisition of egalitarian civic status represented a harbinger of major changes to come.[11] His life contained another paradox. Having been permanently disabled in the fighting by shrapnel wounds in both legs, he belonged to that group of veterans most alienated from the French by their wartime ordeal.[12] Yet, unlike most *mutilés de guerre*, he was afforded post-war opportunities to earn a living in the French economic sector that would have been inconceivable but for his wartime experience. As such, Mboup's life exhibits an unusual range of possibilities, and their complex interplay affords nuanced insights into the meaning of the war for Africans and how it redefined subsequent relations between colonisers and the colonised.

MBOUP'S LIFE HISTORY

Like his ancestors, Demba Mboup was a griot. Explaining the role of this caste in most of the ancient Senegambian kingdoms, he recalled:

In the times before my father ... when the [Senegambian] kings went to a battle, griots were the people in the front line [singing], beating their tam-tams, and telling a lot of [stories] to praise the king. And very often, after the battle, they were the people who described what happened during the fighting. And the griots were [closer] to the king [than anyone else], because when the king [undertook something or] needed something done, the griots were the first to know about the news. They were the ones who informed the people at large about what happened in the king's family – [about their] bravery, their courage, their work, their objectives.

[So], in effect, what a griot tells [about the past] is what happened. You say what you saw and you relate the same thing to your son. And your son will also keep telling [the story to his son], and so on, from generation to generation . . . And I am a part of this family [of griots].[13]

Mboup's family migrated to Kayor in central Senegal from the Futa Toro in the Senegal River valley during the reign of Lat Sukabe Fal (*Damel*) in the early eighteenth century.[14] Although his ancestors came from Kayor, Mboup himself was born in 1897 in the coastal commercial centre and French commune of Rufisque. As one born in – an *originaire* of – one of the Four Communes of Senegal, he was entitled to French citizenship. The second of five children, Mboup was the eldest son. As such, he worked in the fields with his father and other men – growing various strains of millet and maize for family consumption and peanuts to sell to the French traders. He also learned from his father many of the oral traditions of the ruling lineages of Kayor – about the rule of Lat Sukabe Fal and his wars against the invading Muslim Mauritanians, and about the treachery of the French governor Louis Faidherbe, his imprisonment of Samba Fal and the *damel's* subsequent suicide.[15] Mboup also learned about the wider world in other ways. His family, who were Mourides (members of a Sufi fraternity founded by Amadu Bamba in 1883), were recent converts to Islam, and he attended the Koranic school where he was instructed in theology and began learning Arabic. He also went to the local European-style school and was taught by two *originaire* teachers from the Communes, Cleydor Ndiaye and Galandou Diouf.[16]

Mboup's contacts with the French were circumscribed.[17] In addition to having brief exchanges with traders and staff at the European school he attended, he worked intermittently from the age of thirteen as a domestic servant in several French households. In one of these, he was beaten up when he asked for his wages:

So after a thirty-day period, I went to see his wife and asked her about my money. And she told me that I had to wait until M. Lafont came back. So, I insisted. And what did she do? I was sitting down and she came and started slapping me – beating me very hard.[18]

This type of injustice, Mboup felt, sprang from the Europeans' 'disregard, lack of respect and consideration' for Africans and was a hallmark of pre-war colonial rule.[19] It was a world where 'if you had trouble with a white man [and] . . . even though the white man was guilty, [if] you went to the police, he would be released and you would be kept [in jail]'.[20] 'They wanted to treat us as slaves,' he notes. Yet upon the outbreak of the First World War,

Mboup was called upon to defend the French state. In this guise, he was compelled to leave his trade and become a soldier. It was a duty that no griot in his family had ever performed before.[21] It would take him overseas, far from his homeland, and dramatically alter his life.

The eighteen-year-old Mboup was working as a carpenter in Thiès when he first learned that he was being called up. Because he was born in Rufisque and a record of his birth was registered at the office of the *maire* there, he was treated as a citizen of the Republic and conscripted into the French army.[22] The mobilisation process entailed individual notification to recruits of their status by the police before departure for the training camp in Dakar two days later, where they were due to report on 25 October 1915. During this interlude, much had to be done. The potential *originaire* recruits were convoked at the Commandant's residence the day before departure to have physical examinations. There they were stripped naked, and their height, weight, chest expansion, strength, sight, etc. were assessed by a French doctor; most of the potential soldiers were declared fit for service. Meanwhile, the fathers of the recruits procured *gris-gris* (protective charms) for their sons to safeguard them, secured the blessing of local marabouts and gave their sons whatever small amounts of money they could spare. As the train departed for Dakar, the feeling of most of the thirty or forty recruits aboard was one of excitement: 'I was happy [even though] the mothers and fathers were crying because their sons were leaving. But I was [excited] knowing I was going to discover new experiences. I didn't know [what awaited me].'[23]

Like other *originaire* recruits, Mboup was assigned to the bataillon de l' Afrique Occidentale Française (AOF) and began his training at the Caserne de Madeleine in Dakar. There the soldiers conducted military exercises under the instruction of French officers and non-commissioned officers (NCOs) dispatched from Europe for this purpose.[24] During this period, Mboup was introduced to new ways of viewing society. Not only were griots and other caste members of the old order now enlisted as soldiers, but slaves were treated equally with other Africans by the French and no longer publicly bore the social stigma of their servile past.[25]

After three months of preliminary instruction in Dakar, Mboup's unit embarked for France. Having heard about other African troop transports that had been sunk, the soldiers found the two-week passage from Dakar to Bordeaux an ordeal.[26] Mboup arrived in France early in 1916, and spent most of the next two and a half years fighting on various fronts. Initially dispatched with the Armée d'Orient to fight in the eastern Mediterranean, he returned to France in 1917 and participated in the disastrous attack at Soissons on 16 April, where his battalion – part of the 44th Regiment d'Infanterie Coloniale – was 'destroyed'.[27] Assigned to a new unit in the 23rd Regiment where he eventually became a machine-gunner, Mboup fought in Champagne, at Caronne, and Reims.[28] Miraculously, he was never wounded during any of these engagements, despite the chaos experienced by soldiers during attacks:

We were fighting against the Germans. And I was with a white man named Debouse. So the French soldiers around us were attacking. And at a [predetermined] time our cannon – the 75s – -opened fire at [targets] that were not aimed at the right distance. So ... when the French [artillery] fired, the shells fell all around us and [exploded] there. [And] Debouse was [hit and] badly wounded. And I ... took him to the [casualty clearing station]. [So afterwards], we were still trying to take the first line [of German trenches]. And a shell [fragment] came and killed one of [my] friends named Djob Ndiaye; it just flew by and cut off his head.[29]

When not fighting at the front, Mboup spent long periods behind the lines, most notably during the winter when Senegalese units were stationed in the south of France to reduce the ill-effects on them of cold weather. This policy, known as *hivernage*, was the result of an intervention by the Deputy from Senegal, Blaise Diagne, with the French High Command, which had initially opposed it.[30]

By 1917, in the aftermath of repeated military debacles at the front as well as the outbreak of mutinies among French soldiers, the spirit of collective disobedience spread to some *originaires* as well. Mboup recounts how at Perpignan, where his unit was billeted in December 1917, the officers told them to do some outdoor exercises while it was snowing. Some of the men refused and, encouraged by them, the rest of the unit decided not to leave the barracks and instead 'go on strike'. The colonel visited the camp, cutting off the soldiers' ration of tobacco as a punitive measure, and the officers started an inquest to identify the 'leaders of the strike':

So they called the three men ['the leaders'] I mentioned and [when they] talked to them [they] explained that they were very brave soldiers and they should be rewarded ... And they told them that they were going on furlough to Senegal. So the three soldiers were very happy and they were congratulating themselves and inviting us to drink lemonade [with them] and it was very good. And the next day, when they put on their uniforms, they [were joking and] said to the rest of us: 'We are going to Senegal and you are going to the front!' ... And they believed they were going to be taken to Senegal.

[And then] the French officers came and said to them: 'Your furlough in Senegal is in prison!' [laughter] And it was just a trick. When they told them they were going to Senegal, the Frenchmen knew that they were the ones heading the strike. And they put them in prison . . . in Perpignan where they were badly beaten. And [then] they threatened them with ten years in prison [for their actions] . . . . Then, just before [our regiment] returned to the front, the officers asked them if they wanted to stay in prison or go to the first line [i.e., where the danger of being killed was greatest]. And they said they wanted to go to the first line.[31]

Mboup's regiment returned to the front in Champagne in the spring of 1918. The war was at crisis point. The Germans were advancing all along the line intent on bringing the conflict to a victorious conclusion. Indeed, by the early summer, they were so close to Paris that Mboup, who was briefly in the city on leave, witnessed the shelling of the capital by long-range German artillery.[32] In mid-summer, as the tide of the struggle gradually began to turn in favour of the Allies, he encountered Americans for the first time and began to discern significant differences among the French people he met as his unit advanced from Reims and Caronne towards the German frontier. In addition to the Parisians he met on leave, these included Corsicans – who were viewed by the Senegalese as the most racist of the French – and Alsatians, who Mboup was surprised to learn spoke French with a German accent.[33]

As the war neared its end, on the night of 29 October Mboup had an ominous dream:

The night before [we went up to the line] I dreamed I was attacked by two lions. And when the two lions came [toward me] I saw Seriny Touba [Amadou Bamba, founder of the Mouride brotherhood] in my dream. And he put me in a basket and raised me up [out of danger]. [But] one of the lions clawed my left leg [as I was being raised]. And after this dream . . . the next day I told my friend, Murin [Diop]: 'I'm sure something is going to happen to me today, because this dream revealed a lot of things to me.'[34]

In the symbolism of Wolof dream interpretations, the lions' presence portended great danger. But Mboup's dream deeply resonates also with those of European combatants, who also dreamed of aerial flight to escape the dangers of the earthbound trenches.[35] Significantly, the very next day, Mboup was grievously injured:

We were [moving forward, but] the German soldiers were making a [counter] attack – [supported by] artillery – their '77s. [And] I was surrounded by cannon fire. [And] I didn't realise I was wounded when it happened [because] it's not painful at first . . . I just thought there was a lot of smoke around me and I fell down [in a small hole to take cover]. [Then] I looked around and noticed blood pouring out of [my legs]. So I took off my boots and I realised I was badly wounded – I couldn't move [my legs] anymore. [So I took off] my cartridge belt, which I tore [into strips] and tied around my legs to prevent the blood from circulating. I did it myself [to keep from bleeding to death].

[So] I was laying there and soon I couldn't move any longer. But while I was sitting there motionless, I prayed to God and Seriny Touba to help me. If I had to die there, [I was reconciled to it because] it was God's decision, but I hoped they would help me return to my own country someday. And the only thing I had on my mind was that today is the day of death or the day of life. Because there were all kinds of risks. I feared another shell exploding and making things [even] worse. [And I was afraid of being found] by the Germans . . . I was sure if they found me there, they would have killed me and been finished with me.

[But] a *Tubab* [i.e., a European] named Paul, who was a stretcher bearer for the wounded, found me and took me . . . to the *poste de secours* . . . for preliminary medical service. [And afterwards] they took me straight away . . . to Paris and the hospital. But the time between when [I was first discovered] and the time when they returned [with the stretcher] and took me back was almost an hour. And throughout that time the Germans were firing their cannons continuously.[36]

Mboup's convalescence was a mixed emotional experience. Transported from the front via ambulance to Paris, he was conscious that he had survived and gave thanks: 'When I found myself in the ambulance, I [prayed] thanking God and Seriny Touba again [for] coming to my rescue.'[37] After his operation, however, he remained in great pain and, now crippled for life, was conscious of the irony of his situation: 'I had been to many fronts and in different attacks [during the war], and I had never been wounded before this happened to me – 11 days before the signing of the Armistice.'[38] Indeed, his experience during the celebrations in the hospital on 11 November encapsulated his ambivalence:

I was very happy when I heard the war was ended. And that day they cooked a rabbit for me and gave me 15 bottles of lemonade . . . But I couldn't eat [the rabbit] because it was so painful; I just tasted it and had to put it down. [Nevertheless], I wasn't disheartened by the fact that I was wounded just before the end of the war, because I told myself that it was my destiny. But on the day the war ended – the 11th of November – I would have preferred to die instead of living, because my legs were hurting so badly I wanted to die. I even asked a nurse to give me some poison to kill myself. He laughed and said to me: 'Your legs are hurting, but it is not very grave. You will recover your health.'[39]

And he did. After several months in Paris, Mboup's strength returned and he was transferred to another hospital situated near the Marne. The only African in the hospital, he was well treated by the French staff – unlike some unfortunate German counterparts he had seen – and his health continued to improve. Thereafter, he was sent to an infirmary near Nancy, where he began to walk again on crutches. Finally, he entrained for Bordeaux, where he was decorated for bravery with the Croix de guerre and the Medaille militaire.[40] He was also designated a *mutilé de guerre* with a fifty per cent physical disability and issued his back pay before being belatedly demobilised and released from the army. Mbop boarded ship in 1919, longing to return to Senegal and eager to see his family again.[41]

Mboup's voyage home was conducted under vastly different conditions than his earlier passage to France. No longer fearful of being torpedoed, and released from the strictures of military discipline, he and the other former soldiers with him relaxed. Nevertheless, many of the men were determined that their wartime sacrifices on behalf of *la patrie* would lead to a new relationship with the French – one that would end the coercive denigration that had existed before the war. This new mentality among many veterans – and particularly the *originaires*, who were intent on asserting their newly won rights as French citizens – was exemplified in Mboup's mind by an incident on the ship that pitted old attitudes against the new:

One day [we were on] the ship that brought us back to Senegal from Bordeaux . . . There were [many demobilized] soldiers [aboard, and sometimes] they got into arguments with some of the white men who treated them like dirty niggers . . . And one of these men – a citizen from Gorée – was called a *sale nègre* by a white man . . . I think maybe the [French]man was not well-educated, or perhaps he was drunk. [And the soldier] hit him hard . . . and [they] started fighting. [And] we all [joined in] and started to give our friend some help. And we beat the [Frenchman] badly until he asked to be forgiven. He was crying and said that he would never do it again.
    So what happened [afterwards]? Nothing! We were within our rights, because discrimination between people [was no longer tolerated] at that time, [and] we were French citizens like anybody else. [If] the 'white' man wanted to start acting like that, we [could retaliate] and nothing happened. [But], if the same thing had happened before the war, [we] would not have done the same thing. Because we had less power then, and [we] were treated badly like this by the French all the time.[42]

    Recalling his reunion with his family, Mboup said that his mother and father were 'very, very, very happy to see me. [laughter] And my mother was so happy that she wanted to [pick me up and] put me on her back, like a baby. I told her I was too heavy for her [now]. And I gave [them gifts] and a lot of money.'[43] He lived in Thiès for more than twenty years after the war, marrying several wives and having five children. Because of his physical disability and decorations, he received preferential treatment from the French and found work in the public sector of the economy, as a signalman and later as a barrier guard on the railway.[44] As such, he received a salary in addition to his disability pension, and was not obliged to earn a livelihood from the land. He joined the veterans' association in Thiès which was 'a kind of gathering of all of those who came from the war'. The leader of this organisation was Françoise Gningue, who represented the veterans. At the same time, the Office [Nationale] des Anciens Combattants was founded in Dakar.[45]

During the early 1940s, Mboup briefly moved to Louga and Kaolack, where he continued working for the railroad, before changing jobs and permanently settling in Dakar. Hired by the director of the Hôpital principal in Fann, Colonel Dupuis, he worked there until his retirement, making artificial limbs and corrective shoes for other *mutilés de guerre*.[46] His own personal disability allowance was increased from fifty to sixty per cent. Paid quarterly, his allowance was not adjusted for inflation and, frozen at immediate post-war levels, became an increasingly inadequate source of income in his old age.[47]

Despite his permanent physical infirmity and his indignation over the meagreness of his veteran's pension, Mboup, like many of his comrades from the Four Communes, interpreted his experience during the war in a positive light, an attitude much more rare among the African *sujets* recruited in the countryside. Though he possessed only a vague understanding of the origins of the conflict – which he interpreted as a dynastic dispute between rival ruling lineages in Germany, France and Belgium – and stressing his youthful naivety, as well as his unavoidable obligation to serve, he believed the soldiers' contribution brought change.[48] Among the 84 Senegalese veterans and witnesses interviewed with Mboup, most *originaires* believed their wartime service resulted in significant post-war changes, while most *tirailleurs*, and especially those recruited from among the subject population prior to 1918 or who were not NCOs, did not.[49] In Mboup's eyes, the *originaires* received French citizenship in large measure because of their military service, while the respect Africans were sometimes accorded by their European counterparts overseas contrasted favourably with pre-war colonial abuses. In a role reversal he never forgot, Mboup remembered that while he was in Paris, 'I was helped by another French soldier who helped me carry my luggage because I was disabled.'[50] Mboup took pride in his contribution to this new status achieved by Africans.[51] He was also well aware of the extent of the sacrifices that made it possible: of the thirty or forty youthful recruits who left Thiès with him in 1915, fewer than half returned from the war. And though he later downplayed his family's origins – indeed his children broke with Wolof tradition and married into non-caste families – he retained his sense of identity as a griot to the end: 'God has given me a very good memory. So everything that I have told you ... is true.'[52]

In September 2001, one of Mboup's three daughters, Adja Negoye Mboup, as well as one of his grandsons, Mamadou Gueye, discussed the significance of their departed ancestor's service overseas. In so doing, they provided a glimpse into the enduring legacy of the soldiers' wartime contribution to France and how it is variously perceived among the later generations of Senegalese. Their interviews also underscore the importance of recording African oral histories and traditions about the past, and illustrate how individual as well as collective memory is informed by a wide-ranging and complex interplay of factors – including, most obviously, gender, generation, and life cycle – that may be variously interpreted not only by contemporary, but also by future historians.[53]

Adja was born in the 1930s in Thiès but lived in later life in Dakar. A member of the Senegalese middle class, she was also a devout Muslim, having made the hajj to Mecca, and generally interpreted her father's military service favourably. A child of the colonial era, she cited Mboup's acquisition of French nationality, his performance of a 'duty' expected of him – indeed, she emphasised the pride she felt 'that Senegalese were sent to fight for the white man [in Europe]' – and the material benefits accorded their family because of his service overseas as considerations in her assessment.[54] Notwithstanding his 'wound' and the 'pain from the war', she emphasised that he became a French *fonctionnaire* and received a pension.[55] As a result, and unlike other griot children, she and her siblings were not obliged to beg for money. Nor did the family ever go hungry: her father's cash allotment was always sufficient to buy rice and oil. She also recalled that, in later life, her father was able to acquire a second home and, because of his contacts at the Hôpital principal, to procure prescription medicine he needed in old age.[56]

Mamadou Gueye, Mboup's grandson, who was born in 1970 and was university-educated, disagreed with this assessment. He remembered sleeping, as a boy, in his grandfather's bedroom and the pride he experienced in seeing Mboup march on Armistice Day, when he donned his medals and paraded with other veterans. As Gueye became older, however, his views changed. He came to see the fate of his grandfather, and of the tirailleurs sénégalais in general, as but one example of the larger and ongoing exploitation of Africans by France and the West generally. Three points exemplified French injustice toward the former soldiers in his view: the 'inequality' of the Senegalese veterans' pensions compared with those of their French counterparts;[57] the 'killing of many' of the returning African POWs in 1944 at Thiaroye by the colonial authorities – a collective memory significantly transmitted in his case through Ousmane Sembene's film *Camp de Thiaroye* instead of through oral traditions as among earlier generations;[58] and the denial of admission into France to 'the sons' of Senegalese veterans who had fought to defend the country against German aggression during the two world wars. Although he felt pride in the courage exhibited by his grandfather, he was indignant that he had been used by the French in such a way.[59]

As a griot and a meticulous oral historian himself, Demba Mboup would likely have appreciated the differing vantage points (attributable, in the eyes of his grandson, to their 'generational' differences) influencing both his descendants' assessments of his wartime experience.[60] After all, he himself had undergone a similar metamorphosis over time. Despondent and suicidal as he lay in pain in his hospital bed on 11 November 1918, he came to adopt during the *longue durée* of an extended life a different opinion about his wartime fate than he had held more than half a century earlier. Indeed, his own interpretation of the legacy of his service – though not his still-vivid memories of his particular wartime ordeal (inevitably differentiated in so many individual ways from that of other veterans) – was itself the product of a dramatically altered personal perspective.

NOTES

1 A portion of this chapter was presented at the May 2006 meeting of the French Colonial Historical Society/Société d'histoire coloniale française in Dakar, Senegal. The term 'subject peoples', with its sometimes imprecise legal and social connotations, is consciously chosen here in preference to racially based alternatives. For breakdowns of the contingents drawn from the British and French empires, reckoned at between 1,683,000 and 1,462,000, see Christian Koller, *'Von Wilden aller Rassen niedergemetzelt': Die Diskussion um die Verwendung von Kolonialtruppen in Europa zwischen Rassismus, Kolonial- und Militärpolitik (1914– 1930)* (Stuttgart: Franz Steiner, 2001), 87–95. To this must be added approximately 380,000 African Americans and 17,000 Amerindians. In addition, at least 2 million more subject peoples served European armies in labour formations, predominately in Africa, but Koller (96) calculates that 436,000 labourers (including a substantial number of Chinese workers) were imported to serve in Europe between 1914 and 1918. For figures about wartime mobilisation, also see the Introduction to this volume, page 4.

2 See Joe Lunn, 'Male Identity and Martial Codes of Honor: A Comparison of the War Memoirs of Robert Graves, Ernst Jünger, and Kande Kamara', *Journal of Military History* 69, no. 3 (2005), 713–35.

3 Griots were members of a precolonial endogamous caste of bards and storytellers (see below). On the numbers of West African combatants, as distinguished from wartime recruits and the total numbers of soldiers mobilised, see Joe Lunn, *Memoirs of the Maelstrom: A Senegalese Oral History of the First World War* (Portsmouth, NH: Heinemann; Oxford: James Currey; Cape Town: David Philip, 1999), p. 87 nn. 56, 57 and 61, and p. 154, nn. 81, 82. On French West Africans and the First World War, also see Charles Balesi, *From Adversaries to Comrades-in-Arms: West Africa and the French Military, 1885–1981* (Waltham, MA: Crossroads Press, 1979); Marc Michel, *L'Appel à l'Afrique: Contributions et réactions à l'effort de guerre en AOF (1914–1919)* (Paris: Publications de la Sorbonne, 1982); Myron Echenberg, *Colonial Conscripts: The Tirailleurs Sénégalais in French West Africa, 1857–1960* (Portsmouth, NH: Heinemann and London: James Curry, 1991); Iba Der Thiam, *Le Sénégal dans la Guerre 14–18: Ou le prix du combat pour l'égalité* (Dakar: Les Nouvelles Éditions Africaines du Sénégal, 1992); Lunn, *Memoirs of the Maelstrom*; Bakari Kamian, *Des tranchées de Verdun à l'église Saint-Bernar: 80,000 combattants maliens au secours de la France (1914–18 et 1939–45)* (Paris: Éditions Karthala, 2001); Gregory Mann, *Native Sons: West African Veterans and France in the Twentieth Century* (Durham, NC: Duke University Press, 2006), and Richard S. Fogarty, *Race and War in France: Colonial Subjects in the French Army, 1914–1918* (Baltimore, MD: Johns Hopkins University Press, 2008).

4 See Bakary Diallo, *Force Bonté* (Paris: Rieder, 1926) and Joe Lunn, 'Kande Kamara Speaks: An Oral History of the West African Experience in France, 1914–1918', in Melvin Page (ed.), *Africa and the First World War* (London: Macmillan, 1987), 28–53.

5 Bernal Díaz, *The Conquest of New Spain* (London: Penguin Books, 1963).

6 For work on long-term memory, see Francesca Cappelletto, 'Long-Term Memory of Extreme Events: From Autobiography to History', *Journal of the Royal Anthropological Institute* 9 (2003), 241–60.

7 On memory as well as my methodological disagreement with Marc Michel about the value of African oral histories as sources about the war, see Joe Lunn, 'Remembering the *Tirailleurs Sénégalais* and the Great War: Oral History as a Methodology of Inclusion in French Colonial Studies', *French Colonial History* 10 (2009), 125–49.

8 The African historian and linguist Jan Vansina first published *De la tradition orale* (Tervuren: Musée royal de l'Afrique centrale) in 1961. With the subsequent founding of the Oral History Association and the appearance of the *Oral History Review* in 1973, oral history was gradually transformed from a marginal and experimental methodology into a widely accepted research technique and academic discipline. On the evolution of oral history methods, see Luise White, Stephan F. Miescher, and David William Cohen (eds.), *African Words, African Voices: Critical Practices in Oral History* (Bloomington: Indiana University Press, 2001).

9 On field techniques, see Carolyn Keyes Adenaike and Jan Vansina (eds.), *In Pursuit of History: Fieldwork in Africa* (Portsmouth, NH: Heinemann; Oxford: James Currey, 1996) and Donald Ritche, *Doing Oral History* (Oxford University Press, 2003). On my difference with Gregory Mann about the importance of recording interviews for posterity, see Lunn, 'Remembering the *Tirailleurs Sénégalais*'.

10 On griots, see Isabella Leymarie, *Les Griots wolof du Sénégal* (Paris: Maisonneuve et Larose, 1999).

11 On the provisions of the Lois Diagne of 1915 and 1916, which affirmed the French citizenship of *originaires* of the Four Communes of Senegal, see G. Wesley Johnson Jr, *The Emergence of Black Politics in Senegal: The Struggle for Power in the Four Communes, 1900–1920* (Stanford University Press, 1971).

12 Lunn, *Memoirs of the Maelstrom*, 187–236.

13 Interview with Demba Mboup, Dakar, Senegal, 11, 14, 15, 25–29 April, 3 May 1983. Translated from the Wolof by Daouda Fall who, significantly, was himself a descendant of the ruling lineage of Kayor that Mboup's family had served. Direct quotations from the 13 one-hour audio cassette tapes of Mboup's life history, which in this particular reference appear in the transcript as Tape 2, Side A and Tape 7, Side A, will hereafter be cited as Mboup 2A and 7A. Tapes of these 85 interviews with veterans – totalling some 200 hours in length – and the texts of their transcriptions are on deposit with the Archives nationales du Sénégal (ANS), Dakar, Senegal and the Indiana University Archives of Traditional Music, Bloomington, IN.

14 On Lat Sukabe Fal (*Damel*, 1695–1719), see Boubacar Barry, *Senegambia and the Atlantic Slave Trade* (Cambridge University Press, 1998).

15 Mboup 1A, 2A, 2B, 3A and 3B. Also see Barry, *Senegambia and the Atlantic Slave Trade*; Mamadou Diouf, *Le Kajoor au XIX siècle: Pouvoir ceddo et conquête coloniale* (Paris: Karthala, 1990); and James F. Searing, *'God Alone Is King': Islam and Emancipation in Senegal: The Wolof Kingdoms of Kajoor and Bawol, 1859–1914* (Portsmouth, NH: Heinemann; Oxford: James Currey; Cape Town: David Phillip, 2002).

16 Mboup 1A.

17 Though limited, Mboup's contacts as a town dweller with the French were nevertheless more extensive than those of the vast majority of Senegalese living in the countryside. See Lunn, *Memoirs of the Maelstrom*, 10–32.

18 Mboup 13A.

19 *Ibid.* 13A.

20 *Ibid.* 13A.

21 *Ibid.* 3B.

22 *Ibid.* 4A. On the mobilisation of *originaires* and how their experience differed from that of African *sujets*, see Lunn, *Memoirs of the Maelstrom*, 59–90.

23 Mboup 4A. On metropolitan reactions to the declaration of war, see Jean-Jacques Becker, *The Great War and the French People*, trans. Arnold Pomerans (Oxford: Berg, 1993), 3–102.

24 Mboup 3B.
25 *Ibid.* 8B. On the redefinition of servile relationships as a consequence of the First World War, see Martin Klein, *Slavery and Colonial Rule in French West Africa* (Cambridge University Press, 1998), 197–236.
26 Mboup 4A and 4B. On the sinking of the *Athos*, which was torpedoed on 17 February 1917 with the loss of 124 African and 22 European lives, see Archives de la Guerre, Service Historique de l'Armée, Unités 26 N 871, Chateau de Vincennes, Paris.
27 Mboup 12B. On combat in Europe see Michel, *L'Appel à l'Afrique*, 287–343, Lunn, *Memoirs of the Maelstrom*, 120–56, and Fogarty, *Race and War in France*, 55–95.
28 Mboup 5B and 12B.
29 *Ibid.* 9B. On 'short shelling', which may have caused 75,000 French casualties during the war, see Modris Eksteins, *Rites of Spring: The Great War and the Birth of the Modern Age* (Boston and New York: Houghton Mifflin, 2000), 153.
30 On Diagne and the policy of *hivernage*, see Archives de la Guerre, 'État-Major de l'Armée', 7N440. For an account of African soldiers during *hivernage* through the eyes of an exceptionally compassionate and perceptive French witness, see Lucie Cousturier, *Des inconnus chez moi* (Paris: La Suene, 1920).
31 Mboup 11A, 11B and 12B. On collective indiscipline at Perpignan, see Michel, *L'Appel à l'Afrique*, 383–7. For incidents of collective disobedience in other Senegalese units stationed in Bordeaux and Morocco over poor-quality food and work regimen, see also respectively Boubacar Gueye 2A and Mody Sow 4B.
32 Mboup 10A.
33 *Ibid.* 10A and 10B.
34 *Ibid.* 5B.
35 For other references by Senegalese soldiers to the interpretation of dreams, see Mboup 9A and Masserigne Soumare 3B. On dream interpretations among West African Muslims, see Lamin Sanneh, *The Crown and the Turban: Muslims and West African Pluralism* (Boulder, CO: Westview Press, 1997), 39–42. On the psychological responses of European soldiers to the fragmentation of their vision in the trenches and, especially, to their dreams of being raised out of danger through flying, see Eric J. Leed, *No Man's Land: Combat and Identity in World War I* (Cambridge University Press, 1979), 123–38.
36 Mboup 5A. On the massacre of African POWs by Germans during the Second World War and alleged Senegalese atrocities committed during the First World War as a contributing factor, see Raffael Scheck, *Hitler's African Victims: The German Army Massacres of Black French Soldiers in 1940* (Cambridge University Press, 2006), 60–6, 88–97.
37 Mboup 5B.
38 *Ibid.* 5B.
39 *Ibid.* 5B and 6A.

40 *Ibid.* 1A, 5B, 6A and 9B.

41 *Ibid.* 1A, 6A and 6B.

42 *Ibid.* 13A. It is unclear whether the type of 'help' the partially disabled Mboup gave to the soldier from Gorée actually entailed physical intervention or simply moral support.

43 *Ibid.* 6A.

44 *Ibid.* 6A. Mboup also witnessed the formation of the railway workers' syndicate and the first major strike by African workers on the Dakar–Bamako line in the late 1930s.

45 Ibid. 6B. On post-war veterans' associations in French West Africa, see Mann, *Native Sons*, 63–107, and Lunn, *Memoirs of the Maelstrom*, 188–94.

46 Mboup 1A and 6A.

47 *Ibid.* 5A. On the freezing of the pensions of combatants (*retraite du combattant*) by the French in 1960, see Mann, *Native Sons*, 108–45.

48 Mboup 9B and 10A.

49 The rural recruits from Mali interviewed by Mann appear to have shared this latter outlook. Significantly, in the Senegalese sample, interpretations were also highly gendered. Veterans might disagree about the meaning of the war; women witnesses – who interpreted the useless loss of the lives of their loved ones as its only enduring legacy – were uniform in their condemnation of the meaning of the conflict. See Lunn, *Memoirs of the Maelstrom*, 228–36 and Mann, *Native Sons*, 249 n21.

50 Mboup 6B

51 Interview with Demba Mboup's daughter Adja Negoye Mboup and his grandson Mamadou Gueye, 20 September 2001. Douda Fall interpreter, Adja Mboup and Gueye 3C. These interviews were among an additional group of nearly fifty, which were conducted during 2001–2 with descendants of 22 Senegalese veterans originally interviewed in 1982–3.

52 Mboup 6A.

53 This section adumbrates some of the themes that will be more fully developed in Joe Lunn, *African Voices from the Great War: An Anthology of Senegalese Soldiers' Life Histories*, forthcoming. See also White *et al.*, *African Words, African Voices*.

54 Adja Mboup and Gueye, 3C. As a daughter who felt her family benefited from her father's wartime service, Adja Mboup's interpretation offers an interesting counterpoint to the views of women witnesses who were contemporaries of the soldiers and who were uniformly negative in their assessments of the war's legacy (see note 49).

55 *Ibid.* 3B.

56 *Ibid.* 3A, 3B, and 3C.

57 This widespread grievance, repeatedly expressed by First World War veterans themselves, has now entered into contemporary French, as well as African political discourse. See Gregory Mann, 'Immigrants and Arguments in France and West Africa', *Comparative Studies in Society and History*, 45, 2 (2003), 262–85.

58 See Myron Echenberg, 'Tragedy at Thiaroye: The Senegalese Soldiers' Uprising of 1944', in Robin Cohen, Jean Copans and Peter Gutkind (eds.), *African Labour History* (Beverly Hills: Sage, 1978), 109–28.
59 Adja Mboup and Gueye 3B. On the indignation of veterans' sons at their mistreatment as Africans by the French authorities, see also Youssoufa Soumare, Dakar, 22 November 2001, notes.
60 *Ibid.* 3B.

PART II

Perceptions and proximities

CHAPTER 6

Representing Otherness: African, Indian and European soldiers' letters and memoirs

Christian Koller

Writing about his experiences on the Western Front, the Senegalese war veteran Bakary Diallo recalled an episode involving a captured German soldier:

A German mistook his trench and, together with his coffee, was made prisoner by a Senegalese sentry. When he was encircled by African *tirailleurs*, the whole of his body was trembling. You poor man, didn't you anticipate this moment when you already gloated over your future glory? The blacks you thought to be savages have caught you in the war, but instead of killing you, they have made you a prisoner of war. Your fear will hopefully not prevent you from proclaiming in your country tomorrow, after the battle, sentiments of justice that will rehabilitate their name among the savage human races.[1]

The deployment in Europe of more than 600,000 non-white soldiers from the French and British colonies caused a variety of encounters between European and colonial troops. While the Allied policies concerning the employment of these men in Europe and the hopes and racial prejudices surrounding them have been the subject of recent research,[2] their actual experiences in Europe have been explored to a much lesser degree. This chapter uncovers fresh ground in two ways. First, rather than privileging propaganda accounts and official documents, it examines these records alongside personal testimonies – soldiers' letters, diaries and memoirs – to illuminate the colonial experience of combat 'from below'. Second, it is comparative in scope, drawing upon a diverse range of material – German, French and British accounts, as well as letters and memoirs by the colonial troops themselves – in order to understand and examine European perceptions of African and Asian troops alongside the colonial soldiers' view of Europe and its people.

This chapter argues that there are both striking similarities and striking differences among European perceptions of these non-white colonial troops[3] as well as in the wartime experiences of these men from different parts of the world. While such perceptions were shaped by the prevailing colonial racist ideology that stressed European superiority, often for alleged biological reasons, there was also an element of exoticism about the unfamiliar. The two modes of perception, as in colonial discourses in general, often overlapped, both insisting on a yawning gap between Europeans and non-Europeans.[4] The African and Asian soldiers, on the other hand, experienced varying degrees of cultural shock as many of them negotiated European culture for the first time. Some defended their traditional cultural and religious values, while others openly admired and tried to assimilate Western norms, though there were frequent overlaps between these attitudes.

GERMAN SOLDIERS' VIEW OF COLONIAL TROOPS

German propaganda met the introduction of colonial troops on the Western Front with a deeply racist campaign that represented the non-white colonial soldiers as beasts. They were described in terms that negated their quality as regular military forces: 'a motley crew of colours and religions', 'devils', 'dehumanised wilderness', 'dead vermin of the wilderness', 'Africans jumping around in a devilish ecstasy', 'auxiliary rabble of all colours', 'an exhibition of Africans', 'an anthropological show of uncivilised ... bands and hordes' or the catchphrase 'the black shame' which quickly rose to common usage in the early 1920s, when French colonial troops were stationed in the occupied Rhineland area.[5] In summer 1915, the German Foreign Office put into circulation a memorandum titled *Employment, contrary to International Law, of Colored Troops upon the European Theatre of War by England and France*, in which many atrocities were attributed to colonial soldiers, including the poking out of eyes and the cutting off of ears, noses and heads of wounded and captured German soldiers.[6]

Another objection raised by German propaganda against the employment of colonial non-white troops on European battlefields was its alleged impact on the future of colonialism and the supremacy of the 'white race'. If African and Asian soldiers were trained in the handling of modern arms, if they saw the white nations fighting each other and were allowed to participate in these fights and experience the white soldiers' vulnerability, they would lose their respect for the white race once and for ever. After the war, they would turn their weapons against their own masters. German propaganda argued that the French and British policy of deploying colonial troops in Europe was a flagrant breach of white solidarity and should be condemned by every civilised nation.[7]

German propaganda thus fitted in with discourses of imperial racism and social Darwinism common in late nineteenth-century Europe: it drew upon the contemporary notions of racial hierarchies with Europeans at the top, as well as on fears of global racial struggles, which might result in a victory for the 'inferior' races.[8] Similar discourses had dominated German press and propaganda ten years earlier during the Herero and Nama uprisings in German South West Africa (1904–7), when the rebels were portrayed as 'black beasts' or 'devils' and German military leaders legitimised their brutal suppression of the revolt as an element of 'racial struggle'.[9]

Sometimes, German propaganda published soldiers' letters in order to back its claims against the Allied colonial troops. A letter written by the writer Hans Friedrich Blunck, who had volunteered and would later become an important figure in Nazi cultural policy, was published in the newspaper *Vossische Zeitung* as well as in the war chronicle *Der Völkerkrieg* after the 1915 battle of Ypres. In this letter, apparently written for propaganda purposes, Blunck complained:

In this night, the marvellous fighting had become disgusting to me. The foe deployed Senegalese Negroes and Indian auxiliaries against our glorious volunteers, and it was as if, through the stream of blood that covered the battlefield, the trembling beastly smell of the dark-coloured peoples emerged. As if, together with the inferior blood of these strangers, something would pour into the soil plaguing the country, as if the earth knew that it would never again be able to become green after the Africans' feet had touched it . . . I passed the trenches. Some soldiers were handling their colonel's corpse . . . if you looked him in the eyes: shock. Something undescribably horrible must have emerged before he died. He, who had dreamt so much of equal adversaries' fight, . . . the brooder, the German, had seen the black flood, the dark mud, devouring him and his men. He had not been able to fight man against man, as had been the dream of his life; the enemy had sent half-animal peoples of Africa, whom he was expected to take on; the enemy had mobilised Asia and betrayed thousand years old Europe. I suddenly knew where these horrible ideas came from. It was as if the colonel's shaken soul was with us with all its shock about this dark treason of Europe.[10]

Other personal documents, published during the war, mentioned colonial troops as well, but not in such sharply racist terms.[11]

But how were these colonial troops portrayed in German soldiers' letters and diaries not written for propaganda purposes? Did first-person narratives tell stories different from other kinds of documents? Some personal documents mentioned colonial soldiers without much comment. Private Karl

Falkenhain from Naundorf wrote to his wife in September 1914, about his deployment at a prisoner camp in Kleinwittenberg, in which there were 'Russians, Blacks and French, all mixed'. He mentioned a lot of curious civilian visitors but he did not say whether they especially came to see the Africans.[12] Richard Dehmel noted in his diary on 15 October 1914 a similar curiosity:

The sergeant told me yesterday that England's Indian auxiliaries had arrived at the front; one can see them, together with their wives and camels, digging trenches some kilometres from here. As there are also Zouaves [French settlers from North Africa, wearing colourful oriental uniforms] on the opposite side of the front, the big decisive battle will produce a colourful picture of peoples.[13]

Other German soldiers openly looked down on the non-white soldiers, whether they came from Asia, or from North or West Africa. Volunteer Kurt Schlenner, an undergraduate from Berlin who would be killed shortly afterwards, stated in a letter to his parents in December 1914 that the German soldiers were united by a general spirit of comradeship, while the enemy troops were weakened by their racial diversity: 'everybody will first look whether an emerging comrade is from the same tribe as himself. One cannot respect a Negro as a comrade after all.'[14] In his diary Colonel General Carl von Einem referred to the colonial troops as 'riffraff' and a 'menagerie'.[15] Private V. Herzog, a gymnast from Hamburg, described 'Hindus' and 'Zouaves' as 'gory'. Recounting the story of a captured French city, allegedly devastated by fleeing Allied soldiers, he reasoned that 'these must have been Singhalese, so no wonder' (mixing up Senegalese with Singhalese) and further noted that lots of 'Turkos' and 'Hindus' had deserted.[16] Another private wrote in September 1914 that the North African soldiers looked 'forbidding' and that he did not feel sorry for the fallen colonial troops.[17]

Similar notions can be found in the post-war memoirs of the German soldiers. Both leaders of the third supreme command of the German army referred to the colonial troops for propaganda purposes. While Erich Ludendorff, in his memoirs written in the winter of 1918–19, only mentioned that France had made extensive use of African troops, especially in the summer of 1918,[18] Paul von Hindenburg stuck closer to wartime phraseology:

Where tanks were lacking, the enemy drove black waves towards us, waves composed of African bodies. Woe to us, when these invaded our lines and murdered or, even worse, tortured the defenceless. Human indignation and accusation must not be directed against the blacks who commited these atrocities, but against those who deployed these hordes on European soil, allegedly fighting for honour, liberty and justice.[19]

In contrast, the soldiers who, unlike the two generals, had themselves fought against these men used much less of this wartime propaganda-fuelled vocabulary in their memoirs. Instead of pre-conceived notions, trench digger Martin Beradt displayed curiosity and an exoticist attitude towards the colonial soldiers.[20] Ernst Jünger, in his famous *Stahlgewittern*, even dedicated a full chapter to fighting against Indian troops in May 1917.[21] Jünger characterised the Indian sepoys as 'gracile figures', 'having come a long way over the ocean just to have their skulls smashed by Hanoverian fusiliers on this god-damned piece of soil'.[22] Quite similar was the mention of colonial troops in the memoirs of infantryman Otto Maximilian Hitzfeld, written in the early 1980s.[23] Thus, personal encounters with colonial troops seemed to have added to racist perceptions a sense of exoticism.

A very interesting source in this respect is the Alsatian peasant Dominik Richert's memoirs, written probably in the winter of 1918–19, but published posthumously only in 1989. Richert, who had deserted in the summer of 1918, did not share any nationalist or militarist notions but harboured racial prejudices. He considered the Allied European soldiers to be victims of militarism like himself and did not believe in the German atrocity propaganda against alleged French and Belgian *franc-tireurs*.[24] Russian soldiers, however, appeared to him as 'half-cultivated',[25] so that he did not dare to desert at the Eastern Front.[26] Indian troops were even stranger to Richert, who referred to them as 'brown chaps' or 'blacks'. While he condemned killing on nearly every page of his memoir and provided detailed descriptions of wounding and mutilation, he only briefly noted how he made an Indian 'unfit for action' in close combat.[27]

On the whole, front-line soldiers seem to have shared the widespread racist perceptions about the colonial non-white troops; they hardly differentiated among different ethnic groups, and sometimes even confused them. Wartime diaries and letters were not very different from the post-war memoirs in this respect. However, these personal testimonies did not always rehearse the rhetoric of the German propaganda machine. In contrast to the writings of authors close to the state apparatus such as Hans Friedrich Blunck, Erich Ludendorff and Heinrich von Hindenburg, ordinary soldiers' letters, diaries and memoirs hardly mention issues such as the colonial soldiers' alleged atrocities or their war service as a threat to the colonial order. The casual racism of these accounts was also informed by a certain curiosity and exoticism, which distinguish them from the program-matic and vicious racism of German official propaganda.

The image of the colonial troops in the French and British press and propaganda accounts was of course much more positive than in German publications. But at the same time, it was not entirely free of racist imagery. Despite the opposing lines of argument, certain basic racist and imperialist notions were common to French, British and German propaganda.

In the first few months of the war, representations of African troops in the French press did not always differ substantially from German propaganda images. Two weeks after the outbreak of the war, the *Dépêche Coloniale* portrayed African soldiers as 'démons noirs' who would carry over the Rhine, with their bayonets, the revenge of civilisation against 'modern barbarism'.[28] In February 1915, the Marseilles-based journal *Midi Colonial* published a cartoon showing a Muslim soldier wearing a necklace made of German soldiers' ears. The subtitle ran: 'Be silent, be careful, enemy ears are listening!'[29]

It was only at the beginning of 1915 that French officials started promot-ing a revised image of the Africans as infantile and devoted savages in order to counter German atrocity propaganda. The colonial soldiers were depicted as belonging to *races jeunes* and as absolutely obedient to their white masters because of the whites' intellectual superiority.[30] Alphonse Séché, for instance, stated the following in the weekly *L'Opinion*:

For the black man, the white man's orders, the chief's orders are summarised in one phrase that he repeats again and again 'y a service' . . . He won't discuss; he does not try to understand. He would kill his father, mother, wife, child to obey the order he has received. He is not responsible; the will of the superior bends his own . . . In all the blacks' acts, we find this mixture of childlike nature and heroism . . . The Senegalese is brave by nature; as a primitive being, he does not analyse . . . For the Senegalese, his officer is everything; he replaces the absent chief of his village, his father. If the Senegalese has confidence in his chief, he does nothing without consulting him.[31]

Here, the African soldier is at once 'childlike' and 'heroic', intellectually inferior but wholly loyal: the notion of brutality has changed. Whilst the image spread by the French media in the opening months of the war stressed the Africans' 'brutality', implying a possible threat for the French as well, the revised image of the infantile savages insisted on the colonial masters' complete control. African soldiers would be fighters only when told to be so and therefore could only be a threat to the Germans, but never to the French. On the other hand, the British media made a clear differentiation in their representations of their own and of the French army's colonial troops. While France's African troops were depicted as stupid and childlike – 'In his black innocence he seems to be struggling with the things he cannot understand'[32] is how a report in *The Times* (January 1915) described a West African soldier – Indian troops were often characterised as 'picturesque'.[33] The British media emphasised not only the loyalty, martial spirit and bravery of the Indian troops, but also their physical grandeur and cultural practices.[34]

How did European Allied soldiers themselves perceive the colonial non-white troops? While most of the Indian troops were withdrawn from the European theatre of war in December 1915, the French enacted a new policy of 'amalgamation' after their African troops suffered dramatic losses in the autumn of 1914.[35] African troops, whose numbers increased massively in the second part of the war, would now no longer fight as independent units, but were combined with European troops according to the historical model of amalgamation of old troops and volunteer corps during the French Revolution. Yet, was it true, as the German volunteer Kurt Schlenner suggested (see above), that European soldiers did not respect the colonial troops as comrades?

The letters and memoirs of French and British soldiers show an ambivalent attitude towards their non-white allies. Most of them were curious about these 'exotic' soldiers and some even sympathised with them. Louis Barthas, a cooper, trade unionist and socialist, described an Algerian division he encountered at Narbonne as 'magnifique' and even contrasted them favourably to his own unit.[36] Second Lieutenant Roland Leighton, in a letter to his fiancée Vera Brittain in July 1915, mentioned North African troops: 'A company of Turcos has just gone along the road, singing a weird chant punctuated with hand clapping. They all look very Negroid, but are wellbuilt men and march well.'[37] Nevertheless, evidence also suggests that these colonial soldiers were not considered by British soldiers to be comrades on equal terms, but rather were seen as auxiliaries for especially dangerous tasks (which corresponded with the French army's doctrine).[38]

Indian troops attracted the attention of European Allied soldiers. According to Barthas, the news that a 'Hindu army' would soon be arriving at Marseilles caused 'general curiosity' in the autumn of 1914. Barthas described Indian soldiers' habits and customs and especially their way of slaughtering goats.[39] The English officer poet Siegfried Sassoon wrote in his diary: 'I watched the Indian cavalry in the horse-lines by the river: their red head-caps made occasional spots of poppy-colour: the rest was browns and duns and greys – like the huddle of horses and wagons and blankets, and the worn grassless earth.'⁴⁰ Louis Barthas's description of a French military hospital may have been typical of the experience of many Allied soldiers: 'All parts of the world, all races and all colours were represented. Moroccans, Annamites, white and black Americans, Italians, etc., and five or six Frenchmen. When conversation started, a nice cacophony was to be heard.'⁴¹

Only a few soldier-writers explicitly expressed their sympathy towards the colonial soldiers. French infantryman Jacques Vaché, for instance, referred to the Indian soldiers in a 1917 letter as '*poilus de la cavalerie indienne*', thus using a term common for French soldiers and thereby stressing that he considered Indian sepoys as real comrades.⁴² Louis Barthas felt sorry for the North African soldiers who were sent to the front immediately after their arrival in Europe: 'Hardly anyone of these miserable wretches would ever return to Algeria!'⁴³ At the same time, ideas about their alleged brutality lingered on, particularly in the literary imagination. Thus, in his war novel *Le Feu* (1916), the novelist Henri Barbusse, who had spent eleven months at the front, refers to the Moroccan soldiers as 'devils' who are used to 'poking the bayonet in the enemy's belly'.⁴⁴ Stories about the killing of prisoners and the cutting off of enemies' heads by Africans seemed to circulate in the French army. Thus, among the Allied soldiers, there was a wide range of responses, from sympathy and admiration to fear and anxiety. In spite of the significant differences between the French and British attitudes towards their respective colonial troops, certain common perceptions and prejudices were discernible, moving between racism and exoticism. Many of these find their most vicious and exaggerated form in German discourses. Such prejudices could also be found among the neutral voices from the front. Alden Davison, serving with the American Red Cross Ambulance service, in a 1916 letter to his mother described Senegalese soldiers as 'demons at hand-to-hand fighting, but whether the sight of blood maddens them, or the old racial instinctive hatred between black and white crops out, they kill anyone who gets in the way, be he French or German'.⁴⁵

COLONIAL NON-WHITE SOLDIERS' VIEW OF EUROPE

How did the colonial soldiers perceive Europe and the Europeans? The responses of the Indian soldiers have received some attention in recent years, based on censored war letters.⁴⁶ These letters show a variety of responses and coping mechanisms: some soldiers were able to assimilate European mores and habits with their cultural background; a few even thought of marrying European women, though following Indian customs.[47] Some rejected their own customs and habits and formed an unconditional admiration for the European social, economic and gender order,[48] while another group tried to defend their cultural identity and fulfil their religious duties and traditional roles as men and warriors. It was often men from this last group who expressed despair and resignation.[49] There were, however, overlaps between these categories and gradual processes of cultural adaptation.[50]

As for the North and West African soldiers, many of the 'personal' documents published during and after the war were intended to serve propaganda purposes. During the war, Germany arranged the publication in German and French of several texts by the Algerian officer Rabah Abdallah Boukabouya, who had deserted in 1915.[51] The French press, on the other hand, sporadically published African soldiers' letters, demonstrating their loyalty to *civilisation française*.[52] After the war, with Germany staging a massive propaganda campaign against the stationing of African troops in the French occupational zone in the Rhineland, a lot of African soldiers' autobiographical writings were published in France in order to demonstrate these soldiers' loyalty and progress towards civilisation and the alleged success of the French colonial doctrine of assimilation. Thus, colonial periodicals such as the *Dépêche Coloniale et Maritime*, the *Annales Coloniales* and the *Revue des Troupes Coloniales* as well as writers such as René Trautmann published several letters from African soldiers.[53]

At the same time, the first books about the war in French by African authors appeared. Written by former colonial soldiers, they were, at least implicitly, concerned with the colonial relationship and they tended to stress the superiority of European and especially French civilisation. In 1920, the first novel of an Algerian author appeared in French titled *Ahmed Ben Mostapha: Goumier*.[54] Its author Mohammed Ben Chérif had served as a cavalry officer and become a German prisoner of war in October 1914. The novel was strongly autobiographical. The hero of this first-person narrative is an Algerian officer recruited in 1899 for the French campaign in Morocco, fighting subsequently in the First World War and eventually dying in a German prisoners' camp. In this novel, Ben Chérif stressed the need for modernisation of the Muslim community which he portrays as stagnating through the adoration of its glorious past. His hero seems to have studied French history and literature, but is equally well-versed in his own cultural heritage. He admires French culture, but at the same time is proud of being of nomadic descent. As Seth Graebner argues, Ben Chérif's novel tried to show the Muslims' valour and loyalty towards France in order to back post-war claims for political reform in the North African colonies; it also had the purpose of replying to Boukabouya's propaganda texts.[55]

In 1926, the former Senegalese infantryman Bakary Diallo became the first native African to publish a book in French on his war experience. Entitled *Force-Bonté*, for many French colonialists, these memoirs proved the superiority of France's policy of assimilation over other countries' colonial policies.[56] Diallo's confrontation with European culture had started not in 1914 but already in 1911, when he had volunteered for the *Tirailleurs sénégalais*. On the very day he joined up, he was impressed by the recruitment officer's ability to write: 'The rapidity with which his writing multiplied made me wish to imitate him. This, of course, was not possible immediately; but 'I'll learn later' became my overall resolution.'[57] A few days later, Diallo was punished for scribbling on a freshly painted barrack wall whilst on duty as a sentry.

Force-Bonté unconditionally portrays the French as the Africans' benefactors and models.[58] Diallo even mentions proudly that, when his unit arrived in France in the autumn of 1914, they were greeted by French civilians shouting not only 'Bravo les tirailleurs sénégalais! Vive la France!', but also 'Couper têtes aux allemands.' He interpreted this as a proof of their confidence in the colonial troops rather than reflecting on its imperial connotations.[59] Diallo initially describes himself and his comrades as being on the same level as French children, which is how the Senegalese troops were portrayed by French wartime propaganda. He then narrates his progress towards the higher stages of French civilisation through military service, until he and his friends are completely assimilated into French society and even started dreaming in French. When told that war has broken out and that they are being shipped to France, a '*gaîté enfantine*' (infantile joy), in Diallo's words, seizes them.[60]

In France, his communication was initially much easier with children than with adults.[61] However, Diallo did not consider the infantilisation of the Senegalese as a disadvantage, but rather as an opportunity to be integrated into European cultural life under French guidance. When Diallo made friends with a seven-year-old French girl, his comment was: 'Lucky me. I have a French sister.'[62] Through his little 'sister's' family, Diallo became acquainted with a 'force that would completely dominate my mind' – the 'light of goodness'.[63] The gifts he got at his departure to the front appeared to him as 'dons de ma mère'.[64] While it is not clear whether this story is true – for French officials did everything they could to segregate West African soldiers from civilians in the first half of the war[65] – it is nevertheless the leitmotiv of Diallo's war memoirs: Good mother France takes care of her African children, leading them step by step to a higher stage of civilisation. Diallo explicitly compares his birth family's 'fraternité' to the kindness he experienced in France, which he considered to be superior:

Today, we are heading to the front. I don't want to depart without having said goodbye to the Baudry family ... In the few days I spent in Sète, my soul, rocked by pure tender goodness, has encountered loads of affection hitherto unknown to me. My Senegalese sisters, whom I love so much, haven't excited my sentiments so strongly. Nevertheless, they love me with all the goodness, all the tenderness I ever wished to receive from them. Maybe brotherhood encountered by God's grace is more intensive than innate brotherhood?[66]

At the end of his memoir, Diallo observes a French woman feeding birds in the Parc Monceau in Paris and he comments:

What a beautiful scene! For I think, the birds, it's ourselves, the Black, whilst this lady is France! Grateful birds, you can show your joy to everybody coming here in order to enjoy some fresh air ... In front of your benefactor, this lady with a friendly face and golden blond hair, who cared to bring you some bread, I beg you to shout together with me: *Vive la force-bonté de la France!*[67]

According to Diallo, through the good offices of France and her army, all differences between the French and the Africans as well as between the different African ethnic groups would eventually disappear.[68]

   Diallo's war experience, however, differed from that of many of his comrades in several respects. As he had volunteered for the French army as early as in 1911, he did not experience the forced conscription between 1914 and 1917 that traumatised West African populations.[69] Diallo's front-line experience was not representative either. He was at the front for a relatively short time, in September and October 1914. On 3 November 1914, he was wounded. He was subsequently promoted and awarded an honour for bravery and even got French citizenship in 1920. After the war, he remained in France until 1928. By contrast, the average West African soldier would have been forcibly recruited between 1914 and 1917 and would have spent much longer periods at the front. After the end of the war, he would have been shipped back home immediately, without ever getting French citizenship, remaining a 'sujet' without political rights. Joe Lunn's oral history study illuminates the war experience of a larger, more representative, group of West Africans.[70] Most young West African men were not interested in joining the French army: many tried to hide in the bush or to flee to neighbouring British and Portuguese colonies, and in some cases there was even armed resistance against the French recruitment officers. Once forcibly conscripted and arrived in Europe, West African soldiers often did not become unconditional admirers of the *civilisation française*; rather, they adhered to their religion and tried to overcome the fear of being killed with the help of traditional rites and songs.

In conclusion, if we compare the European soldiers' perceptions of colonial non-white troops with these men's views of Europe and Europeans, it becomes apparent that the writings of each side were often influenced by and reflected the contemporary colonial ideology. European soldiers' representations of colonial troops moved between racism and exoticism, notwithstanding the differences and variations in the texts written by German, French or British soldiers. They reflected the imperialist imagination and at times the pattern of wartime propaganda about the deployment of non-white troops in Europe. Very few metropolitan Allied soldiers would unconditionally accept colonial troops as comrades. On the other hand, the writings of the colonial non-white troops also showed a variety of ways of describing otherness. One variant could be characterised as 'traditionalist', stressing their own cultural and religious background in the face of European modernity. Another – 'assimilationism' – included admiration for European civilisation and a readiness to imbibe and emulate European norms. However, as with racism and exoticism in the European soldiers' writing, there were also many overlaps between traditionalism and assimilationism. A comparison of the two kinds of writing also shows the effects of the asymmetry in the colonial relationship. Taking European superiority for granted, the Europeans felt no immediate need of explicit reflections about themselves and their own cultural and social backgrounds. The colonial non-white soldiers, on the other hand, were always acutely conscious of the Other, constantly reflecting not only about Europe and the Europeans, but at the same time about themselves through comparison and contrast.

NOTES

1 B. Diallo, *Force-Bonté* (Paris: Rieder, 1926), 123. All translations from German and French sources in this chapter are mine unless otherwise stated.
2 See C. Koller, '*Von Wilden aller Rassen niedergemetzelt'. Die Diskussion um die Verwendung von Kolonialtruppen in Europa zwischen Rassismus, Kolonial- und Militärpolitik (1914–1930)* (Stuttgart: Steiner, 2001); Koller, 'Enemy Images: Race and Gender Stereotypes in the Discussion on Colonial Troops – A Franco-German Comparison, 1914–1923', in K. Hagemann and S. Schüler-Springorum (eds.), *Home/Front: The Military, War and Gender in Twentieth-Century Germany* (Oxford/New York: Berg, 2002), 139–57; E. Kettlitz,

Afrikanische Soldaten aus deutscher Sicht seit 1871. Stereotype, Vorurteile, Feindbilder und Rassismus (Frankfurt: Peter Lang, 2007); R. S. Fogarty, *Race and War in France: Colonial Subjects in the French Army, 1914–1918* (Baltimore: Johns Hopkins University Press, 2008).

3 In this chapter, the phrase 'colonial troops' is also used to refer to the colonial non-white troops of the British and French empires.

4 See Koller, *Rassismus* (Paderborn: Ferdinand Schöningh, 2009), 59–64.

5 E. Rosen, *England. Ein Britenspiegel. Schlaglichter aus der Kriegs-, Kultur- und Sittengeschichte* (Stuttgart, 1916), 96 and 98; V. Valois, *Nieder mit England! Betrachtungen und Erwägungen* (Berlin, 1915), 7; R. Borchardt, *Gesammelte Werke in Einzelbänden. Prosa V* (Stuttgart: Klett, 1979), (217–64) 243; L. Dill, 'Die Gefangenenlager bei Merseburg', *Gartenlaube*, 63 (1915), 9; *Ein Dutzend englischer Sünden wider das Völkerrecht. Tatsachen und Feststellungen*, no place, 1916, 5; *Kriegschronik. Kriegstagebuch, Soldatenbriefe, Kriegsbilder* (Berlin: Berg, 1915–17), 48; A. Hoffmann, *Illustrierte Geschichte des Weltkrieges*, vol. v (Stuttgart: Union Deutsche Verlagsgesellschaft, 1916), 307; C. H. Baer (ed.), *Der Völkerkrieg. Eine Chronik der Ereignisse seit dem 1. Juli 1914*, 18 vols. (Stuttgart: Hoffmann, 1914–18), vol. x, 107.

6 *Employment, Contrary to International Law, of Colored Troops upon the European Theatre of War by England and France* (Berlin: Auswärtiges Amt, 1915).

7 See E. Müller-Meiningen, *Der Weltkrieg und das Völkerrecht. Eine Anklage gegen die Kriegführung des Dreiverbandes* (Berlin: Reimer, 1915), 68–9.

8 See T. Theye (ed.), *Wir und die Wilden: Einblicke in eine kannibalische Beziehung* (Reinbek: Rowohlt, 1984); M. Wiener, *Ikonographie des Wilden. Menschenbilder in Ethnographie und Photographie zwischen 1850 und 1918* (Vienna/Munich: Trickster, 1990); H. Gollwitzer, *Die gelbe Gefahr. Geschichte eines Schlagworts – Studien zum imperialistischen Denken* (Göttingen: Vandenhoeck & Ruprecht, 1962); H. W. Koch, *Der Sozialdarwinismus. Seine Genese und sein Einfluss auf das imperialistische Denken* (Munich: Beck, 1973).

9 See G. Krüger, *Kriegsbewältigung und Geschichtsbewusstsein. Realität, Deutung und Verarbeitung des deutschen Kolonialkrieges in Namibia 1904 bis 1907* (Göttingen: Vandenhoeck & Ruprecht, 1999).

10 Baer, *Völkerkrieg*, vol. iii, 217–18.

11 See P. O. Höcker, *An der Spitze meiner Kompagnie. Drei Monate Kriegserlebnisse* (Berlin/Vienna, 1914), 78 and 141.

12 F. Schumann (ed.), *'Zieh dich warm an!' Soldatenpost und Heimatbriefe aus zwei Weltkriegen. Chronik einer Familie* (Berlin: Neues Leben, 1989), 14.

13 R. Dehmel, *Zwischen Volk und Menschheit. Kriegstagebuch* (Berlin: S. Fischer, 1919), 33.

14 Witkop, P. (ed.), *Kriegsbriefe gefallener Studenten*, 4th edition (Munich: Verlag Müller, 1928), 26–7.

15 C. von Einem, *Ein Armeeführer erlebt den Weltkrieg. Persönliche Aufzeichnungen des Generalobersten v. Einem*, ed. J. Alter (Leipzig: Koehler, 1938), 108 and 419.

16 Staatsarchiv Hamburg, 622–1/202, Familie Weidehaas, cited in P. Münch, 'Bürgerliche Kriegserfahrungen im Ersten Weltkrieg. Hamburger Turner

zwischen "Kriegsglaubensbekenntnis" und Verzweiflung im Spiegel ihrer Feldpost' (MA thesis, University of Hamburg, 2007), 89–90.

17 Bundesarchiv-Militärarchiv, Freiburg im Breisgau, MSg 1/799, Briefe vom September 1914.

18 E. Ludendorff, *Meine Kriegserinnerungen, 1914–1918* (Berlin: Mittler, 1919), 206.

19 P. von Hindenburg, *Aus meinem Leben* (Leipzig: Hirzel, 1920), 352.

20 M. Beradt, *Schipper an der Front* (Berlin: S. Fischer, 1929), 97–8.

21 E. Jünger, *In Stahlgewittern. Ein Kriegstagebuch*, 16th edition (Berlin: Mittler, 1926), 155–72.

22 *Ibid.* p. 165.

23 O. M. Hitzfeld, *Ein Infanterist in zwei Weltkriegen. Erinnerungen 1898–1980* (Osnabrück: Biblio, 1983), 11.

24 D. Richert, *Beste Gelegenheit zum Sterben. Meine Erlebnisse im Kriege 1914–1918*, ed. A. Tramitz and B. Ulrich (Munich: Knesebeck & Schuler, 1989), 198. On Richert's memoirs, see I. Schmitz, 'Dominik Richert's First World War Memoirs: The Story of a Last Minute Deserter', *War and Literature*, 11/12 (1994), 17–32; Koller, '"Alsacien, Déserteur!" Die Kriegserfahrung des Elsässer Bauern Dominik Richert im Spiegel seiner Memoiren von 1918/19', *Bios*, 13 (2000), 225–39.

25 Richert, *Beste Gelegenheit zum Sterben*, 133.

26 *Ibid.*, 161–2.

27 *Ibid.*, 70–84.

28 *La Dépêche Coloniale*, 18 August 1914.

29 Cited in M. Michel, *L'appel à l'Afrique. Contributions et réactions à l'effort de guerre en AOF* (Paris: Publications de la Sorbonne, 1982), 345.

30 See G. Boussenot, *La France d'outre-mer participe à la guerre* (Paris: F. Alcan, 1916), 23.

31 A. Séché, 'Les Noirs. "L'âme du Sénégalais"', *L'Opinion*, 8/41 (1915), 286–8.

32 *The Times*, 23 January 1915.

33 See *The Times*, 2 October 1914; 25 October 1914; 28 October 1914; 16 November 1914; 9 February 1915.

34 See, e. g., *The Times*, 28 October 1914.

35 C. J. Balesi, *From Adversaries to Comrades-in-Arms: West Africans and the French Military, 1885–1918* (Waltham: Crossroads Press, 1979), 99.

36 L. Barthas, *Les carnets de guerre de Louis Barthas, tonnelier 1914–1918* (Paris: Maspero, 1997), 21.

37 A. Bishop and M. Bostridge (eds.), *Letters from a Lost Generation: The First World War letters of Vera Brittain and four friends. Roland Leighton, Edward Brittain, Victor Richardson, Geoffrey Thurlow* (London: Little, Brown, 1998), 128.

38 See C. Mangin, 'Troupes noires', *Revue de France*, 16 (1909), 61–80 and 383–98, 'Soldats Noirs en Europe', *Questions Diplomatiques et Coloniales*, 13 (1909), 449–60 and *La Force Noire* (Paris: Hachette 1911).

39 Barthas, *Les carnets de guerre*, 22–3.

40 S. Sassoon, *Diaries 1915–1918* (London: Faber and Faber, 1983), 96.

41 Barthas, *Les carnets de guerre*, 528.

42 J. Vaché, *Quarante-trois lettres de guerre à Jeanne Derrien* (Paris: Place, 1991), no. 19.

43 Barthas, *Les carnets de guerre*, 22.

44 H. Barbusse, *Le Feu. Journal d'une escouade* (Paris: Flammarion, 1916), 48–9.

45 *New York Times*, 18 December 1916.

46 S. C. VanKoski, 'Letters Home, 1915–16. Punjabi Soldiers Reflect on War and Life in Europe and Their Meanings for Home and Self', *International Journal for Punjab Studies*, 2 (1995), 43–63; Christian Koller, 'Überkreuzende Frontlinien? Fremdrepräsentationen in afrikanischen, indischen und europäischen Selbstzeugnissen des Ersten Weltkrieges', *War and Literature*, 6 (2000), 33–57, and 'Krieg, Fremdheitserfahrung und Männlichkeit. Alterität und Identität in Feldpostbriefen indischer Soldaten des Ersten Weltkrieges', in M. Bos *et al.* (eds.), *Erfahrung – Alles nur Diskurs? Zur Verwendung des Erfahrungsbegriffes in der Geschlechtergeschichte* (Zurich: Chronos, 2004), 117–28; D. Omissi, 'Through Indian Eyes. Indian Soldiers Encounter England and France, 1914–1918', *English Historical Review*, 122 (2007), 371–96.

47 D. Omissi (ed.), *Indian Voices of the Great War: Soldiers' Letters, 1914–1918* (Basingstoke: Macmillan, 1999), 104.

48 *Ibid.*, 28–9, 33–4, 39, 44–5, 70, 96–7, 105, 129, 134, 156–7, 166, 210, 218–20, 255, 266, 285.

49 *Ibid.*, 48, 206, 271–2.

50 See Santanu Das's Chapter 3 in this volume.

51 R. A. Boukabouya, *L'Islam dans l'armée française (guerre de 1914–1915)* (Constantinople, 1915); 'Die marokkanischen Kaids unter der französischen Herrschaft', *Korrespondenzblatt der Nachrichtenstelle für den Orient*, 3 (1916), 220–2, 271–3 and 328–30; 'Der General Gourand als Generalresident von Marokko', *Korrespondenzblatt der Nachrichtenstelle für den Orient*, 3 (1916), 419–20; 'Das Protektorat über Marokko. General Lyautey und seine Islampolitik', *Islamische Welt*, 1/3 (1917), 57–8 and 1/4 (1917), 253–4; 'Die "Weissen Väter"', *Islamische Welt*, 1/6 (1917), 352–3; 'Der zukünftige Friede und die algerischen Muslims', *Islamische Welt*, 1/9 (1917), 557–9; *L'Islam dans l'armée française (second fascicule)* (Lausanne, 1917).

52 See *Le Temps*, 20 November 1914.

53 See H. J. Lüsebrink, '"Tirailleurs Sénégalais" und "Schwarze Schande". Verlaufsformen und Konsequenzen einer deutsch-französischen Auseinandersetzung', in J. Riesz and J. Schultz (eds.), *'Tirailleurs sénégalais'. Zur bildlichen und literarischen Darstellung afrikanischer Soldaten im Dienste Frankreichs* (Frankfurt: Peter Lang, 1989), 57–71; R. F. A. Trautmann, *Au pays de 'Batouala'. Noirs et Blancs en Afrique* (Paris: Payot 1922), 53–4 and 58–9.

54 M. B. Chérif, *Ahmed Ben Mostapha. Goumier* (Paris: Payot, 1920).

55 S. Graebner, *History's Place: Nostalgia and the City in French Algerian Literature* (Lanham, MD: Lexington Books, 2007), 130.

56 On Diallo's memoirs, see G. O. Midiohouan, 'Le tirailleur sénégalais du fusil à la plume. La fortune de "Force-Bonté" de Bakary Diallo', in Riesz and Schultz (eds.), *'Tirailleurs sénégalais'*, 133–51; J. Riesz, 'The *Tirailleur Sénégalais* Who

Did Not Want to Be a 'Grand Enfant': Bakary Diallo's *Force Bonté* (1926) Reconsidered', *Research in African Literatures*, 27 (1996), 157–97 and 'Die Probe aufs Exempel. Ein afrikanische Autobiographie als Zivilisations-Experiment', in H. Willems and A. Hahn (eds.), *Identität und Moderne* (Frankfurt: Suhrkamp, 1999), 433–54.

57 Diallo, *Force-Bonté*, 33–4.
58 *Ibid.*, 116–22 and 204–8.
59 *Ibid.*, 113–14.
60 *Ibid.*, 109–10.
61 *Ibid.*, 115.
62 *Ibid.*, 116.
63 *Ibid.*, 117.
64 *Ibid.*, 121.
65 See J. H. Lunn, 'Kande Kamara Speaks: An Oral History of the West African Experience in France 1914–18', in M. E. Page (ed.), *Africa and the First World War* (London: Macmillan, 1987), (28–53) 36–8.
66 Diallo, *Force-Bonté*, 119–20.
67 *Ibid.*, 208.
68 *Ibid.*, 42 and 120.
69 See M. J. Echenberg, 'Paying the Blood Tax: Military conscription in French West Africa 1914–1929', *Canadian Journal of African Studies*, 9 (1975), 171–92; M. Michel, 'Le recrutement des tirailleurs en AOF pendant la première guerre mondiale', *Revue française d'histoire d'outre-mer*, 60 (1973), 645–60.
70 J. H. Lunn, *Memoirs of the Maelstrom: A Senegalese Oral History of the First World War* (Portsmouth, NH: James Currey, 1999). Lunn interviewed 85 Senegalese veterans in 1982–3.

CHAPTER 7

Living apart together: Belgian civilians and non-white troops and workers in wartime Flanders

Dominiek Dendooven

In Belgium, the front line ran for fifty kilometres, from Nieuport on the coast to Ploegsteert on the French–Belgian border. The deadlock here began in October 1914 with the Battle of the Yser and the First Battle of Ypres, and ended on 28 September 1918, when the war of movement finally resumed with the 'Liberation Offensive'.[1] The war-stricken zone was the southern part of the province of West Flanders, a sparsely populated rural backwater better known under its unofficial name Westhoek (West Corner). The front line ran through or near the towns of Nieuport (Nieuwpoort), Dixmude (Diksmuide) and Ypres (Ieper), while Furnes (Veurne) and Poperinghe (Poperinge) formed the backbone of the rear area.[2] These five towns were all small in size – none had more than 17,000 inhabitants – but had a rich cultural heritage. The language spoken in this region was a local dialect, one of the many Flemish versions of Dutch.[3] In September and October 1914, many refugees from the more eastern parts of Belgium arrived here, spurred by the German advance.[4] Some stayed in Flanders' Westhoek; most, however, continued their flight and ended up in France or the United Kingdom. The local inhabitants, who held on in their own region, were marginalised not only by the refugees, but also by thousands of troops. In the Yser area (Nieuport–Dixmude), the majority of the military belonged to the Belgian army, but near Ypres and Poperinghe, it was a multinational and multiracial force that occupied the territory. For the local population, most of whom had never before come into contact with foreigners (except French people), it was a most extraordinary situation which was reflected in their diaries and memoirs, and in subsequent interviews. This chapter considers how these men and women experienced, remembered and represented the colonial troops and non-white labourers, particularly the Chinese, who descended upon this tiny part of the world during and after the First World War.[5]

It is difficult to ascertain a definite figure for the local population because of the lack of a census. Consequently, the exact percentage of the local inhabitants to the total temporary population (refugees and military) is unknown,

but it seems that it could not have been more than 10 to 15 per cent.[6] Some
indication may be provided by the few known figures, such as the births
registered in Roesbrugge-Haringe. In 1913, 55 children were born in this large
village northwest of Poperinge on the river Yser. In 1917, no fewer than 285
babies were born here, of which only 41 were registered as 'children from
inhabitants', the remainder being the offspring of 'strangers and war refugees',
and 70 noted as 'illegitimate children'.[7] It is important, in this context, to
stress the international nature of the military forces present in Flanders.
Recent research has shown that during the First World War and the immediate post-war period, representatives of not less than 55 different cultures,
hailing from the same number of states, were present in this little corner of
unoccupied country.[8] The Belgian, French, British, German, Portuguese
and American armies were all involved in the fighting in Flanders, and the
French and the British brought over troops and labourers from every corner
of their respective empires. In the French army, one would meet Moroccan,
Algerian, Tunisian and West African soldiers, later joined by labourers from
Vietnam and Madagascar. The British sent over troops from its dominions
and colonies, including the smaller constituent parts such as Egypt (Egyptian
Labour Corps), the British West Indies (British West Indies Regiment), the
Fiji Islands (Fijian Labour Corps) and Bermuda. Hired Chinese workers, on
the other hand, served in three armies (the British, French and American).[9]

Wartime diaries, memoirs and subsequent interviews, bequeathed by
the local population of the Westhoek, bear rich testimony to the extraordinary circumstances brought about by the war. Some eyewitness accounts
have been published; others still belong to family collections or are housed
in archives.[10] These documents, in addition to the usual methodological
problems arising from their subjective nature, pose specific linguistic problems. Apart from a minority of documents written in French by either a
French-speaking Belgian or an upper-class Fleming, most documents and
interviews are in the local West Flemish dialect. This dialect is virtually
inaccessible to Dutch speakers unfamiliar with the regional language, and
totally incomprehensible to people who do not have Dutch. Consequently,
this exceptional corpus of sources has remained relatively unknown.[11] The
material can be divided roughly into three main groups. First, there are
the records of educated people who did not originate from the Westhoek
and remained there only briefly, such as the writings of the Belgian army
medical officer Maurice Duwez, the nurse Jane de Launoy (both originally
in French) or the celebrated author Cyriel Buysse (who wrote in Dutch).[12]
The second category comprises the reports and diaries of the clergy who did
not necessarily originate from the Westhoek, but lived there before or after

the war.[13] This group includes the diaries of fathers Van Staten, De Cleyn and Joye of the Abbey of Saint-Sixtus in West-Vleteren, mainly written in Flemish (with a few French–Flemish bilingual texts of De Cleyn). These diaries are still preserved in the abbey, but some fragments have been published. The most remarkable and exhaustive account of life behind the front in Flanders is, however, the diary of Achiel Van Walleghem, parish priest of Dikkebus near Ypres. The third and final group comprises accounts by ordinary people – local uneducated Flemings – conveyed to us through post-war interviews conducted in 1970s and in the late 1990s.[14] These various sources together open up the world of the inhabitants behind the front line, and provide insights into the local perception of the non-white workers and troops.

WARTIME WRITINGS OF JANE DE LAUNOY
AND MAURICE DUWEZ

Unlike the inhabitants of the major cities in Great Britain or France, in 1914 the majority of Belgians had never before laid their eyes on a person of a different race. Consequently, an intense curiosity and sense of amazement at the presence of the colonial troops is common to the memoirs of both Jane de Launoy and Maurice Duwez. Both were well-educated, though their experiences of the war were very different.

Jane de Launoy (1881–1953) was the daughter of a Brussels physician and one of the very few graduate nurses in Belgium at the time. During the war, she mainly served in the Red Cross hospital l'Océan in De Panne and her memoir was published in 1937.[15] The memoir is haunted by the presence of the colonial soldiers, particularly the North Africans, whom she met frequently around Christmas Day 1914. Her vivid, almost hallucinatory, descriptions invest the troops with an orientalist romance:

A desert picture! A black dune appears against the backlight where the sun sets. Behind it the sky takes on a fiery red hue. At the top of the dune the silhouette of an Arab stands out. He seems to be walking through fire. He raises his arms . . . kneels, . . . stands up . . . kneels again. It is the Muslim's prayer to Allah. (23 December 1914)[16]

A day later, she writes: 'Arabic fantasy [feigned attack] on the beach. At least fifty horses in a row launch into full gallop in successive waves. Their lively coloured uniforms make it fabulously picturesque.'[17] A strong visual imagination pervades the writing: curiosity, excitement and exoticism are combined in these descriptions, as the Arab troops are turned into objects of far-away romance. But romance is coexistent with racist fears, as the Arab is also portrayed as a brute who murders fellow patients. She recalls a night shift in the hospital when a German patient is brought in and moved into a room with other convalescing soldiers, including an Arab: 'He looks at him, he looks at us and says, while nodding his burning eyes: "You can leave him here, tomorrow he will no longer be." We had to put him somewhere else. Another Arab goes through his pockets and asks: "You want nose of Hun?"'[18] Fact and fiction are closely blended in this 'memoir'. De Launoy fully subscribes to the racist ideas of the day, according to which, ironically, the enemies (German) are less threatening than the non-white allies. Her views about the colonial troops resonate deeply with the opinion of Marie Beck who ran a café and bakery on the French-Belgian border during the war years. In an interview in 1967, she described the *spahis* (indigenous North African light cavalry serving in the French army) as 'beautiful to watch' but stated that 'they howled when they attacked, they were savages'.[19] Like De Launoy's, some of her 'anecdotes' strain at the limits of credibility, but provide fascinating insights into contemporary prejudices and fantasies about the colonial troops. In the interview, she recalled how once a *spahi* extended his arm from underneath his red coat to reveal a wire and 'there were four or five human ears attached to this wire'.[20]

In the memoir, issues of race are often associated with anxieties around gender and sexuality. De Launoy is at once fascinated and repelled by her Arab patients. She describes hearing stories from the Arabs about how they sell women in their country: 'a palm tree for an ugly woman . . . a camel for a beautiful one'.[21] And yet the diary also reveals traces of erotic interest:

For the past few nights a beautiful Goumier has asked me for coffee at one o'clock in the morning. Shrouded in his *burnous* he enters from outdoors and comes up into my office. I am not easily unnerved but when this large devil with his damned seductive eyes appeared before me I was not at ease. He enjoyed his coffee, muttered a few words and looked at me like a sacred object, incomprehensibly taboo![22]

This is a remarkable moment for a nursing memoir: De Launoy feels at once attracted towards and threatened by the 'beautiful Goumier'. According to her, 'he looks at me like an intruder';[23] similarly, Marie Beck notes about the *spahis*, 'Their eyes popped whenever they saw a woman'.[24] However De Launoy does not leap into racial generalisations from individual encounters. Even if she feels that her privacy is being invaded by this particular man, she concedes that 'in general Muslims have a great deal of respect for women in uniform': 'If you come across such a Goumier in a two-metre wide corridor he will press himself against the wall, his arms outstretched, to let you pass.'

This display of courtesy and chivalry flatters De Launoy: 'Belgians should follow their example,' she writes on 29 December 1914.[25] Thus, the racist discourse of the Arab as murderer is interrupted and modified not only by admission of the Goumier's positive attributes but also by active advice to fellow Belgians to adopt the foreigners' practices.

Maurice Duwez (published under the pseudonym Max Deauville, 1881–1966) served in the Belgian army, first as regimental doctor of the Carabiniers and later as medical officer of a Grenadiers battalion. A man of considerable literary talent, he published no less than five books of war reminiscences, and his importance as a witness was highly appreciated by Jean Norton Cru.[26] Duwez comments on the 'strange mixture of races', including 'Arabs and Jews with tanned skin, black beard and the profile of an eagle', but he is particularly fascinated by the tall Wolofs in Kaaskerke near Dixmude:

Long, thin, lanky and smiling Senegalese are on their way stepping like storks. They are exceedingly tall and their long neck protruding from a collar carries a small round head wearing a fez. They wear a short ultramarine jacket and baggy pants. They march barefoot and carry their boots in their hand.[27]

Duwez often uses animal and bird imagery to portray the African troops: their graceful gait is described in subhuman terms. But just as de Launoy's racist assumptions coexist with her occasional admiration for the Arabs, Duwez's descriptions are layered with deep sympathy as he observes the Senegalese pass 'carrying their comrades on their backs': their feet are frozen, they suffer dreadfully and 'thick tears run down their faded cheeks'.[28] This combination of racism and sympathy was shared by Jozef Gesquière who worked as a primary schoolteacher in his thirties in Furnes during the war years and went on to become the headmaster soon after the war ended. In his extensive daily war notes, later assembled into a full-length narrative, he wrote thus of the colonial soldiers:

There are about eight hundred of them. On their heads they wear a red fez with a black tassel. With their tanned faces, their jet-black hair, black moustache and eyebrows, they look quite scary. They are looked at with a degree of fear. And yet they smile at the bystanders in a friendly manner and the fear soon dwindles away. Indeed, they have come to help liberate our country. Poor boys! So far from their home country. How many will never see it again?[29]

The account captures the contradictory emotions these soldiers aroused: they are at once objects of fear and pity. All three commentators share the racist prejudices of the Belgian society at the time, but there is sympathy for the colonial troops as well.

ACCOUNTS OF THE LOCAL CLERGY: THE
DIARIES OF FATHER VAN WALLEGHEM

The contemporary records of the clergy provide some of the fullest accounts
of life behind the front during the war years. The racial diversity of the Allied
troops astonished many clergymen. Father Joye of the Abbey of Saint-Sixtus,
near Westvleteren, noted on 5 September 1917: 'Today I see the first Chinese
in their blue linen costumes ... from India I have already seen men; from
Australia, from Spain, from Algiers, from Scotland wearing skirts, from
Ireland, from Transvaal. There is also one from Russia here.'[30] The large
multiethnic presence in the Westhoek made some of the clergymen feel the
urge to convert these men. Jos Brutsaert, acting parish priest of Rousbrugge,
was one such cleric. After the war, he reported to the Bishop of Bruges how
in September 1917 he realised that there were 'negroes from the island of
Madagascar' quartered at Bombeek, around six kilometres from Rousbrugge,
and how he used to visit them to instruct them in 'European civilisation' and
in the 'Christian religion' three or four times a week.[31] The priest was partly
successful; in October 1917, no fewer than forty Madagascans aged between
18 and 43 were baptised. In his report, he noted that the French officers
were 'exceedingly satisfied' with the 'boys' who had followed 'the lessons in
European civilisation', and that they were 'zealous and obedient'.[32] However,
only a handful seem to have converted to Christianity: most of the troops
kept their own faith.

The most important of these accounts is the remarkable diary of Father
Achiel Van Walleghem. This Catholic priest, 35 years old in 1914, was
appointed to the parish of Dickebusch (now spelled Dikkebus), a mere
5 kilometres west of Ypres. Forced by the continuous bombardments in the
summer of 1915, he moved another 4 kilometres westward to Reninghelst,
though he maintained his daily visits to Dickebusch. He kept up this routine
until 18 April 1918, when the imminent German offensive finally forced him
to go into exile to Rouen, only to return to a devastated Dickebusch in May
1919. Van Walleghem died in 1955, deaf, lonely and suffering from amnesia.
The diary he left behind is the most exhaustive, complete and insightful
document produced by any local inhabitant from war-stricken Flanders
during the First World War. It comprises 1,240 handwritten pages in thirteen
notebooks, with extensive daily entries from 4 October 1914 to 23 April 1918,
and is written in the local dialect.[33] As a priest, Van Walleghem was interested in all aspects of life behind the front line but, apart from the fate of the
local population, he was particularly interested in the non-white troops and
workers.

Van Walleghem was no exception to the contemporary racial prejudices but what distinguishes the diary is his intense curiosity about and detailed engagement with the colonial troops. He provides detailed descriptions of the troops, often with helpful dates. On 22 October 1914, he notes that 'Indian troops arrive to reinforce ... At night the motorbuses of the English pass with Indian troops,' while on 9 December 1914, he records the massive influx of French colonial troops, commenting on the 'Zouaves with their wide red puffy pants' and the *tirailleurs algériens*, with their semi-black appearance, grey puffy pants and cape'.[34] During the Second Battle of Ypres, he observes that 'many Indians as well pass Ouderdom and are billeted in the farms of Maerten, Lievens and Desmarets' (24 April 1915).[35] Even today, the grandson of the farmer Maerten, still occupying the farm, is able to point out the barn in which the Indians had their field hospital. On 10 January 1918, Van Walleghem notes in his diary that 'the negroes from West India have left some days ago'.[36] Such details are helpful but the accounts usually go beyond such factual information into subjective opinions. In his view, the tirailleurs algériens are 'half-wild' and 'they could not be left alone for any period of time'; the Senegalese, on the other hand, are 'courageous and fearless' but are afraid of the sound of guns since, 'according to their superstition, being disfigured by a shell will prevent them from going to heaven' (30 December 1914).[37] It is this careful distinction between the different colonial troops or other racial groups and their perceived habits that makes the diary remarkable.

Consider the following two extracts from his diaries:

Various Indian troops are present in the parish, mostly near Vlamertinghe ... They have a dark skin, are dressed like English soldiers except for their head which is skilfully wrapped in a turban. They speak English and some also speak French, they are very curious, ask many questions and are very interested. They will walk for half an hour to find milk, they observe everything while they are being served, are very distrustful yet cannot be trusted themselves, and if they can somehow manage to run away without paying they will do so ... On the whole they are friendly and polite, yet they can't repress their curiosity and will inspect you from head to toe and are particularly fond of looking through windows. They bake a kind of pancake and also eat a kind of seed with a very strong taste. (6 June 1915)[38]

Negroes (from West India and Jamaica) have arrived to work at the farm of Alouis Adriaen and Drie Goên. They are dressed like English soldiers, are civilised, speak very softly, but they are not much liked because of their sticky fingers, and on the whole the civilians prefer to see the back of them, because when they enter a place for a cup of coffee they can stay anything from five minutes to a couple of hours. (P.S.: I have found a letter written by the mother of one of those blacks. What sincere, Christian and motherly feelings! None of our mothers could write better.) These blacks are terribly frightened by the bombardments. They stare in fear and bewilderment when they hear a shell arriving, and if it drops not too far away, they all flee as if possessed. (26 May 1917)[39]

Both accounts modulate from visual impressions to a detailed analysis of habits and practices, The two groups are carefully differentiated: while the Indians 'cannot be trusted' and can 'run away without paying', the West Indians have 'sticky fingers' and linger unnecessarily in the cafés. Van Walleghem's diary entries are an invaluable guide to the contemporary local perceptions and racist prejudices surrounding the colonial troops. As a priest, Van Walleghem lived in the vicarage, traditionally one of the largest houses in the village. There is little doubt that Van Walleghem regularly listened in on British and French officers, often chaplains, who had been quartered in his house.[40]

However, it was not the Indian or West Indian troops but the Chinese workers who bore the brunt of racist prejudices: 'They are strange fellows and have very childish manners, no better than our 10–11-year-old boys. Yellow of colour, with a flat nose and oblique eyes, they have nearly constantly a foolish grin on their face' (6 August 1917).[41] At the same time, Van Walleghem admits that they are industrious people, working 'as hard as our civilians or as the English soldiers'. When he returns to the ruins of Dickebusch after the war, he employs a party of Chinese labourers for half a week to clear a boys' school of debris and convert it into a 'second church, without windows and with just half a roof' (May–June 1919).[42] Earlier, on Christmas Day 1917, he records the rowdy behaviour of New Zealand troops who 'drink and pour and shout and scream and dispute and search for troubles with the Chinese. The latter become embittered, conspire, and in the afternoon and evening there is fighting in several places. Such wild fellows!' He goes on to report the next day that 'several Chinese who fought with the New Zealanders were executed this morning on Zwarteberg. Is it true? It seems so.' The disturbances in the Chinese camp at Reninghelst are also mentioned by other authors, including Captain J. C. Dunn in his memoirs.[43] Van Walleghem's account of this conflict seems accurate, as it is substantiated not only by an official report of IX Corps and the war diary of signaller David Doe but also by three Chinese graves at Westoutre British Cemetery, just a stone's throw from Zwarteberg.[44]

CHANGING POST-WAR ATTITUDES, ESPECIALLY TOWARDS THE CHINESE LABOUR CORPS

Some of the racial groups including the Chinese Labour Corps and the Indian Labour Corps remained in Flanders for more than a year after the end of hostilities. Opinions of the Belgians on these men were divided and changed considerably during and after the war. In relation to no group was this change in local public opinion greater than over the Chinese labourers. The attitude of the Belgian civilians towards the 'coolies' during the actual war years was moderately favourable, and the 'coolies' could even count on a certain amount of their sympathy. In one late interview, Jeanne Battheu[45] from Poperinge constantly speaks of the Chinese as 'poor fellows' because of their illiteracy and the harsh treatment they received from their British officers.[46] However, this sympathy disappeared after the end of the war, and public opinion completely turned against them.

While Father Van Walleghem in his diary on 6 August 1917 had commented on their great capacity for hard work, Laura Lannoote, representing a post-war generation, noted in an interview: 'They were strange guys, conspicuously dressed, with strange eating habits and a strange language. The only thing they were not able to do was to work.'[47] Some returned refugees always carried a gun 'to defend themselves against the chinks, if necessary'.[48] Many local people believed that gangs of Chinese men, armed with the easily found grenades and guns, wandered in the area. Even Van Walleghem seemed to have changed his opinion: in July 1919, he notes rather cryptically that 'some 350 men [are] back [in Dickebusch]' and 'that the area was made unsafe by all kinds of strange people: front wreckers and especially the Chinese'.[49] The few remaining British officers were supposed to have lost their authority over these men: according to Van Walleghem, in early June 1919 Jules Bailleul, who lived in an area called the Canada, was raided in his house; while he was fleeing, he was shot, and died some weeks later.[50] Stories about armed raids, murders and rapes by Chinese labourers were (and are even now) told. Louis Garrein,[51] who returned to Zillebeke in 1920, described the remaining 'Tsjings' (Chinese) as 'dangerous lads' and recalled how at night they burgled the people living in wooden huts: 'in Houthem they tried to break into the premises of a tobacco cutter. The latter grasped a rifle and shot through the door. One of the Tsjings died on site, the other was able to escape.'[52] Similarly, Gabriëlla Vanpeteghem from Dranouter remembered that the Chinese who had remained after the war to clear the battlefields were objects of fear.[53] They were apparently escorted by British soldiers every five metres, and all the windows of the house they lived in were closed to prevent them from getting out. She further noted: 'Although it was claimed that Tsjings were unable to use weapons, they fired all sorts of rifles and ammunition they found at the front. During the day people were even afraid to go outdoors, and they waited until the evening when [the Chinese] had left. The first girl to be buried in Ypres after the war had been shot by Tsjings on the Kemmel Road.'[54]

While these writings and interviews perhaps testify to a certain degree of violence and misdemeanour on the part of the Chinese workers, it is difficult to separate racist assumptions and stories from memories of actual events. Though the accounts of the murder of Jules Bailleul in Dickebusch, mentioned by Van Walleghem,[55] and the killing of the Ypres girl, mentioned by Vanpeteghem,[56] seem to be based on fact, many of the Chinese horror stories were rumours. In the nearly lawless situation at the former front line right after the war, when the nearest police station was tens of kilometres away and when the few inhabitants who had already returned lived in pillboxes or hastily built wooden huts, the Chinese were ideal scapegoats for unsolved crimes. Moreover, there was xenophobia among the former refugees who returned to a completely devastated area having lost everything and now saw all these foreign men wandering around in their homeland. At the same time, more objective sources such as newspaper articles and other reports bear witness to the degrading behaviour of some of the men from the Chinese Labour Corps. This behaviour can partly be explained by the facts that weapons were indeed readily available, a police force was still lacking and the Chinese felt betrayed by their British employers who had promised them a quick return home after the war.

On the whole, it appears that actual meetings between Belgian citizens and colonial troops or non-white workers were rare. This was mainly due to the politics of segregation as well as the language barrier. Moreover, because of social taboos, some topics are not mentioned in the personal documents, such as the relations between Flemish women and colonial troops (similarly, very little information is available on sexual relations between Flemish women and soldiers of European origin). Moreover, as the number of local witness accounts on a particular racial group is limited, it is difficult to judge how far these stories can be considered as representative of the whole Flemish population at and behind the front. But at the same time, the above evidence suggests that the different racial groups were differentiated by the local people. For example, the attitudes of the Flemish population towards the Indian Labour Corps were largely positive: they felt relieved when the Chinese coolies were finally replaced by Indian labourers. 'In September 1919 the Chinese departed and were replaced by Hindus; the Hindus were somewhat curious and loved to go about and see everywhere, but they were not mean' is Van Walleghem's final comment on the Chinese.[57] While the Indians or the West Indians were understood through existing, if racist, frameworks of knowledge, the Chinese labourers seemed to have defied comprehension. In 1919, Cyriel Buysse described the Chinese workers in classic racist terms, referring to their 'slanting eyes', 'monkey faces' and 'inscrutable smile upon their wooden mugs'.[58] Such words suggest the failure of the local people to understand or relate to the Chinese labourers, resulting in the racist myths about the Chinese workers that haunt the collective memory of the Westhoek of Belgian Flanders even today.

An account by Cyriel Buysse powerfully demonstrates the tense atmosphere of post-war Belgium, exposing the deep links between misunderstanding, wartime terror and racist xenophobia. After over four years of exile the author, having returned to his home in Deurle (ten kilometres south of Ghent), went on a cycle ride to Brussels in March 1919. As he cycled back in the evening, he fell into the water with his bicycle from a blown-up bridge over the river Scheldt, and a farmer came to his help. When Buysse moaned that the situation was dreadful, the farmer warned him of 'far worse things'. In the moonlight, he led Buysse to his farm, and with 'eyes filled with terror', the farmer and his wife opened a closed hatch:

Through a small square-framed window a wonderful spectacle unfolds before my eyes on an inner courtyard.

A milling of men with brown faces, in khaki uniforms and with red chéchias (skullcaps) on their heads, around a flickering wood fire. They are humming and smiling: some of them are dancing in a strange manner, whereas others are playing small musical instruments. Their white teeth and the whites of their eyes are brightly illuminated by the moon: it's an encampment of Moroccan tirailleurs ...

'Are they doing any harm?' I ask, highly interested in the spectacle.

'No Sir, but we are terribly afraid of them. And they don't understand us. When we ask them when they intend to leave, they laugh at us. We daren't even go to bed, sir!'

The farmer closes the hatch with trembling fingers, and I go towards the soldiers through a rear door. Without too much trouble they tell me that they will stay just two more days, and I hasten to bring these glad tidings to the farmer and his wife. They bless me as it were. They grasp both my hands and appear to want to hold on to me.

'We were scared of the Germans, sir,' hiccupped the woman, 'but at least they were human.'[59]

Dread of the racial 'Other', fanned by wartime anxiety, is here stronger than political hostility: the German enemies are perceived to be less menacing than the Moroccan allies who had come to fight for Belgium. The Belgian couple and the Moroccan *tirailleurs* live in the same farm but they are worlds apart.

NOTES

1 The Liberation Offensive is the name given in Belgium to that part of the Final Offensive in which occupied Belgium was liberated. The offensive started on 28 September 1918 and was stopped by the declaration of Armistice on 11 November 1918. See M. Weemaes, *De l'Yser à Bruxelles: offensive libératrice de l'armée belge le 28 septembre 1918* (Brussels: Impr. P. François, 1969).

2 I have used the French names here, as this is how these towns would be known
   to the British (and the French) then and now. However, the recent official
   Dutch version is shown in brackets.

3 P. Chielens, D. Dendooven and H. Decoodt (eds.), *De Laatste Getuige. Het
   Oorlogslandschap van Vlaanderen* (The Last Witness. The War Landscape of
   Flanders) (Tielt: Lannoo, 2006), 12–85. This book, as yet unpublished in
   English, offers an overview of the First World War in Flanders, with the
   landscape as a starting point.

4 M. Amara, *Strangers in a Strange Land: Belgian Refugees 1914–1918* (Leuven,
   Davidsfonds, 2004), 7–36, and M. Amara, *Des Belges à l'épreuve de l'exil. Les
   réfugiés de la Première Guerre mondiale (France, Grande-Bretagne, Pays-bas)
   1914–1918* (Brussels: Université Libre de Bruxelles, 2007), 405. The latter is the
   first in-depth study of the Belgian refugees of the First World War.

5 The phrase 'colonial troops' in this chapter refers to the colonial non-white
   troops of the British and French empires.

6 This is a very rough estimate, based on a wide range of sources, such as the
   reports written by local priests immediately after the war (Bischoppelijk Archief
   Brugge, Verslagen 1914–1918), as well as a comparison of the sizes of military
   units compared to local population figures. For example, at the end of 1914 in
   the district of Furnes, the local population was just 25,000 while 18,822 refugees
   were counted. Moreover, Furnes was home to the headquarters of the Belgian
   army, which at that time comprised 6 divisions, each of between 16,000 and
   24,000 men. See A. Vandenbilcke and P. Chielens, 'Vluchten voor de Oorlog',
   in Chielens *et al.* (eds.), *De Laatste Getuige*, 75.

7 Quoted in J. Gheysens, 'Roesbrugge-Haringe: zijn belang in het geheel van
   wereldoorlog 1914–1918', *Aan de Schreve*, 3 (1973), 30.

8 D. Dendooven and P. Chielens (eds.), *World War I: Five Continents in Flanders*
   (Tielt: Lannoo, 2008).

9 An extensive overview is given in *ibid.*, 23–144.

10 The documentation centre of the In Flanders Fields Museum in Ypres, Belgium
    is particularly rich in Belgian witness accounts.

11 All translations in this chapter are mine unless otherwise stated. I have tried to
    adhere as closely as possible to the original French, Dutch or West Flemish.

12 Buysse stayed in the Netherlands during the war, but the quoted extracts are
    from works he wrote on a visit to the front and about the immediate post-war
    period, specifically about 1919.

13 After the war, every village priest in the West Flemish front region was required
    to submit a report to the Bishop of Bruges.

14 In the 1970s, young people from the Ypres front region set up the Eleventh of
    November Group (Elfnovembergroep) and conducted taped and detailed inter-
    views with senior fellow villagers on civilian and military life in Flanders during
    the First World War. A selection were published as *Volksboek Van den Grooten
    Oorlog* (*Chapbook of the Great War*) (Kemmel: Malegijs, 1978). A second, more
    limited, interview project took place towards the end of the nineties when three
    local volunteers recorded a total of 29 conversations with senior citizens who

had been children during the conflict. The results were published in 2001 under the title 'Getuigen van de Grote Oorlog' ('Witnesses of the Great War'). It is possible that time has occasionally touched up memories, but very often these witness accounts are the only information we have on certain aspects of the war.

15 Jane De Launoy, *Infirmières de guerre en service commandé (Front de 14 à 18)* (Brussels: L'Edition universelle, 1937). A recent Dutch translation is Jane De Launoy, *Oorlogsverpleegsters in bevolen dienst 1914–1918* (Ghent: Snoeck-Ducaju and Zoon, 2001). My translation is from the original French edition.

16 Jane De Launoy, *Infirmières*, 60–1.

17 *Ibid.*, 61.

18 *Ibid.*, 63.

19 Interview of Marie Beck with her nephew Jan Hardeman in 1967. Hardeman noted that the interviewer hardly asked any questions: the interview had the character of a spontaneous conversation. The original tape of the interview as well as a digital copy is kept in the documentation centre of In Flanders Fields Museum. Excerpts from the interview were included in Elfnovembergroep, *Volksboek*, 384.

20 Elfnovembergroep, *Volksboek*, 130.

21 Jane De Launoy, *Infirmières*, 63.

22 *Ibid.*, 63.

23 *Ibid.*

24 Elfnovembergroep, *Volksboek*, 130.

25 Jane De Launoy, *Infirmières*, 64

26 Jean Norton Cru, *Témoins. Essai d'analyse et de critique des souvenirs de combat-tants édités en Français de 1915 à 1928* (Paris: Les Etincelles, 1929), 118–19.

27 Max Deauville, *Jusqu'à l'Yser* (Brussels: Les Editions Rex, 1934), vol.1, 221.

28 *Ibid.*, 229–30.

29 Jozef Gesquière, *Veurne tijdens de Wereldoorlog 1914–1918* (Bruges: Genootschap voor Geschiedenis, 1979), 67.

30 V. Van Staten, L.-M. De Cleyn and E. Joye, *De Abdij-Kazerne Sint-Sixtus 1914–1918. Dagboekaantekeningen* (Poperinge: Aan de Schreve, 2001), 143.

31 Bischoppelijk Archief Brugge, Verslagen 1914–1918 [Bishopric (Bishop's palace) Archives, Bruges, Reports 1914–1918].

32 *Ibid.*

33 These notebooks are still the property of the Van Walleghem family, but are kept in the documentation centre of the In Flanders Fields Museum in Ypres, Belgium. The diary was published in three volumes in the 1960s: Achiel Van Walleghem, *De Oorlog te Dickebusch en omstreken 1914–1918* (Bruges: Genootschap voor Geschiedenis, 1964–7): vol. I (25 July 1914 – 31 December 1915) in 1964; vol. II (1 January 1916 – 21 July 1917) in 1965 and vol. III (22 July 1917 – 1920) in 1967.

34 Van Walleghem, *De Oorlog*, vol. I, 54.

35 *Ibid.*, 109.

36 Van Walleghem, *De Oorlog*, vol. III, 92.

37 *Ibid.*, vol. I, 63.

38 *Ibid.*, 134–5.

39 *Ibid.*, vol. II, 206–7

40 In addition to occasional references to officers in his diary, there is a photograph of Van Walleghem among French and British officers, published in Francis S. J. Irwin, *Stonyhurst War Record: A Memorial of the Part Taken by Stonyhurst Men in the Great War* (Clitheroe: Stonyhurst College, 1927), 442.

41 Van Walleghem, *De Oorlog*, vol. III, 16–18.

42 *Ibid.*, 140.

43 Captain J. C. Dunn, *The War the Infantry Knew* (London: Cardinal Sphere, 1987), 425–6.

44 Report quoted in P. Chielens and J. Putkowski *Unquiet Graves: Execution Sites of the First World War in Flanders* (London: Francis Boutle, 2000), 27–8; David Doe, 'Diary', Imperial War Museum, London, 12171 P326; Row BB, graves 1, 2 and 3 of Chinese labourers Wu Enlu, Zhang Zhide and Zhang Hong'an, dated 25 December 1917, Westoutre British Cemetery, Westouter, Belgium. There are two other graves of the same date in Bailleul Communal Cemetery Extension, Bailleul, France: those of Su Fengshan and Nie Xinghuang, who had originally been buried in Reninghelst Chinese Cemetery, Reningelst, Belgium.

45 Jeanne Battheu (1910–2001) first visited Talbot House in Poperinghe in December 1916. As a Poperinghe resident, she remained a frequent visitor to this famous soldiers' club up until her death, often acting in the latter years as an interviewee on childhood during the First World War.

46 Gwynnie Hagen, 'Eenen dwazen glimlach aan het front', unpublished Master's dissertation, Catholic University of Louvain, 1997, 82.

47 *De Boezingenaar*, June 1993. The account given by Laura Lannoote was recorded by Georges Smagghe in 1993 for the 'village newspaper' of Boezinge and was part of a larger series in which elderly villagers told their life stories. The recording is lost – probably deleted after the publication of the interview. Laura Lannoote was born in Houtem near Ypres in 1904. Between the wars, she worked in a factory in Halluin before settling in Boezinge where she was the landlady of the Café de Sultan. She died at a home for the elderly in Comines on an unknown date.

48 J. Vandemaele and G. Coudron, *Zillebeke, verdoken dorp in de glooiingen van de natuur* (Rekkem: Jomale, 1974), 187.

49 Van Walleghem, *De Oorlog*, vol. III, 142.

50 *Ibid.*

51 Louis Garrein was born in 1906, the son of a small farmer in Zillebeke near Ypres. The family fled early in the war, returning only in 1920. Between the wars, he set up a thriving local trade in coal, beer and other drinks which he continued until his retirement, becoming a well-known figure in the village. He died in 1999.

52 Koen Dumoulin, Steven Vansteenkiste and Jan Verdoodt (eds.), *Getuigen van de Grote Oorlog. Getuigenissen uit de frontstreek* (Koksijde: De Klaproos, 2001), 121.

53 Gabriëlla Vanpeteghem was born in 1908 into a farming family in Dranouter, a Belgian village a few kilometres from the French border town of Bailleul. In 1931, she married a farmer from Zillebeke and settled in that village. She died on 8 June 2002 in Ypres.

54 Quoted in Dumoulin, Vansteenkiste and Verdoodt (eds.), *Getuigen*, 145.

55 Van Walleghem, who only returned to Dickebusch some weeks later, had the date slightly wrong. The national newspaper *Het Nieuws van den Dag* mentioned the hold-up of Jules Bailleul and his family on 12 May 1919, adding the following day: 'It was Chinese coolies, working in these devastated lands, who committed the crime'. Today, Jules Bailleul's name is the last to figure on the local war memorial in Dickebusch.

56 The first note in the city of Ypres's *Register of Deaths* from July 1919, still in use by the town administration, records the death of 13-year-old Martha Staelens on the Kemmel Road. The fact that the deceased was declared by the Ypres police commissioner indicates a violent death. An article in the local weekly paper *De Poperinghenaar* (27 July 1919) describes the attack on the Staelens family by unknown persons, specifically adding that 'there are many Chinese camps in the neighbourhood'. This might validate Gabriëlla Vanpeteghem's account.

57 Van Walleghem, *De Oorlog*, vol. III, 146.

58 Cyriel Buysse, *Verzameld werk*, vol. VII (Antwerp: Manteau, 1982), 734–5 (originally published as a column *Op wandel in Vlaanderen I* in the Dutch newspaper *Haagse Post*, 19 July 1919), quoted in Joris Van Parys, *Het leven, niets dan het leven. Cyriel Buysse & zijn tijd* (Antwerp: Houtekiet; Amsterdam: Atlas, 2007), 557.

59 Buysse, *Verzameld werk*, vol. VII, 689 (originally published as a column *In de Maneschijn II* in *Haagse Post*, 29 March 1919), quoted in Van Parys. *Het leven*, 557.

CHAPTER 8

Nursing the Other: the representation of colonial troops in French and British First World War nursing memoirs

Alison S. Fell

In the late nineteenth and early twentieth centuries, both French and British commentators began to view white middle-class women as an increasingly important element of the 'civilising mission' of the colonial enterprise. In an 1899 address to the Colonial Nursing Association, Sir George Goldie, governor of the Royal Niger Company, spoke for many when he labelled the work of European nurses in British West African colonies as the 'white woman's burden';[1] a year later, French Jesuit priest Jean-Baptiste Piolet wrote in relation to French colonialism that 'woman is made to civilize and police, to inspire and purify, to elevate and exalt all that surrounds her'.[2] At the same time, the presence of white women in the colonies was seen to be fraught with dangers, especially in terms of the protection of 'white prestige', a central component of imperial discourse. White women in the colonies were expected to conform to an idealised model of sexually pure and morally virtuous femininity and were criticised if they were perceived to have failed to do so – some of the nurses Goldie addressed in 1899, for example, were subsequently accused of improper appearance and sexual impropriety, and requests were made for lady nurses 'of mature years and less attractive appearance'.[3] Further it was equally assumed that their presence left them sexually vulnerable to the 'uncontrolled' sexuality and 'primitive urges' of the colonised men.[4] Thus, despite the enthusiasm amongst some for the potential benefits of the 'civilising' influence of white women, their presence abroad was viewed with suspicion and anxiety, reflecting the extent to which colonial discourse was consistently preoccupied by the fear and fantasy of colonies as sites of sexual abandon and excess.

These anxieties surrounding white femininity in a colonial climate reappeared with a vengeance during the First World War.[5] Prior to 1914, contact had been limited to those who travelled to the colonies and to small communities in large cities such as Paris, Marseilles, Liverpool and London. In contrast, the war years witnessed unprecedented contact between a far wider range and larger percentage of the French and British populations and colonised people of colour. White women of all classes encountered the colonised men called upon to defend the French and British empires – on farms and in factories in France where both women and colonised men replaced men at the front,[6] in towns where troops or workers were stationed, and in hospitals, where sick and injured soldiers were cared for by white nurses. As a result, the colonial 'nightmare' of miscegenation and its consequent damage to white prestige was never far from the surface on both sides of the Channel. In their reproductive function, women were thus seen as both the guarantors of the future of the white race and the source of its possible decline or even downfall. Fears about interracial contact during the First World War resulted in the French authorities' 'vigorous interventions' in an attempt to limit any intimacy between men conscripted from the colonies and French women.[7] Soldiers' letters were read for evidence of 'native relations with French women' and, by the end of the war, both troops and workers from the colonies had had their movements restricted (with varying degrees of success).[8] Lucy Bland and Richard Smith describe a similar press response to the presence of Jamaican volunteers in Britain. In 1917, the weekly *Empire News* called for the creation of separate black districts, out of bounds to local white women who might be tempted by 'free-handed Negroes earning good money'.[9] More generally, in both nations white working-class women were accused of displaying uncontrolled public behaviour and sexual wantonness in their alleged overwillingness to consort with non-white troops or workers.[10]

At the roots of such responses were long-standing anxieties about what Smith calls the 'frailty of white [imperial European] masculinity'; negative qualities were projected onto the subject race in order to bolster the self-image of the male coloniser.[11] In this sense, white women and colonised men were both constructed as Other in wartime Europe, having the potential to disrupt the binary assumptions upon which white imperial masculinity was constructed.[12] Yet while these stereotypes prevalent in the First World War clearly betray the imperialist and patriarchal assumptions that underpin them, it is much more difficult to assess the experiences and attitudes of the flesh-and-blood individuals who were actually involved in encounters between white women and these colonial soldiers – to gain a sense, in other words, of the multifaceted and diverse realities that lay beneath the stereotypes.[13] It is to this end that this chapter will consider the representation of non-white soldiers who came from French and British colonies in the letters and memoirs of the usually middle- or upper-class women who worked as nurses, an aspect of their writings which has hitherto received little critical attention.[14] This class distinction is doubly significant: it determined the cultural and official responses to nurses' encounters with colonised men, which differed somewhat from the out-and-out attacks on working-class women's sexual morality; equally, it shaped the nurses' own attitudes to the men as articulated in their autobiographical writings.

On the one hand, nurses' letters and memoirs are deeply marked by dominant gender and imperialist discourses: the colonised soldier appears as an infantilised and loyal 'simpleton soldier', as an exotic ethnographic 'type', or as a bloodthirsty and sexualised 'savage native' who is being looked after by the maternal 'white angel', the benevolent civiliser, or, occasionally, the romantic heroine. At times, however, encounters with Indian, West Indian and African soldiers provoke strong and unexpected responses from nurse-narrators who were often interacting for the first time with non-white men from the colonies. The otherness of the encounter was further height-ened by the potentially intimate setting of a hospital ward. I will argue in this chapter that while some nurse-narrators simply reproduce the existing colonial clichés in their autobiographical texts, others express a fascination with the colonial soldiers' bodies and cultural habits that goes far beyond their official status as 'white angels'. Furthermore, in the case of nurses who spent extended periods of time interacting with their colonial patients, their response sometimes suggests that their experiences led them to question racist and imperialist assumptions. I will begin my discussion by examining populist and propagandistic representations of white nurses and colonial soldiers during the war, before turning to a more detailed consideration of selected letters and memoirs written by the nurses.

WHITE NURSES AND COLONIAL SOLDIERS: CONTEXTS AND CONTROVERSIES

Despite the racial prejudice evident in the attitudes of both the military authorities and wider populations in France and Britain, it was vital that more positive images of colonial men also be produced and circulated in order to boost and justify their recruitment, bolster morale on the home fronts, and allay fears. Thus, in France, ideas of the supposedly innate 'savagery' of the *tirailleurs sénégalais* were combined with notions of their naïve loyalty to the empire and childlike delight in the trappings of civilisation. But the interest for the French consumers of these images was often stimulated by the extent to which the domestication of colonial soldiers was always implied to be superficial. Their savagery could reappear in battle; their 'animal' sexual lust remained just beneath the surface. Thus, even in the patriotic representations of French *tirailleurs*, *spahis* or *goumiers* as loyal, brave and/or essentially childlike, tensions remained, arguably reflecting the inherent instability of the white European masculinity through which such images were filtered.

In January 1915, the populist French weekly *L'Illustration* published Joseph Simont's illustration featuring two nurses giving a present to a wounded *tirailleur* (Figure 4). Simont's drawing contains the key elements of the discourse propagated during the war in France concerning both nurses and colonial soldiers. The soldier's passive and vulnerable position as a bedridden patient and his pleasure in his gift contribute to the widespread construction of the soldier as a 'grand enfant'. Equally, the caption 'Y a bon' (It good), an expression widely associated with West African French troops, also embodied the new stereotype of an infantilised 'simpleton soldier'. Mimicking the pidgin French that the soldiers were taught, it was made famous as the slogan used from 1915 to advertise the Banania drink made from banana flour, ground cereal, cacao and sugar; in adverts, the slogan was accompanied by a grinning *tirailleur*, an image which was reproduced on everything from food products to postcards.[15] In contrast, the smiling benevolence of the nurses positions them as maternal 'white angels', icons of feminine virtue. By 1914, the nurse had become the ultimate female role model for middle-class women seeking a patriotic role in wartime Europe. Nursing in France had traditionally been carried out by nuns, and wartime propaganda and Red Cross recruitment material deliberately played on this tradition, offering a vision of patriotic and sanctified womanhood that appealed to both Republican and Catholic sectors of French society.[16] The stereotypes that appear in Simont's illustration are typical of similar propaganda images produced during the war years. In such images, as Blanchard and Deroo note, 'the African ... becomes a "big child", no longer frightening, that must be led towards adulthood, towards civilization'.[17] In this case, it is the First World War nurse, possessing the qualities of a chaste, maternal and patriotic 'white angel', who is at the forefront of this 'civilising mission'.

Yet despite the widespread circulation of these reassuring stereotypes, the reality of white French women nursing African troops provoked criticism. An example of the controversy surrounding the relationship can be found in the text *Les Noirs* (1919) by Alphonse Séché, a French officer who

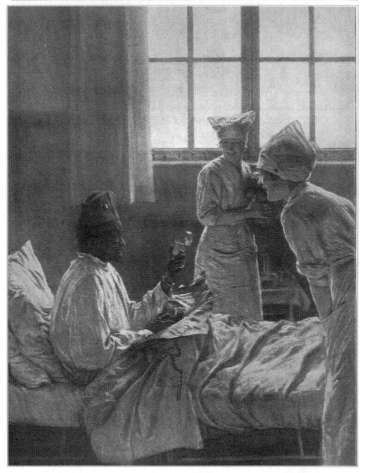

Ce numéro contient en supplément la feuille Sud-Est de la CARTE DU THÉÂTRE OCCIDENTAL DE LA GUERRE EUROPÉENNE.

L'ILLUSTRATION

Prix du Numéro : Un Franc.   SAMEDI 9 JANVIER 1915   73ᵉ Année. — Nᵒ 3749.

« Y A BON ! »
Keletiki Taraoré, qui a donné son sang pour la France, reçoit ses étrennes.
Dessiné d'après nature, par J. SIMONT, dans un hôpital parisien.

4. J. Simont, '"Y a bon": Keletiki Taraoré, qui a donné son sang pour la France, reçoit ses étrennes' ['It good': Keletiki Taraoré, who gave his blood for France, receives his present].

commanded West African troops during the war. In his chapter entitled 'Two hospitals for the Senegalese', the nurses take on a maternal role, keen to 'spoil' their new exotic patients/children. Rather than shoring up this stereotype, however, Séché is keen to point out the dangers of such a nurse–patient relationship, and praises instead the policy of sending troops to establishments in Marseilles and Menton where they were cared for by male army personnel only.[18] For Séché, a vital part of the care of the *tirailleurs* is what he terms their 'resenegalisation', where a medical cure takes place alongside a 'moral' cure, ridding the conscripts of the 'pretensions and arrogance' allegedly accrued during their time in France. Comparing the Red Cross hospital 223 in Marseilles with the military hospital 52 in Menton, run exclusively by men, Séché concludes that:

> The question of nurses caring for *tirailleurs* is ... more complex than it first appears. One cannot treat natives as one treats French troops. Women are making the mistake of insufficiently differentiating between the two ... They are ruled too much by their emotions ... They soften the Senegalese soldier, making him vain and undisciplined ... They are, by their very presence, an obstacle to the cure of 'resenegalisation'.[19]

Thus, while the Simont image testifies to the circulation of positive (albeit imperialist and paternalistic) discursive stereotypes in France, Séché's text points to the underlying fears surrounding the contact between nurses and their African patients. Séché's book aims to reassure its readers that the army had taken steps to guard against the possible negative consequences of interracial mixing. Indeed, in 1915 the military health authorities warned its nurses not to be too 'generous', and not to share in any 'regrettable endearments' with, or to give any photographs to their colonial patients.[20] And as I note above, segregated hospitals for Senegalese soldiers were established by military authorities in the south of France from 1915 onwards, to be staffed by male employees.[21] These directives suggest that French nurses' sexual morality was a common cause for concern among officials and commentators, even if there is scant evidence to suggest this was often warranted.[22] The view of nurses as potentially sexually promiscuous helps to explain the presence of fictional representations, often in newspapers, magazines and popular novels, of nurses as romantic heroines or as glamorous and trivial *mondaines* (society girls).[23] These figures also appear in humorous postcards depicting flirtatious scenes between Senegalese soldiers and their nurses, or with their *marraines* (female pen pals of First World War soldiers).[24] However, although these postcards are potentially subversive in their allusions to interracial sex, in such images the *tirailleur* suitor often has one arm bandaged, and the status of the romantic relationship is thus undermined.[25] While playing on the notion of the vaudeville-like couple of the 'black' soldier-suitor and 'flirtatious' French lady, then, the images also contain a number of props that function to reassure their consumers that an actual sexual liaison, while acceptable material for wartime caricature, lay outside the realms of the possible.

Despite the more positive images presented in Britain of the subject races as brave warriors, the prospect of encounters between Indian and West Indian troops and white British women provoked as much anxiety as it had in France, if not more, and these fears were particularly evident in attitudes to nursing. The image of the 'lady nurse' in Britain, first created by the myth of Florence Nightingale's 'Lady of the Lamp', was instrumentalised to great effect in the First World War, producing the icon of a self-abnegating, devoted and virginal nurse.[26] This image was enhanced by the international outcry that took place after the 1915 execution of Edith Cavell and by the subsequent hagiographic propaganda that surrounded her. Any suggestion of intimacy between nurses and colonial patients was therefore unthinkable. In May 1915, the *Daily Mail* published a picture of an English nurse standing behind a wounded Indian soldier. The photograph caused a scandal – even though the two had been only brought together for the benefit of the photographer as women did not nurse Indian soldiers in that particular hospital.[27] While the official position of the British government was not to base decisions upon race, after the publication of the photograph the Army Council attempted to remove white nurses from the hospitals in Britain that were admitting wounded Indian soldiers.[28] Further, within these hospitals (situated first in Southampton, and then in Brighton and Brockenhurst),[29] Indian patients were not permitted to leave the hospital precincts unless accompanied by male white British personnel. As in France, the fear was that any contact between the Indian convalescents and the civilian population could be subversive in terms of colonial power structures. Sir Walter Lawrence, the commissioner for the Welfare of Indian Troops, echoes Sèche in his concerns that the high standard of treatment received by Indian soldiers in hospital risked encouraging ideas about racial equality, potentially undermining white rule in India: 'as a result of the kindness shown them in hospitals their discipline has gone and they suffer from "swollen head" badly'.[30] Anxieties also surrounded the physical intimacy involved in the act of nursing. An article on the Lady Hardinge Hospital in Brockenhurst that appeared in the *British Journal of Nursing* in 1915, for example, follows the official line, clearly stating that: 'The charge of each sister is 50 beds, 25 in each ward, the two being separated by a corridor.

Their duties consist principally of supervision, and they have two English orderlies working under them – and there are also native servants.' In this way, any potential anxieties about interracial intimacy are anticipated and allayed.[31]

Although at various stages the authorities in both France and Britain attempted to prevent contact between white nurses and African, Indian or West Indian conscripts and volunteers, the nature of the health system during the First World War meant that their efforts were only partially successful. Indeed, it is almost a generic convention of published French nursing memoirs to have a chapter on the nurse's experiences of caring for North or West African troops, and magazines often featured articles about the 'novelty' African patients for white French nurses.[32] Similarly, while there were only a few cases of white British nurses caring for Indian patients in Britain, there was more frequent contact between British nurses who went further afield – to France, to hospital trains and hospital ships, and to other fronts – and conscripts or volunteers from both French and British colonies.

NURSE MEMOIRS

There were more encounters between French and British nurses and the colonial soldiers than the authorities either wanted or anticipated. This was inevitable in a situation in which the thousands of colonial troops who were sick or wounded were bound at some stage to come into contact with the thousands of French and British nurses who worked (on either a professional or a volunteer basis) in the dressing stations and temporary hospitals that were established in schools, hotels and other converted buildings. But how did the French and British nurses themselves feel about nursing colonial troops? Here I explore a wide variety of writing – archival material as well as published letters, diaries and memoirs – to show the range of responses, from a rehearsal of well-worn racial stereotypes to more personalised and nuanced accounts that challenge these dominant tropes.[33]

Examples of negative stereotypes of colonial soldiers, and particularly French African troops, can be found in several letters and memoirs published by nurses during the early stages of the conflict. A highly coloured propagandistic French nurse memoir that appeared in 1915 evokes the myths of African savagery and cannibalism (although the nurse-narrator suggests, as did French propagandists, that these qualities are being positively channelled for the greater good of fighting to save French/Western civilisation). As she carries out her ward round, she cites a loyal Senegalese soldier who, she claims, declares to her that when he sees a German he cries 'You savage! Me serve noble France ... son of France ... Long live France! Me want cut off your head! You hurt France! France civilised, Germany barbaric!'[34] In an account that appeared in the form of a 1915 letter published in the *British Journal of Nursing* Edla R. Wortabet,[35] a British nurse who ran a private hospital in Dieppe, reproduces myths of savagery and voices her evident disapproval at the erosion of 'distinctions' between troops:

It was strange seeing Algerians, and jet black Senegalese sharing alike with the French and Belgian wounded the gorgeous bedsteads in the highly decorated reception rooms, now turned into wards. It is nice of the French to do it, and to treat all their soldiers on the same footing, but one wonders whether the British plan of giving the Indian troops their separate hospitals, and meeting their customs and requirements, is not wiser and more comfortable for both sides. One gigantic Senegalese admitted that in his country they kill their enemies and eat them.[36]

Wortabet clearly feels that Indian and African troops should be exclusively cared for in segregated hospitals by army or 'native' personnel.

It is true that in general terms French nurse-narrators responded more positively to the prospect of nursing colonial troops, wholeheartedly adopting the paternalistic cliché of the brave 'simpleton' African soldier, than the British nurses, whose testimony at times manifests openly racist attitudes. Complaints, for example, occasionally appear in letters to the Edinburgh Committee of the Scottish Women's Hospitals from women working for the Scottish Women's Hospital in Rouaumont. A Miss Stevenson, who stayed for less than a month in 1918, commented that 'anyone who has lived in the East knows well that it is not fitting for white women to wait on natives (men) in practice as they are even less ready than the West for Christianity, and it will only retard matters by lowering the prestige of the white woman'.[37] The reference to the men's 'unreadiness' for Christianity is an interesting one: many trained nurses were inspired by a religious interpretation of their vocation (the British nurses Edla Wortabet and Kate Luard that I refer to were both daughters of clergymen), and some appear to have seen their encounters with non-Christian patients as opportunities for conversion: as an extension, in other words, of missionary work.[38] Volunteer nurses such as Miss Stevenson, however, concurred with the widespread view that any interaction between white nurses and 'natives' was potentially damaging to the goals of Christian imperialism.

Other British nurses, however, appear to delight in the 'novelty' of nursing ethnically diverse patients. Jessie Laurie from the Edinburgh Committee replied to Dr Elizabeth Courtauld at Rouaumont in 1916 that it was 'quite amusing to hear of your warm reception from your nigger patients! They must be quite refreshing to have anything to do with.'[39] This paternalism (or perhaps maternalism) is equally evident in the frequent use of the possessive pronoun by nurse-narrators when discussing their colonial patients. Nurse Alison Mullineaux's diary, for example, consistently refers to a favourite patient as 'my big old Senegalese' and 'my great big Senegalese', and a letter from a British woman nursing Jamaican troops in Alexandria declares 'I do love my darkies'.[40] The nurses' confident appropriation of their African and West Indian patients in this way stands in stark contrast to the lack of authority they experienced in their daily working lives. A strict hierarchy operated in wartime hospitals, at the top of which were the doctors whose orders were never to be questioned. It is clear from nurses' autobiographical writings that some women (and particularly British middle- or upper-class volunteers whose wealth and status meant that in their civilian lives they were not used to silently acquiescing to orders) found the limitations of their roles frustrating. In their encounters with colonised men, whom they often infantilised or objectified, these women were permitted to exercise an authority based upon their supposed superiority as white women – an opportunity some evidently relished.

Their confidence in relation to the colonised men they nursed is also evident in the frequent use in their letters and memoirs of a quasi-ethnographic voice, categorising their colonial patients into national, racial or ethnic 'types' for the benefit of their readers. Lady D'Abernon,[41] a British aristocrat who worked as an anaesthetist in France and Italy during the war, records in her medical notes the characteristics of her patients according to a vague set of ethnic parameters. She talks, for example, of 'usual African difficulties' when describing her patients' responses to treatment, and sometimes offers comparisons between different groups:

July 29 [1916]. 5 Maroccans [sic]. Of these patients none understood anything said to them. They were immensely strong men excepting of the last. My usual induction with closed E. failed. Gave Eth Chl. Followed by E. Much trouble with them but ultimately successful with all. With the exception of the pleural fistula case, which was much wasted, the men were of remarkably fine physique. They compare very favourably with Algerians.[42]

Many French nurse memoirs too adopt the voice of a pseudo-ethnographer, recording extensive details of the physical characteristics, dress, religious habits and customs of their authors' African and Indian patients in a manner reminiscent of colonial travel writing. Geneviève Duhamelet, for example, records in her lively semi-fictionalised account of her experiences as a professional nurse in a hospital close to the front, published in 1917, her fascination with the characteristics of a group of Senegalese and Sudanese soldiers: 'They had glossy black skin, milk-white teeth, woolly hair, arranged in an elaborate style of separated tufts. On their cheeks were regular scars apparently indicating their tribe, village and family. Beneath their French soldiers' uniforms many wore [...] their grigris, their fet- ishes.'[43] Another interesting account is contained in a 1914 journal pub- lished by Mme Emmanuel Colombel who, along with her wealthy mother, raised funds for and set up a Red Cross hospital in a former convent in Arras. She describes a wounded Moroccan soldier as 'being particularly muscular, a "handsome chap", one might say ... During the operation, which was very painful, not a word of complaint from him. His large sad eyes didn't move, his expression remained impassive. They have great courage. The officer who brought him said to me "They fight like lions, but without any discipline. War and pillage is all they know."'[44] The nurse is clearly fascinated by the physical appearance as well as the behaviour of the Moroccan soldier, and her experiences and description appear to contra- dict the ready stereotype given to her by the officer, suggesting instead qualities of quiet courage and endurance.

While, then, nurses often voice the colonial myths they have accepted as ethnographic or scientific fact, the extent to which they dwell on the otherness of the bodies and habits of their patients sometimes leads them to question common myths and stereotypes. Their fascination with and objectification of their patients' bodies, moreover, clearly clashes with the supposedly chaste and maternal gaze of the 'white angel'. It is telling that the only white men whose bodies are discussed in similar terms in French nursing memoirs are the tattooed working-class 'Apaches' (members of Parisian criminal gangs) – young men whose otherness was equally thrill- ingly 'exotic', and who could similarly be easily categorised as 'inferior'. More generally, no doubt keen to refute the rumours that had been circulating in the popular press that romantic/sexual liaisons were common amongst nurses and their patients, and to underline their professional detachment, French nurse-narrators refer to the white men they nursed in terms of their wounds or illnesses.

As I suggest above, the texts written by nurses who had prolonged contact with colonial troops are the ones most likely to question or reject colonial stereotypes in favour of more individualised and nuanced representations. A British memoir published anonymously in 1915 by Kate Luard, an experi- enced military nurse who had worked in the Boer War before nursing

Indian troops on hospital trains in 1914–15, manifests a shift towards greater individualisation and understanding, despite the continued dominance of a confident colonial voice.[45] Early in her text she expresses her frustration at the inability of her Indian patients to articulate their needs and symptoms – 'The badly wounded Indians are such pathetic babies, just as inarticulate to us and crying as if it was a crèche'[46] – and attempts brief characterisations according to 'type' – 'The Sikhs are rather whiney patients and very hard to please, but the little Gurkhas are absolute stoics and the Bengal Lancers, who are Mohammedans, are splendid (57)'. Later, however, she reveals a greater awareness of the potential barriers created by both linguistic and cultural difference:

Three of my sitting-up Indians have temperatures of 104, so you can imagine what the lying-downs are like. They are very anxious cases to look after, partly because they are another race and partly because they can't explain their wants, and they seem to want to be let die quietly in a corner rather than fall in with your notions of their comfort. (88)

A particularly telling episode concerns her encounter with an Indian soldier 'with a S.A. ribbon [who] spotted mine and said "Africa same as you"' (67). Subsequently, Luard expresses a new-found respect for the patients she has tended to infantilise. This is illustrated in the text in the way this episode is followed by a critique of the cold conditions that Indian soldiers had had to face over the Christmas period, showing respect for their bravery and offering a less positive assessment of the military authorities that had added to their suffering by deploying them during the winter months.

French nurses, whilst not producing overtly politicised texts (which would, in any case, have been subject to censorship), also occasionally attack colonial myths and the treatment of African recruits. Thérèse Soulacroix, a patriotic middle-aged nurse who dedicates her 1917 memoirs to her grandson so that he 'might understand the heroism of his people', for example, is nevertheless keen to dispel the common misconceptions of her readers: 'So many things are said about [black Africans]! . . . Apparently they leave a terrible smell behind them, they have bags filled with horrors . . . and they are dangerous for young and pretty women . . .' In contrast, Soulacroix claims that her black patients are 'charming . . . as soft as lambs, not demanding, always happy'. She concludes 'one mustn't laugh at their black faces – they are sacrificing their blood and their lives for the glory of white faces', implicitly criticising racist assumptions on the part of her readers.[47] Another interesting example can be found in the semi-fictionalised memoirs of Madeleine Clemenceau Jacquemaire, the daughter of the French prime minister.[48] Her post-war memoir *Les Hommes de bonne volonté* (1919) is more hard-hitting than most, concentrating on the difficult conditions and heart-wrenching dilemmas faced by nurses who are asked to help heal soldiers only to send them back to the front. One chapter offers a tragic account of the death of Kissis-a-Daouddah, a named Senegalese soldier (unlike many memoirs that merely provide the vague appellation 'tirailleur'). She describes in admiring tones his beauty and dignity when facing death:

> His skin was chestnut brown, very dark and shiny, like the wood of old furniture polished by generations of good housewives, and the damp purple cloth that crowned his head was arranged in such an original way that it was clear that the black soldier had redone the normal bandaging provided by the dressing station in his own fashion . . . A human being could not have more dignity than did this bare naked soldier.[49]

This description is ethnographic in tone, albeit positive and even sexualised in its admiration of the soldier's body. However, what is unusual is the final comment on his fate: 'Kissis will die and man loses his beauty before his life. He will die, in this climate so fatal for his race, for those who defeated his parents and annexed their territory.'[50] Here, Clemenceau Jacquemaire voices the irony of the fate of French African soldiers, who risked their lives for their colonisers in return for very little political or financial reward.

Nurses' autobiographical texts are not to be taken as 'truth' in relation to the 'lies' of pro-war propaganda. Rather, they record what happened when white French and British women encountered the flesh-and-blood equivalents of the stereotypes of colonised men they had seen in magazine illustrations or perhaps read about in novels and travel narratives. As we have seen, in some cases they simply realigned the real-life encounters to fit in with their preconceptions and slipped into available vocabularies or colonial clichés. In other cases, their conceptions were modified, if not transformed. There were a few rare cases when interaction between white women and men conscripted from colonies went further than working side by side or commercial (including sexual) transactions. David Omissi and Richard Fogarty both note cases of marriages between French women and Indian or Indochinese soldiers.[51] Lucie Cousturier, an artist who lived in the South of France near to where *tirailleurs* were stationed, became a campaigner for their rights and travelled to Africa after having her own misconceptions and prejudices rectified.[52] But the majority of nurses' texts reveal more ambiguous attitudes, simultaneously mirroring and revealing the limitations of dominant stereotypes of both nurses and colonial soldiers.

NOTES

1 D. Burkett, 'The "White Woman's Burden" in the "White Man's Grave": The Introduction of British Nurses in Colonial West Africa', in N. Chaudhuri and M. Strobel (eds.), *Western Women and Imperialism: Complicity and Resistance* (Bloomington: Indiana University Press, 1992), 179 (177–91).

2 J.-B. Piolet, *La France hors de la France: Notre emigration, sa nécessité, ses conditions* (Paris: Félix Alcan, 1900), quoted in M.-P. Ha, 'Portrait of the Young Woman as a Coloniale', in M. Evans (ed.), *Empire and Culture: The French Experience 1830–1940* (Basingstoke: Palgrave, 2004), 170 (161–81).

3 Quoted in Burkett, 'The "White Woman's Burden"', 182.

4 A. L. Stoler, *Carnal Knowledge and Imperial Power: Race and the Intimate in Colonial Rule* (Berkeley: University of California Press, 2002), 58.

5 See L. Bland, 'White Women and Men of Colour: Miscegenation Fears in Britain after the Great War', *Gender and History* 17 (2005), 29–61; A. Melzer, 'Spectacles and Sexualities: The "Mise-en-Scène" of the "Tirailleur Sénégalais" on the Western Front, 1914–1920', in B. Melman (ed.), *Borderlines: Genders and Identities in War and Peace 1870–1930* (London: Routledge: 1998), 213–45.

6 See T. Stovall, 'Colour-blind France: Colonial Workers during the First World War', *Race and Class* 35:2 (1999), 35–55; J. Horne, 'Immigrant Workers in France during World War I', *French Historical Studies* 14:1 (1985), 57–88; R. S. Fogarty, 'Race, Sex, Fear and Loathing in France during the Great War', *Historical Reflections* 34:1 (2008), 50–72.

7 T. Stovall, 'Love, Labor, and Race: Colonial Men and White Women in France during the Great War', in T. Stovall and G. Van den Abeele (eds.), *French Civilization and Its Discontents: Nationalism, Colonialism, Race* (Lanham, MD: Lexington, 2003), 298 (297–323).

8 Stovall, 'Love, Labor, and Race', 310.

9 *The Times*, 3 July 1917, p. 5, quoted in Bland, 'White Women and Men of Colour', 34; *Empire News*, 12 August 1917, quoted in R. Smith, *Jamaican Volunteers in the First World War* (Manchester University Press, 2004), 114.

10 See P. Levine, *Prostitution, Race and Politics: Policing Venereal Disease in the British Empire* (London: Routledge, 2003), 147; Melzer, 'Spectacles and Sexualities'; A. Woollacott, '"Khaki Fever" and Its Control: Gender, Class, Age and Sexual Morality on the British Homefront in the First World War', *Journal of Contemporary History* 29:2 (1994), 325–47.

11 Smith, *Jamaican Volunteers*, 25.

12 L. Rice, 'African Conscripts/European Conflicts: Race, Memory and the Lessons of War', *Cultural Critique* 45 (2000), 123 (109–45).

13 The term 'colonial' soldiers in this chapter, as elsewhere in this book, refers to the non-white troops from the British and French empires.

14 On British First World War nursing memoirs, see S. Das, 'The Impotence of Sympathy: Touch and Trauma in the Memoirs of First World War Nurses', *Textual Practice* 19:2 (2005), 239–62; S. Das, *Touch and Intimacy in First World War Literature* (Cambridge University Press, 2005); C. Hallett, *Containing*

Trauma: Nursing Work in the First World War (Manchester University Press, 2010); M. Higonnet, *Nurses at the Front: Writing the Wounds of War* (Boston: Northeastern University Press, 2001); S. Ouditt, *Fighting Forces, Writing Women: Identity and Ideology in the First World War* (London: Routledge, 1994); A. K. Smith, *The Second Battlefield: Women, Modernism and the First World War* (Manchester University Press, 2000). On French First World War nurse memoirs see R. Amossy, 'La femme comme témoin de guerre: les récits des infirmières de 1914–1918', in F. Chevillot and A. Norris (eds.), *Des femmes écrivent la guerre* (Paris: Editions complicités, 2007), 17–34; M. Darrow, 'French Volunteer Nursing and the Myth of War Experience in World War I', *American Historical Review* 101:1 (1996), 80–106; M. Darrow, *French Women and the First World War* (Oxford: Berg, 2000); A. S. Fell, 'Fallen Angels? The Red Cross Nurse in French First World War Discourse', in M. Allison and Y. Rocheron (eds.), *The Resilient Female Body: Health and Malaise in Twentieth-Century France* (Oxford: Peter Lang, 2007), 33–51. However, none of these literary/historical analyses discuss nurses' representations of colonial troops in any detail.

15 Rice, 'African Conscripts', 122.
16 See Darrow, 'French Volunteer Nursing'; Fell, 'Fallen Angels', 35–40.
17 P. Blanchard and E. Deroo, 'Du Sauvage au Bon Noir: Le sens de l'image dans six représentations du tirailleur sénégalais', *Quasimodo* 6 (2000), 169 (167–71) (this and all further translations are my own).
18 From winter 1915–16, the French army implemented a policy of *hivernage*, whereby Africans spent five months in the South of France (November to March). As Sèche shows, in Marseilles and on the Côte d'Azur there existed both segregated hospitals, run by the army, in which troops were cared for by male personnel, and several hospitals run by various charitable associations under the umbrella of the French Red Cross, in which the soldiers were cared for by white French nurses. See M. Michel, *L'Appel à l'Afrique 1914–1918: Les Africains et la Grande Guerre* (Paris: Karthala, 2003), 113–16. African soldiers would also have been cared for by white French nurses in the dressing stations and hospitals nearer to the front.
19 A. Sèche, *Les Noirs, d'après des documents officiels* (Paris: Payot, 1919). Individual chapters were published from 1915 onwards in the magazine *L'Opinion*. The chapter on the Senegalese hospitals in Marseilles and Menton is available online at www.1914–1918.be/service_sante_senegalais.php. Accessed 18 February 2008.
20 See Michel, *L'Appel*, 123.
21 See Michel, *L'Appel*, 114–23; Stovall, 'Love, Labor and Race', 313.
22 This was also true for other First World War nurses; for example, at the 34th Welsh General Hospital at Deolali, India, where Australian Army nurses were accused by a male English doctor of 'immoral behaviour' with Turkish and Indian soldiers, charges which were later shown to be false. See R. Rae, 'Reading between Unwritten Lines: Australian Army nurses in India 1916–19', *Journal of the Australian War Memorial* 36 (2002). Available online at www.awm.gov.auk/journal.j36/nurses.htm. Accessed 19 March 2008.

23 See P. Bazantay, 'Guerre et amour dans le roman français du XXe siècle', in F. Rouquet, F. Virgili and D. Voldman (eds.), *Amours, guerres et sexualité* (Paris: Gallimard, 2007), 108–15.

24 For examples of these postcards see P. Blanchard and L. Gervereau (eds.), *Images et colonies: Iconographie et propagande coloniale sur l'Afrique française de 1880 à 1962* (Paris: Editions Syros-Achac, 1993).

25 See L. Barbizet-Namer, 'Ombres et lumières portées sur les Africains: peintures, gravures, illustrations, cartes postales', in *Images et colonies*, 95 (91–6).

26 Representations of Voluntary Aid Detachments (VADs) in recruitment material, however, designed to appeal to patriotic middle- and upper-class British women, tended to emphasise their role as 'modern women' and played on the possibility of foreign travel. See Ouditt, *Fighting Forces, Writing Women*, 16.

27 J. Greenhut, 'Race, Sex and War: The Impact of Race and Sex on Morale and Health Services for the Indian Corps on the Western Front, 1914', *Military Affairs*, 45:2 (1981), 71–4.

28 The Army Council did not succeed in removing all women from the British segregated hospitals. In addition, Indian troops were cared for by French and British nurses in the dressing stations and hospitals on the Western Front before being sent back (if necessary) for further treatment in Britain. See Greenhut, 'Race, Sex and War'.

29 See D. Omissi, 'Europe through Indian Eyes: Indian Soldiers Encounter England and France, 1914–1918', *English Historical Review* 122:496 (2007), 371–96 (376–7).

30 Lawrence to Kitchener, 8 March 1916, quoted in Omissi, 'Europe through Indian Eyes', 378.

31 Anon., 'The Lady Hardinge Hospital, Brockenhurst', *British Journal of Nursing*, 6 March 1915, 185.

32 For examples of French nursing memoirs including chapters on African soldiers see M. de la Boulaye, *Croix et cocarde* (Paris: Plon, 1919); Geneviève Duhamelet, *Ces dames de l'hôpital 336* (Paris: Albin Michel, 1917); Jeanne de Launoy, *Infirmières de guerre en service commandé* (Brussels: L'Edition universelle, 1936); José Roussel-Lépine, *Une ambulance de gare: croquis des premiers jours de guerre (août 1914)* (Paris: Plon, 1916).

33 I would like to thank Ann Fell for her research into the backgrounds of the British nurses.

34 J. Leune, *Tels qu'ils sont: Notes d'une infirmière de la Croix-Rouge* (Paris: Larousse, 1915), 51.

35 Edla Ralouka Wortabet (c.1863–1940) was of Armenian origin. Before 1914 Edla lived in England as a British citizen and trained in several hospitals and nursing homes both in England and abroad (France and Syria). She wrote *Nursing for Eastern Nurses*, which was translated into Arabic, and was a regular contributor to the *British Journal of Nursing*. Her firm opinions about the hierarchies of nursing are matched by a strong imperialist belief in the hierarchy of races, evident in her letter when nursing for the French Nursing Service in 1915.

36 E. R. Wortabet, 'Dieppe', *British Journal of Nursing*, 24 April 1915, 343–4.

37 Unclassified letter dated 12 June 1918, Tin 42, Mitchell Library, Glasgow, Scottish Women's Hospital Collection.

38 In French memoirs published by Catholic nurses, there is usually a chapter on the deathbed conversion of a non-believing patient. See for example M. Eydoux-Démians, *Notes d'une infirmière 1914* (Paris: Plon, 1915).

39 Unclassified letter dated 26 September 1916, Tin 11, Mitchell Library, Glasgow, Scottish Women's Hospital Collection.

40 Alison S. Mullineaux, 'Diary', Imperial War Museum (hereafter IWM), 78/36/1; letter from Susie Joy published in *The Gleaner*, 10 May 1916.

41 Before 1914, the aristocratic Lady Helen Venetia d'Abernon (1865–1954) and her husband Sir Edgar Vincent (1st Baron D'Abernon of Esher) were at the centre of London's social life. She was famously beautiful, and there is a 1904 portrait of her by John Singer Sargent. Childless, she worked as an anaesthetist with Red Cross hospitals in the First World War. She boasted that she had never lost a patient in 1,137 operations.

42 Lady D'Abernon, IWM, 92/22/1.

43 Duhamelet, *Ces dames de l'hôpital 336*, p. 225.

44 E. Colombel (pseudonym of J. Taillandier), *Journal d'une infirmière d'Arras Août–Septembre–Octobre 1914* (Paris: Bloud et Gay), 1916, 82.

45 Kate Evelyn Luard trained in London in the 1890s, and served in the Queen Alexandra's Imperial Military Nursing Service Reserve (QAIMNSR) in the Boer War. She then held senior positions in several hospitals before going to France in 1914. She received the Royal Red Cross Medal in 1916, and a bar in 1919, and was twice mentioned in despatches. Unlike many professional First World War nurses, she praised the work of VADs (in a 1922 letter to the *British Journal of Nursing*). In addition to the anonymous diary, she published *Unknown Warriors*, a collection of further diary extracts, in 1930.

46 Anon. [Kate Luard], *Diary of a Nursing Sister on the Western Front 1914–15* (London: William Blackwood & Sons, 1915), 53. Page numbers of further references are placed after quotations.

47 T. Soulacroix, *Notes de guerre et d'ambulance* (Paris: P. Lethielleux, 1917), 126–9.

48 Madeleine Clemenceau Jacquemaire (1870–1949) was the daughter of Georges Clemenceau (1841–1929) and his American wife Mary Plummer (1850–1923). She joined the French Red Cross in 1914 in Bordeaux, where she was living with her father. See J.-B. Durosell, *Clemenceau* (Paris: Fayard, 1988), 360–6.

49 M. Clemenceau Jacquemaire, *Les Hommes de bonne volonté* (Paris: Calmann-Lévy, 1919), 150–2.

50 Clemenceau Jacquemaire, *Les Hommes*, 166.

51 Omissi, 'Europe through Indian Eyes', 388; Fogarty, 'Race, Sex, Fear and Loathing', 58, 63.

52 L. Cousturier, *Des Inconnus chez moi*, ed. R. Little (Paris: L'Harmattan, 2001).

CHAPTER 9

Imperial captivities: colonial prisoners of war in Germany and the Ottoman empire, 1914–1918

Heather Jones

The First World War resulted in radically new encounters between colonial subjects and the imperial sphere which have only recently become the focus of historical research.[1] Yet one key aspect of this wartime interaction has remained overlooked: how First World War captivity led to new exchanges between African and Asian colonial troops and Europeans. This chapter explores captivity as a site of cultural interaction between African and Asian colonial subjects and white Europeans by juxtaposing two imperial case studies, Wilhelmine Germany and Ottoman Turkey, to see how captivity influenced ideas of 'race' and identity and disrupted existing power hierarchies.

An enormous range of diverse imperial–colonial encounters (that is, interactions between colonial subjects and the imperial sphere) occurred in these two environments. In Germany, this chapter will explore how African and Asian colonial prisoners, captured on the Western Front, encountered German captors, German civilians, and representatives of Germany's Turkish ally, who visited their prison camps, as well as numerous prisoners of war from different ethnicities and nationalities, both non-European and European. In Ottoman-controlled Mesopotamia, this study will show how British and Indian soldiers shared a common captivity during the initial phase of capture following the fall of Kut-el-Amara in 1916, which led them to view each other in new ways as they responded to Turkish captors, as well as Arab and Kurdish guards, and the myriad different civilian ethnic groups of the Ottoman Empire. Taken together, these two captivity histories allow us to draw new conclusions about different wartime understandings of 'race.'

DIFFERENT CONTEXTS: GERMANY
AND OTTOMAN TURKEY

To begin, it is necessary to provide a brief historical overview of the two case studies, starting with Germany. The notion of 'race' was central to how

Germany viewed its African and Asian prisoners, juxtaposing a popular representation of colonial troops as the savage Other on the battlefield, against a propaganda discourse that portrayed Germany as the protector of Islam. Thus German impressions of colonial prisoners depended upon a discursive tension: between the racial Other as the embodiment of uncontrolled violence and the racial Other as ally. This played itself out in an ambivalent German treatment of non-white colonial prisoners, who were both privileged and mistreated during different phases of the war.

We do not have total figures for how many colonial prisoners were held captive or died in Germany. However, during the first half of the war, an attempt was made to centralise all non-white prisoners at a camp at Wünsdorf, near Zossen, which, at its peak, contained some 4,000 colonial captives, mainly Muslims, but also including Sikhs, Hindus and some Christians.[2] Wünsdorf, known as the *Halbmondlager* (the crescent moon camp), was intended as a show camp. It was located beside another propaganda camp at Weinberg for Muslim prisoners from the Russian empire.

In both the Wünsdorf and Weinberg camps, Germany catered for the prisoners' religious and cultural traditions, in particular Islamic practices, in an attempt to convince them to volunteer to fight for Ottoman Turkey.[3] Muslim prisoners were provided with a mosque, halal meat and a propaganda newspaper called *Al-Ǧihād*: there were pan-Islamist and pro-Turkish propaganda lectures. Some prisoners were even taken on a tour of Berlin in September 1915; during the encounter, Berliners reacted 'sympathetically' and the prisoners behaved 'impeccably'.[4] In 1916, the first colonial prisoners from Wünsdorf camp, trained by Germany, were sent to Istanbul as volunteer 'jihadists' for the Ottoman army. In total, 1,084 Arab prisoners and 49 Indians from the camp made this journey, the last volunteers arriving in Turkey in April 1917.[5] Overall, however, this policy was a failure. The Ottoman army did not know what to do with these men and the prisoner-volunteers were unhappy, receiving little food and no pay. A German military doctor stated that the volunteers were beaten and felt betrayed: 'In Germany [...] they had good treatment, good pay and good food. Here they have not been paid; they are left hungry and mistreated. Three of their comrades have already been shot by Turkish officers!'[6] Eventually the volunteers were sent to the Mesopotamian front, via Ras-el-Ain and Baghdad, from where many deserted to British lines. Ironically, British and Indian prisoners of war coming in the other direction after their capture at Kut, encountered these colonial volunteers from Wünsdorf serving with the Ottoman army.[7] A British prisoner, Colonel C. E. Colbeck, spoke with several Algerians who told him that

They had been given very scanty food in Germany but were all well fed and clothed on undertaking to go to serve with the Turks. One Algerian officer [. . .] excused himself by saying that in spite of his having educated himself he could never rise to the same position and rank of a Frenchman and was always considered by them as 'indigene' and inferior whereas in the Turkish army he was as good as anyone else.[8]

Former Wünsdorf prisoners who deserted back to the Allies stated that those who refused to sign up to go to Turkey were sent into special harsh disciplinary units at Wünsdorf and were badly treated.[9] In contrast, those who volunteered received 5 marks a week, 20 cigarettes and better food.[10] One prisoner-volunteer, Binhamed Bey El Hadj, who deserted in Baghdad, stated in an interview after his repatriation to France that he had gone to fight for Ottoman Turkey because of 'the pressure of the propaganda and also [because he] did not want to miss an opportunity to escape'.[11]

Overall, life in Wünsdorf camp was not particularly easy: the camp death rates in October 1915 were 1.2 per cent for Arabs and a very high 16.8 per cent for the Indians.[12] In 1917, Wünsdorf was largely emptied. Of those inmates who had not volunteered for Turkey, some 2,910 colonial prisoners were sent to camps in Romania, a transfer that the German authorities stated was for 'climatic reasons' but which some of the Arab prisoners described as a reprisal.[13] Reprisals were, in fact, not unknown: uncooperative colonial prisoners were sent to secret reprisal camps such as that at Weiler in Alsace, uncovered by the International Committee of the Red Cross in October 1917 after a tip-off.[14] Muslim prisoners who refused to renounce France or Britain were sent here; most were wounded or ill but had been denied access to the neutral medical commissions that selected prisoners in poor health for internment in Switzerland or exchange to their home country.[15] Practically nothing is known regarding the experience of those black, Asian and Arab prisoners in Germany who were held in camps or hospitals other than Wünsdorf.

The colonial–imperial interactions that occurred in Ottoman captivity after the siege of Kut-al-Amara were very different: when Kut fell in April 1916, the Ottoman army captured some 2,678 European British other-rank prisoners (including 13 naval ratings) and 284 British officers; of these 2,962 European British prisoners, 1,782 were later reported dead or were never traced and were presumed dead.[16] Alongside these men, at Kut the Ottoman army captured a large number of colonial soldiers from Britain's territories in India; however, while a separate breakdown of figures is given in the *Statistics of the Military Effort* for Europeans captured at Kut, the only figures in this post-war source for Ottoman captures of Indians relate to the whole of the Mesopotamian campaign: overall, some 10,686 colonial soldiers from India, including 200 Indian Army officers, were captured in Mesopotamia; of these captives, 1,698 other ranks and 10 officers were reported dead and 1,324 were recorded as untraced at the end of the war – 3,032 men in total.[17] A wartime pamphlet published in Delhi estimated that 10,486 Indian other ranks and 222 Indian officers were captured at Kut; other post-war estimates put the figure at 9,300.[18] Thus survival statistics for the Indians captured at Kut remain difficult to verify.

Many prisoner deaths occurred during the brutal forced march north-wards from Kut-al-Amara immediately following their capture, via Baghdad and Mosul, to the railhead at Ras-el-Ain. Three key differences between this experience and the colonial–European encounter in German prison camps must be stated at the outset: first, the levels of violence towards British and Indian prisoners during their first weeks of Ottoman captivity were far higher than those experienced by colonial troops in the German prisoner-of-war camps. Second, Ottoman captivity involved a more complex inversion of representations and power hierarchies: after Kut, British captives perceived both the Indian prisoners who shared their fate and their captors, Ottoman guards, as racially other. The Kut prisoners simultaneously embodied multiple imperial identities: as British soldiers, both European and Asian, they were concomitantly the representatives, and the colonial subjects, of British imperialism, as well as the captive victims of Ottoman Turk imperialist forces. Finally, compared to the German case, there is far less source material available – and that which exists is largely British.

'RACIALISING' THE ENCOUNTER WITH THE COLONIAL PRISONER

The understanding of 'race' was also not the same in the German and Ottoman cases. At the outset of the war, 'race' was a defining cultural paradigm that underpinned the hierarchies of European imperialism.[19] However, it would be an error to define the wartime meaning of 'race' solely in terms of this imperial definition or its later, interwar meanings. In reality, for many Europeans between 1914 and 1918, 'race' meant multiple things – not only biological 'race' but also ethnicity or nationality – and understanding of the term also changed during the war. Within the wartime world-view, not only the non-European or imperial world was defined in terms of racial hierarchies: under the influence of social Darwinism, the different nationalities and ethnicities of Europe itself were also seen as distinct 'races'.[20] This confused plural meaning of the term 'race' – encompassing both imperial and intra-European racial hierarchies – is crucial to understanding how Germany saw its prisoners of war. By August 1915, Germany had captured over a million prisoners.[21] During the war, at least thirteen different nationalities were represented in German prisoner camps, encompassing numerous ethnicities.[22] As a German expert on prisoners, Wilhelm Doegen (1877–1967), later wrote: 'Germany did not fight against a world of armies [...] but rather against a world of races [*eine Welt von Völkern*].'[23] The war changed the meaning of 'race' in Germany where the conflict lent increasing weight to the idea that each enemy had a biological 'racial', as well as a political, identity, even if this was only vaguely articulated.

Captivity provides one example of an area where this shift was occurring. We can identify a significant 'racialising' process which was part of the encounter with the prisoner of war – particularly the colonial prisoner. In 1915, the Kaiser approved the establishment of a Royal Prussian Phonographic Commission to travel around German prisoner-of-war camps, recording the songs, languages and music of the various ethnicities held captive there.[24] The commission, a group of ethnologists, linguists and anthropologists led by Doegen, recorded an impressive range of Slavic, Yiddish, African and Asian folk music and languages, as well as French patois and British and Irish dialects.[25] Anthropologists were also involved in an associated project: Felix von Luschan (1854–1924), a professor of anthropology in Berlin, was funded by the Prussian Cultural Ministry to send students into camps to carry out body measurements and to photograph captives in an attempt to classify Germany's enemies 'scientifically' from a 'racial' perspective.[26]

Given the belief in different intra-European races, such research was not limited to colonial captives but was undertaken for all prisoners. However, it highlights how 'race' was an increasingly important dimension in how prisoners were perceived. The general flood of postcards, photographs and drawings of the different 'races' held in German camps provided further evidence that captivity was becoming associated with a racialised discourse. Typical was the series of drawings of prisoners of war defined according to racial 'type' by the German Jewish artist Hermann Struck or the propaganda book of portrait photographs of prisoners, produced by Otto Stiehl, to highlight the different 'races' in German camps.[27] While some sketches of different German prisoner 'types' were also produced in France, the 'racial' classification of prisoners in German popular discourse went much further.[28] In part this was for propaganda purposes – to attack the French and British claim to be defending civilisation by presenting their armies as a hotch-potch of perceived 'inferior' colonial races.

It is important to emphasise that the understanding of 'race' in the Ottoman empire before and during the war was different to that outlined above for Germany. The two states' circumstances contrasted greatly: Germany was an aspiring imperial power; Ottoman Turkey, an older empire in decline. However, in Ottoman Turkey, concepts of 'race' and identity also began to change during the immediate pre-war and wartime period: after Enver Pasha came to power in a putsch in 1913, the ideas of the Young Turks, who advocated ethnic Turkish nationalism and pan-Turanist expansion, took hold, challenging older, traditional ideas of Ottomanism, based on tolerance within a multinational empire.[29] Yet despite these changes, 'race' did not play a determining role in Ottoman treatment of the Kut prisoners and, in contrast to Germany, enemy prisoners of war do not appear to have been a factor in changing popular ideas of 'race' and identity – rather in the Ottoman empire, wartime nationalism radicalised through the persecution of internal civilian minorities, such as the Armenians.

Why did the 'racialised' discourse develop so strongly in the German case and not in the Ottoman empire? Here it seems that a wartime fear of the colonial Other was particularly powerful in Germany; one explanation for this may be the earlier depictions of Germany's African colonial subjects as savages – depictions which were used to justify the harsh German repression of the Herero and Nama people in 1904–7; another possible origin is the particular late-nineteenth-century German anthropological interest in racial theory.[30] In 1914–18, however, the impulse to 'classify' colonial prisoners in Germany racially also clearly stemmed from a particularly widespread German discourse of fear that developed around the non-white colonial soldier on the battlefield: to classify was to regain a sense of power over the feared captive, through labelling and categorising him. Racialisation thus developed differently largely because fear determined the colonial–imperial encounter in different ways in the Ottoman and German cases, as this chapter will now explore.

FEAR OF THE NON-WHITE COLONIAL SOLDIER IN GERMANY

Fear of the racial Other was the initial German response to the encounter with non-white colonial prisoners. In German propaganda in 1914, the Allied use of non-white colonial troops on the European battlefield was presented as a war crime because, Germany claimed, they practised illegal forms of warfare such as the mutilation of the wounded or taking body parts as trophies. Highly mythologised, these German beliefs appear to have drawn upon 1914 atrocity rumours that the German army was cutting off children's hands in France and Belgium, as well as from the pre-war association of the colonial sphere with barbaric practices: in particular, the mutilation of German soldiers' corpses during the Herero genocide or the pre-war Belgian atrocities in the Congo.[31] The accusations against colonial troops did have a non-racial parallel: Germany also accused white Allied soldiers and civilians of mutilating the German wounded in 1914.[32] However, as the war continued, a specific German discourse of fear came to be powerfully associated with non-white colonial troops.[33]

The discourse was a homogenising one: it did not distinguish between Indian troops, fighting for the British on the Western Front from 1914, and French North African Arab or Black West African Tirailleurs sénégalais units. It was officially promoted: in 1915 and 1919, the German Foreign Office published reports cataloguing accusations of war crimes by Entente colonial troops.[34] The 1919 text reveals a widespread German discourse of racial fear. For example, it cited the commandant of Münster prisoner-of-war camp in June 1915: 'French prisoners of war from the Moroccan division say that the combat behaviour and conduct of Moroccans is to take no prisoners, but to massacre everyone. For example, one prisoner stated that he had seen how 200 Germans who had already surrendered were cut down [*niedergemacht wurden*].'[35] Another typical account, by Emil Spaet, a former civilian internee in Britain, related that he was told by an English lieutenant named Fenn that:

In Le Havre a closed train wagon arrived which had been loaded with some 40 badly wounded Germans and 3 wounded Indians at the front and when the wagon was opened all 40 Germans were found dead. They had been killed by the Indians who had not had their knives taken from them. Lieutenant Fenn recounted that he had been present at the opening of the wagon. Moreover, he stated that the Indians always come back from battle with the cut-off ears and heads of German soldiers. The British officers are powerless to stop this behaviour.[36]

Another German stated in 1914 that he had seen '100 Indian cavalry wearing necklaces of cut-off ears around their necks and with cut-off heads in their knapsacks.'[37] An intelligence officer from Landshut reported that 'the black troops have been ordered not to take prisoners, but instead to kill everyone'.[38] These statements bear all the hallmarks of myth making. Whether an initial incident of combat ruthlessness by a colonial unit actually originally served as the starting point for this discourse is impossible to ascertain. What is clear is that projecting atrocious acts onto colonial troops provided a way to narrate wartime violence that justified German victimhood. This fear of the colonial soldier was not confined to Germany; the *belief* that colonial troops were more violent formed a pan-European cultural representation of the colonial Other, which fitted with pre-war assumptions that colonial peoples were cannibals or savages. In 1915, even the International Committee of the Red Cross 'shared this ideology of suspicion' against non-white troops.[39]

In Germany, this fear of the colonial soldier was a key determinant in how Germans saw the French use of colonial troops to guard German prisoners of war sent to prison camps in France's North African colonies. By January 1916, there were some 5,300 German prisoners of war in camps in Morocco and 12,000 in Tunisia and Algeria.[40] In 1916, the German government protested to the International Committee of the Red Cross, accusing the French of placing German prisoners under the 'control of fanatical Arabs who enjoy harassing Christians'.[41] Such accusations caught the German public's imagination: the Cologne branch of the Red Cross even reported to the Vatican that German prisoners in Algeria and Morocco 'were placed at the mercy of the vengeful animal passions of the blacks [*tierischen Rachegelusten*]'.[42] One German commandant informed French prisoners of war that it was 'inhuman' that German prisoners of war should be guarded by black troops in Africa, stating, 'while you French consider the black race as your equal, we Germans place it a little above the level of the monkey and have always considered it as inferior'.[43]

Tales of violence by non-white guards against German prisoners were grossly exaggerated in Germany: significantly, where German interviews with former prisoners repatriated from North Africa during the war refer to beatings, these were carried out by *white* French guards.[44] However, fuelled by a small number of real incidents, the belief grew in Germany that the treatment of German prisoners in North Africa breached the accepted racial hierarchies. By 1 January 1916, five German prisoners had been killed by Arab guards during escape attempts.[45] In Algeria, rumours that the German army burned the bodies of dead Muslim soldiers led to hostile demonstrations against the first German prisoners of war arriving at Tizi-Ouzou.[46] In addition, at the start of the war, forms of punishment used by the French to discipline indigenous colonial troops were employed against German prisoners of war in North Africa, although the French claimed that this had occurred at the initiative of local commanders, without authorisation.[47] Such stories fed the widespread German racialised fear of non-white troops.

The belief that colonial troops were brutalising prisoners or mutilating Germans on the battlefield was very rarely substantiated with credible proof in this German discourse of fear. However, in the racially interpreted world of 1914–18, this lack of corroborating evidence did not matter. Moreover, the atrocity image of the colonial soldier fulfilled a need. It created a safe space for articulating thoughts about fear, wartime violence, killing and atrocity which could not be expressed with regard to one's own combat actions. Faced with the shock of battlefield killing, Europeans feared that they were regressing into a primitive or savage state. Thus the discourse about how 'real' colonial 'savages' behaved provided a means of articulating this other, deep-seated fear about European barbarisation. For white soldiers, categorising non-white colonial troops' behaviour as 'savage' offered reassurance – it stigmatised colonial killing while drawing attention away from the brutality of white European acts of battlefield slaughter. It reasserted racial hierarchies: white troops killing the enemy could be excused by being presented as superior to the illegitimate mutilations that colonial soldiers were accused of carrying out.

In some cases, this atrocity discourse against colonial troops may have led German units to give no quarter to black soldiers. In July 1915 and July 1917, German soldiers told the writer Gregor Huch that army commanders had told them they did not wish to see any black prisoners of war taken.[48] A popular joke in the German army in 1914 related how a Bavarian NCO killed a large number of black prisoners.[49] There is a lack of evidence generally regarding battlefield killings of colonial troops: overall, the total number of colonial prisoners held in Germany remains unknown, and thus it is impossible to verify whether colonial troops were under-represented in captivity relative to the number serving on the Western Front. However, it is clear that the German atrocity discourse about colonial troops had real long-term effects – re-emerging in the German propaganda campaign against the use of black troops during the occupation of the Ruhr and in the form of racist propaganda and German atrocities against colonial troops during the invasion of France in 1940.[50]

A corollary of the fear discourse was the curiosity towards the Other which emerged once the colonial soldier was captured; this often resulted in infantilisation. Thus in late 1914, Indian prisoners in Wittenberg camp en route for Wünsdorf were depicted as naïve and childlike in a German report: 'the overall impression of these prisoners is that they are like big children.'[51] The focus upon the prisoners' food and toilet habits enhanced this infantilised image. The prisoners refused the food offered to them: an expert in Oriental Studies, Herr Vacha from Berlin, was called in to explain the religious dietary rules before separate food was organised and instructions were issued explaining that Muslims did not eat pork and Hindus did not consume beef.[52] The report pointed out that the Indians were 'very clean' and did not use toilet paper, preferring water. The prisoners were depicted as passive: they told the Germans that they had not been informed in India that they were bound for Europe, believing they were going to a neighbouring country to put down an uprising.[53] The report noted that they were 'very grateful' for their good treatment and said they 'would pray for us'.[54]

An infantilisation process is also clear in the image shown in Figure 5, where humour is used to deflect the fear response to the colonial Other and trivialise it. The printed caption on the reverse of the postcard, presented as a message from the German guard in the photograph, reads:

My latest portrait with my two 'new' friends, two Senegalese, who have not been prisoners long. The Negro wearing the hard hat with the less friendly face aroused my particular curiosity because he has three wives at home. I can only describe this as lamentable. I am sure that you will all pity him because he looks far from proud.[55]

Such humour was a way of making safe what was feared, the direct corollary of the widespread German discourse mythologising the violent non-white soldier. It removed the agency of the 'savage' colonial fighter through captivity and reinforced belief in the superiority of German civilisation.

5. 'Fister's New Friends'. Postcard of a German guardsman with prisoners, on whose reverse is printed: 'My latest portrait with my two "new" friends, two Senegalese, who have not been prisoners long.'

How do these German discourses compare to the British description of the
Ottoman case, where the non-white colonial figure was both captor and
prisoner of war during the horrendous march into captivity from Kut-el-
Amara via Baghdad and Mosul to the Ras-el-Ain railhead? If we consider the
overall British depiction of the non-white 'captor' figure first, a number of
patterns emerge. There is some use of pre-war stereotypes of the 'barbaric'
colonial subject which is similar to the German case: political explanations
such as the role of the Young Turks, ideological mobilisation, the malad-
ministration of the Turkish war effort or wartime brutalisation were rejected
by some British witnesses in favour of essentialist orientalist or 'racialised'
explanations for prisoner mistreatment. Private D. Hughes's account of the
march illustrates this:

Terrible cases of sickness were met with [. . .] Cowsheds were filled with men the
majority of whom would never come out alive again. It was an indirect massacre.
Most of the men, too ill to go to draw their ration of flour and salt, were left to die of
starvation [. . .] orderlies were the most inhuman types of the Oriental race. I have
seen them pull and throw about men hovering between life and death [. . .] Almost
in the last stages of every disease of a filthy country lay our men, unable any longer
to fight against the cruelty of the victorious Oriental.[56]

Orientalism thus provided an explanatory framework for some former
British prisoners for what was an extremely traumatic, brutal initial captivity, endured by men already weakened by the siege. However, in contrast to
the German situation, the association of the Ottoman guards with violence
during the march was not exaggerated into broader mythologised mutilation narratives nor did it produce a widespread discourse of 'fear' of the
racial Other in wartime Britain, in the way that occurred in Germany. This
was despite the ample verifiable first-hand evidence that the Kut prisoners
were horrifically treated.

There were two key reasons for this difference: first, the dominant scandal
around Kut in Britain was the conduct of the British and Indian officers who
were separated from the other ranks and relatively well-treated by their
captors, while the ordinary soldiers – both British and Indian – endured a
horrific march. Non-Muslim other-rank Indian prisoners were eventually
segregated at Ras-el-Ain to work on the railway line; Muslim and British
other-rank prisoners were transported on from Ras-el-Ain by train to separate camps in Turkey proper. The disparity in treatment between officers

and other ranks helps explain the reluctance to discuss Kut in Britain: class remained the predominant paradigm, not 'race'. Second, Britain had long employed colonial troops; thus a general racially based vilification of all non-white soldiers would have been counterproductive. In many British accounts of Ottoman captivity, careful distinction is made between the different captor ethnicities encountered, particularly Turkish, Kurd and Arab – there is no one vague yet homogenous violent colonial stereotype, as in the German discourse. For example, the British ex-prisoner P. W. Long specified in his memoir how a Turkish lieutenant viciously beat one of the Arab guards.[57] Long also distinguished between friendly Chaldean and Armenian women and hostile Arab women.[58] Above all, it was the fact that Indian colonial troops were sharing the same hardships on the march that made it necessary for British prisoners to distinguish continually in their accounts between different non-white colonial subjects. The Indian prisoner became a complex figure of sympathy, pity and, at times, suspicion in these narratives.

Prior to capture, British troops in Kut had close working relationships with Indian soldiers; many had already served in India. Long described how a 'lingua franca,' a Hindi slang, existed between British and Indians:

The Indians [orderlies] [. . .] lifted me on to a bed that had only a blanket covering the springs. 'Kutch nay mattrish, sahib?' queried one of the Indians. 'Kutch nay' was the answer. [Lit. 'No mattress sir?' 'None.'][59]

However, mutual tensions had arisen during the siege: some British troops resented the Indians' special ration requirements and suspected their loyalty; evidence suggests that some Muslim Indian troops were unhappy at fighting fellow Muslims.[60]

Long's account of captivity generally depicts Indian fellow prisoners positively, admiring, for example, how an Indian prisoner stole a ration tin from a captor: 'he told me that he had put it upside down on his head before winding on his turban and they hadn't thought of searching the turbans! Very neat, I thought.'[61] Long also described friendship between the Indian prisoners on the march:

[. . .] a sepoy, who had been helped for several miles, finally collapsed and could not rise again, not even when the Onbashi [commander of the guard] tried kicking him to his feet. He was a Hindu, and a naik (corporal) of his regiment pleaded to be allowed to stay with him. I knew a fair amount of Hindustani and interpreted his wishes to the Onbashi [. . .].[62]

The request was refused; the prisoners were forced to leave the Indian behind to die. A similar incident occurred at Tikrit, when an Arab civilian tried to steal a sepoy's kit and 'slashed the wrists of the unfortunate Indian': 'he was crying pitifully and holding his hands, dripping with blood in front of him. The right hand was almost severed from the wrist and blood was spurting from severed veins in both wrists.' This sepoy was left behind at Tikrit, and Long did not know what happened to him subsequently.[63]

Significantly, Long was a British prisoner from the other ranks. In contrast to his generally sympathetic depiction of Indian prisoners, British officers regularly insisted in their post-war accounts of Kut that the British captives had suffered more than their Indian counterparts. Thus Major-General Sir Charles Melliss stated that 'at every Arab village I came to our poor fellows, British and Indian (the British suffered the worst), were lying in the most terrible state of dysentery and starvation.'[64] According to Major E. W. C. Sandes, 'Our Indian rank and file suffered severely it is true, but not to the extent of the British who could not live on the rough food given them by their captors.'[65] Sandes had enjoyed a privileged captivity as an officer, and his memoirs generally ignored the suffering of the other ranks, both Indian and British.[66]

The post-war belief, among British officers, that Indians suffered less on the march appears to have two causes: first, officers drew this conclusion from post-war claims that a higher proportion of the British prisoners taken at Kut had died in captivity than their Indian counterparts. But the available death statistics for Indians are only overall figures for the whole period of wartime captivity in Ottoman Turkey; they do not tell us comparative Indian and British death rates for the *initial* march from Kut. In 1919, a letter to the Under-Secretary of State for India admitted it was not possible to 'give even approximate figures of the after siege mortality amongst the Indian native troops. That the mortality was very heavy is certain but probably not so heavy as the mortality of the British Tommies as the Turkish policy prompted them to treat the Indian native troops better than they did our fellow countrymen.'[67] In the absence of more detailed statistics on Indian mortality during the march, such claims remain speculative.

In contrast, the evidence from British other-rank survivors does not support the view that the Indian other ranks suffered less during the march itself, although Muslim prisoners, on occasion, were allowed valuable privileges such as the right to distribute the food or milk. It was only once the prisoners were sent on to camps from the Ras-el-Ain railhead that the Turks fully implemented a policy of favouritism towards Muslims – a policy which the British prisoners had anticipated and resented.[68] During the march, many Indians actually suffered badly: one officer, H. C. W. Bishop, was told by an Indian other-rank prisoner who 'had evidently had a hard time' that 'on the way to Baghdad the guards had flogged men who fell out to see if they were really ill'.[69] The chaplain, Revd Spooner, was told that 'troops (British or Indian) falling out on the line of march from sheer exhaustion were left to perish either of starvation or the probability of being murdered by the Arabs'.[70] Major E. A. Walker, a medical officer, described many Indian and British other ranks dying of starvation and sickness in horrific conditions along the route.[71] Crucially also, the available mortality statistics do not distinguish between Muslim and non-Muslim Indian death rates. Indeed, Hindu and Christian Indians were not sent on from Ras-el-Ain but were kept working on the Berlin–Baghdad railway line, where Walker claimed they had 'no shelter; only their own blankets, bare Turkish ration to live [. . .] 75 per cent died in the first year'.[72] Ras-el-Ain was an unpleasant site – a key killing location for victims of the Armenian genocide. British prisoners described seeing massacred Armenian corpses in the wells there.[73] In July 1916, Walker found Indian sepoy prisoners in a holding camp at Ras-el-Ain had with them a 'small Armenian boy of about ten or so' who was the sole survivor of thousands of Armenian women and children who had been massacred.[74]

The second reason for the belief that Indians had suffered less was that British officers had travelled along the same march route as the other-rank captives, but under much better conditions. They had seen other-rank prisoners dying and had been unable to help them. This created a post-war sense of guilt. Melliss stood out as a particularly humane officer who had done his very utmost to assist the dying prisoners he encountered, by buying food and medicine for them; yet, according to Walker, even Melliss had ordered in Tikrit that the scarce resources he was able to procure should only be given to British prisoners. Walker recalled finding at Tikrit 'about 170 Indians and 80 British crammed in a dirty little Serai nearly all with dysentery and diarrhoea starving on a diet of flour salt and parched wheat. Melliss had left money with Crichton to buy milk (for *British* only – rotten of him) and we put up some more but it was only a drop in the bucket.'[75] Melliss may well have taken comfort from a post-war belief that the Indians had been coping better on the march, rather than acknowledge that at times during the crisis he had chosen to privilege white prisoners.

To conclude, captivity clearly was a key sphere of colonial–imperial wartime interaction. However, this interaction evolved differently in different empires. In both the German and Ottoman cases, the captivity encounter drew upon 'racial' stereotypes. However, it is evident that in Germany a mythology of 'race' and colonial atrocity developed in response to the encounter with colonial troops on the battlefield and in the prison camp, a mythology which was more widespread and extreme than the British reaction to the mistreatment of prisoners after Kut. This 'fear discourse' led to a racialised representation of the prisoner of war in Germany in a way that did not occur in the case of the British–Ottoman Turkish captivity interaction. The relatively nuanced British discourse on the non-white captor – the Turkish or Arab guard – also contrasted greatly with German representations of the North African Arab guard.

Yet in both cases one fundamental similarity emerges: race was not the key determinant of the physical treatment of prisoners; class or political strategy was. Even in Germany, where the discourse of 'race' evolved most powerfully, the treatment of colonial prisoners was still dictated by political-strategic interests, not the rapidly evolving paradigm of 'racial' perceptions. Germany's strategic need to impress its Turkish ally and prove its credentials as a new imperial power determined its prisoner policy. Hence we see the privileging of the colonial troops' religious and cultural needs at Wünsdorf. This privileging was politically, not racially, driven; it mirrored the policy towards strategically useful categories of white European prisoners – such as the Irish, who were also encouraged to change sides by being centralised in one prisoner-of-war camp.

Similarly, in the Turkish case, political-strategic interests dominated policies regarding prisoners of war. Policy towards the Kut prisoners cannot be considered 'racialised' – Indian Hindus, Sikhs and white soldiers were treated practically identically, and the favouritism that occurred towards Muslim prisoners after the Kut march was on strategic-religious, not racial, grounds. Moreover, both British and Indian officers were spared the horrors of mistreatment; class was the motive here, not race. Finally, in the case of Kut, political-strategic interests were fundamental to why the overall British reaction was so muted. After the war, Kemalist Turkey was seen as an ally that Britain did not wish to offend – even some post-war accounts by prisoners who survived Ottoman captivity emphasised that they were very fond of the 'new' Turks.[76] Ultimately, although the colonial–imperial interaction led to different levels of 'racialised' perceptions and representation in the two cases, it was the dominance of political-strategic considerations which defined the treatment of colonial prisoners of war in both Germany and the Ottoman empire.

NOTES

1 For African troops, see Joe Lunn, *Memoirs of the Maelstrom: A Senegalese Oral History of the First World War* (Portsmouth, NH: Heinemann, 1999); Marc Michel: *Les Africains et la Grande Guerre. L'Appel à l'Afrique (1914–1918)* (Paris:

Éditions Karthala, 2003); and Hew Strachan, *The First World War*, vol. 1, *To Arms* (Oxford University Press, 2001). On Indian soldiers, see David Omissi (ed.), *Indian Voices of the Great War: Soldiers' Letters, 1914–1918* (Basingstoke: Macmillan, 1999). My thanks to Eden Knudsen for commenting on a draft of this chapter.

2 Gerhard Höpp, *Muslime in der Mark. Als Kriegsgefangene und Internierte in Wünsdorf und Zossen, 1914–1924* (Berlin: Verlag das Arabische Buch, 1997), 44.

3 *Ibid.*, 44–5.

4 *Ibid.*, 55.

5 *Ibid.*, 83–5.

6 *Ibid.*, 84.

7 P. W. Long, *Other Ranks of Kut* (London: Naval and Military Press, 1938), 33.

8 Imperial War Museum [henceforth IWM], London, 91/25/1. Colonel C. E. Colbeck.

9 Service Historique de l'Armée de Terre [henceforth SHAT], Paris, 16 N 2947, 'Compte-rendu sur la propagande musulmane faite parmi les prisonniers Arabes en Allemagne', 4 June 1918.

10 *Ibid.*

11 SHAT 7 N 2107, Tirailleurs deserteurs, El Hadj Binhamed Bey, matricule 4269.

12 Höpp, *Muslime in der Mark*, 50.

13 *Ibid.*, 45; see also Wilhelm Doegen, *Kriegsgefangene Völker: Der Kriegsgefangenen Haltung und Schicksal in Deutschland* (Berlin: D. Reimer, 1919 [1921]), 30. SHAT 16 N 2947, 'Compte-rendu sur la propagande musulmane'.

14 Archives du Comité International de la Croix Rouge, [henceforth ACICR], Geneva, 446/III/c.62, Camps de propagande et d'éliminés en France, Propagande individuelle, Comité International de la Croix Rouge, letter to General Verand, 18 January 1918.

15 *Ibid.*

16 Figures from *Statistics of the Military Effort of the British Empire during the Great War, 1914–1920* (London: HMSO, 1922), Note to Table XVI(a), 330–31.

17 *Ibid.* 'Indian' in this context refers to ethnic Asians from pre-partition British India. Although in *Statistics of the Military Effort* the table of prisoners of war taken in different theatres mentions a column for 'Indian Native Kut' (330), the figure actually given is the combined one for 'Indian Native Kut' and 'Indian Native' (i.e. Indians captured elsewhere during the Mesopotamian campaign).

18 IWM, *Treatment of British Prisoners of War in Turkey* (Delhi: Government Printing, n.d.) K.4938, Ref: 77/3.0. Long, *Other Ranks of Kut*, preface, and Martin Gilbert, *The First World War* (London: HarperCollins, 1994), 248, give slightly lower figures: 2,500–2,592 British prisoners, of whom 1,750 died in captivity and 9,300 colonial soldiers, 2,500 of whom perished. For an estimate based on contemporary Turkish papers see: E. W. C. Sandes, *In Kut and in Captivity with the Sixth Indian Division* (London: John Murray, 1919), 261.

19 Annette Becker, *Oubliés de la Grande Guerre: humanitaire et culture de guerre, 1914–1918: populations occupées, déportés civils, prisonniers de guerre* (Paris: Noêsis, 1998), 318.

20 *Ibid.*, 350.

21 Uta Hinz, *Gefangen im Großen Krieg* (Essen: Klartext, 2006), 92.

22 *Ibid.*, Table 3, 238.

23 Doegen, *Kriegsgefangene Völker*, Vorwort. See the similar argument in Leo Frobenius, *Der Völker-Zirkus unserer Feinde* (Berlin: Eckart, 1917).

24 Susanne Ziegler, 'Stimmen der Völker. Das Berliner Lautarchiv', in Horst Bredekamp, Jochen Brüning and Cornelia Weber (ed.), *Theater der Natur und Kunst, Katalog, Eine Ausstellung der Humboldt-Universität zu Berlin 10. Dezember 2000 bis 4. März 2001* (Berlin: Humboldt University and Henschel Verlag, 2000), 117–28.

25 The recordings survive at the Lautseminar at the Humboldt University, Berlin.

26 Andrew D. Evans, 'Capturing Race: Anthropology and Photography in German and Austrian Prisoner-of-War Camps during World War I', in Eleanor M. Hight and Gary D. Simpson (eds.), *Colonialist Photography: Imagining Race and Place* (London: Routledge, 2002), 226–8.

27 Hermann Struck, *Kriegsgefangene: ein Beitrag zur Völkerkunde im Weltkriege: 100 Steinzeichnungen* (Berlin: Reimer, 1916); Otto Stiehl, *Unsere Feinde. 96 Charakterköpfe aus deutschen Kriegsgefangenenlagern* (Stuttgart: Hoffmann, 1916).

28 See, for example, Marcel Eugène Louveau-Rouveyre's prisoner sketches at the Bibliothèque de Documentation Internationale Contemporaine, Les Invalides, Ref Or F3 1311–1320, Paris.

29 Alan Kramer, *Dynamic of Destruction: Culture and Mass Killing in the First World War* (Oxford University Press, 2007), 147; Donald Bloxham, *The Great Game of Genocide: Imperialism, Nationalism and the Destruction of the Ottoman Armenians* (Oxford University Press, 2005), 19.

30 H. Glenn Penny and Matti Bunzl, *Worldly Provincialism: German Anthropology in the Age of Empire* (Ann Arbor: University of Michigan Press, 2003).

31 John Horne and Alan Kramer, *German Atrocities, 1914: A History of Denial* (New Haven: Yale University Press, 2001). Isabel V. Hull, *Absolute Destruction: Military Culture and the Practices of War in Imperial Germany* (Ithaca and London: Cornell University Press, 2005), 136, 210.

32 Politisches Archiv des Auswärtigen Amtes [henceforth AA], Berlin, Akten betreffend den Krieg 1914. Grausamkeiten in der Kriegsführung und Verletzungen des Völkerrechts, Aug.–Sept. 1914: R 20880.

33 See Christian Koller, 'The Recruitment of Colonial Troops in Africa and Asia and their Deployment in Europe during the First World War', *Immigrants and Minorities*, vol. 26, nos. 1/2. March/July 2008, 111–33.

34 AA, *Völkerrechtswidrige Verwendung farbiger Truppen auf dem europäischen Kriegsschauplatz durch England und Frankreich* (Berlin, July 1915); AA, *Liste über Fälle, die sich auf planmäßige Ermordung und Mißhandlung einer größeren Zahl von deutschen Kriegsgefangenen durch farbige Truppen beziehen* (Berlin: Reishoder, 1919).

35 AA, *Liste über Fälle*, no. 3, 13 June 15 – N 5481.15.z.v., Die Kommandantur des Gefangenenlagers Münster, 13 June 1915.

36 *Ibid.*, No. 19. Eidesstattliche Versicherung des früheren Zivilinternierten, Kaufmanns Emil Spaet aus Mannheim, Spelzenstr. 17, 11 September 1916 – Nr 18370.16.z.v.I.

37 *Ibid.* 36. eidliche Vernehmung Becker – Nr 1322.12.17.z.v.I.

38 *Ibid.* 16. Bericht des Nachrichtenoffiziers Paul in Landshut, 18 March 1916 – Nr 4075.16.z.v.- auf Grund von Angaben des französischen Fliegers Follot.

39 Becker, *Oubliés*, 324.

40 Odon Abbal, 'Le Maghreb et la Grande Guerre: les camps d'internement en Afrique du Nord', in Jean-Charles Jouffret (ed.), *Les Armes et la Toge, Mélanges offerts à André Martel* (Montpellier: CHMEDN, 1997), 623–5; 631.

41 Marc Michel, 'Intoxication ou brutalisation. Les représailles de la Grande Guerre,' in Nicolas Beaupré and Christian Ingrao (eds.), *14–18: Aujourd'hui, Today, Heute. Marginaux, Marginalité, Marginalisation* (Paris: Noêsis, 2001), 179–81.

42 Vatican Archive Rome, Segretaria di Stato, Guerra 1914–1918, rubrica 244, Fasc. 132, Prigionieri tedeschi, folio 41. Letter from the War Aid Fund of the United Branches of the Red Cross, Cologne, Abt. IV, 10 March 1916. Enclosed report: Geheimrats Greve.

43 French complaint to Gustav Ador, directly citing German comments, 23 July 1915, ACICR, 60/445/III, cited in Michel, 'Intoxication ou Brutalisation', 181.

44 Bundesarchiv-Militärarchiv [henceforth BA-MA], Freiburg, PH2/33, f. 16, interview with Oskar Wachler and f. 76, Interview with Erl. Arnold. Also Gerhard Rose, 'Feuilleton. Aus den Erfahrungen einer vierjährigen Gefangenschaft in Algerien und Frankreich. Ein Beitrag zur Humanität der Franzosen gegen ihre Kriegsgefangenen', *Deutsche Medizinische Wochenschrift*, 10 July 1919, pp. 771–3.

45 Abbal, 'Le Maghreb et la Grande Guerre', 628.

46 *Ibid.*, 630.

47 Baron A. d'Anthouard, *Les Prisonniers Allemands au Maroc* (Paris: Hachette, 1917), 24.

48 Gregor Huch, 'Die belgische Schande. Ein Briefwechsel', *Der Deutsche*, vol. 1, JG 1 (1919), 69–70.

49 Württembergisches Hauptstaatsarchiv, Stuttgart, M 660, Nachlass Gleich, Meine Erlebnisse im Feldzug 1914, part III: Die Verlängerung des rechten Heeresflügels, Diary, 22 September 1914, 27.

50 Raffael Scheck, ' "They are just Savages": German Massacres of Black Soldiers from the French Army in 1940', *Journal of Modern History*, 77 (2005) 2, 325–44. Keith L. Nelson, 'The "Black Horror on the Rhine": Race as a Factor in Post-World War I Diplomacy', *Journal of Modern History*, vol. 42, no. 4 (December, 1970), 606–27.

51 BA-MA Msg.200/224.

52 *Ibid.*

53 *Ibid.*

54 *Ibid.*

55 Postcard: author's own collection.

56 Dorina L. Neave, *Remembering Kut: 'Lest we forget'* (London: Arthur Baker, 1938), 158–64.

57 Long, *Other Ranks*, 28–9.

58 *Ibid.*, 26.

59 *Ibid.*, 17.

60 IWM 73/133/1 Dr W. L. Nute; IWM 04/24/1 J. McK Sloss; IWM 76/115/1 Diary of Major E. A. Walker [enclosed in Revd Spooner papers]. Omissi, *Indian Voices*, 15.

61 Long, *Other Ranks*, 47–8.

62 *Ibid.*, 63.

63 *Ibid.*, 56.

64 Major-General Sir Charles Melliss, comments made to the Geographical Society, cited in E. H. Keeling, 'In Northern Anatolia, 1917', *Geographical Journal*, vol. 55, no. 4 (April 1920), 286. A wartime letter from Melliss to Lloyd George does not refer to Indians doing better: 'our men, British and Indian, lying exhausted and nearly all desperately ill'. India Office Records, IOR/L/MIL/7/18454, 1 February 1918, British Library, London.

65 Sandes, *In Kut and in Captivity*, 451.

66 *Ibid.* See also Sandes's travel book *Tales of Turkey* (London: Murray, 1924).

67 IOR/L/MIL/7/18454, T. D. Cree, Major Assistant Political Officer to Under-Secretary of State for India, 8 January 1919.

68 IWM 76/115/1, Papers of the Revd H. Spooner, letter to the Secretary of State for War, 18 July 1917.

69 H. C. W. Bishop, *A Kut Prisoner* (London: John Lane, 1920), 48.

70 IWM, 76/115/1, Spooner, Letter to the Secretary of State for War, 18 July 1917.

71 IWM 76/115/1, Diary of E. A.Walker, 17 July 1916.

72 *Ibid.*,

73 *Ibid.*, On Ras-el-Ain see Bloxham, *The Great Game*, 88–9. Near Aleppo, H. C. W. Bishop saw Armenian civilians 'looking very wretched'. His guards said they would be 'marched off into a waterless spot in the hills and kept there till they died'. Bishop, *A Kut Prisoner*, 69.

74 IWM 76/115/1 Diary of E. A.Walker, 17 July 1916.

75 IWM, 76/115/1, Diary of E. A.Walker, 14 June 1916.

76 See Sir Arnold Wilson MP's preface and P. W. Long's introductory comments in Long, *Other Ranks*; also Dorina Neave's preface in Neave, *Remembering Kut*; Major-General Sir Charles Melliss decried this British desire to placate Turkey: see Melliss, cited in Keeling, 'In Northern Anatolia, 1917', 286.

CHAPTER 10

Images of Te Hokowhitu A Tu in the First World War

Christopher Pugsley

Te Hokowhitu A Tu – the Maori Contingent to the First World War and its successor contingents and reinforcements that became the Pioneer Battalion and then in September 1917 the New Zealand (Maori) Pioneer Battalion – was the public face of Maori military contribution in the First World War.[1] A total of 2,227 Maori and 485 Pacific Islanders served in the Maori Contingent and its subsequent incarnations; 336 died on active service and 734 were wounded.[2] This number was drawn from a male Maori population that was estimated to number no more than 30,000 in the 1911 census.[3] An unknown number of Maori also served in the ranks of the provincial units of the New Zealand Expeditionary Force (NZEF), enlisting with their Pakeha (white New Zealander) mates from their home town and district. Although New Zealand introduced conscription in November 1916, the Pioneer Battalion remained a volunteer unit for Maori throughout the war. Government attempts to coerce the Waikato and Taranaki tribes, who mindful of the land confiscations of the New Zealand Wars of the 1860s refused to support the war effort, by introducing selective conscription for those tribes were unsuccessful.[4] Yet the scale of the Maori war effort that managed to sustain a 1,000-strong unit for much of the war from such a limited population base has never really been appreciated by New Zealand, nor has its story been widely told.[5] Rikihana Carkeek's *Home Little Maori Home* is a unique published personal memoir by a member of the Maori Contingent, and as I do not read Maori, the private letters and correspondence of the Maori soldiers is a story for someone else to explore.[6] This chapter examines how this contribution was reported and, more specifically, what was seen of the Maori contribution by the New Zealand public at home. How was this contribution interpreted by both Maori and Pakeha audiences, and is it possible to assess the differing interpretations between them?

My emphasis will be on the portrayal of Maori on film as, by 1914–18, New Zealand was a country where 'going to the flicks' was a national pastime, one more popular than going to church. The First World War is one where film played an important role in portraying national endeavour and was used as a propaganda tool to unite the population behind the war effort in every belligerent nation. New Zealand was no different. Indeed, New Zealand was a trailblazer in the government use of film and was one of the first countries in the world deliberately to commission film as a government publicity tool.

SELLING NEW ZEALAND TO THE WORLD

From initial contact, images of Maori fascinated European audiences and encapsulated some of the allure of New Zealand first in photographs and then in film. Prime minister Richard 'King Dick' Seddon's Liberal government (1893–1906) deliberately threw government resources into areas that other countries saw as the preserve of private enterprise. In 1901 Seddon set up the Department of Tourists and Health Resorts under the energetic leadership of its first General Manager, T. E. Donne, who determined to employ all means possible to broadcast the delights of New Zealand to the world in order to attract both tourists and migrants.[7] From the beginning, Maori featured in showing what was exotic and different about New Zealand. Maoris had featured in the first film taken of New Zealanders overseas as part of the New Zealand contingent to Queen Victoria's Diamond Jubilee celebrations in London in 1897.[8] The 54-strong contingent drawn from volunteer companies throughout the colony included 20 Maori raised by the Native Affairs Department, forming the Heretaunga Mounted Rifles.

In Wellington, Seddon and the Governor, Lord Ranfurly, were in the audience at the Opera House on the opening night in September 1897 when the Kinematograph Company of Christchurch presented 'the wonderful Kinematograph Reproduction of the Diamond Jubilee Procession'. The announcement that the 'Maorilanders would be shown with the New Zealand Premier' was greeted with 'a louder burst of enthusiasm than ever'.[9] This was the first contingent to be sent overseas as representatives of New Zealand; it was also the first New Zealand official body to be captured overseas on film. To the audiences of the day, the film was living proof that New Zealand was establishing itself as a presence in the world, albeit as part of the British empire. In this ceremonial event, Maori and Pakeha were seen together representing one proud, distinctive, but small colony of the empire.

However, this was a deliberately cultivated image that did not represent the reality within New Zealand. There was no sense in this portrayal of a declining race, beset by land disenfranchisement and health and education problems; rather these were noble savages of a higher order.[10] Maori had an exotic 'postcard' image within New Zealand and that reflected the reality of contact or rather the lack of contact for many New Zealanders, particularly in the South Island where Maori were few.[11] Theirs was a ceremonial role. This was made clear during New Zealand's participation in the war in South Africa against the Boers (1899–1901). Maori chiefs offered to form a Maori Contingent, but were refused as the British government would not permit native races outside South Africa to fight in a 'White Man's War'.

Nevertheless, Maori were given a principal role in New Zealand's welcome to the Duke and Duchess of Cornwall and York (later King George V and Queen Mary) when they visited New Zealand, 10–21 June 1901, to thank the colony on behalf of the empire for its efforts in the Boer War. The visit was the subject of the New Zealand government's first officially commissioned film.[12] Central to this film were scenes of the Maori reception to the royal couple at Rotorua. It is a film of one of the largest Maori gatherings in the twentieth century, and shows the pride of a race against a backdrop of geysers and mud pools; it fascinated New Zealand audiences as much as it fascinated the world.[13]

The Maori was also the subject of overseas' film producers' interest when Gaston Méliès, with his American-based Star Film Company, visited New Zealand in 1912.[14] Working with the Reverend Bennett's Maori Mission Choir and Entertainers at Rotorua, Méliès filmed three fictional narratives with a largely Maori cast including a one-reel film version of the popular Maori legend *Hinemoa*.[15] The outbreak of war in 1914 spurred a multi-reel version of *Hinemoa* filmed by George Tarr who also used the Reverend Bennett's Rotorua Maori Mission Choir and Entertainers for his cast.[16] This was the first New Zealand fiction film to receive star billing and record audiences throughout New Zealand. It fitted in with the accepted 'postcard' image of the Maori. One could argue that outside the centres of Maori population, New Zealanders' own images of Maori were also influenced by the illustrations in the weekly papers and the filmed images, and were almost as much divorced from reality as those of an overseas viewer.

VOLUNTEERING FOR A WHITE MAN'S WAR

In 1914 New Zealand mobilised volunteers from its Territorial Forces to form a New Zealand Expeditionary Force (NZEF). Britain declared war on

New Zealand's behalf, and as a loyal self-governing dominion within the empire, New Zealanders were proud to show that country and empire were indivisible. The Maori people again offered a Maori Contingent to fight for New Zealand and it was again refused by the British government on the grounds 'that the Maoris should not take part in the wars of the White Race against a White Race'.[17] However this argument vanished with the deployment of Indian army units to France in late 1914. Permission was reluctantly given for a special Maori Contingent, 500-strong, half of which was to go to Samoa and the other half to Egypt as garrison troops.[18]

The practical realities of Maori soldiers bored and frustrated at being in a backwater away from the war and the anticipated tensions between them and the native Samoans were soon realised and it was decided that the Maori Contingent should join the New Zealand Expeditionary Force (NZEF) in Egypt.[19] It was raised and trained at Narrow Neck Camp, Devonport, Auckland and organised into two 250-strong companies – 'A' Company, drawn from the west coast of the North Island, north of Auckland and the South Island; 'B' Company, drawn from the east coast of the North Island – and commanded by a Pakeha New Zealand regular officer Major Henry Peacock, New Zealand Staff Corps (NZSC). The highest-ranked Maori officer was the Contingent's Medical Officer, Captain Peter Buck (Te Rangi Hiroa) who appeared in the role of 'spokesman' in the Government's film on the visit to Rotorua in 1908 by the officers of the United States White Fleet.[20]

On 10 February 1915, Te Hokowhitu A Tu paraded through the crowded streets of Auckland before sailing to the capital, Wellington. On Saturday 13 February 1915, the Contingent disembarked and marched with the Third Reinforcements of the NZEF to Newtown Park for the official farewells. It was a time when the papers were full of news of the bombardment of the Turkish forts guarding the Straits of the Dardanelles and of the Turkish attack on the Suez Canal that would soon see New Zealanders in action for the first time. It was against this background that the Contingent received their farewell which was captured on film and survives in the Pathé vaults in the United Kingdom.[21] One can identify Major Peacock, the Pakeha Maori Contingent commander, leading his officers and men. The film shows the Third Reinforcements, numbering 1,712 personnel, and the 509-strong Maori Contingent or Te Hokowhitu A Tu marching down Adelaide Road and through the city to the wharves where they would depart the following day for Egypt on the SS *Wairrimo*.

The film immediately featured at the local cinemas and was advertised as *Our Maori Contingent (Native Volunteers for the Front)*, 'which vividly depicts our native volunteers for the Front as they appeared last Saturday afternoon'.[22] It was screened repeatedly in the cinemas. This and other departure films continued to circulate around local theatres in the Hayward's and Fuller's circuits for the duration of the war, until worn out with repeated screenings. In January 1917, two years after the event, the *Akaroa Mail* advertised that Hayward's Weekly Pictures in the Oddfellows' Hall was 'showing the departure of the Maori Contingent and the Third Reinforcements for the Front'.[23] This kind of film never dated for New Zealanders, so long as their men remained overseas; for the families of those who died, the images remained etched in memory forever: 'They swing across the screen in brave array'.[24] Only one wharfside departure film still survives in the New Zealand Film Archive.[25]

For everyone present at the park on 13 February 1915, it was an occasion to say farewell to loved ones, but for the Maori Members of Parliament who had engineered the Contingent's existence, it was something more:

The Europeans, who had seen that 500 march, have never forgotten: they still speak in high praise of them, of the splendid condition of the men, of their marching and of their general appearance which compared favourably with the best troops in the world. Some went as far as to say that they were even better than the white soldiers seen at Newtown Park. It is only right that it should be so. The heritage of their ancestors had been inherited by them, such as the haka, the tutu-ngarahu, canoe-paddling singing the performance of which in those days meant the rhythmical motion of the legs and swinging of the arms and the singing of the 'waiata'. That quality was already in them while they were learning these 'hakas' of the white races.[26]

Both Maori and Pakeha saw something special in the commitment of New Zealand youth to war: it would show the world something of the quality of New Zealand. To Maori legislators, however, the sending of the Maori Contingent was a message not just to the wider world but to New Zealand that the Maori contribution was of a standard that marked them equal to or above their Pakeha peers.

The unique nature of the Maori Contingent continued to catch the attention of cameramen, and it is the only unit for which film survives of its departure from New Zealand, its exploits in Egypt and on the Western Front and then, importantly, its return to New Zealand in 1919 as the New Zealand (Maori) Pioneer Battalion.

IN EGYPT AND GALLIPOLI

The first year of the war had already seen the NZEF embark for the war in Europe only to find themselves offloaded in Egypt with Turkey's entry into the war as an ally of Germany. The transports docked at Alexandria after passing through the Suez Canal, on 3 December 1914, seven weeks to the day after sailing through the Wellington heads. The two forces, consisting of the New Zealanders and of the Australian Imperial Force (AIF), made up of the 1st Australian Division, were formed into the Australian and New Zealand Army Corps under the command of Lieutenant-General Sir William Birdwood.[27] Because the 8,500 New Zealanders were not enough by themselves to form a viable division, which normally numbered between 15,000 and 20,000, Godley, the commander of the NZEF, found himself commanding a mixed division of New Zealanders and Australians. It was a most curious combination, being two brigades of infantry and two brigades of mounted rifles, lacking the normal amount of artillery and missing many of the specialist units normally found in a division.[28]

The New Zealand public was hungry for news. The newspapers were full of events on the Western Front, and every cinema vied to get scenic film of Egypt to show where the boys were training. The first film shown of New Zealanders was of the voyage out; then on 28 April 1915 the *Evening Post* advertised at the King's Theatre:

Our Boys in Egypt – A Grand Parade of New Zealand Forces in Cairo before Major General Godley, General Birdwood and Mr T. Mackenzie. Infantry, Mounted Ambulance, Transport, etc, all New Zealand's sons are in it, also the Australian Boys.[29]

The film was screened in New Zealand cinemas in the same week that news arrived of the landings on the Gallipoli Peninsula of Turkey.[30] It shows the final parade of the New Zealanders before embarking for the Dardanelles and ends with a haka by the Maori Contingent with the cameraman taking full advantage of the drama of the war dance.

The Maori Contingent had just arrived in Egypt and to their chagrin found that, instead of being integrated into the Anzac Corps going to Gallipoli, they were to go to Malta for further training. The remainder of the division, less the Mounted Rifles, however, were earmarked for General Sir Ian Hamilton's Mediterranean Expeditionary Force that was to undertake the landing on the Gallipoli Peninsula. Major H. Hart, second-in-command of the Wellington Infantry Battalion, summed up in his diary the Maori role as once again being an important part of the public face of the NZEF, but sidelined when it came to operational performance:

On the 3 April the Maori contingent gave a haka. The Maori have been giving displays, haka, etc to Generals and other big guns since their arrival. Today one exhibition was witnessed by Sir H. McMahon, Chief Commissioner, General

Maxwell, Birdwood, Godley and all the chief people of Cairo – and myself. On Monday the Maori go on to Malta for more haka displays presumably.[31]

Hart's cynicism is evident, but the Maori too wanted to be more than a sideshow. The NZEF War Diary reported: 'During the entertainment one of the officers, Capt Buck made a speech on behalf of the Maori asking that their claims for seeing active service may be favourably considered. At the conclusion of his speech, Sir John Maxwell [Commander-in-Chief Egypt] replied that they might rest assured that in due course they would be given an opportunity of proving their worth on the battle field, which statement met with universal approval.'[32] Buck's plea included the words: 'Though we are only a handful the remnant of a remnant of a people yet we consider that we are the old New Zealanders. No division can truly be called a New Zealand Division unless it numbers Maoris amongst its ranks.'[33] Yet the titling of the Maori contribution as 'The Maori Contingent' suggested something separate to the rest of the New Zealand endeavour. In 1915, that separateness was emphasised by the sending of the Maori Contingent to Malta on what seemed to Contingent members as something of a travelling show – 'a kind of Williamson company' as one of the soldiers said.[34] None of these undercurrents are evident on the film. But while the rest of the NZEF are indistinguishable, it is the Maori once again who stand out and provide the logical climax to the filming: not trained well enough to fight, for the public at home they are still the showpiece of New Zealand's contribution.[35]

The film was shown throughout New Zealand. Indeed it, with the film taken of the New Zealand convoy, was perhaps one of the most viewed films in New Zealand in 1915, capturing as it did the last glimpse of a body of New Zealanders who in four months from late April to late August 1915 suffered almost 100 per cent casualties. Three out of every ten New Zealanders seen on this parade would be dead by the end of the year. This was the last view of New Zealanders before they landed on Anzac Cove on 25 April 1915, and because there was no film from Gallipoli shown that year, this film of the last parade in Egypt became its substitute. This film, along with that of the troopship departures, the voyage out and the parade scenes of the New Zealanders and the Australians at Mena, Egypt, was edited and re-edited; titled and re-titled, and released over and over again throughout the year of the Gallipoli campaign. The public wanted more but despite advertisements that promised 'GENUINE PRESENT DAY WAR PICTURES – not Spectacular Parade and Review pictures taken years ago', all that was available was just that, the same pictures seen before. Despite this, the promise of the chance to recognise 'relatives and friends who are fighting for our liberty' worked, and the crowds came.[36]

No moving-film cameramen landed with Hamilton's Mediterranean Expeditionary Force on the Gallipoli Peninsula. It was the written word and photograph that the public had to rely upon for news from the battle-front at Gallipoli. Official reporters, including Ellis Ashmead-Bartlett from England and C. E. W. Bean from Australia, were attached to the contin-gents, and it was their reports of the landings that captured the imagination of the empire and overshadowed the landings of the British and French forces at Cape Helles. Ashmead-Bartlett's despatches, vividly 'eyewitnessed' from a battleship offshore, cemented the image of Anzacs as natural soldiers that the Australian and New Zealand public wanted to believe, and his role as an official British correspondent gave it a validity that no Australian or New Zealand reporter would have earned.[37] This image was matched by C. E. W. Bean's reports, but a New Zealand voice was missing. This was belatedly supplied by Malcolm Ross, the official correspondent for the NZEF, who did not get to Gallipoli until June 1915.[38] Ashmead-Bartlett returned to Gallipoli in June 1915, bringing with him a moving-film camera. His is the only film taken of the British effort in the Gallipoli campaign, and while New Zealanders appear in the film, the inter-titles generalised them into amorphous Anzacs; it was the same for the Maori Contingent. The great sap, the major communication trench linking up the isolated outposts north of the ANZAC Corps perimeter which they dug, is shown but they do not feature.[39]

The Maori had landed on 3 July 1915 to be employed in a Pioneer role but took part as infantry in the August offensive, with 48 dead, 126 wounded, and 234 hospitalised sick in August and September 1915.[40] Because of the extensive New Zealand casualties, the Maori platoons were absorbed into those of the New Zealand Mounted Rifles to make up the numbers. This loss of identity was compounded by Godley's decision to return to New Zealand four Maori officers whose performance he decided was unsatisfactory.[41] This had enormous repercussions among the Maori tribes in New Zealand. Te Hokowhitu A Tu represented Maori achievement and the willingness to perform alongside other New Zealanders in support of the empire, and now Maori effectiveness to lead in battle was being called into question. This public slight threatened the supply of reinforcements to the Contingent; Maori Members of Parliament resorted to enlisting reinforce-ments from Rarotonga and Niue to maintain numbers.[42] Godley belatedly realised the political ramifications of his actions and compromised, allowing the return to the front of some of the Maori officers sent home.[43]

The nine-month Gallipoli campaign had raised questions about Maori leadership, and the casualty rates confirmed that Maori could not sustain a separate infantry battalion or for the moment an independent 500-strong Pioneer unit in its navvy and light engineering role. Fellow New Zealanders on the Gallipoli Peninsula recognised their prowess, but in New Zealand, Maori politicians feared that Maori amalgamation into existing units would diminish public appreciation of their effort

MAORI IN THE UK AND FRANCE

The surviving film of New Zealanders training in the UK was the result of the efforts of the High Commissioner, Thomas Mackenzie, and T. E. Donne, the Trade Commissioner at the High Commission in London, who were Minister in charge, and first General Manager of the Department of Tourists and Health Resorts respectively. Both had long seen film as the medium to put New Zealand in front of the world. They cemented this in 1912 when they initiated an agreement between the New Zealand government and Pathé Frères for the distribution of New Zealand government film through the Pathé network.[44] This association continued when New Zealand troops arrived in the UK in 1915 and convalescent and training camps were established to deal with the New Zealand wounded from Gallipoli.

The inevitable 'charity' rugby matches were subject of newsreel attention, as were the convalescing soldiers of the Maori Contingent. One of the earliest Pathé newsreels of late 1915 is of a Maori Contingent rugby team at Boscombe playing in a charity match, with three segments of film of the same event being used as separate items and two inevitably featuring a haka.[45]

The Maori soldier became a focus of newsreel interest and this continued throughout the war. Film survives of the funeral of a Maori soldier at Walton-on-Thames in October 1916; it was released by Pathé under the title *Maori Funeral*. It shows the gun-carriage cortege marching from the hospital, with those inmates who can march following in threes, along with nurses and medical staff. A party of Maori soldiers carries the flag-draped coffin to the graveside where the firing party fires three volleys over the grave while the band plays.[46] Despite the title, it is a military funeral serviced largely by Pakeha who were no doubt dispatched from Codford or Hornchurch. The film projects the image that for the soldiers abroad, there was no racial distinction in death. As a Maori soldier is buried by his mainly Pakeha comrades, it is almost a coming-true of Te Rangi Hiroa's ideal: 'No division can truly be called a New Zealand Division unless it numbers Maoris amongst its ranks.'[47]

Sir Thomas Mackenzie was keen to see the formalisation of filming of New Zealand activities in England, and he used Donne to approach Pathé Frères 'with regard to the taking of Cinematograph Films in this Country that may be of interest to New Zealand'.[48] Pathé Frères provided one of its top cameramen as the New Zealand official photographer and cinematographer with the New Zealand Division in France (see below), and they produced another one of their best cameramen, Sergeant T. Scales, 'an expert Cinematograph Operator in the New Zealand Expeditionary Force', and 'a camera and all the necessary film stock'.[49] Scales would take thousands of feet of film of New Zealanders in 'Blighty' in the eighteen months that he worked as the NZEF's official cameraman in the UK. New Zealanders would see Maori in the many films taken and their faces along with the distinctive New Zealand 'lemon squeezer' headdress in photos and on film. Maori are evident in the arrival scenes at Liverpool in *With the New Zealand Expeditionary Force in the United Kingdom, Part 1*: a 7000-feet multi-reel feature, a compilation of Scales's filming that encompassed all aspects of a New Zealander's experience in war from his arrival in England for training, to his despatch to the front in France and Belgium, to his return to New Zealand as a wounded convalescent.[50] Other film companies also continued to film New Zealanders, some having a distinct Maori focus. There is the Gaumont Graphic item *Maori War Dance*, showing members of the New Zealand (Maori) Pioneer Battalion doing the haka, that was released on 19 January 1919, immediately prior to their return to New Zealand.[51]

The missing elements in all of this are the local films commissioned by local theatre managers in the UK. One rare example survives. The Strawberry Fête was a day of fun and sports promoted by the 'Dairymen, Fruiterers, Grocers and Bakers' of Torquay on Alexandra Day, 27 June 1917; a film was taken of the events and screened in the local cinema. Torquay was the site of the New Zealand Discharge Depot for the evacuation back home of the permanently unfit, and New Zealanders feature prominently in the crowds and events. People exit the Town Pavilion after watching the 'Maori War Dance', and a group of Maori Pioneer Battalion veterans walk towards the park for the 'evening performances of the Maori Nature Dances'. Visually, for most of the film they are part of the crowd which included civilians and soldiers, Maori and Pakeha in their uniforms, mingling together, taking part in the sports events, collecting prizes from the mayor's wife and sitting at tables with female friends. It is only at the end that the

Maori Pioneers stand out: when performing their haka. If the town's relationships can be judged by what we see on the film, then it seems Maori and New Zealander are merged into one in the public perception.[52]

The New Zealand Division had been formed in Egypt in February 1916. In forming the three infantry brigades and three artillery brigades that constituted the core of the division, its commander, Major-General Sir Andrew Russell, also had to form myriad minor units to provide essential support to the division. One of these was the Pioneer Battalion, just over 1,000-strong, the same size as an infantry battalion; it was to be a working group of practical engineers who would assist the Engineer field companies within the division.[53] Maori losses on Gallipoli had shown that they could not sustain an infantry role and, despite the arrival of the Second Contingent as reinforcements, could not provide the numbers necessary for a complete Pioneer Battalion.

On the formation of the New Zealand Division, the members of the Maori Contingent were grouped with former members of the Otago Mounted Rifles, who were reduced in numbers to one mounted squadron. Lieutenant Colonel G. A. King, NZSC, was appointed Commanding Officer of the Pioneer Battalion. The Maori formed two companies in the four-company battalion. The Second Maori Contingent arrived in France as reinforcements in April 1916 and, like its predecessor, was featured on film. Two brief Gaumont Gazette segments showing the inspection of the Second Maori Contingent by Major-General Henderson, Director of Medical Services, survive from late September 1915. They show the Second Maori Contingent on parade at Narrow Neck Camp in Auckland. These were distributed around the world in both English- and French-language versions.[54]

In France, arrangements were made for British official cameramen to include the New Zealand Division in their filming. One film was made under these arrangements, with an official cameraman filming the visit to the New Zealand Division of the Secretary of State for the Colonies in March 1917. This coincided with efforts by Mackenzie and Donne in London to secure a New Zealand cameraman from Pathé Frères. The arrangement saw Henry Armytage Sanders 'appointed official photographer to the New Zealand Expeditionary Force with rank of Lieutenant'; he joined the New Zealand Division in France in April 1917.[55]

The sole official British film of the New Zealand Division taken in March 1917 gives a snapshot of the work of the division; we see the Secretary of State inspect a guard of honour made up of men from Pioneer Battalion, part Maori, part Otago, with Major Peter Buck (Te Rangi Hiroa) as the escort officer. The film deliberately shows all aspects of the division, its infantry and artillery units, life in the line and inevitably a rugby match against the 38th Welsh Division. In the film taken before Gallipoli, there had been a focus on the Maori Contingent that is missing here; now they are integrated into the work of the division, and their being part of the guard of honour might have escaped many viewers.[56] The British official cameraman is responding to the programme given to him by the divisional staff, and from what we see it is clear that Russell, the New Zealand commander, wanted New Zealand to see an overview of the work of the division on the Western Front.

Sanders took a series of films of the New Zealand Division between May 1917 and January 1919. What stands out in these films is the degree of integration that is achieved. One is conscious of the Maori presence: this is not because they feature more than the other units, but being the only Maori unit they naturally stand out, particularly in the film of the visit of William Massey, the New Zealand prime minister, and Sir Joseph Ward during a quiet period in early July 1918.[57] There are two segments featuring what was now the New Zealand (Maori) Pioneer Battalion: one shows Ward offering a large cigar to a Maori soldier who accepts it with considerable aplomb, the second shows the battalion giving three cheers, followed by an energetic haka. However, in the dozen or so surviving films taken by Sanders of the New Zealand Division, this is the only one where Maori stand out.

Rugby played a prominent part in the filming of the NZEF, but few Maori players made the divisional representative team which played a number of games against other divisions as well as French selections throughout the war. In October 1918, with victory certain, it was again time for rugby with the New Zealand Divisional 'All Blacks' playing France at the Parc de Princes before a capacity crowd. Once again, there was no Maori team member but on film we see a young Maori corporal of the New Zealand (Maori) Pioneer Battalion leading the team in the haka while a fellow Pioneer stands by holding his lemon squeezer hat. The New Zealanders won 14–0.[58] The film captures a sensitive and important issue: the haka was a standard feature before most games against non-New Zealand teams, but here we see evidence that, in the New Zealand Division at least, it was a borrowed ritual and, in this rare example, due deference is being shown to its rightful owners.

The *Westmorland* berthed at 9 a.m. on Sunday morning 6 April 1919, bringing the New Zealand (Maori) Pioneer Battalion home: it was the only unit, apart from the Tunnelling Company, that would return to

New Zealand as a complete entity, the others returning according to their original reinforcement drafts. The press reported on the 'greatest Maori ceremony of its kind held since the royal visit to Rotorua in 1901';[59] it was one where, for the first time in history, thousands gathered within the Auckland Domain to welcome home a body of Maori that New Zealand had sent abroad to fight as New Zealanders. The acting prime minister Sir James Allen took the salute, but all attention was on the welcome to the warriors of Te Hokowhitu A Tu returning home. The welcome is captured on film and this and the film of the Gisborne Hui Aroha (welcoming ceremony by the East Coast tribes), which has not survived, toured New Zealand cinemas. It is an important film because it closes the loop and ensures that Te Hokowhitu A Tu is the only New Zealand unit in the First World War to have on film a record of its existence from departure in 1915, to its work in Egypt and France and then return to New Zealand. The return home film, though brief, captures the emotion of the moment.[60] The press reported:

The chief ceremony of the afternoon was a tangi for the departed. The soldiers of each tribe sat in the midst of an enclosure in the camp adjoining the sports ground and around them were gathered the sorrowing ones. With low wailing and chants of sorrow, led by their chiefs, the mourners grieved for those who would never return. It was a scene of real pathos and emotion, the significance of which seemed to be lost to the crowds of white people who pressed in upon the mourners, seeming to regard it as a scene of entertainment, instead of one of solemnity and grief.[61]

Maori images on film before 1914 had conformed to a racial, tourist-inspired stereotype that portrayed them as noble savages living at peace in an idyllic land. It was an image that many New Zealanders were as prepared to believe as its intended audience in Australia, the United States and Europe. New Zealanders had to journey to Gallipoli and France for Maori and Pakeha to identify each other's worth as soldiers and individuals and to see themselves as New Zealanders. This integration was understood and reflected in the film taken by the official British cameraman and the British-recruited NZEF cameramen, all of whom worked to the directions given by New Zealand Expeditionary Force headquarters in France or the UK. While scenic images of Maori continued to be produced in New Zealand, the emphasis within the New Zealand Expeditionary Force was to tell a story of New Zealand's war effort. The Maori Pioneer Battalion's story was integral to that story. The respect that Pakeha New Zealand soldiers had for their Maori counterparts can be read in that single surviving image of the New Zealand Division's 'All Blacks' doing the haka before the start of the game in Paris against a French selection.

Maori attracted the attention of the overseas cameramen, particularly in the UK, but this was balanced by the cameramen's interest in New Zealand's participation in sports, particularly rugby, and in the New Zealanders' interaction with the British public. In most cases, New Zealander and Maori became interchangeable in the overseas film editor's eye. The return of Te Hokowhitu A Tu in March 1919 became a focus of cinematic attention, but for most of the viewing Pakeha civilians at home, the welcome scenes were curiosity pieces, with Maori being still largely seen as stereotypes, if not figures of fun. It would take fifty years and another major war before this image changed.

NOTES

1 I am grateful for the support of the staff of the NZ Film Archive in the research and writing of this chapter. The following are the accounts in English: James Cowan, *The Maoris in the Great War: A History of the New Zealand Native Contingent and the Pioneer Battalion* (Christchurch: Whitcombe & Tombs, 1926); Christopher Pugsley, *Te Hokowhitu A Tu: The Maori Pioneer Battalion in the First World War* (Auckland: Reed/Raupo, 2005); Ashley Gould, 'Maori and the First World War', in Ian McGibbon (ed.), *The Oxford Companion to New Zealand Military History* (Auckland: Oxford University Press, 2000), 296–9; P. S O'Connor, 'The Recruitment of Maori Soldiers 1914–1918', *Political Science*, 19, 2, 1967, 48–83.

2 Pugsley, *Te Hokowhitu A Tu*, 81.

3 'Maori and Half-Caste Population', in *The New Zealand Official Year Book 1915* (Wellington: Government Printer, 1915), 120–3.

4 O'Connor, 'Recruitment of Maori Soldiers 1914–1918'.

5 The establishment of the Pioneer Battalion was 29 officers and 1,001 other ranks, Chief of General Staff, Headquarters New Zealand Military Forces, *War 1914–1918 New Zealand Expeditionary Force: Its Provision and Maintenance* (Wellington: Government Printer, 1919), 9, 14 and 41.

6 Rikihana Carkeek, *Home Little Maori Home: A Memoir of the Maori Contingent 1914–1916* (Wellington: Tōtika Publications, 2003).

7 Margaret McClure, *The Wonder Country: Making New Zealand Tourism* (Auckland University Press, 2004), 26.

8 A fragment survives in the New Zealand Film Archive (henceforth NZFA), Wellington: 'Queen Victoria's Diamond Jubilee Procession, 22 June 1897', F11225.

9 *New Zealand Times*, 14 September 1897, quoted in Clive Sowry, 'Eighty Years of Film Exhibition in Wellington', Part Two (1897–1900), *Sequence*, July 1977.

10 The ambivalence of this image of Maori in photography is suggested in Anne Maxwell, *Colonial Photography and Exhibition: Representations of the 'Native'*

and the Making of European Identities (London: Continuum, 2000). For a view of Maori political, cultural and social issues in this period, see Angela Ballera, *Iwi: The Dynamics of Maori Tribal Organisation c1769-c1945* (Wellington: Victoria University Press, 1998); Lindsay Cox, *Kotahiangi: The Search for Maori Political Unity* (Auckland: Oxford University Press, 1993); Harry C. Evison, *Te Wai Pounamu, the Greenstone Island: A History of the Southern Maori during the European Colonisation of New Zealand* (Christchurch: Aoraki Press, 1993); Raeburn Lange, *May the People Live: A History of Maori Health Development from 1900 to 1920* (Auckland University Press, 1999).

11 'Maori and Half-Caste Population'.

12 See correspondence, 1901 Royal Visit, IA I, 1908/864, Archives New Zealand, Wellington.

13 'Royal Visit of the Duke and Duchess of Cornwall and York to New Zealand, 1901', NZFA, F2468.

14 'Personal Matters', *Evening Post*, 13 September, 1912, 7.

15 'The "Lost" Méliès New Zealand Films', NZFA. See individual films, Progressive Silent Film List, Silent Era, www.silentera.com. Accessed 15 January 2008.

16 Interview with George Tarr, 'Film Making in New Zealand', T259, Radio Sound Archives, Copy NZFA; also see Programme, 'The Maori,' Rotorua Maori Mission Choir and Entertainers, Town Hall, Wellington, Tuesday 26 July 1910, photo image 71610-ac-1–1, Alexander Turnbull Library, Wellington.

17 'A Description concerning the Maori Contingent of Aotearoa and Te Waipounamu who took part in the Great War Collated by the Committee of the Maori Members of Parliament' in Pugsley, *Te Hokowhitu A Tu*, 30.

18 Pugsley, *Te Hokowhitu*, 21–2.

19 *Ibid*.

20 'American Officers' Visit to Rotorua', 1908, NZFA, F3033. Peter Henry Buck (1877?–1951) was a pioneering Maori doctor, sportsman and Member of Parliament, who would gain world renown as an anthropologist and Director of the Bernice P. Bishop Museum in Hawaii. Of Ngati Mutanga descent, the name Te Rangi Hiroa, from one of his illustrious ancestors, was conferred upon him by his tribal elders. M. P. K. Sorrenson, 'Buck, Peter Henry 1877? – 1951', *Dictionary of New Zealand Biography*, updated 22 June 2007, www.dnzb.govt. nz/ accessed 1 November 2010.

21 'New Zealand Reinforcements Leaving', 13 February 1915, Pathé Gazette, British Pathé No. 1860.48. ITN Archive, London.

22 *Evening Post*, 18 February 1915, 2–3; 29–31 March 1915, 2.

23 *Akaroa Mail*, January 1917.

24 Florence Ripley Mastin, 'At the Movies', in Catherine Reilly, *Scars upon My Heart: Women's Poetry and Verse of the First World War* (London: Virago Press, 1981), 70.

25 'Off to the Front', 1914, NZFA, F1820.

26 'A Description concerning the Maori Contingent', 30.

27 Christopher Pugsley, *Gallipoli: The New Zealand Story* (Auckland: Raupo/ Penguin, fourth edition, 2006), 70.

28 *Ibid.*, 83.

29 *Evening Post*, Wednesday, 28 April 1915, 2.

30 *New Zealand Herald*, 19 March 1915 – 25 April 1915.

31 Major H. Hart Diary, Wellington Infantry Battalion, 3 April 1915, National Army Museum New Zealand/Alexander Turnbull Library, Wellington; see also John Crawford (ed.), *The Devil's Own War: The First World War Diary of Brigadier-General Herbert Hart* (Auckland: Exisle Publishing, 2008).

32 3 April 1915, NZ Defence Forces, *NZEF War Diary 1914* (Wellington: Government Printer, 1915).

33 J. B. Condliffe, *Te Rangi Hiroa: The Life of Sir Peter Buck* (Christchurch: Whitcombe & Tombs, 1926), 27.

34 Pugsley, *Te Hokowhitu A Tu*, 35. The Williamson company was one of the largest touring theatre companies in Australia.

35 The film's purchase for the New Zealand government was at Godley's initiative. The 'world rights' of the 505-metre film were purchased for £160 and it was despatched to New Zealand on the SS *Willochra* addressed to the Tourist Department, arriving on 16 July 1915.

36 Advertisement, 'NZ Troopship to the Dardanelles', *Evening Post*, 30 September 1915, 2. See also advertisement, Shortt's Theatre, 'The Heroes of the Dardanelles' and The Empress Theatre, 'Trentham to Mena's Great Camp', *Evening Post*, 12 July 1915, 2.

37 Ellis Ashmead-Bartlett, *Ashmead-Bartlett's Despatches from the Dardanelles* (London: G. Newnes, 1915).

38 His first despatch 'In Action … "The White Ghurkar"', in four columns, appeared in the *Evening Post*, 3 July 1915, 18.

39 'With the Dardanelles Expedition: Heroes of Gallipoli, 1915', retitled and recaptioned by C. E. W. Bean for the Australian War Memorial in the 1920s, Australian War Memorial, Canberra, F00069.

40 Pugsley, *Te Hokowhitu A Tu*, 42–5.

41 P. S. O'Connor, 'Recruitment of Maori Soldiers, 1914–18', 57.

42 *Ibid.*

43 *Ibid.*

44 Memo for the Ministry of Internal Affairs, dated 9 October 1912. Kinematograph Films, Dominion Museum, Museum of New Zealand, Wellington.

45 Boscombe, 'New Zealand Maori "Haka" for Deserving Charity', Pathé Gazette, 1915–16, Pathé, 1902.42; 'Maori soldiers R & R aka Maori Contingent Resting' ('New Zealand Maori Soldiers who took part with the Anzac Forces in the Gallipoli Campaign are resting for a while in England'), 1915–16, Pathé 1850.05; 'Maori "Haka" War Cry', 1915–16, Pathé 2346.12. All ITN Archive, London.

46 'World War I Funeral Procession for a New Zealand Soldier', October 1916, NZFA, F48685.

47 Condliffe, *Te Rangi Hiroa*, 27, quoted in Pugsley, *Te Hokowhitu A Tu*, 34.

48 Mackenzie to Prime Minister and Defence Department, 'Cinematograph Films', dated 1 November 1917, Personal Papers, 32700 Sgt T. F. Scales,

ZWR 9/18. Archive New Zealand, Wellington. Mackenzie had been knighted in 1916.

49 *Ibid.*

50 'With the New Zealand Expeditionary Force in the UK', Part 1, 1917–1918, NZFA, F1001.

51 BGT407052726, 815(2), 'Maori War Dance' 18 January 1919, New Zealand-related Material in the Gaumont Graphic Newsreels (UK) (Reuters–ITN), BGT407052726, 815(2) and Gaumont-Journal, France, Gaumont Pathe Archive, 93400 Saint-Ouen, France.

52 'Strawberry Fete: Promoted by the Four Allied Trades Dairymen, Fruiterers, Grocers and Bakers, Held at Torquay on Alexandra Day', 27th June 1917, Torquay Public Archives.

53 *War 1914–1918 New Zealand Expeditionary Force. Its Provision and Maintenance*, 9, 14, and 41. John Studholme, *New Zealand Expeditionary Force, Record of Personal Services during the War of Officers, Nurses, and First-Class Warrant Officers; and other facts relating to the NZEF* (Wellington: Government Printer, 1928), 15–17.

54 'Major General Henderson Inspects Maori Troops, 1915', Gaumont Graphic, NZFA F48604; see BGT407040844 0, 'Maori Troops in New Zealand: Major General Henderson inspects the Second Contingent of Maori Troops before they leave New Zealand for the Front', 15 November 1915 Reuters–ITN Archives; 1549GJ 00005 'Nouvelle Zélande: Le Major General Henderson passé en revue un Contingent Maori avant son depart pour le Front', Journal Gaumont, France; BGT407040891, 495.1 'New Zealander's Response: The 2nd Maori Contingent on Parade', 20 December 1915 Reuters–ITN Archives; 1606GJ 00003, 'Nouvelle Zélande: Parade par le Deuxieme Contingent de Soldats Maori', 1916, Journal Gaumont, France.

55 High Commissioner to Minister of Defence dated 6 January 1917; Allen to G. W. Russell dated 8 January 1917; Minister of Defence to High Commissioner dated 11 January 1917; High Commissioner to Minister of Defence dated 23 March 1917, D12/113, Archive New Zealand, Wellington.

56 'Review of New Zealand Troops by Hon. Walter Long, 1917', NZFA, F4330.

57 'Visit of the Hon. W. H. Massey and Sir J. Ward to Western Front 30 June – 4 July 1918', NZFA, F1068.

58 'Seeing Sights of Paris Before Football Match 1918', NZFA, F4517.

59 'The Maori Battalion', *Auckland Weekly News*, 10 April 1919, 17. Illustrations, 31, 34–5, 38–9.

60 'Maori Contingent Home, 1919', Australian Gazette 451, NZFA, F29570.

61 'The Maori Battalion', 17.

PART III

Nationalism, memory and literature

'He was black, he was a White man, and a dinkum Aussie': race and empire in revisiting the Anzac legend

Peter Stanley

For over ninety years, Australia has been interpreted, defined, celebrated and criticised through the idea of 'Anzac'. The word – and particularly its many meanings that have changed over time – can mystify. Dale Blair, an astringent critic of the simple-minded acceptance of Anzac and the author of a frank analysis of its expression through one battalion's experience, took as the epigram to his *Dinkum Diggers* a complaint by a soldier in the Great War. Frank Gates, a 1st Division machine-gunner, as the Australian War Memorial's condescending catalogue entry put it, was a 'young man of limited life experience, who rarely engaged in self-reflection'. Even so, he wrote to his mother how

It does not matter where one goes or what paper one reads, there seems to be hardly anything but Anzac and the Anzacs. Anzacs this and Anzacs that until we have become sick of the word.[1]

Many Australian historians may echo this cry of frustration and despair. Can we not evade the complexities and the dominance of the word? Can we not set aside its gravitational pull in drawing attention to the Great War and what it entailed? Sadly, it is neither possible nor desirable to evade the word or its meanings. It is not possible to understand Australia's experience of war in the twentieth century without also understanding the idea of Anzac.

'Anzac' as a word was originally coined as an acronym (supposedly the first such formation in the English language) by military clerks in Egypt early in 1915. It rapidly passed from the functional to the symbolic. Soon after the Australian and New Zealand Army Corps took part in the invasion of Gallipoli from April 1915, 'Anzac' spawned a legion of meanings. It signified both the area of Turkey the invaders held ('Anzac area', or simply 'Anzac') and the name of those comprising the force ('the Anzacs'). Even before the end of the campaign (which ended in defeat and disgrace with the evacuation of Anzacs in December 1915), it came to represent an idea, even an ideal. 'Anzac', wrote the war correspondent Charles Bean, the chief necromancer of the word, 'stood, and still stands, for reckless valour in a good cause, for enterprise, resourcefulness, fidelity, comradeship, and endurance that will never own defeat'.[2] This celebrated declaration is heard in Anzac Day addresses each year and is the classic statement of what has come to be seen as the 'Anzac legend'.[3] But the legend is not timeless. While Anzac as an idea remains a part of Australia's understanding of itself, its expressions have changed.

'ANZAC, RACE AND EMPIRE': THE HISTORY OF THE LEGEND

Charles Bean was Australian-born (in Bathurst in 1879) but British-educated. Rediscovering his homeland in the decade after federation in 1901, and especially its bush workers, Bean revered the men of the bush especially. Here is the root of the persistent but unduly emphasised connection between the Anzac legend and the bush legend.[4] Bean survived Gallipoli (where he was wounded) and the Western Front. On his return, he devoted his life to understanding and recording what Australia had done in the Great War. His most important achievements were the writing of the official history (which took him to 1942) and the creation of the Australian War Memorial, which opened in Canberra in 1941. By the time of his death, in 1968, he was widely regarded as one of the greatest Australian historians.

Bean's 1916 *Anzac Book* became the first and classic statement of the Anzac legend. It was an expression of how Australians stood up to the challenge of Gallipoli and how they would face the greater ordeals the Great War would bring. Bean is central to the genesis of the legend, by what he chose to stress and celebrate and what he decided to omit or underplay. In the early 1980s, a debate raged over whether by selecting contributions from soldiers on Gallipoli, Bean consciously sought to define the qualities displayed by the men already called Anzacs.[5] For those unfamiliar with the concept, Alistair Thomson provides a concise summary in *Anzac Memories* (1994):

At Gallipoli, and then on the Western Front, the Anzacs proved the character of Australian manhood for all the world to see and, through their victories and sacrifices, established a nation in spirit as well as in name. The Australian soldier of the legend was enterprising and independent, loyal to his mates and to his country, bold in battle, but cheerfully undisciplined out of the line and contemptuous of military etiquette and the British officer class ... According to the legend these qualities, fostered in the Australian bush, discovered and immortalised in war, typified Australians and Australian society ... the nation that 'came of age' at Gallipoli.[6]

Thomson does not endorse or advocate the legend – indeed, his own work challenges it – but he states its standard expression. Note that the legend has been adopted by 'Australians and Australian society' as a whole, regardless of whether individuals served in the Great War, or any war. While commitment to the legend is expressed in many ways (by reading family or military history or visiting military museums), the principal expression of the legend became the observation of Anzac Day, the national day of commemoration, namely 25 April.

The survivors of Gallipoli marked the first anniversary of the invasion of Gallipoli ('the Landing at Anzac') in Britain and Egypt on 25 April 1916. Soon it became a day of mourning and commemoration in Australia. In the 1920s, paralleling New Zealand's adoption of the anniversary, the day coalesced as the distinctive Australian expression of remembrance and was accorded a much greater adherence than 11 November, Armistice (and later Remembrance) Day. Anzac Day, for instance, soon became an official public holiday, unlike Remembrance Day. Though universally observed, Anzac Day saw the expression of different forms of commemoration. Graham Seal, in *Inventing Anzac*, distinguishes between a formal 'Anzac Tradition' (a phrase coined originally by Charles Bean) – the expression of commemoration by governments and official bodies – and 'the Digger Tradition' – the informal, demotic expression of remembrance by communities, ex-servicemen and generally unofficial bodies.[7] Seal argues that the formal Anzac tradition has virtually subsumed the informal tradition. The Anzac legend we know today is very different to the idea that evolved in the Great War and the 1920s. It has been and can be turned to accommodate new needs expressed by parts of Australian society.

The classic expression of the legend has in the past twenty years or so come under sustained scrutiny and criticism as part of the discovery of Australian military history by academics. Historians have explored the origins, nature and implications of the legend, gender and war, commemoration and memory.[8] One of the most successful of these ventures resulted in Elena Govor's book *Russian Anzacs in Australian History* (2005) – a discovery of the thousand Anzacs in the Great War who came from the old Russian empire.[9] The legend is much more ethnically diverse than we might suppose. Despite this vigorous scrutiny and re-evaluation, two aspects that have not been investigated with much rigour are in fact race and empire. Stephen Garton, in a valuable survey, observes that lost in this obsession with 'nation' is any sense that, in 1915, 'nation' was neither necessarily the most prominent nor the most important 'meaning' of Anzac: 'Race and Empire were equally prevalent'.[10] They were indeed, but the modern configuration of the Anzac legend gives little emphasis to them. This article argues that a reconsideration of the historical reality on which the legend is based is merited. This is justified, whether on the empirical ground that race and empire were more important to contemporaries than they are to modern Australians or on the theoretical ground that they constitute useful categories by which to interrogate the omissions and emphases in the popular and scholarly historiography. Either way, in order to understand the historical experience and significance of the legend, we need to explore the relationship between Anzac, race and empire.

'HIS FATHER'S EMPIRE ZEAL': ANZAC AND EMPIRE

The evolution of Anzac into an Australian civic religion has diminished and concealed the prominence of imperial sentiment in its initial form. The Australian army in the Great War (and indeed, for much of the Second World War) was the Australian *Imperial* Force (AIF). The middle word is today variously ignored or derided. It is certainly difficult for twenty-first-century Australians to comprehend the duality of identity at the heart of early-twentieth-century Australia.

At federation in 1901, Australians were a proud constituent of the British empire. By the centenary of the federation, not only had the empire eroded, but Australia's attachment to it had almost entirely disappeared. The gradual separation from the empire became the dominant motif of the national story in the twentieth century. Visible fissures in wartime – the Breaker Morant case in the Boer War, the evident mishandling of Australian (and indeed imperial) forces in the Great War, on Gallipoli and the Western Front, and the debacles of Greece and Crete and Malaya and Singapore in the Second World War – accelerated this process.[11] Wartime defeats and disasters (even within ultimately victorious coalitions) helped to turn Australians from a sentimental and benign view of empire to a suspicion and even dislike of the idea that they could ever have once been comfortable with a subordinate position.

At the time, however, many Australians saw the qualities of their troops displayed in the Gallipoli campaign as a vindication of their membership of the empire. Leonard Mann, who served in the AIF and wrote one of the most sensitive fictional evocations, *Flesh in Armour*, explained the motivations of one of his characters, Charl Bentley:

He had been brought up on such stuff as Green's *Short History of the English People*, *Westward Ho*, Tennyson's *Revenge* and *Deeds that Won the Empire* . . . Charl had come to smile a little of late years at his father's Empire zeal, but he too was proud of his English blood.[12]

W. H. Fitchett's imperial history-cum-homily *Deeds that Won the Empire* (1897) crops up repeatedly in discussions of Australian attitudes to the imperial relationship, but it alone does not explain the degree or depth of attachment to the empire, a bond that the blunders and slaughter of the war strained and weakened but did not break.

Many contemporary expressions of imperial loyalty can be found. For example, Peter Board, the Director of Education in New South Wales, saw the Australian contribution to an imperial war effort as proof that the new nation had became 'an active partner in a worldwide empire'. For Board, 25 April became 'an Australian Empire Day', marking the emergence of a nation whose 'men and women have striven and fought and died in an Empire struggle'.[13] Few Australian historians have considered Gallipoli or the Great War in terms of this relationship. The few include the late John Robertson in *Anzac and Empire*, and the late Eric Andrews in *The Anzac Illusion*.[14] Neither has been followed in the twenty-first century by anyone sceptical of nationalist claims (unless it is myself, who sought to place this most fiercely contested part of the Anzac line in a New Zealand and British perspective in my *Quinn's Post, Anzac, Gallipoli*).[15]

Australia's preoccupation with national identity points to the single most pervasive trope in the literature. Australia, from even before the 25 April landing, has always freighted the war with national identity. Wilbraham Fowler, an Innisfail bank clerk about to go ashore with the 15th Battalion, described 25 April 1915 in his diary at the time as 'the most Historical date in Australian History'.[16] For Charles Bean, whose official history hinged on the question of how 'the Australian people – and the Australian character . . . come through the . . . test of this, their first great war', nationhood stood at the core of what Gallipoli meant.[17]

The unambiguously independent, assertively nationalist Australia of the early twenty-first century finds it uncomfortable to acknowledge that the AIF was an 'Australian Imperial Force'. Billy Hughes, prime minister for the last three years of the war, was a 'King and Empire man'. However, this simple assertion of imperial unity did not outlast the defeats in Greece and Singapore in the Second World War. Even what became the Returned Soldiers, Sailors and Airmen's Imperial League of Australia dropped the 'Imperial' in 1965. This transformation in attitudes toward the empire did not primarily occur as a result of academic books or scholarly debates.

Australian understanding of Anzac, and of war as a whole, has always been deeply influenced by journalism, and especially by journalists interpreting Australian war history. There has been a strong connection between the Gallipoli campaign and journalists since 1915 and much of the popular history of Anzac has been written by them. Ellis Ashmead-Bartlett's celebrated despatch describing the 25 April landing galvanised Australian opinion. It not only shaped Australians' perceptions of their troops' performance, but contributed to recruiting and laid the foundation of the Anzac legend created, as we have seen, by another war correspondent on Gallipoli, Charles Bean.[18]

While journalists have always comprised a segment of the authors in the field, in the past few years they have emerged as a particularly notable force. Les Carlyon's *Gallipoli* became a best-seller in 2001, though its inflated rhetoric and simplistic depictions of commanders and their decisions (especially British ones) attracted derision from serious historians.[19] Carlyon, however, became the court historian to John Howard (conservative prime minister from 1996 to 2007), who awarded Carlyon his inaugural (and only) award for history in 2007. Carlyon received the award for his 2006 book *The Great War*, an even more otiose effort than *Gallipoli* in national celebration of the Anzac (that is, Australian) achievement.[20] The result is that in popular understanding and public memory, early twentieth-century Australia is relentlessly interpreted through the prism of the assumptions and concerns of early twenty-first-century nationalist Australia. The distorting consequences of this unwelcome but seemingly ineradicable process can also be seen in the way 'race' as an idea has been practically expunged from the modern Anzac legend, compared to the historical reality.

'BLACK JOHNNIE' AND 'WHITE JOHNNIE': ANZAC AND A RACIAL IDEAL

During the Great War, Australians fought Ottoman Turkey and imperial Germany. The Germans, though denigrated as 'Huns' and accused by wartime propaganda of appalling atrocities (all but a few later found to be gross exaggerations) were European and therefore worthy opponents. The Turks were not regarded as a 'White' opponent, though early forebodings that they were a savage enemy were allayed by their bravery and by the relative absence of atrocities, except those perpetrated against the helpless prisoners of war. A grudging respect between antagonists acknowledging the other's courage grew up on Gallipoli, though it has been exaggerated in popular romantic writings in the past decade or so.

Racial pride occupied an unspoken centrality in the AIF's identity. Recalling a comrade killed early in the Gallipoli campaign, Joe Maxwell remembered that 'a whiter man and a better soldier never lived'.[21] The phrase recurs, both in contemporary record and in modern Australia, as an ironic throw-back to a time when the phrase represented the highest praise. What Bean called 'the battle of race' was instead fought out between members of the AIF and the inhabitants of the non-white countries through which Australians passed. In practice, this meant German New Guinea, Ceylon, South and West Africa and, above all, Egypt and Palestine. There, elements of Australian experience and reaction which occurred have been largely suppressed in the classic modern manifestation of the Anzac legend and, more surprisingly, in its analysis.

A volunteer Australian Naval and Military Expeditionary Force occupied Germany's colonies in New Guinea in the war's opening weeks. It remained to garrison Rabaul and its dependent posts until the war's end, when New Guinea became an Australian mandate territory under the League of Nations. The Australians, from 1915 comprising Tropical Force, adopted the demeanour of Australian colonial administrators in neighbouring Papua, and essentially continued the German colonial administration. Indeed, they emphasised the white man's dominance by publicly punishing 'natives' who challenged the new regime, notably in a celebrated flogging in Rabaul in 1915. Tropical Force has largely been overlooked in the construction of Anzac, as has been its part in enforcing the racial regime of White Australia.[22]

On Gallipoli, Australians served alongside Indian troops. There could be few more dramatic contrasts between protagonists in the Gallipoli campaign than between Australia and India, on almost every level. Australia, a politically progressive and consciously European self-governing dominion with a small population, sent a large force of volunteer citizen-soldiers to fight on Gallipoli (of perhaps 50,000 men). India, disenfranchised, non-European and a vast patchwork of possession and protectorate, sent a small part of its huge volunteer professional army to Gallipoli: just over 3,000 combatant troops and 1,800 non-combatant 'followers', as the Indian Army called its mule drivers, cooks and laundrymen.[23] The disparity in numbers between the Australians and the Indians – roughly ten to one – suggests the relative significance of their respective experience and memory. The disparity is reversed when considering the cost the two forces paid in terms of lives lost. Just over 8,000 of the Australians died as a result of the campaign, a loss rate of about one in six. But 1,624 of the Indian combatants were killed, a loss rate of greater than one in two.[24] This was the heaviest casualty rate of all the protagonists in the campaign: much heavier than the Turkish and British empire loss rates, grievous though they were.

Australian (and New Zealand) diaries of Gallipoli invariably mention the Indian troops favourably. Indian mule drivers were 'most painstaking and patient in everything they do', sharing their oatmeal cakes or simply seen as admirable because 'it was a treat to see them work'.[25] Indians were seen as martial and manly, good comrades. Indian camp followers regarded Anzacs as customers: 'It is said that one of these Indian mule drivers made a fortune by using his clippers to cut the soldiers' hair,' John Treloar recorded in August 1915.[26] Remarkably for a nation in which racism was so deeply ingrained, personal, if temporary, friendships grew up between men of two very different forces. Arthur Hallam, a former scoutmaster from South Australia, wrote home (in a letter published in the local newspaper) how 'yesterday evening I was chatting to a Hindoo gunner ... and after writing his name in my autograph book, he cooked me some chuppetees [sic], and again this breakfast ... a very pleasant change'.[27] Indian troops, a New Zealand gunner recorded at the time, were 'the finest type of coloured men that it was possible to meet'.[28]

The impression of comradeship surmounting the constraints of race, language, diet and religion prevailed in the decades following the Great War. In 1919, 'A Returned Soldier' offered a long, dramatised account of an encounter between an Australian and 'Indian' soldiers (ethnicity unspecified), supposedly on the eve of the August 1915 battle on Gallipoli. Despite the limitations of a common language, 'the two soldiers, vastly different in aspect and build', nevertheless strike up an acquaintance. The Australian greets the Indian 'Salaam Johnnie!' and asks 'Johnnie! – you got curry?' The two share a meal and a conversation rendered ludicrous by neither speaking more than a few words of the other's tongue, but as fighting men, 'the black Johnnie is on a level with the white Johnnie'.[29] In the decades after the war, ex-service journals praised 'Indians' as fighting men, especially the Indian Mountain Artillery batteries that served at Anzac throughout the Gallipoli campaign.[30] Often the recollections carried the edge of condescending humour, and described generic 'Indians'. For example, in a memoir of the Imperial Camel Corps, an Indian – also called 'Johnnie' – supposedly observes of a two-up game that Australians were 'most religious men' because they followed the toss of the pennies with 'Jesus Christ, he's headed them again'.[31]

Encounters with Indian troops during the war were relatively rare after Gallipoli, but the seemingly universal regard they attracted may have helped to break down common white Australian assumptions and prejudices. At the same time, Indian soldiers, however admirable, were also manifestations of an empire that became increasingly unpopular among Australians, including readers of history, and the Indian part in the campaign remains largely overlooked.[32]

'THEIR COMPETENCE AS SOLDIERS': ABORIGINES AND ANZAC

The Australia that raised and constituted the first Australian Imperial Force was a deeply racist society. Almost the first act of the first federal parliament in 1901 was to enact a 'White Australia' policy. It was a society paradoxically both secure of its standing as 'White' and deeply insecure as a small settler colony on the edge of Asia. The vast majority of its people (about 95 per cent) claimed descent from English, Irish, Scottish or Welsh settlers (whether convict or free). Most regarded themselves as 'Australasian Britons' and thought of Britain as 'home'. Indigenous Australians were denied citizenship, were not counted in the census, and indeed were expected to die out or be absorbed as a race within the near future, and no great qualms were entertained on that score. Non-British migrants were not encouraged, and the colour line was drawn very closely indeed. During the Great War, Maltese workers (attracted by a wartime shortage of labour) had been denied permission to land as 'non-white'.[33]

Under the Defence Act of 1903, the legislation governing the composition of the armed services, only white volunteers were to be allowed. As a result, no specifically Aboriginal units were formed, but Aboriginal Australians still volunteered and were accepted. These men included full Aborigines as well as men then known as 'half-castes'. Because Aborigines served in AIF units more or less surreptitiously, it has been difficult for families, communities and scholars to identify Aboriginal servicemen.

The Aboriginal presence in the AIF attracted attention during the war. *The British Australasian* in 1916 reported on the consternation caused by a 'lordly-looking aboriginal Anzac' [*sic*] passing through an English village in a taxi, smoking a cigar. The sight puzzled onlookers, some of whom had just been persuaded that Australians were, in fact, mostly Europeans. Aboriginal Australian soldiers were so rare that 'those with the AIF might be counted on the fingers'; the one Aborigine in a battalion might be nick-named 'Abo'.[34] Later in 1916, the newspaper brought to its readers' attention 'one of the most remarkable' of the Aboriginal soldiers, Douglas Grant of the 13th Battalion. Grant, who had been adopted as a baby by a white family, had trained as a draughtsman and was described as 'a man of high attainments with a great love for Shakespeare and poetry generally;' he was said to play the bagpipes 'as well as any Scot'.[35]

Soon after this report appeared, Grant was captured in the battle of Bullecourt. In captivity, he became the subject of ethnographic curiosity among German scholars, who modelled his bust in ebony and allowed him comparative freedom in wartime Berlin.[36] After the war, Grant became disillusioned by the Australian government's failure to meet its obligations to the 'returned man'. He published an article in the ex-service magazine *Reveille* in 1929, 'The Broken Pledge', arguing for just treatment for all ex-servicemen.[37] Grant became celebrated as 'probably the only full-blooded aborigine [*sic*] . . . in the AIF', gaining a reputation as a 'scholar, speaker and humorist'.[38] A paragraph in *Reveille* in 1931 reporting on Grant's post-war life (he had built a model of the Sydney Harbour Bridge, then just about to open) disclosed that he was not only the secretary of an ex-service organisation but also a patient at a hospital specialising in mental disturbances.[39] This report sparked a running discussion on the number of Aborigines who had served. Successive issues of *Reveille* brought further names to light, disclosing that, at least in New South Wales, dozens of Aborigines had volunteered and been accepted in defiance of the Defence Act.

'Despite their service and their competence as soldiers', the principal chronicler of the Aboriginal servicemen writes, 'Aborigines were excluded from the "digger legend" '.[40] Not until 1973, when Chris Coulthard-Clark wrote a pioneering article, was the subject broached again.[41] This brought the presence of Aborigines in the AIF to the attention of scholars as a whole, and numerous studies followed.[42] Bob Hall and Chris Coulthard-Clark showed in their pioneering work that some four hundred Aborigines were accepted by recruiting officers more eager to enforce their quotas than maintain the AIF's ideal of racial purity. Following the lead of Coulthard-Clark and Hall, from the 1990s a string of local studies documented the service of Aboriginal individuals, families and communities in the Great War and after.[43]

But Grant and the several hundred other Aboriginal Diggers were very much an anomaly. Accordingly, the AIF as an institution and Anzac as an ideal embodied the tenets of the White Australia its volunteers thought they were protecting. This was no remote spectre. Japan's victory over Russia in 1905 had obliged many to ponder the prospect of a war between a remote, thinly populated 'White' dominion and a populous Asian power with a growing fleet. Charles Bean, as a young feature writer for the *Sydney Morning Herald* in 1907, had given British readers of the *Spectator* a series of propositions that he claimed represented Australians' views. Bean argued that 'the probability of an Oriental invasion ... is enormous' and that Australians believed 'a fierce racial war ... to be ahead of them'. He urged British politicians to state unequivocally that Britain 'would not leave [them] to fight the battle of her race by [themselves]'.[44]

'DIGGERS AND NIGGERS': RACE AND THE ANZAC LEGEND

Australian reinforcements reached Britain by two convoy routes: one via Ceylon and Egypt and the other via South Africa and ports in British West Africa. The troops' encounters with 'natives' in ports en route reflected their racial assumptions and their belief in the essential superiority of what they thought of as the White Race. Australian contingents calling at Ceylon gained a reputation for disorder and indiscipline, and especially for outrages against the inhabitants; these actions are documented in the diaries of many soldiers who recorded what was for most of them their first overseas trip. One of the reasons for the authorities' concern was that Australians failed to understand that they were expected to maintain the prestige of the imperial race. In mid-January 1915, ships of the second Australian contingent travelled via Colombo in Ceylon. Many of the reinforcements aboard some of the transports became 'troublesome to manage'. At least 200 men slipped down ropes and made for the town, heading for Colombo's bars. Reports circulated of men in the streets half-dressed and drunk, lying with their arms around the necks of rickshaw coolies. Reports from the officers of the Royal Garrison Artillery, whose men had formed pickets to round up the absconders, gave a detailed and damning picture. They described Australians 'wandering about the town, half naked and drunk'.[45]

Charles Smith, whose troopship called into Colombo on the way home in 1919, recalled his fellow troops as they 'carried on like school-children at a picnic', and 'often wondered what the natives in Egypt, Ceylon and such places thought of our chaps'.[46] Their behaviour may look like simple youthful, alcohol-fuelled high spirits on the part of men restive after long voyages. However, when examined in detail, a more complex picture emerges, revealing a web of racial and imperial relationships. On one level, visiting troops became complicit in the dubious attractions offered by local people who lived off passing trade. George Evans recalled his troopship calling at Colombo on the way to Europe, remembering Colombo as 'a bit startling'. He described how a dozen 'native boys' came aboard his ship and masturbated for the men's entertainment, with 'the winner' receiving sixpence. In this he witnessed an existing commercial sexual practice.[47] Another Evans, Eric, describes how, on the way home in

1919, men aboard his troopship 'got a lot of amusement by making the young locals box each other'. Evans and his mates were not drawn into an existing practice; in his diary, he records that it was 'very funny to watch'.[48] Eric Evans noted that understandably, by the war's end, 'the Australians' name stinks in Colombo'.[49]

The troops' depredations in Ceylon are relatively well known; not so their encounters with Africa. In ports such as Cape Town, Durban, Dakar and Freetown, Australian reinforcements met Africans for the first time. 'The blacks naturally form one of the newest of experiences to us all,' Frank Roberts wrote to his wife Ruby when his troopship, the *Ascanius*, called at Durban in June 1917. He described the Africans as 'little kiddies in their antics performed to entice pennies from the boys hanging over the ship's side'.[50] Naturally, the visiting troops encountered mostly dock labourers, 'rickshaw runners' and people who sold cheap liquor and sex in the 'native quarter' of the ports. They conformed to the view of Africans as physically strong but morally debased. Frank and two friends took a rickshaw ride. The 'zooloo' who pulled them kept up 'a steady jog trot up the whole way there and back' for about a mile and a half. 'My word, did your native play up,' Frank wrote, describing how he 'bucked', 'whistled' and 'shied' at other runners and pedestrians, beating to their destination other rickshaws with only two passengers. There:

we gave him three shillings . . . and my word he deserved it. When we got out the perspiration was rolling from his black face and he grinned at us with his lovely white teeth and slapped himself on the chest and said strong fellow me . . .[51]

Few troopships spent much time at West African ports for fear of malaria, but the troops' fascinated observations of what they could see of the very edge of the Dark Continent and its people revealed their view of the relationships between races. At Freetown in August 1917, journalist Frank Brewer, on the way to become a bomber with the 20th Battalion, observed with disgust that a drunken Australian officer had to be helped aboard by Africans. This he felt was 'shocking', indeed 'degrading', an insult to the dignity of the white race.[52] Philip Tarlinton, a gunner who spent almost his entire service in hospital in Britain before being discharged with gastritis, had seen Freetown when the *Ascanius* called there the year before. He observed the 'Diggers and Niggers' meeting in 'The Black Man's Paradise'.[53] Wilfred Gallwey, one of the most acute observers of the AIF, wrote about the Australian reinforcements visiting Dakar in 1916 who became drunk and disorderly and were 'badly kicked' by French colonial 'Turkoes' policing the port. 'There is nothing that hurts the pride of an

Australian more than to be ... roughly handled by a coloured man,' Gallwey noted.[54] Here again, Australian soldiers undressing in public prompted calls (from French officers) to observe the proprieties of an imperial power.

In France, Australians encountered and observed men from all over the British empire, both as combatants and as labourers, including Egyptian, Chinese and South African labour companies. The contemporary Australian definition of 'non-white' troops encompassed forces whose inclusion might seem surprising to modern sensibilities. They included not only colonial French and British troops, but also Portuguese, known disdainfully to Australians as 'Pork 'n' Beans'. Sadly, no one has asked what the encounters in France involved, or what they meant either for Australians or for the largely unrecorded colonial subjects. Indeed, with the exception of the Australian encounter with Egypt, ably documented and analysed by Suzanne Brugger in *The Australians and Egypt* (1980), none of the other contacts between Australian troops and non-white inhabitants or troops has been explored, despite the relative abundance of evidence available. Given the rich heritage of prejudice Australians had entertained toward the Chinese in Australian society for the previous fifty years, it might be salutary to discover how they regarded and treated the Chinese labourers they met in France. It was said that when Chinese labour units were ordered to cut off their Manchu pigtails, Australians obtained them and wore them as wrist-watch straps.[55] Eric Evans, despite his indifference to the young men of Colombo whom he would watch battering each other for his amusement, commented sympathetically on the imperial labour units he encountered in France. In August 1917, he noted how South African 'Capes' (labour battalions of so-called Cape Coloureds) were 'constantly having rows with Chinese workers'. He thought that 'both seem to be treated pretty badly' and concluded 'one has to question the morality of imposing this war on such peoples'.[56]

Encounters between non-white Australians and other empire forces suggest fascinating insights into the politics of race. Sparked by stories about Douglas Grant, a member of the 56th Battalion, Henry Raine, recalled an illuminating incident near Ypres in September 1917. Raine's company included an Aborigine, Mick King, a boxer before enlistment but 'one of the quietest and gamest men' in the unit. A carrying party of a West Indian labour company brought ammunition up the position. Mick King was standing by smoking when 'three or four of the niggers passed offensive remarks' about him, such as 'Australian nigger – live on the banks of creeks and never wash themselves'. King took this insult in silence for 'a long time'.[57] Then, putting out his pipe, he walked over and punched his tormenters, one by one, driving them away. Soon after, 'poor Mick' was supposedly 'blown to pieces by a shell'. Raine's epitaph on him was that 'although he was black, he was a White man, and a dinkum Aussie'. The complexities of racial, national, unit and personal allegiance and identity in this incident make for profound reflection. It is significant, perhaps, that only in death were these diverse imperial contingents at peace. In many war cemeteries, men of different forces and ethnicities were buried regardless of race. Commonwealth War Graves Commission cemeteries continue this practice of integrated interment.[58]

And yet, despite the massive gap in the historiography, the relationship of non-white peoples and Australians was clearly of huge importance at the time. During the war, former prime minister Alfred Deakin spoke at recruiting rallies, urging men to enlist to 'keep Australia white and free'.[59] At the war's end, the wartime prime minister Billy Hughes returned to tell a cheering crowd in the Bendigo town hall that 'those boys fought to keep Australia white and free'.[60] At Versailles, Hughes had alienated the Japanese delegation both by insisting on the maintenance of the White Australia policy and by regarding the newly acquired island mandate territories as 'Australia's ramparts'.[61]

The consequences of the neglect of or lack of curiosity in other races can be seen in an anecdote recorded by Frank Brewer in his diary. In June 1918, Brewer and his comrades met 'some West Indian blacks belonging to a Labour Battalion' camped nearby. They produced 'an improvised mando-line [sic]' and sang, though 'the darkies' singing became very monotonous', he noted with distaste. Brewer was interested to find that 'most of them had the Aussie turned-up hat set on their black heads'.

All the Coloured Soldiery appear to have taken a violent fancy to the 'Aussie chapeau'; for I have seen Chinamen, Indians, Cape boys, Jamaica blacks and many other[s] in possession of our hats.[62]

This offers a classic instance of what we might call Australian particularism. By 1918, Australians had become famous, not least for their distinctive turned-up hat. But Brewer seemed not to be aware that the slouch hat had been worn by a great range of troops, both imperial and colonial, white and non-white, for some fifty years. The slouch hat had been adopted more or less simultaneously across several empires (British, Belgian, American and German), worn by American rough-riders, German African *askari*, British imperial yeomanry, Gurkhas and all Australian colonial forces. Brewer assumed that it had passed from Australians to others (presumably as a token of admiration), whereas in fact it had originated in Central Europe and been adopted in the mid nineteenth century, spreading to North America in homage to the Hungarian revolutionary Kossuth before reaching various colonies in the century's last quarter. Australians, lacking an interest in the AIF's meetings with and attitude toward non-white soldiers, lacked an awareness of Australia's relationship to the empire.

There is, therefore, a pressing need to revisit the Anzac legend. Not only does it need to be monitored to comprehend the changes through which it is passing as Australian society changes, but we need to understand how the assumptions and preoccupations of the past contributed to the history of this pervasive and tenacious idea.

NOTES

1 Frank Gates, quoted in Dale Blair, *Dinkum Diggers: An Australian Battalion at War* (Melbourne University Press, 2001), epigram.

2 C. E. W. Bean, *Anzac to Amiens* (1916; Canberra: Australian War Memorial ((hereafter AWM)), 1983), 181.

3 For a concise survey of the meanings of Anzac, see my contribution to the Victorian Parliament's 2002 re-examination of its Anzac Day legislation, 'The Anzac spirit', at www.parliament.vic.gov.au/sarc/Anzac/Anzac%20Report%20Ch2.htm

4 Russel Ward's *The Australian Legend* (Melbourne: Oxford University Press, 1958) offers the classic interpretation of the influence of the bush ethos in shaping white, male Australian culture.

5 David Kent argued that 'the Anzac Legend was always didactic' and that 'the *Anzac Book* was an important text in disseminating the values he idealised' (D. A. Kent, 'The Anzac Book and the Anzac Legend: C. E. W. Bean as Editor and Image-maker', *Historical Studies*, vol. 21, no. 84, April 1985, 376–90).

6 Alistair Thompson, *Anzac Memories: Living with the Legend* (Melbourne University Press, 1994), 26.

7 Graham Seal, *Inventing Anzac: The Digger and National Mythology* (St Lucia: University of Queensland Press, 2004), 3–6.

8 For example, see Joy Damousi and Marilyn Lake, *Gender and War: Australians at War in the Twentieth Century* (New York: Cambridge University Press, 1995); Alistair Thompson, *Anzac Memories: Living with the Legend* (Melbourne University Press, 1994); Dale Blair, *Dinkum Diggers*; K. S. Inglis (assisted by Jan Brazier), *Sacred Places: War Memorials in the Australian Landscape* (Melbourne University Press, 2008).

9 Elena Govor, *Russian Anzacs in Australian History* (Sydney: UNSW Press, 2005).

10 Stephen Garton, 'War and Masculinity in Twentieth-Century Australia', *Journal of Australian Studies*, no. 56, 1998, 86–105.

11 Harry 'Breaker' Morant was a British-born Australian officer who, as a member of a South African irregular unit, was convicted of killing unarmed Boers seeking to surrender, and was executed in 1902. Deluded Australians persist in considering this war criminal a hero, unjustly tried by 'English' generals. For contrasting interpretations, see Nick Bleszynski, *Shoot Straight You Bastards!: The Truth Behind the Killing of Breaker Morant* (Sydney: Random House, 2002) and Craig Wilcox, *Australia's Boer War* (Melbourne: Cambridge University Press, 2002).

12 Leonard Mann, *Flesh in Armour* (Sydney: Angus & Robertson, 1973), 7.

13 Peter Board, quoted in Gavin Souter, *Lion and Kangaroo: The Initiation of Australia* (Sydney: Pan Macmillan, 1992), 229.

14 John Robertson, *Anzac and Empire: The Tragedy and Glory of Gallipoli* (Melbourne: Pen and Sword, 1993); Eric Andrews, *The Anzac Illusion: Anglo-Australian Relations during World War 1* (Melbourne: Cambridge University Press, 1993).

15 Peter Stanley, *Quinn's Post, Anzac, Gallipoli* (Sydney: Allen & Unwin, 2005).

16 Memoir, Corporal Wilbraham Fowler, 15th Bn, 3 DRL 6136, AWM, Canberra.

17 Charles Bean, 'The Writing of the Australian Official History of the Great War: Sources, Methods and Some Conclusions', *Royal Australian Historical Society Journal and Proceedings* vol. 24 (1938), Part 2, 91.

18 Kevin Fewster, 'Ellis Ashmead-Bartlett and the Making of the Anzac Legend', *Journal of Australian Studies*, vol. 10, 1982, 17–33.

19 Les Carlyon, *Gallipoli* (Sydney: Macmillan, 2001).

20 Carlyon is only the most notable of a clutch of journalists who tried their hand at celebratory history. Other accounts include John Hamilton's *Goodbye Cobber, God Bless You: The Fatal Charge of the Light Horse, Gallipoli, August 7th 1915* (Sydney: Pan Macmillan, 2005);. Jonathan King, *Gallipoli: Our Last Man Standing: The Extraordinary Life of Alec Campbell* (Milton, New South Wales: John Wiley & Sons, 2004); and Jonathan King (with Michael Bowers), *Gallipoli: Untold Stories from War Correspondent Charles Bean and Front-line Anzacs: a 90th Anniversary Tribute* (Sydney: Transworld Australia, 2005).

21 J. Maxwell, *Hell's Bells and Mademoiselles* (Sydney: Angus & Robertson, 1939 [1932]), 17.

22 Besides S. S. Mackenzie's volume of the official history of Australia in the 1914–18 war, *The Australians at Rabaul: The Capture and Administration of the German Possessions in the Southern Pacific* (Sydney: Angus & Robertson, 1940), there is little besides Michael Piggott, 'Stonewalling in German New Guinea', *Journal of the Australian War Memorial*, no. 12 (1988), 3–15, which does address relations between Tropical Force's members and the recolonised 'natives' of the German Pacific territories.

23 *Statistics of the Military Effort of the British Empire During the Great War*, 777.

24 *Statistics of the Military Effort*, 778.

25 Letter, Sgt Keith Melvyn Little (15/58) Main Body HQ, 2003.409, Queen Elizabeth Memorial Library, Waiourou; Letter, 11 June 1915, Pte John Atkins, Auckland Battalion, B 1989.199; typescript recollection by Pte Raymond Baker, Canterbury Battalion, Peter Liddle Collection, University of Leeds.

26 J. L. Treloar, *An Anzac Diary* (Armidale: privately printed, 1993), 173.

27 *West Coast Recorder*, 25 August 1915.

28 MS-Papers-1676–1, 2/123 Gnr Frank Cooper [NZFA], Alexander Turnbull Library, Wellington.

29 'A Returned Soldier', *Recollections of Gallipoli, France and Flanders* (Sydney: privately published, 1919), 9–12.

30 For example, [Frederick] Cunliffe-Owen, 'Indian Mule Driver: Sublime Heroism', *Reveille*, 31 March 1932, or 'Indian Mountain Batteries', *Reveille*, 1 March 1933.

31 Frank Reid, *The Fighting Cameliers* (Sydney: Angus & Robertson, 1934), 104. Winning in the gambling game of 'two-up' depends on which way up two pennies fall.

32 I attempted to redress this neglect in articles such as 'An Entente … Most Remarkable: Indians at Anzac', *Sabretache: Journal of the Military Historical Society of Australia*, April–June 1981, 17–21, and in references in *Quinn's Post, Anzac, Gallipoli*, and in a paper, 'Indians on Gallipoli', presented to the International History Congress in Sydney in July 2005, on which this portion of the chapter is based.

33 Gavin Souter, *Lion and Kangaroo: The Initiation of Australia* (Sydney: Pan Macmillan, 1992), 255–6.

34 *The British Australasian*, 16 October 1916.

35 *The British Australasian*, 2 November 1918.

36 C. D. Coulthard-Clark, 'Grant, Douglas (1885?-1951), *Australian Dictionary of Biography*, online edition, www.adb.online.anu.edu.au.

37 *Reveille*, 31 July 1929.

38 *Reveille*, 31 March 1930.

39 *Reveille*, 30 June 1931.

40 Robert Hall, *The Black Diggers: Aborigines and Torres Strait Islanders in the Second World War* (Sydney: Allen & Unwin, 1989), 1.

41 Chris Coulthard-Clark, 'Aborigines in the First AIF', *Army Journal*, no. 286, March 1973, 21–6.

42 See the AWM Aboriginal servicemen and servicewomen bibliography, www.awm.gov.au/research/bibliographies/aboriginal.asp

43 These include, for example, Kenny Laughton (ed.), *Aboriginal Ex-Servicemen of Central Australia* (Alice Springs: IAD Press, 1995) and Doreen Kartinyeri, *Ngarrindjeri Anzacs* (Adelaide: Aboriginal Family History Project, South Australian Museum, and Raukkan Council, 1996).

44 Bean, quoted in Thomas Tanner, *Compulsory Citizen Soldiers* (Sydney: Alternative Publishing Co-operative, 1980), 148. See Peter Stanley, *Invading Australia: Japan and the Battle for Australia, 1942* (Melbourne: Viking/Penguin, 2008), 33.

45 'Behaviour of 2nd Australian Contingent in Colombo', 233/2, AWM, Canberra, 25.

46 Charles Smith, 'Five Years in the AIF', *Reveille*, 1 April 1933.

47 G. V. Evans, *Recollections of the 1914–18 War* (Brisbane: Springhill, 1982), 4.

48 Patrick Wilson (ed.), *So Far From Home: The Remarkable Diaries of Eric Evans, an Australian Soldier during World War I* (Sydney: Kangaroo Press, 2002), 247.

49 *Ibid.*, 248.

50 Frank Roberts to Ruby Roberts, 16 June 1917 in N. M. Roberts (ed.), 'The Dream on the Wind', n.d., 17. Manuscript in private hands.

51 *Ibid.*, 20–1.

52 'The War Diary of No. 6765 Private Brewer F. J., 20th Bn', ML1536 (CY4066), Mitchell Library, Sydney.

53 P. W. Tarlinton, 'Diggers and Niggers', *The Sun*, 16 February 1919, clipping in the papers of J. G. Roberts, MS 8508, State Library of Victoria.

54 Wilfred Gallwey, 'The Silver King', vol. I, 516, MSS 1355, AWM.

55 N. Cole, 'The Chinese in France', *Reveille*, 1 October 1932.

56 Wilson (ed.), *So Far From Home*, 113.

57 *Reveille*, 31 July 1931.

58 I noticed Chinese labourers and Indian (Muslim) camp followers buried beside Australian and British troops in the St Sever Cemetery at Rouen, one of the largest in France. This aspect of race relations at war deserves to be investigated more fully. See Michèle Barrett's Afterword, 'Death and Afterlife: Britain's Colonies and Dominions'.

59 *Age*, 21 December 1917, quoted in C. H. M. Clark, *A History of Australia*, vol. VI (Melbourne University Press, 1987), 77.

60 *Age*, 1, 2 September 1919, quoted in Clark, *A History of Australia*, vol. VI, 126.

61 W. J. Hudson, *Billy Hughes in Paris: The Birth of Australian Diplomacy* (Melbourne: Thomas Nelson, 1978), 125.

62 'The War Diary of No. 6765 Private Brewer F. J., 20th Bn', ML1536 (CY4066), Mitchell Library, Sydney.

CHAPTER 12

The quiet Western Front: the First World War and New Zealand memory

Jock Phillips

The story of the Great War and public memory is now much-trod, if contested, territory, and the title of this chapter picks up on some crucial markers of that debate. What is new is the application of these issues to New Zealand. In particular, we need to wrestle with the politics of a colony, or more exactly a dominion, of the British empire. This raises questions of cultural imperialism. As a result, the timing and the conclusions of the story are subtly different from the more familiar narrative in the old world.

The works referred to in the title are, first, Erich Maria Remarque's novel and the subsequent film, *All Quiet on the Western Front*, which sparked off the fashion for antiwar literature in Britain from 1928. Second, there is Brian Bond's monograph *The Unquiet Western Front* (2002). Bond argued that the memory of the Great War in Britain was largely captured by this antiwar writing. Mud, blood and horror became the war's enduring memory, promoted particularly by the public-school writers Siegfried Sassoon, Robert Graves and Edmund Blunden, whose books came out simultaneously with the translation of Remarque's novel in 1929. The image was reinforced in the 1960s by popular successes such as '*Oh, What a Lovely War*' and in the 1990s by novels such as Sebastian Faulks's *Birdsong* (1993) and Pat Barker's *Regeneration* trilogy (1991–5). This memory, says Bond, has obscured the very real achievement of British forces in the Great War.[1] I will argue that exactly the reverse took place in New Zealand and that the horrors of the Great War were for a long time obscured in public memory. The third reference is of course to Paul Fussell's path-breaking work *The Great War and Modern Memory* (1975), against which Bond was clearly reacting. Fussell saw the antiwar writers as representing a modernist rebellion against the genteel tradition. They undermined 'high diction' through a savage use of irony and destroyed the heroic image of war which had impelled men to the front in the early years of the conflict.[2] My question is

231

how far, if New Zealand's war memory is 'quiet' rather than 'unquiet', the genteel tradition and heroic language of war were critiqued by New Zealanders. The last reference, more indirect, picks up the quietness of New Zealand's war and links to Ormond Burton's history, *The Silent Division*, which as we shall see sparked some 'unquiet' reflections on the war after 1935.

My suggestion that the public memory of the Great War in New Zealand focused less on 'futility and waste' than that in Britain (although the extent of this focus can be questioned in Britain's case too) is not because New Zealand soldiers failed to experience the horrors of war. Between 1914 and 1919, about 100,000 New Zealand soldiers served overseas. They suffered over 18,000 deaths, with total casualties of over 59,000.[3] In a war in which over 8 million people died, these are tiny numbers. Yet in proportionate terms they were high – 8 per cent of the New Zealand men of eligible age died, a higher figure than for any country in the empire except Britain. New Zealand soldiers endured the heat, the flies, the stench and the awful tension of the Gallipoli front in 1915 and then were thrown into the Western Front. From 1916 to 1918, they confronted the hopeless quagmire of that sector. They were at the cutting edge of the Passchendaele push in October 1917, suffering several thousand casualties in a two-hour period.[4]

SOLDIERS' WRITING

One cannot explain the apparent absence of a 'horrors of war' perspective on the fact that New Zealand lacked a literary culture or a group of well-educated writers capable of challenging heroic traditions of war. It is true there were few published poets or writers amid the ranks and it was never easy getting published at all from New Zealand. But Kiwi soldiers were a literate lot whose abundant letters and diaries, not to mention their contributions to campaign newspapers and publications, provided opportunities to reflect on their experiences. In examining these writings, we quickly encounter a deep vein of irony and cynicism. The binary opposition of heroic expectation and horrifying reality was a staple of much wartime writing by New Zealand soldiers. As early as June 1915, for example, while newspapers at home were congratulating the boys on being 'true to British traditions of valour',[5] at Gallipoli George Bollinger, a former bank clerk who had enlisted the day war was declared, wrote in his diary: 'The world outside has great confidence in their men but I often wonder if they realise or try to realise what a hell the firing line is and know that every man desires and cannot help desiring immediate peace.' Six days later, when he received the newspaper accounts, Bollinger noted, 'The stench from our own dead lying out in front is terrific. It is hard to think that each of these men is some Mother's son. We see such scenes as this and still some newspapers have the audacity to suggest we like this life.'[6]

Similarly, on the Western Front, ordinary New Zealand soldiers expressed disillusionment with chivalric ideals. Much writing in the two volumes of *New Zealand at the Front*, anthologies of writings and drawings produced by the soldiers themselves first in 1917 and again in 1918, works on this contrast. K. L. Trent is no Wilfred Owen, but his 'A Digger's Disillusion' shares the ironical perspective and contrasts heroic language and muddy reality:

> When I first thought of enlisting
> And courageously assisting
> In this game the poet calls the sport of Kings,
> > I had dreams of martial glory
> > Dashing charge with bayonet gory,
> And a host of other brave and stirring things.
>
> But, alas! For dreams deceiving,
> And imagination weaving
> Such a web of utter falsehood in my brain!
> > For my visions all are shattered,
> > And I've just became a tattered,
> Weary digger, working knee-deep in a drain.[7]

Two other sentiments come through in the soldiers' writings. One is a strong anti-officer sentiment which belies the public image much promoted during and after the war that officers and men were an egalitarian fellowship. In *New Zealand at the Front*, officers come across as cowardly parasites enjoying a soft life of good food, wine and armchair comforts. The other sentiment is hostility to the English balanced by regard for the Australians. This begins with the view that English soldiers were physical squirts – in George Bollinger's words, 'a lot of half-grown boys'.[8] At Gallipoli Rifleman John Moloney recorded that the main topic of conversation among the New Zealanders was their disillusionment with regard to the standard of British soldiery: 'Their bodies have been stunted and their outlook cramped.'[9] When the troops reached France, such opinions were confirmed. Eric Miller judged the Tommies 'diminutive men of poor physique' and Allan Watkins saw the success of New Zealand tug-of-war teams over English teams as 'a startling reminder of the decadence of the English physically'.[10] Such attitudes developed into a contempt for English officers, who were seen as foppish idiots, and NCOs, who were judged to be brutal disciplinarians. When the soldiers reached England, their attitudes further evolved into a dislike for England itself. By 1917, Peter Howden, brought up in the highly Anglophile society of upper-class Wellington, was concluding, 'Most of the arrivals including myself are wondering what sort of a country *this* is that we are fighting for. The general conclusion is that we should hand it over to the Germans and apologise to them for having nothing better to give them.'[11] On the other hand, diaries and letters are sprinkled with admiration for their Aussie mates. Initially they had been dismissed as an undisciplined rabble, 'a loose beery lot'.[12] Trooper Claude Pocock wrote that, before Gallipoli, in Egypt when Kiwis and Aussies met 'in a restaurant or anywhere in town there is generally a row of some kind.'[13] But once the heat of battle began, Anzac mateship came to the fore. After the evacuation from Gallipoli, the New Zealanders camped briefly on Lemnos island. When the Australians arrived, one soldier recalled, 'our New Zealand camp cheered to the echo'.[14]

The acceptance of the Aussies came partly from recognition that the Kiwis too had become a rather loose beery lot. There was the evidence of the high levels of venereal disease[15] and of drunken riots at New Zealand camps at Armistice and after, but even in the diaries (where self-censorship operated), New Zealand soldiers admitted the enjoyment of alcohol and sex. George Nuttall, from a Methodist teetotal family, confessed in February 1917: 'The morning after the night before ... Last night under the influence of little light wine. The sergeants had a bet and the result was Sergeant Robertson put a stone through the Colonel's window and then rolled into the billet.'[16] On 30 December 1916, Sergeant Parmenter went out to purchase some drinks for sixty men for a New Year's Eve party. He bought 22 gallons of beer, a case of whiskey and an undisclosed quantity of wine. The next day, to be certain of having enough drinks, he bought another 10 gallons of beer. Unsurprisingly he reported on New Year's Day, 'All had a very merry time.'[17]

Obviously, one must be careful about generalising from isolated examples, but in many of their writings during the war, published and unpublished, New Zealand soldiers shared certain attitudes: front-line experience is an horrific ordeal, officers are not to be trusted, the English are despised, Aussies are good mates, and the compensations of war come in good times with the boys away from the front. Above all, the heroic image of war was gone forever. In *New Zealand at the Front*, there is a story which contrasts the veteran's view of war with the civilian image. A convalescing veteran goes off to a patriotic revue: 'a crowd of chorus girls in travesties of the full-dress uniforms of our best regiments minced across the stage in a style that was about as unmilitary as could possibly be imagined'. The veteran's mind shifts to memories of the front. When the pianist plays 'The gallant boys of the old Brigade, They live in Old England's heart', he jumps up and screams, 'For God's sake, stop that damned tune!' Then, after calming down, he wonders if any performer could make him laugh like his mates from the infantry, who 'used to foregather in the estaminet in the rest area, and talk and talk over a bottle of Vin Rouge?'[18] Such were the views of ordinary colonial men confronted by mass war.

WAR MEMORIALS

How far did such attitudes become part of New Zealand's 'public memory' of the war? We begin with a debate which took place immediately after the war, as New Zealanders discussed how to commemorate it. The issue was whether or not to put up stone war memorials, which traditionally had been a prime medium for the expression of genteel and heroic sentiments. The soldiers themselves had definite views. Given the evidence of the diaries, it is no surprise they were not interested in high-flown language or stone memorials. George Cain recalled of the Western Front in 1916: 'I saw little evidence that anyone wanted the posthumous award of "sweetness" so neatly chizelled [*sic*] in stone by the living . . . instead I saw . . . those lucky enough to have a copped a "good one" – no more than a broken arm perhaps – grinning broadly and cheerfully as they marched in the opposite direction.'[19] To the extent that veterans participated in debates about memorials, they opposed stone monuments and wanted the primary commemoration of the war to be jobs and good care for the veterans themselves. One veteran wrote to a Christchurch paper that 'the idea of wasting a minute in thinking about memorials, etc., is to me utterly idiotic'.[20] The priority was to find work for returning soldiers. But in 1919, while the debate raged, many soldiers were still overseas; those back home were often too exhausted, coping with war injuries or trying to re-establish themselves, to take part. Their interests were represented by the Returned Soldiers Association (RSA) which drew up plans for soldiers' clubs and suggested homes for disabled soldiers, which it argued should take precedence over public statuary.[21] Some local groups also argued that the best way of remembering the war was buildings or facilities which might improve community life, such as local halls.

A third viewpoint came from local stone masons and artists who had a vested interest in favouring stone memorials. They insisted that locals should create the memorials, for only they could represent distinctive

New Zealand attitudes. In February 1919, the magazine *New Zealand Building Progress* attracted 19 entries for a competition for war memorial designs.[22] Two local sculptors, W. H. Feldon and Frank Lynch, asked the authorities for memorial work, while in Christchurch a stone mason and sculptor, W. T. Trethewey, entered in the art society's annual competition a clay cast of a New Zealand soldier as a model for local memorials. Trethewey's work was interesting. The surviving photo shows a Kiwi soldier tossing a bomb, hand-made from a jam tin. His clothes are totally dishevelled, his socks are down, his face is lean and strained, and he is standing on rough ground with sandbags. War is presented as a physical ordeal. 'The Bomb-thrower' was a talking point, and a public subscription purchased it for the society. But it was not considered appropriate for a war memorial because it was too disreputable. The statue was subsequently lost.[23]

None of these points of view – the soldiers', the utilitarians' or the nationalists' – had much impact. Instead, European-style ornamental memorials expressing spiritual values and language came to capture the public memory of the Great War. How did this happen? The chief exponents of this view were the acting prime minister in early 1919, Sir James Allen (who was Minister of Defence throughout the war), and his son-in-law, William Hugh Montgomery. Allen was an Anglophile, educated in England at Clifton College, St John's College Cambridge and the Royal School of Mines. Montgomery had also been educated in England and had studied art in both Paris and London. Montgomery, then in the Defence Department, warned two days before the Armistice against 'unworthy memorials of a utilitarian nature, which will fail to commemorate adequately the great national effort ... the spirit in which our soldiers fought ... and the sacrifices which they have made'.[24] Montgomery wanted to preserve the view that the war had served spiritual, not material, purposes. Allen gave support. He wrote that a 'beautiful piece of statuary' might embody 'one of the great ideals that come out prominent owing to this war – loyalty, self-sacrifice, duty, freedom, the assurance that right will prevail over might'.[25] Once Allen had spoken, others fell into line. The *Dominion* newspaper proclaimed of war memorials: 'In these high regions art and religion clasp hands ... A great work of art should be an abiding witness to the supremacy of the things of the spirit.'[26] Thus, to preserve high ideals, the idea of the utilitarian monument was largely vanquished. Of 452 recorded civic memorials, there were 23 memorial halls, several bridges and 7 libraries (the latter could be justified as inculcating 'higher values'). The vast majority of New Zealand memorials were ornamental.

If so, did they provide an opportunity for local artists expressing a New Zealand perspective? Again, hopes were dashed. From the outset, there had been a high degree of cultural cringe in Allen and Montgomery's arguments. They argued that New Zealand as a young and new society needed lasting monuments to national ideals – 'we may learn a lesson from the older civilisations'. Therefore New Zealand, 'the land of the galvanised iron makeshift', could not produce high art. 'No narrow parochial feeling should induce the government to employ local artists,' Montgomery wrote.[27] At a town planning conference in May 1919, overseas memorials were put on display as models.[28] Cultural cringe was reinforced by economic forces. Communities found it cheaper to choose a mass-produced memorial from a monumental mason's catalogue than to patronise a local artist. The New Zealand mason would order the memorial from an Italian mason or provide an obelisk or an angel that he had already imported. The upshot was that few memorials were done by local artists, such as Frank Lynch and W. T. Trethewey, hoping to express a distinctive national perspective.

What happened to these men? Lynch completed one war memorial – a soldier figure in Devonport which was later cast in bronze for use in Masterton. Lynch was a returned soldier, and there is much in his memorial expressive of the soldiers' viewpoint. The statue is a digger about to leave Gallipoli. 'As he leaves his unfinished job, he takes a last look back at the heights and doffs his hat to the memory of his dead "cobbers".'[29] The digger carries the distinctive New Zealand 'lemon-squeezer hat', his shoelaces are undone, his socks are drooping round his ankles. A returned soldier could easily identify with the 'untidy soldier', as the memorial was known. But Lynch received no more commissions and in 1924, before leaving the country, he wrote to the Prime Minister complaining that sculptural work had been put into the hands of 'Italian workmen'. As for Trethewey, in the town of Kaiapoi in 1922 a marble war memorial was unveiled which he had completed (Figure 6). The enthusiastic mayor described it thus:

The figure was a soldier in full kit, and his Digger friends assured him it was complete in every detail, even to the broken boot-lace! The soldier was resting after a desperate charge, the torn sleeve and wounded arm showing what he had been through … the face was lined and careworn: it was the face of a man who had looked into the face of hell and had yet been undaunted.[30]

Trethewey had modelled his statue after conversations with a veteran, James Douglas Stark. Together, these two local sculptors, producing what we might call the 'broken shoe-lace school' of memorials, captured something

6. Marble war memorial at Kaiapoi, New Zealand

of the realistic, anti-heroic spirit of the soldiers themselves. Yet they were isolated examples. The other war memorials were largely a mixture of classical, Christian and chivalric symbols heavily drawn from British examples. There were obelisks and columns, arches and crosses, copies of the Whitehall cenotaph, and over thirty soldier figures smartly dressed and standing to attention – the work of Carrara craftsmen. As for the inscriptions, heroic phrases such as 'The Glorious Dead' or 'made the supreme sacrifice' were common. There were phrases of biblical origin – 'Their name liveth for evermore' or 'Greater love hath no man . . .' and there was the poetry of British imperialism – Rudyard Kipling's 'Lest we forget', Rupert Brooke's 'These laid the world away . . .' and Laurence Binyon's 'For the fallen'. There were few signs that the war might have inspired anti-British sentiments. The words 'New Zealand' appear on three memorials, the word 'Empire' on thirty-one. The Union Jack appears as often as the New Zealand ensign, and we find such phrases as 'The Motherland called, and they went'.[31]

Given that the Great War left the soldiers themselves with a powerful yearning for peace, and a cynicism about high diction, why did this not leave its mark on the public memory expressed in memorials? Partly it was cultural insecurity. There was a desire to emulate older civilisations, and in England too the iconography and inscriptions on war memorials largely followed classical and Christian models.[32] New Zealand followed the old country. The classical and biblical sentiments worked in New Zealand for the reasons they worked overseas. As Jay Winter has eloquently suggested, families wishing to remember their dead found comfort in the traditional iconography and in the sentiment that the death was for a noble purpose.[33] New Zealanders' need to honour the dead was particularly strong. The graves of almost 17,000 fallen were 12,000 miles across the other side of the world; it was very difficult to visit them. One-third had no known grave. The war memorial became a surrogate tomb which relatives could visit and decorate with flowers. Much of the energy expended in raising funds for memorials came from parents, especially the mothers of dead soldiers. Sir James Allen himself had lost his son on the Western Front. He insisted that memorials be raised by voluntary subscription, not public grants, to express the spirit of sacrifice. 'High diction' gave meaning, a spiritual purpose, to a son's death. Unlike Australia, New Zealand memorials overwhelmingly recorded only the names of the dead and not the names of those who served.[34] The most common name for war memorials in the 1920s was 'fallen soldiers' monument'.

After memorials, the major carrier of the war's public memory in New Zealand was Anzac Day, 25 April, the date when Australian and New Zealand soldiers landed on the Gallipoli Peninsula in 1915. By 1921, the day had become in law a national day and public holiday: it was seen as sanctifying high ideals, it became 'holy'. From 1921, all commercial activities, race meetings and hotels were closed to express a 'universal sacrifice' in the cause of spiritual values, echoing the attitudes expressed in the war memorials. The ceremony itself was modelled on a wartime burial at the front.[35] Unlike Australia, where the march of the veterans became the ritual centrepiece, in New Zealand the laying of wreaths on the memorial beneath the names inscribed in stone was the high point. In the immediate post-war years, much was made of New Zealand's service to the British empire, which was seen as being consistent with, not opposed to, the claim that Gallipoli represented the birth of nationhood. New Zealand was a nation defined in terms of service to the empire, not revolt from it. Anti-British sentiments did not surface. While Anzac Day addresses often praised the distinctive relationship with Australia, the meaning was different from the pro-Australian sentiments to be found in soldiers' diaries. For soldiers, mateship with the Aussies accompanied a critique of British generals and men. On Anzac Day, the Anzac relationship became a ritualised statement of common service to the imperial cause. Further, Anzac Day commemorated the Gallipoli experience, rather than the Western Front: thus, it had the effect of magnifying that campaign's importance. In fact, about ten times more New Zealanders served on the Western Front from 1916 to 1918 than on the Gallipoli Peninsula in 1915. The Gallipoli fallen were only about 16 per cent of New Zealand's losses.[36] Yet Gallipoli took on an importance in the public memory which hid the more typical experience of Flanders and France.

The public memory of war within New Zealand thus became very different from the soldiers' wartime reflections. Why was this so? It began during the war itself. From the first news about the Gallipoli landings, New Zealanders at home received their impressions of the war from British sources – from British newspaper correspondents and commentators. When thinking about Gallipoli, they recalled the writings of Ashmead-Bartlett, and the words they quoted were the King's that the Anzacs had 'proved themselves worthy sons of Empire', or Sir Ian Hamilton's that they had 'upheld the finest traditions of our race' or John Masefield's that they were 'the flower of the world's manhood'.[37] New Zealanders continued to receive the plaudits on their soldiers from the mother country and, flattered, allowed these views to determine their understanding of the war. In 1920, the Prince of Wales toured the country, continually praising the veterans. When the All Blacks national rugby team visited Britain in 1924–5, the souvenir booklet sold at matches said: 'The New Zealand soldier on the heights of Gallipoli and on the flooded fields of Flanders of 1914–18 is the New Zealand Rugby footballer of 1924, who is equally distinguished for gallantry, deportment and demeanour in Great Britain.'[38] With such flattery, any hostility to Britain created by the war soon disappeared.

The soldiers had written home, but their letters were censored. There was also an unusually long time, much longer than in the case of the English, between battle-front experience and a soldier's return home, when he could recount what it was like at the front. Because of shipping shortages, it was sometimes a year after the Armistice before the New Zealand soldiers reached home.[39] By then the horrors of the front may have receded slightly from memory, and people at home were not inclined to ask about it.[40] There was a desire to forget and move on. John A. Lee wrote that after Passchendaele, it was too horrible to do other than try to forget.[41] The same amnesia occurred after other wars – the American Civil War, even the New Zealand Wars.[42] The Returned Services Association, which had some 50,000 members in 1920, dwindled to under 7,000 by 1927. The association was dominated by officers, and it learnt to exploit the heroic image of war to heighten public respect. Other communications from the front hid rather than revealed. Official war photographs which toured New Zealand immediately after the war showed few signs of the mud or devastation of the Western Front and plenty of photos of the wounded grinning from stretchers. A war artist was eventually appointed in 1917 but with strict instructions not to show dead bodies.[43] In the same year the prime minister, William Massey, authorised a national war museum, but unlike Australia there was no C. W. Bean to push the idea through to completion. Of course, there was much myth making at the Australian War Memorial, but at least in the magnificent dioramas Australians had a visual sense of the Western Front. When Auckland did build a museum as its war memorial, the displays were largely of old equipment.

WAR WRITING

The post-war years did not see a flurry of writing from New Zealand, unlike the years following the Second World War, when there was a flood of reminiscences and novels by ex-soldiers. No memoirs appeared until the late 1930s and they were few.[44] There were some unit histories published in the 1920s, and four 'official' histories. These consisted of campaign volumes on Gallipoli, the Western Front, and Sinai and Palestine, and a volume on the war effort. Officers wrote the three campaign histories. The best was Fred Waite's on Gallipoli (*New Zealanders at Gallipoli*, 1921) which further emphasised that theatre in public memory. The volume on the Western Front was written by Colonel Stewart who noted in his preface that a historian of the campaign might 'have been able to interview participants' and 'catch the atmosphere of the time'. But 'the opportunity was overlooked. The actors are now dispersed, and the historian must fall back on written records.'[45] The result was an impenetrable chronicle of movements written from an officer's perspective. The voice of the digger was unrepresented.

By the end of the 1920s, the public memory of war obscured rather than reflected the view from the front. That cynicism about the war ideals, that suspicion of officers, that growing contempt for things British, and the consolation of nights 'on the piss' with the boys – these had few traces in the public record. Gallipoli had become more important than the Western Front. Anzac mateship was purely a rhetorical gesture. Private memories remained and it is doubtless that diggers shared their perspective in personal conversations. Yet, as Alistair Thomson has suggested, the diggers' private memories may well have been reshaped by the public memory.[46] There was little overt hostility to war in 1920s New Zealand. When the Chanak crisis erupted in 1922, the cabinet took three minutes to declare the country ready for war with Turkey again, and 12,000 men instantly volunteered. Love of the empire and respect for imperial traditions of war were stronger in the 1920s than ever before. The ecstatic response to the visit by the Prince of Wales in 1920 suggested this. The most reprinted school text of the 1920s, *The Story of the British Nation*, devoted 80 of its 137 pages to the martial traditions and successes of the British empire.[47]

In the early 1930s, the antiwar books of Remarque and Graves arrived from Britain. Yet in those years, when the Christchurch Cathedral chapter were planning a second Christchurch war memorial and George Gould suggested a peace memorial incorporating an incumbent figure such as the Royal Artillery memorial at Hyde Park, the cathedral chapter decided this would be 'sad and quite uninspiring'. They wanted a cross or something suggesting high ideals – 'effort, high purpose and endeavour, self-sacrifice, achievement or attainment'.[48] The result, it has to be said, was that the local sculptor, our old friend W. T. Trethewey, produced the country's finest war memorial with figures of Sacrifice, Youth, Justice, Peace and Valour standing beneath Victory who is breaking the sword of war.

It was not until 1935 that the first of four books appeared – six years after the antiwar books made their appearance in Britain – presenting a picture rather closer to the views of the soldiers. In that year, Ormond Burton produced *The Silent Division*, a complete history of the New Zealand Expeditionary Force in the Great War based largely on Burton's own experiences. Burton had previously written a conventional war panegyric, *Our Little Bit: A Brief History of the New Zealand Division* (1918), and a commissioned history of *The Auckland Regiment* in 1922 but *The Silent Division* was different. Told in an intense, almost breathless, literary style, it vividly described the New Zealand experience, with the division itself as the major character. Several aspects were important. One was the use of irony, with Burton playing off the expectations of the soldiers against the trench realities. Second, while he accepted the place of the war in inspiring a new nationalism, he specifically linked this to the experience at Chunuk Bair during the August offensive on Gallipoli when, echoing the judgement of soldiers at the time, he believed that New Zealand valour was betrayed by British incompetence. For Burton, New Zealand nationalism meant a rejection of the old country. Third, he described the growing pacifism among the soldiers at the front and concluded that the Great War was 'beyond reasonable doubt the major insanity and the most profoundly immoral act of our time.' [49]

The same year, 1935, Robin Hyde, a female journalist, completed *Passport to Hell* – indeed she finished it on Anzac Day. The book was based on extensive conversations about the war experiences of James Douglas Stark or 'Starkie' as he was known – the very same veteran who had assisted Trethewey to represent the Kiwi digger on the Kaiapoi war memorial. In Hyde's powerful account, Starkie was at one level a war hero, who carried out extraordinary feats of courage and was once recommended for a VC. But he was far from the conventional hero of gentlemanly virtues. Hyde had first heard about Starkie when preparing a story on Mount Eden prison – Starkie had been a jailbird, a hot-tempered drifter ready with his fists and always running up against authority. No Anglo-Saxon hero, he was the son of a Delaware Indian father and a Spanish mother. But in war his character paid off. Sentences condemning him to years in military prisons were cancelled as officers called upon his skills in no-man's-land. His hot-tempered pugilism and his anti-authoritarian spirit were the keys to his battlefield success. In *Passport to Hell*, high ideals are absent. Alongside terrifying feats of arms, there is the boozing, the wenching, the swearing and the gambling which were also Starkie's world. War is a moral chaos of untamed men. [50]

Two years later, in 1937, John A. Lee, Member of Parliament, published *Civilian into Soldier*, based on his wartime experiences. Like Starkie, John Guy the hero had been a drifter quickly condemned to military prison. He too discovered to his astonishment that his wild habits were successful in war – 'He was more out of harmony with the military machine than any man in his Battalion, yet of all he got a decoration.' War was a brutalising experience, so that in battle a soldier learnt to 'become a beast'. As the digger left the trench and raced forward, he 'sloughed off a million years of human repression . . . in those hours he had gone from civilisation to slime'. Far from expressing chivalry, war reversed moral pieties: 'All was atrocity, and the game was to survive.' Further, John Guy noticed how men coped. They did not cry, for tears were 'uncomradely'. So men released tension through swearing, and found tenderness in the arms of a prostitute. In a world of moral chaos, 'a whore was at least a step on the road to normality. Excess profits were good business, murder was nobility, bungling was generalship, getting drunk or sleeping with a girl were sin.' Yet Guy found that after a night with a prostitute he 'radiated happiness.'[51]

One more publication gave a rather different view of the Great War from that memorialised in stone. This was Archibald Baxter's powerful autobiographical account *We Will Not Cease* (1939). The book was an unostentatious account of Baxter's war as a conscientious objector. It was a story of starvation diets and gross beatings. When Baxter was sent on a troopship to join the men at the front, he suffered a terrifying ordeal ironically called 'the crucifixion'. This involved the objector being taken to no-man's-land and tied to a post with his arms behind him while shells fell all around. In addition to presenting the message that there was as much courage in being a pacifist as in going to war, and possibly more, Baxter claimed that the soldiers he met understood his position and were sympathetic to his stand.[52]

These four books, each an impressive literary achievement, echoed the view of the Great War to be found in many soldiers' wartime writings. Each had little time for high moralities; each was explicit about the anti-authoritarian instincts of New Zealand soldiers and the way they found relief in brothels and beer dives. Each expressed strong pacifist views. In all of them, Britain and the empire were empty concepts. Yet there is no evidence that these four books had much impact on public memory. Burton's book, published in Sydney, was never reprinted. *Passport to Hell* caused some notice in England where it sold so well that few copies were available for shipment to New Zealand. At home, it was serialised in *Radio Record* and was regarded as a success – yet, even so, in September 1936 the publishers reported a total sale of only 5,750 copies. It was not a runaway seller.[53] Lee's volume clearly did not do very well, since the sequel, *Soldier*, was not published until 1976. As for *We Will Not Cease*, it was published in England in 1939 and only a few books reached New Zealand before the outbreak of the Second World War. The unsold books were destroyed in the London blitz.[54] None of these books were republished until the 1960s – and Burton's book has never been.

One should not conclude, however, that, by the end of the 1930s the soldier's view of war had no place at all in New Zealanders' consciousness. Through the private conversations of soldiers and the evidence of their injuries, people were aware of the costs of war. The British antiwar books of the early 1930s had some impact. John Mulgan, born in 1911, wrote in 1945: 'We felt the tragic waste and splendour of this first Great War and grew up in the waste land that it produced.'[55] But the distinctive New Zealand content of those private experiences, especially the critique of Britain, had been forgotten. The public memory, largely shaped by the sentiments expressed in memorials and Anzac Day addresses, made inaccessible the experience of the Great War for later generations. For two decades after 1945, New Zealand war writings and public memories were dominated by the official histories, war memoirs and novels produced by the Second World War. No one bothered to examine the Great War afresh. When the fiftieth anniversary of Gallipoli occurred, New Zealand, unlike Australia, did not take the opportunity to explore the event again. As the veterans died off, only the public memory remained. Some young New Zealanders grew up believing that the major New Zealand experience of the Great War was a 'victory' at Gallipoli.[56]

Rediscovery did not begin until the 1980s, just as the last veterans were dying. Significantly the rediscovery began with Gallipoli in the form of an outstanding military history by Chris Pugsley, drawn heavily from soldiers' diaries and letters, and a powerful series of oral histories with veterans put together by Maurice Shadbolt.[57] Time and again, the former soldiers told Shadbolt that this was the first time they had talked in detail about their wartime memories. Soon after, Nicholas Boyack and Jane Tolerton systematically interviewed fifty surviving veterans, and Nicholas Boyack and myself, with the assistance of E. P. Malone, put together a volume of extracts from dairies and letters.[58] The first decade of the twenty-first century has seen a flood of publications and a growing interest in the Western Front. In November 2004, an unknown warrior was disinterred from a cemetery in France and laid to rest in front of the National War Memorial in Wellington. There was an astonishing public response with 100,000 people in the streets and saturation television coverage. Anzac Day 'season' of 2005 saw no less than seven major books on the First World War and three full-length television programmes. The overwhelming tenor of public discussion was the horror of the Great War. At last, the soldiers' story entered into public memory, although other people's war (such as that of women, objectors, and war workers) remained largely untold and forgotten.[59] However the Great War was no longer 'quiet' or 'silent'. It had taken over eighty years to make a noise.

NOTES

1 Brian Bond, *The Unquiet War* (Cambridge University Press), 2002.
2 Paul Fussell, *The Great War and Modern Memory* (Oxford University Press, 1975).

3 H. T. B. Drew, *War Effort of New Zealand* (Christchurch: Whitcombe and Tombs, 1923), 50; Ian McGibbon (ed.), *The Oxford Companion to New Zealand Military History* (Auckland: Oxford University Press, 2000), 80, 367.

4 Glyn Harper, *Massacre at Passchendaele: The New Zealand Story* (Auckland: Harper Collins, 2000).

5 *Evening Post* (Wellington), 29 April 1915.

6 George Bollinger, Diary, 9, 15 June 1915, MS-Papers-1419, Alexander Turnbull Library, Wellington.

7 *New Zealand at the Front* (London: Cassell, 1918), 112.

8 Bollinger, Diary, 19 December 1914.

9 John Moloney, Diary, early August 1915, MS-Papers-1194, Alexander Turnbull Library.

10 Eric Miller, *Camps, Tramps and Trenches: The Diary of a New Zealand Sapper 1917* (Dunedin: A. H. & A. W. Reed, 1939), 84; Allan Watkins, Diary, 23 February 1916, MS-Papers-2355, Alexander Turnbull Library.

11 Peter Howden letters in Jock Phillips, Nicholas Boyack and E. P. Malone (eds.), *The Great Adventure: New Zealand Soldiers Recall the Great War* (Wellington: Allen & Unwin, 1988), 169.

12 W. G. Malone, Diary, 26 December 1914, MS-Papers-2198, Alexander Turnbull Library.

13 Trooper Claude Pocock, Diary, 25 March 1915, Accession No. 1991: 2136, Queen Elizabeth II Army Museum, Waiouru.

14 George Ewing Pilling, Diary, 13 February 1916, quoted in Nicholas Boyack, *Behind the Lines: the Lives of New Zealand Soldiers in the First World War* (Wellington: Allen & Unwin, 1989), 47.

15 In the first six months of 1917, for example, the venereal disease rate for all troops in England was 34 per 1,000. Among the New Zealand troops, the rate was 134 per 1,000. AD 24/46/11, Archives New Zealand, Wellington.

16 George W. Nuttall, Diary, 7 February 1917, MS-papers-2192, Alexander Turnbull Library.

17 H. E. Parmenter, Diary, 30, 31 December 1916, 1 January 1917, MS-1760, Alexander Turnbull Library.

18 *New Zealand at the Front* (London: Cassell, 1917), 125.

19 George Cain, *Packsaddle to Rolls-Royce* (Penrose: Foveaux, 1976), 62.

20 Undated clipping in AD1, 15/189/2, Archives New Zealand, Wellington.

21 *New Zealand Herald*, 27 June 1919.

22 *New Zealand Building Progress*, February 1919, 421.

23 Chris Maclean and Jock Phillips, *The Sorrow and the Pride* (Wellington: GP Books, 1990), 130.

24 IA1, 32/1/19, Archives New Zealand, Wellington.

25 AD1, 15/189/2, Archives New Zealand, Wellington.

26 *Dominion*, 28 August 1920; see on this debate Maclean and Phillips, *Sorrow and the Pride*, 74–8.

27 IA1, 32/1/19, Archives New Zealand, Wellington.

28 *Press* (Christchurch), 6 January 1919.

29 *New Zealand Building Progress*, December 1921.

30 *Kaiapoi Record*, 26 February 1922.

31 Maclean and Phillips, *Sorrow and the Pride*, 106.

32 Alex King, *Memorials of the Great War in Britain: The Symbolism and Politics of Remembrance* (Oxford & New York: Berg, 1998); Catherine Moriarty, 'Christian Iconography and First World War Memorials', *Imperial War Museum Review*, 6 [n.d.], 63–75.

33 Jay Winter, *Sites of Memory, Sites of Mourning: The Great War in European Cultural History* (Cambridge University Press, 1995), 115, 223.

34 Jock Phillips and Ken Inglis, 'War Memorials in Australia and New Zealand', in John Rickard and Peter Spearritt (eds.), *Packaging the Past? Public Histories* (Melbourne University Press, 1991), 186.

35 Maureen Sharpe, 'Anzac Day in New Zealand', *New Zealand Journal of History*, October 1981, 104.

36 McGibbon (ed.), *Oxford Companion to New Zealand Military History*, 80.

37 See for example, *Otago Daily Times*, 13 May 1915 or *Evening Post* (Wellington), 23 April 1983; Maureen Sharpe, 'Anzac Day in New Zealand 1916–1939: Attitudes to Peace and War', MA thesis, Auckland University, 1981, 21.

38 Roger Dansey (ed.), *Special Souvenir, All Blacks in England, Ireland and Wales* (n.p., 1924), 9.

39 By 31 December 1918, 28,182 men had returned but 56,684 were still overseas. 52,833 of these were returned during the year following the Armistice, leaving over 3,000 still overseas at that point. See W. H. Montgomery, 'Repatriation', in Drew, *War Effort of New Zealand*, 164.

40 For example the families of two returned veterans, Randolph Gray and Leonard Hart, reported that no one asked about their war experiences and neither talked about them. See Jock Phillips, Nicholas Boyack and E. P. Malone (eds.), *The Great Adventure: New Zealand Soldiers Describe the First World War* (Wellington: Allen & Unwin, 1988), 72, 130.

41 Quoted in Erik Olssen, *John A. Lee* (University of Otago Press, 1977), 15.

42 Tony Horwitz, *Confederates in the Attic* (New York: Pantheon, 1998), 180; James Belich, *The New Zealand Wars and the Victorian Interpretation of Racial Conflict* (Auckland University Press, 1986).

43 Tony Martin, *New Zealand Images of War* (Palmerston North: Dunmore Press, 2000), 47–53.

44 C. A. L. Treadwell, *Recollections of an Amateur Soldier* (New Plymouth: T. Avery, 1936); Miller, *Camps, Tramps and Trenches*.

45 Colonel H. Stewart, *The New Zealand Division 1916–1919* (Auckland: Whitcombe & Tombs, 1921), iii.

46 Alistair Thomson, *Anzac Memories: Living with the Legend* (Oxford University Press, 1994).

47 Jock Phillips, *A Man's Country: The Image of the Pakeha Male – a History* (Auckland: Penguin, 1987), 193.

48 Undated clipping from *Christchurch Sun* in the Trethewey collection (privately held).

49 Ormond Burton, *The Silent Division* (Sydney: Angus & Robertson, 1935), 326.

50 Robin Hyde, *Passport to Hell* (London: Hurst & Blackett, 1936).

51 John A. Lee, *Civilian into Soldier* (London: T. Werner Laurie, 1937), 205, 65, 155, 168, 283, 294.

52 Archibald Baxter, *We Will Not Cease* (London: Gollancz, 1939).

53 Derek Challis and Gloria Rawlinson, *Book of Iris: A Life of Robin Hyde* (Auckland University Press, 2002), 344, 346, 364, 394.

54 David Grant, 'Baxter, Archibald McColl Learmond 1881–1970', *Dictionary of New Zealand Biography*, updated 22 June 2007 www.dnzb.govt.nz.

55 John Mulgan, *Report on Experience* (London: Oxford University Press, 1947), 33.

56 Memory of Bronwyn Dalley, Chief Historian, New Zealand Ministry for Culture and Heritage.

57 Christopher Pugsley, *Gallipoli: The New Zealand Story* (Auckland: Hodder and Stoughton, 1984); Maurice Shadbolt, *Voices of Gallipoli* (Auckland: Hodder and Stoughton, 1988).

58 Nicholas Boyack and Jane Tolerton, *In the Shadow of War: New Zealand Soldiers Talk about World War One and Their Lives* (Auckland: Penguin, 1990); Phillips, Boyack and Malone, *Great Adventure*.

59 See Janet S. K. Watson, *Fighting Different Wars: Experience, Memory and the First World War in Britain* (Cambridge University Press, 2004).

CHAPTER 13

'Writing out of opinions': Irish experience and the theatre of the First World War

Keith Jeffery

One of the most celebrated Irish literary spats of the early twentieth century arose when, in 1928, the poet W. B. Yeats rejected Sean O'Casey's play *The Silver Tassie* for production in Dublin's Abbey Theatre, of which Yeats was a director. The play follows the journey of Harry Heegan from Ireland to serve on the Western Front and his return home crippled by war wounds. 'You are not interested in the great war,' Yeats told O'Casey, 'you never stood on its battlefields or walked its hospitals, and so write out of your opinions'. Arguing, furthermore, that the inherent dramatic power of a work was the chief consideration, rather than any possible 'message', Yeats went on to declare that 'among the things that dramatic action must burn up are the author's opinions; while he is writing he has no business to know anything that is not a portion of that action'.[1] Beyond his assertion that O'Casey was apparently unequipped to write about the Great War, Yeats had a more general uneasiness with the topic of war as a suitable subject for literary works, as most famously demonstrated in his editorial approach to the 1936 *Oxford Book of Modern Verse*, in which he chose to omit work now regarded as quintessential Great War poetry (including, for example, poems by Wilfred Owen). 'If war is necessary, or necessary in our time and place,' he wrote in the preface, 'it is best to forget its suffering as we do the discomfort of fever, remembering our comfort at midnight when our temperatures fell.' 'Passive suffering', he added, 'is not a theme for poetry';[2] nor, evidently, was it one for drama either.

At the time Yeats rejected O'Casey's play, the island of Ireland was recovering from a decade or so of intermittently violent political turmoil. From the mid nineteenth century, Irish politics had been dominated by the issue of Home Rule, the desire of Irish nationalists for some measure of political autonomy. By 1912 Britain had agreed to establish a subordinate Irish parliament in Dublin (to come into effect in 1914), which would legislate for domestic matters while Ireland as whole remained within the United Kingdom. This was too much for Irish unionists, who were predominantly Protestant (comprising about a quarter of the whole Irish population) and concentrated in the northern province of Ulster. Characterising Home Rule as (among other things) 'Rome Rule' (the majority Catholic population was overwhelmingly inclined to nationalism), from 1912 Ulster Unionists set up a paramilitary Ulster Volunteer Force, apparently prepared to resist Home Rule by force of arms. In turn, the nationalists created their own, parallel Irish Volunteers, and by the summer of 1914 Ireland looked to be on the brink of civil war. But local Irish political divisions were temporarily swept away by the outbreak of the Great War when both nationalist and unionist leaders, representing the overwhelming majority of Irish political opinion, committed themselves behind the British imperial war effort, fighting (for example) 'for the freedom of small nations', encouraging many Ulster and Irish Volunteers to enlist in the British army.

For the tiny (and in 1914 completely unrepresentative) extreme of Irish nationalism – republicans who sought complete independence from the British empire – the war brought a chance to strike for Irish freedom. 'England's extremity', it was said, 'is Ireland's opportunity,' and they launched a military rebellion at Easter 1916 which after a week was suppressed by government forces, leaving parts of central Dublin devastated. But alienation from the war, ham-fisted British responses to the Rising, the postponement of the introduction of Home Rule while the war continued, and an abortive attempt to apply military conscription to Ireland contributed to a sea-change in Irish nationalist opinion, so that in the UK general election of 1918 the republican separatists of Sinn Féin soundly defeated their Home Rule rivals. This, in turn, effectively legitimised a military campaign mounted by the Irish Republican Army against British rule which resulted in the Irish Free State in 1921 being granted autonomy within the British empire (along the lines of Canada or Australia), while six counties of Ulster remained within the UK as the 'province' of Northern Ireland. Irreconcilable republicans challenged the new Dublin government, but were defeated after a nasty and inevitably bitter civil war in 1922–3. Relative calm had descended on Ireland by the late 1920s, but O'Casey's subject matter, and the responses to his work, have to be seen within the legacy of Ireland's fraught recent history.[3]

Despite Yeats's views on the need for direct experience to underpin literary endeavour (and to avoid the supposed error of writing merely 'out of opinions'), or, indeed, on the suitability (or not) of war as a subject at all, a significant number of Irish playwrights – of whom only one had served at the battlefront – have used the Great War as the basis for their work. An exploration of some of this work (which can only be properly understood when considered in the light of the contemporary political context and changing historical attitudes to the First World War) can illuminate contrasting, and sometimes challenging, perceptions of the Great War and its social, political and historical impact. Irish writers' opinions about the 'meaning' of the war (in a broad sense, beyond mere 'war aims'), and also the reception of their work, have been powerfully coloured by the changing political circumstances of twentieth-century Ireland, north and south, and, certainly, by the experience of the authors themselves. Thus, an exploration of Irish Great War 'opinions', 'experience' and 'theatre' provides us with a case study of how the impact of that titanic global conflict resonated in a particular place, whose people were both integrated and engaged with the British imperial war effort, but who also, over time (though not at all as simplistically as is sometimes asserted), in part became detached from both the empire and the 'memory' of the conflict.

O'CASEY'S *THE SILVER TASSIE* AND MACGILL'S *SUSPENSE*

Sean O'Casey's play *The Silver Tassie* follows the experience of Harry Heegan, a Dublin working-class lad and captain of the trophy-winning Avondale football team. The name Avondale was evidently chosen for its association with the nineteenth-century Irish nationalist leader Charles Stewart Parnell, whose family home was at Avondale, County Wicklow. Heegan and his team-mates, therefore, are implicitly identified from the start with the Home Rule nationalism which the Parnellite tradition represented. Like Parnell, too, at least some of the characters appear to be Protestants. Susie, for example, who has an unrequited regard for Harry, begins the play as a bible-thumping fundamentalist Christian of a recognisably Protestant sort. Like O'Casey himself, Susie is a member of the once sizeable Dublin Protestant working class.[4] Whether Heegan and his pal Barney are Protestant or not (this is not made clear), they are Dubliners in the British army who have already seen war service – Heegan having won the Distinguished Conduct Medal – and are about to return to the front after a period of leave.

The Silver Tassie is dominated by the strikingly expressionist second act, set 'in the war zone: a scene of jagged and lacerated ruin of what was once a monastery',[5] a location that was made all the more impressive by a celebrated stage set designed and painted by Augustus John. 'At the back, in the centre,' continued O'Casey's carefully detailed instructions, is 'the shape of a big howitzer gun, squat, heavy underpart with a long, sinister barrel now

pointing towards the front at an angle of 45°. Here we have all the
dehumanising impact of modern mechanised warfare: the industrialised
mincing-machine of the Western Front. In this act, moreover, all the
individual men (apart from Barney) become mere ciphers: '1st soldier',
'2nd soldier' and so on. The dialogue is interspersed with a series of chants,
giving the whole thing a quasi-religious and dreamlike (or nightmarelike)
quality.[6] As O'Casey had never 'stood on the battlefield', this act was
certainly written out of his imagination; it was, to use Samuel Hynes's
resonant phrase, indubitably 'a war imagined'.[7] Declan Kiberd, indeed, has
argued that O'Casey's 'imaginative sympathy' for the soldiers in his play was
possible precisely because he had no experience of the battlefield. Kiberd
furthermore suggests that O'Casey's *less* sympathetic treatment of the rebels
in his play set around the 1916 Rising, *The Plough and the Stars*, may stem
from the fact that he *had* been on that particular battlefield.[8]

Yet, although the second act is especially powerful and memorable, it is
worth observing that the other three acts are set in Ireland. Thus, three-
quarters of the play is situated in circumstances of which O'Casey, who lived
in Dublin throughout the war, was very well aware. Act I depicts the Dublin
inner city where O'Casey himself was reared. And despite Yeats's assertion to
the contrary, moreover, O'Casey *had* 'walked the war's hospitals'. Act III is set
in a Dublin hospital, just like the one (St Vincent's) in which, for a fortnight
in 1915, O'Casey himself was treated alongside soldiers invalided home from
the front. Here, he had tubercular lumps removed from his neck by a surgeon
who had lost his only son on the Western Front. 'The whole city was sadly
coloured now', recalled O'Casey in his memoirs, 'with the blue [uniform] of
the wounded soldier. They were flowing into St Vincent's as room could be
made for them.'[9] O'Casey, too, was familiar with the military in general. His
elder brothers, Tom and Mick, had been in the British army before the war,
and Mick re-enlisted in 1915. The last act of the play is set during a post-war
'victory' dance at the Avondale Football Club, a social and sporting milieu
familiar enough to O'Casey from his hurley-wielding days with the Gaelic
League before the war.[10] So it was that O'Casey, despite Yeats's criticism
(along with his underlying assumption that the omnipresent Great War only
occurred on the battlefield), was not entirely 'writing out of opinions'; he was
also, certainly, writing out of experience.

But there are 'opinions' too. The war and the experiences depicted by
O'Casey in *The Silver Tassie* are predominantly hateful, costly and destructive. Harry Heegan begins as an heroic figure, but a war wound leaves his
legs paralysed, and at the end he has become a helpless, embittered cripple.
His best friend, Barney, meantime, has won the Victoria Cross for saving

Harry's (now useless) life on the battlefield and stolen Harry's girlfriend
Jessie. Harry is the spectre at the victory dance – the human cost of the war –
a conventional enough representation in the context of the late 1920s wave
of antiwar literature. But with its Dublin scenes, *The Silver Tassie* also
powerfully reminds us of the domestic, civilian impact of the war. Unlike
some other, 'classic' war plays (notably R. C. Sherriff's famous *Journey's
End*), moreover, the work has parts for women – as in the actual war
experience – mothers, sisters, lovers, nurses and the rest.

In April 1930, just over six months after *The Silver Tassie* was first staged at
the Apollo Theatre in London, another Great War play by an Irish author
opened at the Duke of York's Theatre: *Suspense* by Patrick MacGill. This
was more of an archetypal war play, evidently written out of experience, as
MacGill had served in France (though not actually for very long), and the
drama takes place wholly at the front line. Like *Journey's End*, it is set during
the great German spring offensive of March 1918 and has an all-male cast,
though in this instance it was one of ordinary, rank-and-file British soldiers
(apart from the 'CO', Captain Wilson). Unlike the intensely English, public-
school officers in *Journey's End*, MacGill's characters are more democratically
representative of everyman, and one of his five principal characters, Lomax,
was played as an Irishman in the first production.[11] The soldiers in *Suspense*
are subjected to the constant and eventually unnerving sound of German
sappers mining beneath their trench. The tension mounts steadily until, to
the soldiers' intense relief, they are stood down. But as they withdraw, the
mine goes off and they turn back to what appears to be certain death. It is a
rather static play; there is not much action, but the work certainly presents the
costly futility of the conflict. The eighteen-year-old rookie Pettigrew, who is
in the front line for the first time, begins as a keen young soldier, but a week's
experience sends him 'off his chump', though not before he eloquently voices
the depression which has engulfed him: 'All through the war, yesterday,
tomorrow, now, men have gone, are going to their death, always with the
black beast over their heads, waiting for them, scraping under the ground –
you can hear it now – (*tapping suddenly evident*) – waiting to come up, to
catch us in its claws. We are afraid. All are afraid . . .' Later, Pettigrew adds:
'We are making England safe for democracy . . . But it is all a lie! How can it
be made safe for the thousands who are dead?'[12]

CRITICAL RESPONSES

Neither *The Silver Tassie* nor *Suspense* were money-spinners – each ran for
only about sixty performances – but O'Casey's play was much the greater

critical success. Ivor Brown in the *Saturday Review* praised O'Casey for his 'heroism', precisely for moving the action from a familiar Irish situation to the Western Front. 'Mr O'Casey', he wrote, 'could have kept the tragi-comedy of Heegan, the footballer-soldier, cup-lifter and broken hero, safe and sound by sticking to Dublin. But Mr O'Casey, no less heroic than Heegan, has evidently decided that such a victory is too easy; accordingly he has followed Heegan to the guns in Flanders, justly remembering that countless Irishmen did make that journey.'[13] In the *Nation*, Matthew Norgrave called *The Silver Tassie* 'a passion play', 'by far the finest and most complete attempt at dramatising the war from the Tommies' point of view'.[14] The most intriguing commentary on *The Silver Tassie* was that by his fellow Irishman, St John Ervine, long-time chief drama critic of the *Observer*. Ervine, a Belfast Protestant, made a name for himself as a critic, playwright and novelist in the years before the First World War when he lived in London and began to move in radical political circles. Briefly manager of the Abbey Theatre, Dublin, in 1916, Ervine enlisted in the army, was drafted to the Western Front and lost a leg in the conflict. Thus, by the time he came to enter the lists on behalf of O'Casey's play, Ervine was a man of both experience and opinions.

Ervine greatly admired 'Mr Sean O'Casey's passion play'. O'Casey, he wrote, was 'a poet whose heart is stirred by the unsought and undeserved sorrows of the people among whom he was born'. *The Silver Tassie* was 'a cry of pain wrung from the lips of an onlooker at the war who has been deeply moved by the spectacle of human suffering'. While it was 'a bitter and cynical play', and 'occasionally unjust', it was 'also intensely human'. Ervine (who had been a commissioned officer) thought the play was 'cruelly unjust to all but the private soldiers'. Perhaps recalling the modest circumstances of his own childhood, he added that 'poor men and women have learnt to accept the facts of life without whimpering. They are able to reconcile themselves with the small comforts that may be extracted from them.'[15] Indeed, embedded in the review is a nice symmetry (though one which would have only been apparent to a few British and Irish *cognoscenti*), with St John Ervine, himself a war-crippled Irishman, passing judgement on this play about a similarly afflicted victim of the Great War.

And what of *Suspense*? W. A. Darlington of the *Daily Telegraph* described it as 'remarkable' and 'absolutely realistic'; Alan Parsons in the *Daily Mail* observed that MacGill's play had 'been called the "Journey's End" of the private soldier', which he thought was 'an apt enough description'.[16] The *Observer*'s reviewer – not Ervine on this occasion, though apparently a Western Front veteran – heartily disliked the play and criticised it for its unconvincing description of trench life. He complained, for example, that no steps were taken to counter the threat posed by the German tunnellers:

Men went mad or deserted wholesale while waiting, waiting for the mine to go up. Was the CRA [Commander Royal Artillery] appealed to, or the CRE [Commander Royal Engineers] agog? Did anyone so much as consider, let alone take any steps whatever to retaliate? No. Any man who had ever passed nights in a sap listening for faint echoes as such sounds as here interrupted the loudest conversation must have wondered to what culpable suicides he had been attached.[17]

Other critics were less dismissive. While conceding the play's weaknesses, J. T. Grein in the *Sketch* asserted that 'as a human document this play is of as great a value as "Journey's End", as Barbusse's "Feu" and "Sergeant Grischa". In form', he continued, 'it may be less perfect, at times diffuse, but it hits home because . . . it sounds true, as if it had welled up from a heart and mind seeking outlet in wild effusion.'[18] As in his similarly bleak battle-front novel *Fear!* (published in 1921), which describes the progressive moral degeneration of an English conscript drafted to the battlefront in the last year of the war,[19] in *Suspense* MacGill manipulated his narrative, sacrificing factual accuracy for dramatic effect – altering 'history', if you like – to convey a specific message, to wit the essential futility of the war. It was a theme which was certainly more resonant in 1930, by which time grimly realistic and disillusioned accounts of the war had become more common, than it had been ten years before. But the fact remains that a Western Front drama created by a man who had *actually* been there (and presumably informed by his opinions of what it had *actually* been like) did not, for whatever reason, strike a particular chord with the theatre-going public.[20]

IRISH 'NATIONAL AMNESIA'?

The Silver Tassie and *Suspense* are remarkable in that they are two of the very small number of 'Irish' First World War plays in which the action, or a significant part of it, is set on the battlefield itself. The literary scholar Heinz Kosok has identified over twenty Irish plays with a First World War resonance.[21] The overwhelming majority of these are set in Ireland. Many focus on the Easter Rising of 1916, when the Great War merely serves as a kind of distant backdrop. In others, such as Lennox Robinson's *The Big House* (1926), the war is scarcely more than a convenient hook on which Irish domestic concerns may be hung. Robinson's play, for example, opens at the moment the war ends on 11 November 1918, the battlefield losses of the Anglo-Irish in the war (including the heir to the estate) becoming a kind of metaphor for the passing of the old Protestant Ascendancy order at home.[22] Kosok argues that, apart from Northern Protestants, after Easter 1916 the 'role of Irish soldiers in the British army' in retrospect appeared 'as questionable if not downright treasonable, and for many years the allegiance was passed over in silence, except where it was belittled, denigrated or treated with outright contempt'. In the context of Irish drama, he asserts, 'it took Irish dramatists, for obvious political reasons, more than 60 years to come to terms with the First World War'.[23] In *historical* terms this is simply not true, in two senses. In the first place, O'Casey clearly 'came to terms with' the war in the 1920s and the myth of 'national amnesia' regarding Ireland's engagement with the Great War, implicit in Kosok's analysis, needs to be interrogated a little before it may be assumed. Second, if we are to take Kosok's assertion at face value, the First World War with which Irish dramatists apparently 'came to terms', after sixty years or so, was a war which existed in a particular cultural universe, which does not entirely match what we know of the historical reality.

The notion of a 'national amnesia' about nationalist Ireland's involvement (perhaps *non-unionist* Ireland's involvement would be a better way of putting it) with the First World War has been ascribed to F. X. Martin in a famous essay '1916 – Myth, Fact and Mystery'. Martin, in fact, described 'the attitude of the various governments in [independent] Ireland since 1923' to the Irish Parliamentary Party – the constitutional nationalists who before 1914 had primarily campaigned for a separate Irish parliament *within* the United Kingdom – as the 'Great Oblivion'. In a passage contrasting the support for constitutional nationalism with that for separatist republicanism, Martin observed that 'how little hold the Irish separatists had on the people can be clearly shown by cold statistics – in mid-April 1916 there were 265,600 Irishmen serving, or in alliance, with the British forces'. At the same time, he noted that there were an estimated 16,000 Irish Volunteers in the separatist paramilitary organisation. Thus, for every Irishman with the separatists, 'there were sixteen with the British; over eighty percent of the people', he continued, 'were in sympathy with England's war effort'. Writing in the mid-1960s, Martin observed that in independent Ireland it was 'difficult to find men and women who will acknowledge that they are children of the men who were serving during 1916 in the British Army'. This, he wrote, 'is the "Great Oblivion", an example of national amnesia'.[24]

The idea has had considerable currency, especially among cultural commentators. Writing in the 1990s, for example, Declan Kiberd asserted that 'for decades after independence, the 150,000 Irish who fought in the Great War (for the rights of small nations and for Home Rule after the cessation of hostilities, as many of them believed) had been officially extirpated from the record'.[25] 'Extirpate' is a strong word, and clearly inappropriate. For nearly two decades after independence, there were large public demonstrations on Armistice Day (tens of thousands paraded in Dublin in the 1920s), official Irish government representatives laid wreaths at the London Cenotaph, the Fianna Fáil government after 1932 provided a publicly acknowledged state subsidy for the completion of the Edwin Lutyens-designed Irish National War Memorial, and Eamon de Valera himself agreed in principle to attend the opening of the memorial (though the onset of the Second World War prevented this).[26] This is not to say that Ireland's engagement with the First World War was enthusiastically and openly commemorated and celebrated in the way which has more recently become commonplace. There were limits to what the Irish government would do, but from the early 1920s to the late 1930s the Great War was by no means 'officially extirpated'. A real watershed in the public acknowledgement of nationalist Ireland's engagement with the Great War, however, took place during the Second World War,[27] and from the 1940s to the 1960s (when Martin wrote his essay) – and beyond – there was indeed a greater degree of disengagement, even 'forgetting', about the issue. In short, many writers who discuss the alleged 'national amnesia' have themselves 'forgotten' that the phenomenon was both patchy and scarcely, if at all, existed for at least twenty years after the war had ended.

OBSERVING ULSTERMEN AT WAR

What Heinz Kosok calls the 'tabooisation of the First World war by Irish dramatists' effectively lasted until February 1985 when a notable play, Frank McGuinness's *Observe the Sons of Ulster Marching Towards the Somme*, was premiered by the Abbey Theatre in Dublin. The historian George Boyce has suggested that the increased Irish cultural interest in the Great War illustrated by this play was in part a response to the Northern Irish Troubles since the late 1960s. The violence 'provoked new explorations of Irishness, and the Great War was now perceived, rightly if belatedly, as central to the forging of Irish identities'.[28] But the increased Irish cultural interest in the Great War also reflects a wider phenomenon in Britain and beyond, with public interest and cultural engagement intensifying at a time when the last veterans of the Great War were dying out.[29] Reflections on the social cost of the war, prompted by a contemplation of the war memorial in Coleraine, in Northern Ireland, where Frank McGuinness was writer-in-residence at the University of Ulster, are said to have provided the 'emotional germ' of his critically acclaimed work.[30]

The play follows the experience of eight men who volunteer to serve in the 36th (Ulster) Division, an almost entirely Protestant and unionist formation. The characters represent the diversity of the northern Protestant community. Two from Belfast city are hard men from the shipyards who have little in common with salmon-fishing lads from Coleraine. Set apart from the rest is Pyper, a child of the Ascendancy, who acts as the devil's advocate (or perhaps the devil himself), a clever young man who cynically satirises (but does not shake) his comrades' fervent faith. The Belfast men wish only to root out Papists and beat their big Lambeg drum, a traditional symbol of Protestant virility. In a carefully staged dreamlike sequence at the start of Act II, the soldiers, home on leave, voice fears largely suppressed at the front. One, a former preacher, believes himself to be transfigured into the Son of Man; others muse on sacrifice, and one of the Belfast men compares their fate to that of the Belfast-built *Titanic* – one of the few secular allusions in a play suffused with a rich and suggestive religious symbolism.

Observe the Sons of Ulster reaches a climax at the start of the Battle of the Somme on 1 July 1916, when the Ulster Division suffered very heavy casualties. Exploring the place of the Somme in the loyalist–Protestant mind – the Union sealed with blood – in McGuinness's vision, the play also investigates an essentially Presbyterian Reformation mentality, dominated by notions of pilgrimage, suffering, individual responsibility and personal salvation. At the time of its first production, perhaps the most striking thing about this powerful work was the evidently astonishing combination of subject matter – sympathetically treated loyalists (hitherto regarded by the Irish theatre-going classes as a species of leper or pariah people) – and authorship, a Catholic from Donegal, one of the three Ulster counties in independent Ireland. McGuinness's Ulster background, indeed, may have helped to give him a more complete appreciation of the loyalist mind-set than might otherwise have been the case. His play undoubtedly contributed to bringing loyalists in from the cultural cold, though its initial success, especially in Dublin where the play has always attracted better audiences than in Belfast, may have been reinforced by what might be called its 'anthropological' dimension. Guided, Margaret Mead-like by McGuinness, audiences could glimpse the doings of some primitive, remote tribe, with loyalist Orangemen celebrating the shibboleths of their antique religion and parading (literally in 'Part II', where the Twelfth of July celebrations are recreated) a quaint and touching faith in God, King and Ulster, until death or disillusionment sets in.

However remote McGuinness's tribe may be, in literary terms there is much that is familiar. The play is informed by a vision of the war similar to that promulgated by Paul Fussell in his hugely influential book *The Great War and Modern Memory*. Fussell's overstated vision of the 'realities of war' focused (to the exclusion of all else) on the trench experience of the Western Front and on the perceived futility of the conflict as conducted there. Here innocent young soldiers are sent to their deaths for no discernible or worthwhile purpose. Conditions in the trenches, where the ordinary soldiers were forced to spend the majority of their time, are unspeakable; senior commanders are remote and irresponsible; casualties are grievous and constant.[31] 'The war is cursed', says McGuinness's soldier McIlwaine, a Belfastman: 'It's good for nothing. A waste of time. We won't survive. We're all going to die for nothing.' On the eve of the Somme, Craig, a Fermanagh man, declares that 'this is the last battle. We're going out to die.' And so they do, all except Kenneth Pyper who, as an old man, opens the play with a meditation on the apparent 'sacrifice' of his fellow soldiers and asks, 'why we did it. Why we let ourselves be led to extermination?'[32]

McGuinness's conception of the war also accepts the traditional loyalist assumption that Ulster's engagement with the war was a purely Protestant matter. The Coleraine war memorial sits in a predominantly Protestant town, and is emblematic of the purely unionist wartime 'blood sacrifice'. At the memorial's dedication the first prime minister of Northern Ireland, Sir James Craig, conscious of the new state's uncertain status, declared bluntly to the assembled crowd that those who had passed away had 'left behind a great message to all of them to stand firm, and to give away none of Ulster's soil'.[33] But the soldiers commemorated on the monument are *not* all Protestant, and it is very unlikely that they were all unionists.[34] Yet by the time Frank McGuinness came to contemplate the memorial and write his play, the 'memory' of that nationalist engagement with the war (especially that of Ulster nationalists) had faded, and he can perhaps be forgiven for embedding in his work assumptions that, so far as Ulster was concerned, the Great War was an exclusively Protestant affair.

In a critique of Frank McGuinness's plays, Eamonn Jordan has categorised *Observe the Sons of Ulster* as a 'history play', adding that 'the history play is neither obliged to tell the historical truth nor is it restricted to historical facts'. It is, rather, 'an imaginative engagement with the past, an engagement which both re-constitutes history and re-presents it, while never pretending to be a real historical document'.[35] Apart from raising the thorny question of what actually constitutes 'history' and 'historical truth', and ignoring the possibility that the text of a 'history play' might itself be 'a real historical document' (whatever that means), this conclusion is extremely convenient for the author of any 'history play' since it neatly absolves him or her from engaging with historical 'facts' (alas, another slippery term) while purporting to embody some enduring historical truth. There is a distinction to be made between the marvellous drama of *Observe the Sons of Ulster* and the historical 'opinions' which it conveys. From the historian's perspective, the play now looks like a rather dated, one-dimensional exploration of the Somme, which assumes only a Protestant unionist involvement with the battle, a reading, moreover, which draws on Paul Fussell's lopsided understanding of the war, including constant casualties, incessant misery and the rest. McGuinness's undoubtedly daring and imaginative work (especially as a non-Protestant) can be challenged not only as being insufficiently understanding of the Irish engagement with the Great War and the Somme battle, but also, ironically, as being too uncritically accepting of the unionist version of events, a version which excludes the participation of nationalist (or any other) Ireland from the war.

THE FIRST WORLD WAR AND MODERN IRISH HISTORY

It is scarcely possible to discuss any Northern Irish-related plays (or any other cultural product for that matter) produced in the last third of the twentieth century without considering their relationship to the violence which afflicted the province during those years. As has been noted, the revival of interest in the First World War has been linked to the Troubles, and so too was the transformation of O'Casey's *Silver Tassie* into an opera by Mark-Anthony Turnage, premiered by English National Opera in February 2000, and staged in Dublin with a different production by Opera Ireland in April 2001. The opera inevitably embodies the 'opinions' of Turnage and his librettist, Amanda Holden, about both the First World War and the contemporary Irish political situation. In terms of the former, the work is generally faithful to the text of the play, except that most of the humorous episodes in O'Casey's original have been removed. One commentator revealingly observed that the libretto pared the story down to 'its tragic essentials'.[36] Only tragedy apparently is 'essential' to the story of the war. The Irish staging of the opera was significantly bleaker than the English, though this may have been the result of a smaller budget rather than any explicit directorial choice. But the largely unremitting glumness of the opera's action rather confirms the tendency for contemporary perceptions and treatments of the Great War (and not just the Irish dimension) to become more serious, pious and sombre as time passes.[37] This is true even in explicitly humorous treatments of the war. The BBC television comedy series *Blackadder Goes Forth* (1992), for example, was very funny but also savagely satirical and concluded with the principal characters being slaughtered in what is clearly a wholly futile attack.

It is difficult to conceive of any comedic treatment of the Great War being produced today without some darker element of satire or irony. Yet this was evidently not the case in the 1920s. In November 1924, during the week of Armistice Day, cinemagoers in Cork had the opportunity to see *Old Bill Through the Ages*, a 'merry film burlesque' featuring the Great War character created by Bruce Bairnsfather.[38] In August 1928, the Pavilion Cinema in Sligo advertised a Great War comedy, *Lost at the Front*, starring the 'Field-Marshalls [*sic*] of fun', Charles Murray and George Sidney. 'The humorous side of the great war', reported the local paper, 'is one that must be reckoned with. In fact a lot of those who participated in the conflict prefer to remember only those phases that were humorous.' It was claimed to be 'the funniest war film ever filmed . . . From one thrilling love affair to another. And when they lost their way in NO MAN'S LAND – with shells from both armies screaming past their ears – they were positive that they were in ONE war that wasn't everything the recruiting sergeant said it was. Come and have a good long laugh. Doors open 7.30.'[39]

Regarding the relationship of his work to the politics of late-twentieth-century Ireland, Turnage declared that he was very concerned about the 'Irishness' of the original play. Reflecting on the Northern Ireland ceasefires of the 1990s, he observed: 'I think, living now, to ignore the Irishness of it is almost obscene,' and despite Amanda Holden's libretto originally specifying that the operatic version would be set in 'a town somewhere in Britain', Bill Bryden's staging in London returned the action to Dublin.[40] Rather than the opera being prompted, at least in part, by political and social turmoil in Northern Ireland (as *Observe the Sons of Ulster* may have been), Turnage saw the reworking of *The Silver Tassie*, and the recovery of an Irish First World War story which might as easily have been located in 'a town somewhere in Britain', as reflecting the happily improved situation and the normalisation of public attitudes (or 'opinions') about Ireland's involvement with the Great War. Perhaps the most significant thing about the Opera Ireland production in Dublin is that none of the critics even thought to remark about the sympathetic portrayal of Dublin Irishmen in British army uniforms, which in the original play made the work so problematic for Yeats and other observers.[41]

Unlike the history of Ireland's engagement with the First World War, which in recent years has progressively been recovered and, in the process, become more nuanced and complete, staged representations of the conflict have continued to tell a familiar, traditional and even clichéd story: the war was futile; slaughter and injury was continuous and comprehensive (though *The Silver Tassie* men do get home alive, if not all in good order); the whole affair was desperately serious; only Protestants and unionists fought at the Somme; and the violence of the war appeared to have had no moral justification, unlike, apparently, that of the 'fight for Irish freedom' back at home.[42] This is not to say that 'writing out of opinions' necessarily invalidates continued cultural responses to the Great War; Yeats was clearly wrong on that score, and a dogmatic application of his rule would prevent any Irish Stephen Crane (for whom read Frank McGuinness or Sebastian Barry) from readdressing Ireland's engagement with the Great War in rewarding literary ways.[43] But, by detaching their work from the historical realities of the time and ignoring or even suppressing the complexities of Ireland's First World War experience, today's dramatists and directors threaten to do us all a disservice. However poignant, painful or moving may be the drama of particular theatrical productions, by staying in the 'comfort zone' of the familiar, traditional story, they neglect challenging dimensions of the actual experience of the war and confirm the danger (in this case) of writing out of received *historical* opinions.

NOTES

This chapter is a revised and expanded version of 'The Last Battle: "Writing out of opinions": Irish experience and the theatre of the Great War', *Times Literary Supplement*, no. 5510 (7 November 2008), 13.

1 Yeats to O'Casey, 20 April 1928 (*Letters of Sean O'Casey*, ed. David Krause (London: Cassell, 1975), 268). The correspondence was published in the *Observer*, 3 June, and the *Irish Statesman*, 9 June 1928.
2 W. B. Yeats (ed.), *Oxford Book of Modern Verse, 1892–1935* (Oxford University Press, 1936), xxxiv–xxxv. For a thoughtful reflection on Yeats's attitude to the war, see R. F. Foster, 'Yeats at War: Poetic Strategies and Political Reconstruction from the Easter Rising to the Irish Free State', *Transactions of the Royal Historical Society*, 6 ser., 11 (2001), 125–45.
3 For Ireland and the Great War generally, see Keith Jeffery, *Ireland and the Great War* (Cambridge University Press, 2000). For the political context, see Paul Bew, *Ireland: The Politics of Enmity, 1789–2006* (Oxford University Press, 2007).
4 For this sometimes underrecognised social group, see Martin Maguire, 'The Organisation and Activism of Dublin's Protestant Working Class, 1883–1935', *Irish Historical Studies*, 29 (1994), 65–87.
5 Stage directions and quotations from the play are taken from the text in Sean O'Casey, *Three More Plays* (London: Macmillan, 1965).
6 The religious resonances of the play are illuminatingly discussed by Nuala Johnson in her *Ireland, the Great War and the Geography of Remembrance* (Cambridge University Press, 2003), especially 118–26.

7 Samuel Hynes, *A War Imagined: The First World War and English Culture* (London: Bodley Head, 1990) is the best single work on the subject.

8 Declan Kiberd, *Inventing Ireland* (London: Jonathan Cape, 1995), 246–7.

9 Sean O'Casey, *Drums under the Windows* (London: Macmillan, 1945), 290–300.

10 For O'Casey's family and early life, see Garry O'Connor, *Sean O'Casey: A Life* (London: Hodder & Stoughton, 1988).

11 See the review in *The Times*, 9 April 1930.

12 Patrick MacGill, *Suspense* (London: Herbert Jenkins, 1930), 40, 50.

13 *Saturday Review*, 19 October 1929.

14 *The Nation and Athenaeum*, 26 October 1930.

15 *Observer*, 13 October 1929.

16 *Daily Telegraph* and *Daily Mail*, 9 April 1930.

17 *Observer*, 13 April 1930.

18 *Sketch*, 23 April 1930. The allusion to 'Sergeant Grischa' was possibly prompted by the fact that a film version of Arnold Zweig's novel *The Case of Sergeant Grischa* had been released in February 1930.

19 For discussion of this novel, and other of MacGill's prose works, see Keith Jeffery, 'Irish Prose Writers of the First World War', in Kathleen Devine (ed.), *Modern Irish Writers and the Wars* (Gerrards Cross: Colin Smythe, 1999), 9–13.

20 A film version of *Suspense*, released in September 1930, was not a commercial success although it was critically admired. See *The Times*, 24 September 1930, and E. G. Cousins, *Filmland in Ferment* (London: Archer, 1932), 145.

21 See Heinz Kosok, *The Theatre of War: The First World War in British and Irish Drama* (Basingstoke: Palgrave, 2007). Even Kosok's list (as perhaps inevitably must be the case with such catalogues) is incomplete, since it includes neither Louis J. Walsh's *Going West* (1915) nor Percy French's short play *The Letter from the Front*, in *Prose, Poems and Parodies of Percy French*, ed. Mrs de Burgh Daly (Dublin: Talbot Press, 1929), 157–63.

22 There is a brief discussion of the play in my *Ireland and the Great War*, 69–70.

23 Kosok, *The Theatre of War*, 55.

24 F. X. Martin, '1916–Myth, Fact and Mystery', *Studia Hibernica*, 7 (1967), 7–124 (68). Rather than 'national amnesia', Roy Foster uses the term 'therapeutic voluntary amnesia', which (usefully) is not quite the same thing (Foster, 'Yeats at War', 125).

25 Declan Kiberd, *Inventing Ireland*, 239. 150,000 is a considerable underestimate, unless only Catholic nationalists are being counted. Historians, too, can be afflicted by this 'amnesia', which is sometimes manifest in curious ways. In Ian McBride (ed.), *History and Memory in Modern Ireland* (Cambridge University Press, 2001), in which aspects of the 'memory' of the First World War are discussed in at least five separate chapters, while the index contains an entry for 'Easter Rising (1916)', there is none for the First World (or Great) War; this is a sin of omission indeed. An entry for 'Somme, Battle of', indicating a few of the relevant pages, is all that is provided.

26 Jeffery, *Ireland and the Great War*, 109–23; Jane Leonard, 'The Twinge of Memory: Armistice Day and Remembrance Sunday in Dublin since 1919', in

Richard English and Graham Walker (eds.), *Unionism in Modern Ireland* (London: Palgrave, 1996), 99–114.

27 A point made in my *Ireland and the Great War*, 134–5.

28 George Boyce, *The Sure Confusing Drum: Ireland and the First World War* (University College of Swansea, 1993), 24. A revised version of this lecture was published under the title '"That party politics should divide our tents": Nationalism, Unionism and the First World War', in Adrian Gregory and Senia Pašeta (eds.), *Ireland and the Great War: 'A War to Unite Us All'?* (Manchester University Press, 2002), 190–216.

29 This phenomenon was stimulatingly explored in Brian Bond, *The Unquiet Western Front: Britain's Role in Literature and History* (Cambridge University Press, 2002).

30 Nicholas Grene, *The Politics of Irish Drama: Plays in Context from Boucicault to Friel* (Cambridge University Press, 1999), 246.

31 Paul Fussell, *The Great War and Modern Memory* (London: Oxford University Press, 1975). For a robust historians' critique of Fussell, see Robin Prior and Trevor Wilson, 'Paul Fussell at War', in *War in History*, 1 (1), 63–80.

32 Frank McGuinness, *Observe the Sons of Ulster Marching Towards the Somme* (London: Faber, 1986), 12, 50, 74.

33 *Belfast Telegraph*, 11 November 1922.

34 Of the 171 names on the war memorial, 15 have been identified as definitely Catholic. See Robert Thompson, *Coleraine Heroes 1914–1918* (Bushmills: privately published, 2004).

35 Eamonn Jordan, *The Feast of Famine: The Plays of Frank McGuinness* (Berne: Peter Lang, 1997), xxii.

36 Richard Morrison in *The Times*, 8 February 2000.

37 This process has been reinforced by the conflation of the war with 'the Holocaust and the Gulag' (Jay Winter and Antoine Prost, *The Great War in History: Debates and Controversies, 1914 to the Present* (Cambridge University Press, 2005), 56).

38 *Cork Weekly Examiner*, 8 November 1924.

39 *Sligo Champion*, 8 September 1928.

40 Programme notes for ENO production; *The Times*, 8 February 2000.

41 See, for example, the *Irish Times*, 3 April 2001.

42 Jennifer Johnston's play *How Many Miles to Babylon* (1993), based on her 1974 novel of the same name, rather gives this impression. Jerry Crowe, a Catholic republican, only enlists in the British army, he says, in order to learn to shoot a gun to use for the fight for Irish freedom.

43 As Barry has done in his novel *A Long, Long Way* (London: Faber, 2005); see my review in the *Times Literary Supplement*, 22 April 2005.

CHAPTER 14

'Heaven grant you strength to fight the battle for your race': nationalism, Pan-Africanism and the First World War in Jamaican memory

Richard Smith

In 1981 the Iran–Iraq war (1980–8) had become mired in the trench warfare and gas attacks of an earlier era. The Jamaican writer John Hearne was moved to reflect on the nature and impact of twentieth-century warfare. Although he had been born eight years after the Armistice, the First World War had loomed as a 'grey fear' for Hearne, a stain on his childhood representing the abiding anxiety that his father, twice wounded in the conflict, would heed another call of Empire and not return.[1] This overwhelming anticipation of loss marred an otherwise idyllic journey from boy to man, which Hearne often spent in the company of a father he clearly adored. His upbringing in the higher reaches of Jamaican society was reflected in a nostalgia for mountain treks, horse riding, cricket and boxing, pastimes Hearne enjoyed during a decade of smouldering resentment at colonial rule which exploded in the 1938 labour rebellion.[2] But Hearne's race and class interests were outweighed by more universal concerns. The imagined death of his father in some future war represented a lost innocence: a personal symbol for the millions Hearne believed had needlessly died in the name of 'religions, political ideologies and national sovereignties' during the twentieth century.[3]

In 1925, Frank Cundall, pioneering historian of the island and chairman of the Jamaican War Memorial Committee, listed by parish the 1,130 or so Jamaicans who died in the First World War.[4] Most had seen service in the British West Indies Regiment (BWIR) which enlisted nearly 10,300 from the island. Established for the duration of the war only, the BWIR eventually comprised twelve battalions and recruited over 16,000 men from the West Indies, British Honduras, the Bahamas and Bermuda. The majority of Jamaica's contribution were black and 'coloured' men of the peasantry, working or middle classes.[5] All were volunteers and represented a fraction of the 135,061 men aged between 16 and 45 registered for enlistment under the Jamaica Military Service Act of 1917, full conscription never having been implemented. However, Jamaica's veterans came to occupy a pivotal place in the national identity which became more prominent during the decades of Hearne's youth and which continues to be negotiated after the death of Stanley Stair, the last Jamaican veteran of the war, in May 2008.[6] Jamaica's contribution to the war effort was deployed to support a gamut of demands from constitutional change and self-government to African liberation. Consequently, popular Jamaican war memories did not tend to accord with the 'grey fear' described by Hearne, a minority voice closer to the tragic representations dominant in Britain. However, a grey quality certainly abounds in the ambiguities and contradictions in Jamaican war memory and its politics of commemoration and sacrifice.

Although national commemorations of war and private processes of grief can initially seem to be at odds, a more fluid definition of mourning may regard post-war national or social struggles as collective grieving processes, striving to ensure that death, disfigurement and military service in general were not in vain.[7] The place of the war in Jamaican memory points to this latter interpretation. In Jamaica, a colonial society whose dominant ideological forces were especially concerned to glorify imperial military achievement, the 'political symbolism'[8] of war memory was particularly potent and conventional grieving was marginalised. Instead, the popular imagination appropriated the martial rhetoric and symbolism to seek rewards for wartime sacrifice. Consequently, war memory in Jamaica has a complex relationship with statehood. The meaning of Jamaican sacrifice in the First World War, although later recognised and even requisitioned by the nation-state formed in 1962, was at first contested between the imperial power and the mass movements central to its overthrow. But with the rise of a Pan-African dimension to Jamaican politics, particularly after the Italian invasion of Ethiopia in 1935, the symbolism of military service could transcend nationalist preoccupations and be mobilised in the service of more universal aims. This chapter examines the unstable nature of Jamaican war memory which has mirrored the changing preoccupations of veterans, political movements and diasporic communities.

EMPIRE, WAR AND JAMAICAN IDENTITY

In 1906, the travel writer and journalist John Henderson recorded the remarks of an unnamed Jamaican intellectual who epitomised growing aspirations to representative government:

The people of this island have every moral right to govern themselves . . . we are an educated people with ambitions . . . we recognise it is a fine thing to be part of the great Empire . . . but . . . a finer thing to be a free, unfettered nation. England will always have our heartiest support and affection.[9]

Among the Jamaican middle classes in general, affection for Britain and empire, and apprehension that enfranchisement of the peasantry and working class might impinge on their interests, muted the desire for self-government.[10] On the eve of war in August 1914, intellectuals and progressives established the Jamaica League to promote Jamaican cultural achievements and campaign for social and economic reform within the existing imperial relationship. The League believed that self-government could only be considered once the masses had been thoroughly educated and infused with a sense of civic responsibility.[11] Almost simultaneously, Marcus Garvey founded the Universal Negro Improvement Association and African Communities League (UNIA) to 'promote the Spirit of Race Pride and Love'[12] and to 'establish educational and industrial colleges for the education of our boys and girls' and 'reclaim the fallen and degraded . . . and help them to a state of good citizenship'.[13]

Many Jamaicans looked to Britain to dispense equity and justice, particularly to curb the power of the local planter class and its representatives in the Jamaican Legislative Council. Faith in professed imperial values was underpinned by a strong identification with the monarchy, linked to the popular perception that William IV and Queen Victoria had delivered emancipation.[14] This belief was exploited by speakers at wartime rallies seeking support for the war effort: they argued that a 'Prussian victory' would end the 'benign rule of the Empire'[15] and lead to the reintroduction of slavery. 'Men of the Island of Jamaica, be not branded as cowards if you are needed for active service,' counselled Ivanhoe Harry, a member of the Kingston fire brigade, urging fellow countrymen to 'be courageous, be firm, be resolute, prepare to defend your country with your life's blood'.[16]

Acknowledging this growing pro-war sentiment, UNIA declared its belief in 'the great protecting and civilizing influence of the English nation and people . . . express[ing] our loyalty and devotion to His Majesty the King, and Empire . . . pray[ing] for the success of British Arms on the battlefields of Europe and Africa, and at Sea'.[17] In a letter to the *Daily Gleaner*, Sidney Moxsy urged Jamaican 'Sons of Liberty' to heed the 'Motherland's Call' to enlist and ensure they did not become 'slaves beneath a foreign sway'.[18] In the midst of these pro-imperial sentiments, nascent Jamaican national identity and Pan-Africanism were increasingly evident. There was an expectation that both would be invigorated by military service and post-war redemption would ensue. The trade unionist and early UNIA activist W. G. Hinchcliffe exemplified this mood when, in 1916, he praised Jamaicans who had heeded calls to volunteer, for 'on them the laurels will fall, which must eventually lift the standard of the African race, and cause oppression into oblivion to fall'.[19]

But the politics of war identity for Jamaican volunteers would be more complex than Hinchcliffe had envisaged as they faced a continual struggle to be regarded as front-line soldiers rather than plantation labourers. On 28 August 1914, the Indian Expeditionary Force 'A' was dispatched to France, presenting an opportune moment for the Colonial Office to suggest the raising of West Indian overseas contingents to the War Office. The proposal was rebuffed: many in the military establishment remained hostile to the deployment of non-white troops in Europe, fearing the imperial racial hierarchy might be called into question. Others resorted to racial stereotypes, as in the Army Council's assertion that 'coolness, courage and initiative are at premium [in the front line] – qualities of which the ordinary coloured labourer is deficient'.[20] Such pronouncements did not dissuade Jamaicans and other West Indians from journeying to Britain to enlist. But their offers of service were accepted according to the whims and prejudices of local recruiting officers because military law was unclear whether a volunteer regarded as 'a negro or person of colour' was a British subject or an alien.[21]

Fearful of the potential for disaffection if such volunteers were rejected, the West Indian governors collectively promoted the formation of West Indian contingents. But only in May 1915, after King George V declared his support for West Indian recruitment, did the War Office adopt a more pragmatic approach. The creation of the British West Indies Regiment (BWIR) was subsequently announced in the *London Gazette* on 26 October 1915. By the spring of 1916, the West Indian contingents had arrived in sufficient numbers in Seaford on the south coast of England to enable the dispatch of two battalions to Egypt. The first Jamaican contingent for the new regiment departed in early November 1915, an event captured on newsreel by the Fox Film Company, which was making the first $1 million movie, *A Daughter of the Gods*, on the island. The newsreel was shown to Jamaican audiences from February 1916, with shots of the many thousands who gathered to bid farewell to the troops.[22] Interest in the contingent was also kept alive by the publication of letters from Jamaicans once they arrived in Egypt. Private Seaford Johns reported the expectation of battle, affirming: 'we all have a fixed determination that we unite under the same old flag to fight for one King and one Empire, with one hope and one desire and with gallantry we'll march along, until we conquer, win or die'.[23]

Formally regarded as an infantryman, a BWIR private received the shilling a day paid to his counterpart in other British units. However, separation allowances paid to wives and dependants, determined by colonial governors rather than the War Office, were set at lower rates on the grounds that the cost of living in the colonies was cheaper. British commanders and officials tended to regard the BWIR as an inferior 'native' unit, despite its infantry designation. Medical and recreational facilities were generally substandard, and increases in pay and allowances, granted to the rest of the British army from 1917, were withheld until conceded after lengthy protests.[24] Men who were not believed to be of pure European descent were unable to rise beyond non-commissioned rank.[25] More significantly, a continued reluctance to deploy West Indian soldiers on the front line meant that nine of the twelve BWIR battalions were deployed as labour units on the Western Front and later at Taranto in southern Italy, a key port for the British Mediterranean lines of communication. Duties included road building and railway construction, digging trenches, unloading ships and trains, and carrying shells to the front line.

The first, second and fifth (reserve) battalions, however, eventually saw front-line action in Palestine and Jordan. They won some official praise, most notably from Major-General Edward Chaytor, who led the successful campaign against the Turkish forces in 1918. Chaytor remarked that the BWIR had 'won the highest opinion of all who have been with them during our operations'.[26] A small detachment of the regiment also served alongside the 2nd West India Regiment (WIR) in the East African campaign.[27] The Jamaican press reproduced medal citations alongside official reports of actions involving local volunteers, including the 'spirited bayonet charge' by the 1st BWIR in September 1918 at Jisr Ed Damieh, a key bridgehead on the river Jordan.[28] For the majority of the veterans, struggling with the disappointment and humiliation of not being recognised as front-line troops despite routine exposure to shellfire, such accounts would provide a ready vocabulary and imagery for years to come. In 1938, a former BWIR sergeant recalled how the volunteers had sung 'we are going to catch the Kaiser if we only get a chance' as they left Jamaica. Some had made the 'supreme sacrifice', while others returned 'with Victory on the point of our Bayonet'.[29] Such sentiments showed how these colonial veterans had become attached to the European heroic discourse which conflated 'war' with 'combat'.[30] Expressed in conventional military argot, the post-war Jamaican memory tended to neglect the contribution of those deployed on auxiliary duties and those who had succumbed to disease, rather than to wounds.[31] However, the adherence to such narratives also illustrated how it was necessary to highlight the front-line heroism in order to stress post-war entitlement.

POST-WAR RADICALISATION AND DEMANDS FOR LAND

While Jamaican popular sentiment celebrated the front-line achievements of the men serving abroad, the reality in the war zone was different. Discrimination in pay and conditions, the dishonour of being treated as labourers rather than fighting men, and poor access to recreational and medical facilities contributed to the mutiny of BWIR battalions stationed at Taranto shortly after the Armistice. Wage and ration improvements were granted to disgruntled Italian and Maltese labourers employed by the British in the supply lines. Alongside them, BWIR troops were increasingly humiliated by the harsh disciplinary measures and the increasingly menial duties they were expected to perform. On 6 December 1918, Lieutenant-Colonel Willis, commander of the 9th Battalion and a notoriously brutal officer, ordered his men to clean latrines used by Italian labourers. They refused and some men surrounded his tent, slashing it with knives and bayonets, before dispersing. There was some 'promiscuous shooting' as well as threats 'to kill every white man' if measures were not taken to complete demobilisation and repatriate men to the West Indies by Christmas.[32] The next day, the 9th and 10th battalions refused to work, but were forcibly disarmed and ordered on a route march. A battalion of the Worcestershire Regiment, accompanied by a machine gun company, was dispatched to forestall further unrest.[33] Although the mutiny was brought swiftly to an end, harsh sentences were meted out to the forty-seven men found guilty of involvement. Private Arthur Sanches, regarded as the ringleader by the military, received a death sentence which was later commuted to twenty years' imprisonment.[34]

On 16 December, sixty West Indian sergeants at Taranto formed the Caribbean League to promote 'all matters conducive to the General Welfare of the islands constituting the British West Indies and the British Territories adjacent thereto'.[35] The League was greeted with cautious approval by the military authorities, who obtained a report of the inaugural meeting from an informer. However, the reported assertion at a subsequent meeting 'that the black man should have freedom to govern himself in the West Indies and that force must be used, and if necessary bloodshed, to attain that object'[36] gave more cause for concern. Cited in reports circulated by the War Office to the Colonial Office, it prompted some panic among the West Indian governors.

Closer analysis suggests that many League members adopted a non-violent, reformist approach that anticipated working alongside, or at least not in direct opposition to, the colonial governments. This was evident when some members suggested that the recently mutinous rank and file should not be canvassed for support lest they 'not understand the peaceful purpose of the league'.[37] Whereas the convicted mutineers had been private soldiers to a man, the League wholly comprised non-commissioned officers, many of whom seemed intent on preserving the limited authority they held within the military hierarchy. The domination of the League leadership by the Jamaican sergeants – Cecil Collman, Harold Leopold Brown and Arthur P. Jones – caused some dissatisfaction and dissent among members from the other West Indian territories. Sergeant Leon Pouchet, the Trinidadian informer who kept the military abreast of the League's activities, was clearly rankled by this issue.[38]

The Caribbean League did not survive demobilisation, which was completed by August 1919. However, although the League was short-lived, it demonstrated the emergence of a distinct racial consciousness brought about by the hardships of war and by discrimination at the hands of the military establishment. A certain confidence had also developed from having served alongside white European troops abroad and having observed their human frailties at first hand. This mood was captured in a poem written during the rebellion by Sergeant Henry Benjamin Monteith of the mutinous 9th battalion:

> Lads of the West, with duty done, soon shall we parted be
> To different land, perhaps no more each other's face to see,
> But still as comrades of the war our efforts we'll unite
> To sweep injustice from our land, its social wrongs to right.[39]

These words reflected a personal transformation for Monteith. As an elementary teacher in civilian life, he had contributed poems of a distinctly pro-imperial tone to the *Jamaica Times*, praising the heroism of Britain and her allies, 'Who, ere we sheathe our sword shall see – A beaten, powerless Germany.'[40] But in 1919, Monteith expressed a nascent Pan-Africanism and the aspiration for federal West Indian self-government.

The modest collectivist vision of veterans such as Monteith was at odds, however, with that of the colonial state, which reiterated the discourse of individual industry and tended to downplay any direct suggestion of entitlement by virtue of military service. But the options for enterprising endeavour were limited, and most returning veterans faced either backbreaking casual work at low pay or unemployment. In the face of these demoralising circumstances, and despite the injustices endured in the army and the rejection of military authority at Taranto, the veterans clung to the rhetoric of heroic military sacrifice as both an emotional and a strategic tool to demand economic improvements and citizenship rights in the post-war decades.

Many Jamaican veterans – 4,036 of the 7,232 who returned – chose to migrate to Cuba, encouraged by a government keen to disperse potential agitators.[41] For those who remained, cultivable land – the mainstay of peasant self-sufficiency since slavery – became the central demand. In May 1919, Governor Probyn hailed the first group of demobilised Jamaicans and announced employment and land settlement schemes, promising a future of prosperity 'to run from the day on which Jamaica's brave sons came back from the war.'[42] But it was not until 1924 that the Jamaican Legislative Assembly began to make tentative steps to implement the settlement hinted at in Probyn's welcoming platitudes. In that year, the Governor and soldier representatives from the Old Comrades' Association agreed a scheme for five-acre allotments to be offered to veterans with savings of at least £10 and means of support before the first harvest. Loans, repayable over twelve years, were available to purchase additional acres. The Jamaican government also allocated £20,000 for road-building and bridges on the three Crown estates earmarked for the scheme.[43] However, the settlements at Rio Grande in Portland failed to thrive. Most plots were many miles from the nearest main roads. Poor communications were compounded during the five-month rainy season when two local rivers became impassable and the legislature's pledge to fund improvements was overruled by the Secretary of State for the Colonies. Seventy-two veterans acquired allotments, but just three endured the five years necessary to earn full title to the land.[44]

By the early 1930s, the ranks of the veterans were augmented by men forcibly repatriated as the Great Depression afflicted the Cuban sugar industry. In May 1933, the Ex-British West Indies Regiment Association led several hundred veterans, including some in wheelchairs, on a hunger march from the Kingston racecourse to the Legislative Council chamber. A petition to Governor Ransford Slater outlined the hardships endured by Jamaicans and insisted that the sacrifices in the First World War should be recognised:

We are quite sanguine of the acute depression which the island is passing through at the moment, but we are asking most respectfully that immediate relief, however small it may be, be granted to the men who served their King and country during the Great World War and who are now in dire need! We are now beseeching the members of the Council to help us financially as the men and their families are starving and many of them shelterless, while our children cannot go to school for want of clothes and food.[45]

In July, the Association met with Sir Ian Macpherson MP, a former British minister of pensions who was touring Jamaica, and demanded new lands be made available with a fund to assist cultivation. The delegation also suggested that the Jamaica War Contribution, paid annually at the rate of £60,000 to the imperial government since the end of the war, be suspended for five years and the funds diverted to benefit ex-servicemen.[46] Under the terms of the land settlement scheme which the government approved after these protests, 3,406 ex-servicemen received free plots of five acres and a loan of £5, advanced in thirty-shilling instalments. These included members of both the BWIR and the WIR, the latter having been disbanded at the end of 1926. Some 400 ex-soldiers in a model settlement at Coolshade, Saint Catherine, received an additional loan of £4.[47]

Peasant proprietorship had become ideologically attractive to some sections of the colonial administration. A self-sufficient and relatively prosperous peasantry, with an emotional attachment to the land, was regarded as a buffer against the increasingly turbulent disenfranchised working class and rural poor. Sir Edward Denham, governor from 1934 until his death in June 1938, epitomised this attitude, asserting, 'The saving grace in Jamaica is the Jamaican's passion for the land and to own a bit of it, and the provision of land settlement is the best bond between Government and governed.'[48]

But the new settlement scheme, like those preceding it, was beset by poor land quality, deficient water supplies and inadequate communications. By 1938, of 2,506 men still in possession of their lands, only 1,800 were actively cultivating and barely 400 were residing on their properties.[49] The poor quality of land and lack of sufficient financial support was highlighted by Hubert Reid, a veteran of the West India Regiment who had received the Distinguished Conduct Medal for gallantry in the East African campaign.[50] He noted:

[I]t has taken 17 years of untold petitions, marchings through the streets of the City as well as agitations, before we were told off to some of the most remote parts of worthless lands without even a well-needed £5 note to assist in making a ramshacle [*sic*] place of abode, much less in trying to cultivate the place for an existence . . . In some cases, not even wild birds would care to inhabit them. Not even an inch is suitable for cultivation, and as far as roads are concerned, the inaccessibility of the places renders that impossible.[51]

Reid was leader of the Jamaica Ex-Service Men Labour Union founded by Canute McKenzie in 1935. The Labour Union represented the former regular soldiers of the disbanded WIR, rather than the BWIR veterans of 1914–19. The professional soldiers of the WIR felt a degree of superiority over the former volunteers of the BWIR. As a result, the Labour Union tended to pursue privileges for its members rather than forging links with other Jamaican workers. During the labour rebellion of May 1938, the Labour Union opportunistically forged closer ties with the white employers, working as strike-breakers on the United Fruit Company wharves.

CITIZENSHIP OR PAN-AFRICANISM?

While the Labour Union sought primarily to benefit those who had undertaken military service, the war memory could not be contained within such limited bounds and ultimately resonated far beyond Jamaican shores. The labour struggles of the late 1930s, in which veterans had played a fundamental part, gave rise to further industrial militancy during the Second World War, leading to the introduction of the universal franchise in 1944. This was a major concession to the citizenship claims of the Jamaican masses. Previously, the electorate had been dominated by the white elite and the 'coloured' middle classes who could meet the prohibitive property and tax qualifications. Thus, in the 1935 elections, only around 10 per cent of the adult population was registered to vote for the fourteen electable seats on the Legislative Council. Low voter turnout meant that active participation in the electoral process was closer to 4 per cent.[52] Jamaicans who fought in the First World War were granted a temporary dispensation entitling them to vote in the Legislative Council elections of 1920, regardless of property. Alfred Mends, a pioneering trade unionist and later adviser to Reid's Labour Union, led subsequent demands to extend the franchise to all Jamaicans in recognition of the island's participation in the war effort.[53] In 1923 Mends recalled how 'Jamaicans fought heroically ... Many gave up their lives, others [were] permanently disabled, to uphold the glory of the British Empire, to keep floating proudly in the breeze the Royal Standard, the Union Jack,' and asked 'Where is the reward?'[54]

Mends was strongly influenced by the struggles of African Americans to obtain the vote and cited Frederick Douglass's plea to President Johnson after the Civil War (1861–5): 'Your noble and humane predecessor placed in our hands the sword to assist in saving the nation, and we hope that you, his able successor, will favourably regard the placing in our hands the ballot with which to save ourselves.'[55] Demanding the fulfilment of pledges made in the empire's hour of need and underlining the implicit links between military service in the First World War and the expectation of citizenship, Mends portrayed Jamaica as '[a]n Island shouting ... across the broad blue waters of the Atlantic ... for Full Extended Representation, commensurate with the much vaunted boast 'Civis Britanicus sum' (I am a British citizen).[56] He was echoing the sentiments of the Jamaican volunteers who had been encouraged to believe that war service would lead to greater political and economic participation. Significantly, Mends also led a campaign against the death sentence imposed on Rupert Smalling, a veteran of the WIR who had murdered a fellow soldier. Smalling, who had been mentioned in dispatches for bravery in East Africa and remained in uniform after the war, was said to have suffered temporary insanity caused by shell shock.[57]

The strategic use of war service to press the case for self-determination could transcend this limited aspiration, however, and was embraced by the broader vision of Pan-Africanism which evolved during the 1920s and 1930s. This was evident in the transition of Marcus Garvey from an advocate of imperial citizenship to the leading Pan-Africanist figure before the Second World War. Having left Jamaica in 1916, Garvey re-established the Universal Negro Improvement Association (UNIA) in 1917 in Harlem, New York, home to a burgeoning community of African Americans and Caribbean and African migrants.[58] Recognising that the Allies' post-war vision of self-determination and freedom did not extend to African Americans or imperial subjects of African descent, Garvey called for blood to be shed to secure an African homeland. At a mass meeting in Brooklyn, New York, in January 1919, Garvey declared:

Our sacrifices, as made in the cause of other people, are many . . . it is time that we should prepare to sacrifice now for ourselves . . . Africa will be a bloody battlefield in the years to come . . . we are determined . . . to fight . . . to a finish. That finish must mean victory for the Negro standard . . . I feel sure that my blood shall have paid that remission for which future generations of the Negro race shall be declared free.[59]

In March 1921, Garvey arrived in Jamaica from Cuba where he had addressed thousands of Jamaican migrant labourers, many of whom were war veterans. Declaring that the Jamaican was a 'citizen of Africa' and not 'a British born subject', Garvey argued that true independence could only be achieved through the establishment of a 'dominion of Negroes' in Africa. Until then, Jamaican veterans should press their claim for enfranchisement as the first step toward African liberation.[60]

In the following decade, Pan-Africanist ideas took a firmer hold among the Jamaican war veterans. The coronation of Ras Tafari as Haile Selassie, Emperor of Ethiopia, in November 1930 underlined the place of Africa as a spiritual homeland. The failure of the League of Nations to prevent Mussolini's invasion of Ethiopia in 1935 provided a potential opportunity for Jamaicans to heed Garvey's sacrificial message.[61] Petitions and resolutions were organised as Jamaican citizens demanded the right to fight for the Ethiopian cause, denied to them by the Foreign Enlistment Act (1870) and the Ethiopian Order in Council (1934). In October 1935, some 1,360 Jamaicans signed a UNIA petition to George V, vowing as 'members of the Negro Race, and the descendants of African slaves' to ensure 'the preservation of any part of Africa which is free of foreign domination' and to defend 'our ancient and beloved Empire'.[62] A further petition was organised by St William Wellington Wellwood Grant, a veteran of the First World War. Referring to Ethiopia as the 'only relic of the great African Empire' and to the contribution of the BWIR in the First World War, the petition demanded 'that in the same way as we helped to safeguard the integrity of other races, we are asking that our race be protected at this crucial moment'.[63]

Grant epitomised the shift to a global consciousness among Jamaican war veterans, but also continued to adhere to some facets of imperial subjecthood, especially those related to military service. He returned to Jamaica in 1934 after over a decade of involvement with UNIA in the United States, and his role in the campaign to defend Ethiopian sovereignty placed him temporarily at the forefront of radical politics. In May 1938, he led the first march in protest at the shooting down of striking sugar workers at Frome, the event which signalled the beginning of the labour rebellion. Grant was rapidly eclipsed as the partisan struggle between Norman Manley's People's National Party and Bustamante's Jamaica Labour Party took hold.[64] However, his adherence to Garveyism and concern for the plight of the masses meant that he continued to be held in high regard. Until his death in 1977, he wore the uniform of the paramilitary UNIA Tiger Division upon which were pinned the British War Medal and Victory Medal earned during his service with the BWIR.[65]

Since the late 1960s, the history of the West Indian contribution in the First World War has largely been regarded as lost, suppressed or forgotten. However, the sacrifices of Jamaican volunteers *were* commemorated and celebrated, although within the limits of post-war imperial relations. Memorials were erected in each of Jamaica's three counties. The first, a Calvary cross of imported Portland stone at Montego Bay, St James parish, Cornwall, was unveiled in September 1921.[66] Smaller memorial tablets were erected in many Jamaican parishes by public subscription.[67] The principal Jamaican memorial was unveiled in Church Street, Kingston, on Armistice Day 1922. Dedicating the memorial, Acting Governor Bryan declared that fallen Jamaicans formed part of an imperial brotherhood whose graves 'girdled' the world. But he also implicitly acknowledged the more distinct Jamaican identity to which the war had contributed, symbolised by 'our memorial . . . designed, fashioned and wrought by island hands, from island stone'.[68] The *Daily Gleaner* also recognised this transition, echoing Rupert Brooke in suggesting that the war dead had left a 'little part of Jamaica in a foreign soil'.[69]

The shifting geography of the Kingston memorial reflected the movement of war memory from empire to the nation-state. In 1953, it was relocated in George VI Memorial Park, renamed National Heroes Park after independence.[70] But controversy around the burial of St William Grant underlined how, even after independence, many Jamaicans claimed identities beyond those of nationhood. Grant, like noted veterans before him – Hubert Reid and the journalist and impresario Vere Johns – was buried with full military honours.[71] However, the Pan African Secretariat of Jamaica, who the previous year had presented Grant with an award for his contribution to Pan-Africanism, believed interment at Up Park Camp military cemetery was not sufficient to commemorate his achievements.[72] The Secretariat argued a tomb in National Heroes Park, alongside Marcus Garvey, whose remains had been returned from England in 1964, would have been a more fitting tribute.[73] Subsequently, Victoria Park in Kingston was rededicated in Grant's honour.

The First World War raised the hopes of Jamaican volunteers in terms of citizenship rights, employment opportunities and autonomous land proprietorship. These expectations were expressed through the discourse of military sacrifice, despite the exclusion of many from the front-line settings to which heroic narrative alludes. The failure of imperial government to meet these expectations increased veteran militancy, although the dispersal of ex-servicemen through the Americas initially diluted the political impact in Jamaica. The increasing exposure, particularly of émigré Jamaicans, to an emerging global Pan-African consciousness transcended the boundaries of colonial subjecthood, leading to the reinterpretation of military service with more radical consequences. However, as the development of Hubert Reid's Ex-Service Men Labour Union shows, the demands of veterans could also be of a limited and parochial nature.

Over the past twenty-five years, Jamaica's war memory has moved even further from a narrow association with a single nation-state. Alongside other diasporic communities in Great Britain, Jamaicans have affirmed their citizenship in the former imperial power through the recovered memory of ancestral sacrifice in the world wars.[74] The contribution of imperial subjects was commemorated by the unveiling of the Memorial Gates on

Constitution Hill, London, in 2002. More recently, the Imperial War
Museum, London, presented 'From War to Windrush' (13 June 2008 to 1
November 2009), its first exhibition acknowledging the contribution of
West Indians in the world wars. These claims for recognition depend partly
on a reworked post-imperial nostalgia which continues to privilege military
service, and especially front-line duty, within discourses of national belonging. Jamaican war memory therefore needs to be framed within empire *and*
its unravelling in the post-imperial era following the Second World War.
While Jamaicans ostensibly volunteered to defend the British empire,
within the popular imagination, they also served the cause of Pan-
Africanism, the future Jamaican nation and its diaspora.

NOTES

1 John Edgar Caulwell Hearne, author of *Voices Under the Window* (1955), served
  in the Royal Canadian Air Force during the Second World War. His father
  Maurice Vincent Hearne served as a sergeant in the Royal Fusiliers in the First
  World War before joining the civil service in Jamaica, having migrated there
  from Canada in the late 1920s. J. Hearne, 'The Democracy of Death', *Sunday
  Gleaner*, 5 July 1981, 12.
2 R. Hart, *Rise and Organise: The Birth of the Workers and National Movements in
  Jamaica (1936–1939)*, (London: Karia, 1989).
3 Hearne, 'Democracy', 12.
4 F. Cundall, *Jamaica's Part in the War, 1914–1918* (London: West India
  Committee for the Institute of Jamaica, 1925).
5 'Coloured' was the contemporary term for Jamaicans of mixed African and
  European heritage. For a discussion of the race and class dynamics of Jamaican
  society see B. L. Moore and M. A. Johnson, *Neither Led Nor Driven: Contesting
  British Cultural Imperialism in Jamaica, 1865–1920* (Mona: University of the West
  Indies Press, 2004), especially pp. 1–50.
6 Personal correspondence with Nola Stair, June 2008. Around 400 white
  Jamaicans gained commissions in other British and imperial units and perhaps
  a few hundred Jamaicans of all skin shades served as NCOs and privates in other
  British regiments. R. Smith, *Jamaican Volunteers in the First World War: Race,
  Masculinity and the Development of National Consciousness* (Manchester
  University Press, 2004), 80–1.
7 T. G. Ashplant, G. Dawson and M. Roper, 'The Politics of War Memory and
  Commemoration: Contexts, Structures and Dynamics', in Ashplant *et al.* (eds.),
  The Politics of War Memory and Commemoration (London: Routledge, 2000),
  7–16. J. Damousi, *The Labour of Loss: Mourning, Memory and Wartime
  Bereavement in Australia* (Cambridge University Press, 1999), 1–2.
8 J. Winter, *Sites of Memory, Sites Of Mourning: The Great War in European
  Cultural History* (Cambridge University Press, 1996), 93.
9 J. Henderson, *Jamaica* (London: A & C Black, 1906), 105.

10 For background, see P. E. Bryan, *The Jamaican People 1880–1902: Race, Class and Social Control* (Basingstoke: Macmillan, 1991); T. C. Holt, *The Problem of Freedom: Race, Labor, and Politics in Jamaica and Britain, 1832–1938* (Baltimore: Johns Hopkins University Press, 1992); Moore and Johnson, *Neither Led Nor Driven.*

11 *Jamaica Times* (henceforth *JT*), 8 August 1914, 9.

12 Marcus Garvey, 'A Talk with Afro-West Indians: The Negro Race and Its Problems', in R. A. Hill (ed.), *The Marcus Garvey and Universal Negro Improvement Association Papers*, vol. 1 (Berkeley: University of California Press, 1983), 62.

13 'Circular Appeal' enclosed with Marcus Garvey to Booker T. Washington, 8 September 1914, in Hill (ed.), *Marcus Garvey . . . Papers*, vol. 1 (Berkeley: University of California Press, 1983), 69.

14 Moore and Johnson, *Neither Led Nor Driven*, 273–4.

15 *Daily Gleaner* (henceforth *DG*), 12 October 1915, 13.

16 *JT*, 12 September 1914, 4.

17 Marcus Garvey, UNI and Conservation Ass. & African Communities League to Rt. Hon. Lewis Harcourt MP, 16 September 1914 – Resolution passed at Collegiate Hall, Kingston 15 September 1914, The National Archives, London (hereafter TNA) CO137/705.

18 *DG*, 29 November 1915, 14.

19 *DG*, 12 May 1916, 10.

20 Memorandum from Military Members of the Army Council 6 February 1917 to Commander in Chief, British Armies in France, TNA WO32/5094.

21 *Manual of Military Law* (London: HMSO, 1914), p. 471; Smith, *Jamaican Volunteers*, 64–5.

22 *DG*, 24 February 1916, 8.

23 *DG*, 6 May 1916, 13.

24 Smith, *Jamaican Volunteers*, 125–6.

25 *Manual of Military Law*, p. 471. At least one Jamaican, described as 'coloured,' breached this restriction. Hubert Austin Cooper, Deputy Clerk of the Courts for the parish of Westmoreland, was commissioned as a Second Lieutenant of the BWIR in 1917 (*DG*, 1 August 1942, 1; *The Voice* (St Lucia), 28 June 1919, 4).

26 War Diary 1BWIR. June 1917–April 1919, entry for 13 October 1918, TNA WO95/4732.

27 Not to be confused with the BWIR, the WIR emerged from the West India Regiments formed during the wars with France from 1793. Although, uniquely among colonial units, the WIR was a line regiment of the British army, it too was usually regarded as a 'native' unit. See B. Dyde, *The Empty Sleeve: The Story of the West India Regiments of the British Army* (St Johns, Antigua: Hansib, 1997).

28 *DG*, 29 March 1919, 18. The original report, 'British West Indies Regiment', appears in TNA WO95/4732 War Diary 1BWIR. June 1917–April 1919.

29 Memoranda from British West Indies Regiment Association, Sergeant W. Johnson to Royal Cm. (n.d.), TNA CO950/93.

30 James Campbell, 'Combat Gnosticism: The Ideology of First World War Poetry Criticism', *New Literary History*, 30 (1999), 203–15.

31 The majority of BWIR casualties occurred away from the front line. 1,071 died of disease, 178 men were killed or died of wounds, and 697 were wounded (*West India Committee Circular*, 539, 29 May 1919, 128).

32 War Diary Camp Commandant Taranto Base entries for 6–12 December 1918, TNA wo95/4255; 'The First World War Memoirs of Lieutenant D. C. Burn', f. 136. Imperial War Museum (IWM) PP/MCA/173. There was only one reported fatality during the mutiny period – when Acting Sergeant Robert Richards negligently discharged his rifle, killing Private Samuel Pinnock (War Diary of 7BWIR, entry for 9 January 1919, TNA wo95/4262).

33 War Diary Commandant Taranto Base entries for 6–8 December 1918, TNA wo95/4255; TNA wo95/4262 War Diary 7BWIR, January 1918 – January 1919 entry for 9 January 1919; E. Dupuch, *A Salute to Friend and Foe* (Nassau: Tribune, 1982).

34 Register of Field General Courts Martial and Military Courts to 27 February 1919, TNA WO213/27. Second Lieutenant Hubert Austin Cooper (see note 25) is reported to have served as a military prosecutor during these hearings (*DG*, 1 August 1942, 1). He had previously defended Private Albert Denny who was executed for murdering a fellow soldier (TNA wo71/675 Army Form B. 122).

35 Notes of meeting held at Cimino Camp, Italy, 17 December 1918, TNA co318/350/2590.

36 Major Maxwell Smith to Major-General Thuillier, GOC, Taranto, 27 December 1918, TNA co318/350/2590.

37 Major Maxwell Smith (8BWIR) to GOC, Taranto, 3 January 1919, TNA co318/350/2590.

38 Notes of meeting held at Cimino Camp, Italy, 17 December 1918; Major Maxwell Smith (8BWIR) to GOC, Taranto, 3 January 1919, TNA co318/350/2590. Sergeant Cecil Collman returned to civil life in Jamaica as the deputy clerk of court in Portland, having helped oversee the final stages of demobilisation. Sergeant Harold Leopold Brown devoted the remainder of his life to benevolent societies and became a leading advocate of Jamaican agricultural initiatives (*DG*, 7 May 1919, 10; *DG*, 11 March 1946, 9).

39 'The Song of Our Returning Soldiers', *JT*, 28 June 1919, 8.

40 'The Kaiser after His Kind', *JT*, Christmas number, December 1914, 9. Returning to Jamaica from Taranto in the summer of 1919, Monteith immersed himself in progressive social activism for the remainder of his life. Central to his vision was a desire to revitalise Jamaica through comprehensive education and agricultural investment. He served as a president of the Jamaica Union of Teachers, officer of the Jamaica Agricultural Society and parish councillor for his native St Ann (*DG*, 23 June 1970, 1, 5).

41 'BWIR Ass. Witnesses', TNA co950/93, J33 26th Session; 'Memorandum on Unemployment and Rates of Wages', TNA co950/944, Written Evidence, Serial No. 169.

42 Extract from Sir Leslie Probyn's welcome speech to returning soldiers, 2 May 1919, TNA co950/93.

43 A. S. Jelf to William Bennett, C. H. Eastwood and others, 15 February 1933, TNA CO137/799/10; *ExService Man*, n.d., 5 enclosed with British West Indies Regiment Association Memorandum to Moyne Commission', TNA CO950/93. The Jamaica Old Comrades Association (formerly known as the Jamaica Ex-Service Men's Association) was dominated by white and light-skinned Jamaicans, many of whom had served in regiments other than the BWIR. The future prime minister, N. W. Manley, who served as a Royal Artillery gunner, was a member of the executive committee (*DG*, 21 December 1923, 6).

44 A. S. Jelf to William Bennett, C. H. Eastwood and others, 15 February 1933, TNA CO137/799/10; British West Indies Regiment Association Memorandum TNA CO950/93.

45 *DG*, 18 May 1933, 15. The Ex-BWIR Association was founded in 1919 and remained active until the early 1940s. After the Second World War, the Jamaica Legion became the main veterans' organisation. It remains affiliated to the Royal Commonwealth Ex-Services League and maintains the Curphey Home for veterans.

46 *DG*, 15 July 1933, 7; William Bennett and others to Gov. R. E. Stubbs, 19 October 1932, C. H. Eastwood and others to Gov. Sir Ransford Slater, 7 December 1932, TNA CO137/799/10; Gov. Denham to Ormsby Gore, SSC 4 January 1938, CO137/818/3; *Jamaica War Contribution* (Cd. 8695), London, 1917.

47 Minute by Surveyor-General, 10 January 1938, TNA CO137/828/5.

48 Denham to Sir Cosmo Parkinson, Colonial Office 30 July 1937, TNA CO137/818/3.

49 Minute by Surveyor-General, 10 January 1938, TNA CO137/828/5.

50 Reid's citation appears in the *London Gazette*, 30 October 1918, 12,835.

51 Memorandum of Jamaica Ex-Service Men Labour Union, TNA CO950/240.

52 R. Hart, *Towards Decolonisation: Political, Labour and Economic Developments in Jamaica 1938–1945* (Mona, Jamaica: University Press of the West Indies, 1997), 3.

53 Notice, King's House, 22 May 1919, TNA CO318/348/38685.

54 A. A. Mends, *Can There Still Be Hope for the Reformation in Jamaica?* (Kingston: Temple of Fashion Printery, 1923), 11–12.

55 Quoted in *ibid*.

56 *Ibid.*, 5.

57 *DG*, 10 January, 1924, 6.

58 On the West Indian presence in Harlem see L. J. Parascandola (ed.), '*Look for Me All Around You': Anglophone Caribbean Immigrants in the Harlem Renaissance* (Detroit: Wayne State University Press, 2005); J. M. Turner, *Caribbean Crusaders and the Harlem Renaissance* (Urbana: University of Illinois Press, 2005).

59 *West Indian* (Grenada), 28 February 1919. Also see M. A. Stephens, *Black Empire: The Masculine Global Imaginary of Caribbean Intellectuals in the United States, 1914–1962* (Durham, NC: Duke University Press, 2005).

60 See *DG*, 25 March 1921, 11; 26 March 1921, 6; 29 March 1921, 10.

61 On the Italian invasion's wider impact in the Anglophone Caribbean, see R. G. Weisbord, 'British West Indian reaction to the Italian–Ethiopian War: an episode in Pan-Africanism', *Caribbean Studies*, 10:1 (1970), 34–41; K. A. Yelvington, 'The War in Ethiopia and Trinidad 1935–1936', in B. Brereton and K. A. Yelvington, *The Colonial Caribbean in Transition: Essays on Post-Emancipation Social and Cultural History* (Gainesville: University Press of Florida, 1999).

62 Petition of Kingston UNIA October 1935, TNA CO318/418/4/71062.

63 Copy Petition to Secretary of State for the Colonies 5 October 1935, TNA CO318/418/4/71062.

64 On the legacy of the long-standing rivalry between the PNP and the JLP, see A. Sives, 'Violence and Politics in Jamaica', PhD thesis, University of Bradford, 1998, and Carlene J. Edie, *Clientelism in Jamaica* (Boulder, CO: Lynne Rienner, 1991).

65 Hill (ed.), *Marcus Garvey ... Papers*, vol. VII (Berkeley: University of California Press, 1990), 309–10; N. White, 'St William Wellington Grant: A Fighter for Black Dignity', *Jamaica Journal*, 43 (1979), 56–63; K. Post, *Strike the Iron: A Colony at War: Jamaica 1939–1945*, vol. 1 (Atlantic Highlands, NJ: Humanities Press, 1981) 63–4.

66 *DG*, 23 September 1921, 9.

67 See for example DG, 24 October 1921, 9; 26 October 1921, 6; 21 November 1921, 4; 2 December 1921, 4.

68 *DG*, 13 November 1922, 6.

69 *DG*, 13 November 1922, 8.

70 *DG*, 15 July 1953, 3.

71 *DG*, 5 November 1969, 21; 16 September 1966, 4.

72 Up Park Camp also contains the graves and memorials to Jamaican volunteers of both world wars in the care of the Commonwealth War Graves Commission.

73 *DG*, 7 June 1976, 15; 2 September 1977, 15.

74 Jane Bown's photograph of a black British veteran at the Cenotaph, chosen for the cover of Paul Gilroy's *There Ain't No Black in the Union Jack* (London: Routledge, 1987), strikingly recorded this shift.

CHAPTER 15

Not only war: the First World War and African American literature

Mark Whalan

In a column for the *Chicago Defender* published just following the Second World War, the African American poet Langston Hughes has his Harlemite barfly Jesse B. Semple (or 'Simple') say the following:

'You know Buddy Jones' brother, what was wounded in the 92nd in Italy, don't you? Well, he was telling me about how bad them rednecks treated him when he was in the army in Mississippi. He said he don't never want to see no parts of the South again. He were born and raised in Yonkers and not used to such stuff. Now his nerves is shattered. He can't even stand a Southern accent no more.'

'Jim Crow shock,' I said. 'I guess it can be as bad as shell shock.'

'It can be worse,' said Simple. 'Jim Crow happens to men every day down South, whereas a man's not in a battle every day.'[1]

Although ostensibly written about a different conflict, Hughes's association of battlefield trauma with the traumas of racial segregation in the USA was one forged in the experiences of the First World War. Shell shock troubled distinctions between organicist and psychological notions of trauma; it was exacerbated by feelings of helplessness in conflict situations.[2] Such a blend of psychological and physical stress and coercion was familiar to African Americans living under Jim Crow, and Hughes's bleak humour suggests that its everyday status only prolonged that trauma rather than dulled it.

More broadly, Simple's (typically deceptive) simple statement suggests two things about the African American reaction to the First World War. First, it voices a sense common in African American cultural reactions to the two world wars: that, in the words of Jessie Redmon Fauset, African American soldiers had 'fought a double battle in France, one with Germany and one with white America'.[3] Second, if for the European combatants the war resulted in a 'Victorian world of respectability, predictability, and heroes' being replaced by 'a culture of experience, surprise, and victims', for African Americans it bequeathed instead a range of new experiences and phenomena which resembled depressingly familiar emotional, physical and political situations which often centred on victimhood.[4] As Hughes noted, shell shock was one such 'novelty'; and as I shall discuss later, no-man's-land was another. The war therefore gave a conceptual vocabulary to racial conflict, which would be both influential and resourceful in the continuing struggle for African American self-assertion and civic status in the years following 1918.

This vocabulary only augmented a tendency for African American writers to talk about the racial politics of the USA in terms of military conflict. As Richard Wright put it:

Our black boys do not die for liberty in Flanders. They die in Texas and Georgia. Atlanta is our Marne. Brownsville, Texas, is our Château-Thierry. It is a lesson we will never forget; it is written into the pages of our blood, into the ledgers of our bleeding bodies, into columns of judgment figures and balance statements in the lobes of our brains.[5]

Yet the Great War was absorbed by African American culture in other ways too, ways more progressive and occasionally even celebratory. It introduced thousands of veterans to the political leverage of cosmopolitanism, a leverage particularly associated with meeting a white French population who often welcomed them as liberators and people worthy of respect. It encouraged masculine identities grounded in self-assertion, courage, decisiveness and physical prowess – qualities which Jim Crow sought to suppress in African American men. And if the celebratory spirit of African American culture of the 1920s – the era of the Harlem, or New Negro, Renaissance – was predicated largely on an optimistic vision of the potential of urban modernity for African American people, a transformation Alain Locke referred to as the move from 'medieval America to modern', then participation in modernity's greatest spectacle of carnage was sometimes viewed as a necessary rite of passage.[6] Of course, the great migration of millions of African Americans from rural South to urban North which was kick-started by the labour shortages in northern industries during the war was the major demographic, cultural and social consequence of the Great War for African American life.[7] Yet, contrary to what has sometimes been claimed, that was only a part of a broader cultural engagement.[8]

AFRICAN AMERICAN SERVICE IN THE FIRST WORLD WAR

The war provided ample reminders of the second-class status African Americans occupied in the national collective. At all phases of the state apparatus for war, they faced policies of segregation, subjugation, and downright hostility – despite the expectation that they would fully contribute to the war effort in financial and physical terms. Initially it appeared that no additional African American officers would be commissioned, despite hundreds of thousands of African Americans being inducted in the draft (almost 2.3 million registered, and 357,000 were inducted into the US forces in the war).[9] Pressure was brought to bear on the War Department, particularly by the fledgling National Association for the Advancement of Colored People, who argued forcefully that African American officers should be allowed to lead African American troops into combat. In the end, a segregated camp was opened at Des Moines, Iowa, but its only graduating class produced the meagre total of 639 officers – and many of these would later be removed from their units by racially motivated 'efficiency boards'.[10] Elsewhere, as the US geared up for full-scale mobilisation, the tensions involved in the new conditions of increased labour mobility, and African American men under arms in the South, did not take long to flare into conflict. In July, East St Louis witnessed three days of what was, effectively, a racial pogrom. Some 39 African Americans were killed, including women and children, and half of the town's 6,000-strong African American population were forced to evacuate. In Houston in August, after prolonged provocation from local whites and city police, a detachment of African American soldiers from the 24th Infantry – one of the oldest and most illustrious African American units, rather than draftees – marched into the town under arms; in the firefight 17 local whites, including 5 policemen, were killed. Governmental justice for these soldiers was swift and summary; 13 were hanged without appeal, and a total of 156 were court-martialled.[11]

Original plans had projected for sixteen new African American regiments, but this was deemed too risky after the events at Houston. Instead, a plan was implemented to give most African American draftees minimal combat training, and ship them to France as soon as possible to work as labour troops.[12] Eventually, this was how 80 per cent of African American troops would be deployed, compared to about 33 per cent of white troops. These labour troops experienced long working hours, poor equipment and accommodation, harassment from white military police, being under an officer cadre drawn disproportionately from the South, and an assortment of unattractive jobs (including reburying the dead in military cemeteries). The resulting dissatisfaction is fictionalised in Claude McKay's novel *Home to Harlem* (1928), whose protagonist Jake deserts his labour unit at the busy harbour at Brest because he 'was disappointed. He had enlisted to fight. For what else had he been sticking a bayonet into the guts of a stuffed man and aiming bullets straight into a bull's eye? Toting planks and getting into rows with his white comrades at the Bal Musette were not adventure.'[13]

Two African American divisions did see combat, accounting for approximately 42,000 African American troops, but their experiences were very different. The 93rd (never actually assembled as a full division) contained National Guard units which had existed before the war, including the 15th New York and the 8th Illinois, from Chicago. Somewhat perplexed about how to handle these units, the commander of the American Expeditionary Force (AEF) John Pershing handed them over to the French, who were desperate for manpower (an action in contrast to his generally stubborn refusal to assign command of American units to his European allies). Equipped with French helmets and weapons, the 15th, rechristened the 369th regiment of the 93rd Division (or colloquially the Harlem Hellfighters), arrived in France from December 1917 and eventually spent 191 days in the line – the longest of any American unit during the war. They undertook defensive actions near Château-Thierry during the German spring offensive of 1918, assisted the American assault in the Argonne in September 1918, and were also the first Allied troops to reach the Rhine following the Armistice, on 26 November; for their actions in taking the town of Sechault during the Argonne offensive in late September, the entire regiment received a citation for the Croix de Guerre.[14]

Similarly distinguished records were achieved by the other regiments in the division, a fact which caused some consternation in a general staff reluctant to shower praise on African American soldiers in the fashion of the French. Indeed, 'secret' memos circulated by the AEF Headquarters urged French commanding officers not to praise these troops too extravagantly, not to receive them on terms of equality, and to discourage their access to local civilian populations – especially French women.[15] Despite the issuing of the memo and similar events (and indeed partly because of them), the actions of the 93rd were greeted with wild enthusiasm in the African American press, and their welcome-home marches – in New York, Chicago, Cleveland and Pittsburgh in the early months of 1919 – were attended by hundreds of thousands of people. In contrast, the 92nd gained an unwarranted reputation for failure after one of its regiments performed poorly in one engagement at the Argonne – an engagement for which they had deficient equipment, and highly questionable leadership from their white senior officers. Despite heroic actions in other, later engagements, especially at Metz in the closing days of the war, the entire division was branded a failure by its commanding general, and by contemporaneous historians of the AEF.[16] As William N. Colson, an African American lieutenant in the 92nd, observed in the socialist African American monthly *The Messenger*, 'It was not to be expected that any class except the war traders would get anything more than suffering out of the war. But the Negro division was the object of special victimisation superimposed upon its sacrifice.'[17]

PARTISAN POETRY: THE WARTIME CULTURAL RESPONSE

America's African American press reacted variously to the events of the war, dependent on local conditions and editorial politics; nevertheless, many printed what Mark Van Wienen has called 'partisan poetry,' namely occasional poetry written quickly by editors, clergymen, soldiers, or other professional readers and/or contributors.[18] During the war, such poetry became an important vehicle for voicing African American patriotism, but a patriotism consistently allied with statements of African American political and social aspiration which its authors hoped would materialise into policy as a result of their sacrifices in the conflict. A host of minor poets published in African American newspapers and magazines; particularly important venues for such poetry were *The Crisis*, the NAACP's house magazine, and from the second half of 1918 *The Crusader* and the Universal Negro Improvement Association's *Negro World*. Much of this poetry was later published in collections, and it shared a number of consistent themes. As Van Wienen notes, one such was the trope of the superior heroism and patriotism of African American soldiers, as they were effectively fighting two battles – one against the Germans, and one against domestic racial prejudice.

One such example is Roscoe Jamison's 'Prayer to the Flag':

> Thou art my Flag. I love thee still,
>   In spite of them who rend, and smear
> Thee with base crimes; who seek to kill
>   My People's hopes with baleful sneer
> I love thee still, and now I lift
>   My eyes to thee on high, above,
> To pray thee for the promised gift
>   Of Freedom for the Race I love.
>
> E'er thy stars mount dim Europe's skies,
>   To cheer brave hearts to Victory,
> I pray thee hear my People's cries,
>   Here in the Home-land, set men free.[19]

Such poetry stressed two arguments: that African American sacrifices in the war should be rewarded with fairer domestic policies towards African

Americans, as they had proved their thoroughgoing Americanness through their actions in the conflict. The second argument took up a dominant strand of Woodrow Wilson's rhetoric justifying the conflict. This argued that the war was being fought to make the world safe for democracy, which seemed hypocrisy to taxpaying African Americans prohibited from voting in much of the US. As Jamison continues, 'must we starve while aliens feast?'

These poems frequently took an essentially liberal perspective on race relations in the war, hoping that proof of African American bravery and service would change white American attitudes towards African American identity. As Leslie Pinckney Hill put it in a poem about 'Dixie's black men':

> They said they were too slow, too dull, too this and that to do it,
> They couldn't match the method of the Hun,
> And then to arm a million – why, the land would surely rue it
> If a million blacks were taught to use a gun.
> But right won out, and they went in at all detractors smiling;
> They learned as quick as any how to shoot,
> They took the prize at loading ships, and riveting and piling,
> And trained a thousand officers to boot.[20]

This type of poetry revealed the tensions involved in African American subscription to a rhetoric of patriotism and chauvinistic nationalism, as such a rhetoric was frequently used elsewhere to deny African Americans a voice in civic participation. This issue became even more acute when African American writers reflected on the sometimes hysterical anti-German propaganda circulated at the time, dwelling on purported German atrocities against women and children in occupied Belgium. To many African American observers, such atrocities seemed little different from the accounts of lynchings which emerged almost every week from the South, or in the reports from East St Louis. As a character in Alice Dunbar-Nelson's short play *Mine Eyes Have Seen* reflects, after hearing of the murder of children in Belgium, 'What's that to us? They're little white children. But here, our fellow-countrymen throw our little black babies in the flames.'[21] Outright opposition to the war on the part of African American writers during the war years was rare, due in part to the harsh legislation pushed through by Wilson that made criticism of US entry into the war liable to charges of sedition. (Socialist newspapers such as *The Messenger*, which published articles criticising US hypocrisy in conducting a global war for democracy whilst disfranchising its African American citizens at home, saw its editors arrested under the Espionage Act; Marcus Garvey, who made similarly forceful statements, was placed under Bureau of Investigation surveillance).[22] During the war, most writers therefore had to make the difficult negotiation between subscription to a patriotic rhetoric which monopolised public statements on the war, and a refusal to endorse their nation's racial politics.

One result of this tension was the emergence of a second theme in such 'partisan poetry', one which generally appeared in the more radical magazines. In a move which many white intellectuals also undertook in these years, several articles and poems by African American authors critiqued Western European claims to cultural and racial superiority. For example, in 'Civilization', Andrea Razafkeriefo exclaimed:

> With all your boasted culture
>   Your armies you have led
> To scientific slaughter
>   And left ten millions dead.
>
> With all your talk of justice
>   And grand Democracy,
> The weak are still exploited
>   And robbed of liberty.[23]

Such poetry linked up the aesthetics of Enlightenment discourse with the nationalism and racial theory which several commentators felt had brought the Western world to such a catastrophic war.

The most sophisticated theorisation of this was undertaken by W. E. B. Du Bois, a writer and civic leader who expressed a range of complex and sometimes contradictory responses to the conflict.[24] However, one persistent strand of his response was the desire to link the aesthetic with the political; as he remarked in an editorial in *The Crisis* before US entry into the war:

Behind all this gloss of culture and wealth and religion has been lurking the world-old lust for bloodshed and power gained at the cost of honor.

The realization of all this means for us the reassembling of old ideals. Honor which has had no meaning for us in this land of inconstant laws, takes on a new aspect; mediocrity, so long as it does not mean degradation, is sweet; peace – not at 'any price' – is a precious boon; old standards of beauty beckon us again, not the blue-eyed, white-skinned types which are set before us in school and literature but rich, brown and black men and women with glowing dark eyes and crinkling hair.[25]

As Russ Castronovo has recently argued, this was just a part of Du Bois's long-standing effort to configure the aesthetic as a site of African American political engagement, whereby 'aesthetics was retheorized so that beauty no longer appeared as an ideal beyond practical purpose but was revealed as a formal matter saturated by the historical content of racial atrocity'.[26] The

First World War gave Du Bois his most globalised and bloody historical grounding for that retheorisation and, well after 1918, his sense persisted that Western hierarchical schemas of evaluating different cultures would be greatly unsettled by the war.

In 1917 and 1918, much of the 'partisan poetry' and the editorials that accompanied it had carried a sense of progressive hope: that African American sacrifices to the US war effort would result in better conditions for African Americans in peacetime, and that the interlinked aesthetic, political and social practices of Western Enlightenment racial theory would be seriously altered by the war. Such hopes largely vanished during the events of 1919. As veterans returned and looked for work, and as industry attempted to erode some of the concessions to organised labour advanced during the war, the resultant tensions flared into violence. Race riots terrorised African American communities in many of the nation's major cities; African American veterans fought back in running battles with vigilante whites and white authorities, especially in the riots in Washington and Chicago. The so-called 'red summer' of that year also saw a hike in the number of lynchings; at least sixteen veterans were lynched between November 1918 and the end of 1920, some still in uniform.[27] A tone of bitterness and betrayal began to dominate African American journalism and writing about the war; as one African American newspaper claimed, 'for valor displayed in the recent war, it seems that the Negro's particular decoration is to be the "double-cross"'.[28]

THE WAR AND THE NEW NEGRO RENAISSANCE

Such reactions fed into the outpouring of cultural productivity in the 1920s known as the Harlem, or New Negro, Renaissance. Feelings of betrayal and disappointment at the US government for not doing more for African Americans after the conflict were widespread across the political spectrum, and this has led some commentators to see the major energies of the New Negro Renaissance as essentially uninterested in the war, and more focused instead on the nuances and mechanics of class and cultural mobility in the transition from a Southern rural to a Northern urban culture.[29] Yet New Negro poets, novelists, photographers, painters, musicians and intellectuals continued to be fascinated by the experiences of the war. They were generally unconvinced about the liberal narrative of service which had predominated during the war years, namely that proof of African American martial ability and loyalty would effect a change in national racial politics. But they were interested in how the war had affected conceptions of radicalised masculinity, how experiences in France could recast American discourses which sought to naturalise racial segregation, and even how the war had disrupted the experience of race as an embodied phenomenon. Examples of material dealing with these issues abound, but for the remainder of this chapter I will focus on two New Negro Renaissance novels: Jessie Redmon Fauset's *There Is Confusion* (1924) and Victor Daly's *Not Only War* (1932).

Despite James Weldon Johnson's claim in his 1930 cultural history *Black Manhattan* that 'the Negro novel of the World War is still unwritten', in fact the book often claimed to have begun the tradition of the New Negro Renaissance novel devotes its final third to a fictional account of the war.[30] The first of Jessie Fauset's four published novels, *There Is Confusion* focuses on issues which preoccupied her career: the lives of middle-class African American families, how to reconcile notions of racial duty with those of personal ambition, and the complex terrain of identification imposed by the colour line. *There Is Confusion* also engages topics which interested other African American writers in the 1920s: how women responded to the social and political shifts of wartime; how African Americans related to the symbolic apparatus of American nationalism; a fetishisation of the African American Des Moines officer as a role model for post-war masculinity; and the disappointment of returning veterans.[31] Here, I shall focus on perhaps the novel's most provocative reflections on the meaning of the conflict for African Americans, namely its depiction of battle scenes, and of African American combatants' experiences in France.

These centre around Peter Bye, a character who struggles throughout the text to assume the mantle of the industrious, sober, 'race man' which is expected of him – especially by his imperious sweetheart Joanna Marshall.[32] A medical student, at the war's outbreak Peter trains as an officer at Des Moines before departing for France. On the troopship he meets the white Meriwether Bye, the great-grandson of a slave-owning Quaker who had owned his great-grandfather, Joshua Bye. As the two converse, their shared familial and economic history becomes clear, as does Peter's anger at the history of enslavement that provided Meriwether's family with their foundation of wealth, and Meriwether's own guilt at these events ('it's a rotten story', he exclaims at one point).[33] Even at this initial stage of their relationship, their similarities are stressed: 'it was true that while there was no facial resemblance, the two men were built almost exactly alike, tall, with broad shoulders, flat backs and lean thighs'.[34] Meriwether was even Peter's father's name. As the novel progresses, Peter is sent up to the line in France and volunteers for a dangerous reconnaissance mission. Slowly advancing in a night-time foray in

no-man's-land, he sees Meriwether in hand-to-hand combat with a
German soldier. Peter kills the German, but is wounded himself, and
ministers to the fatally wounded Meriwether – whom he has to tend in
complete darkness, sensing his wounds solely by touch and finding that his
'heart was beating faintly and just above it was a hole, with the blood
gushing, spurting, hot and thick'. He drags Meriwether away from immediate danger, and Meriwether dies in his arms intoning the words
'Grandfather, this is the last of the Byes.' Peter loses consciousness, but
stretcher-bearers find them the following day, locked in an embrace. The
chapter closes as a white stretcher-bearer remarks, 'I've seen many a sight
in this war, but none ever give me the turn I got seein' that smoke's hair
dabblin' in the other fellow's blood.'[35]

So extraordinary is this moment that even such an eminent critic of the
Harlem Renaissance as George Hutchinson confesses, 'I do not know
exactly what to make of this scene.'[36] Yet it is just one of several pieces
written at the time in the US which use a distinct set of motifs about the
racial implications of combat. The first is the exposure of the vulnerability
of the white body in such combat, its propensity to being wounded and
dismembered, which often comes as a shock or a surprise to African
American observers used to a discourse of whiteness as something beyond
the body. This was disorienting in two ways; first, it challenged a particular
aspect of white racial identity, namely its association with qualities beyond
the physical. Richard Dyer has discussed the reliance of notions of white
superiority on qualities which go beyond the corporeal and the visible; as he
notes, whiteness often claimed as the source of its uniqueness a particular
'spirit' which emanated from but also transcended the body. As he remarks,
'the white spirit could both master and transcend the white body, while the
non-white soul was a prey to the promptings and fallibilities of the body'.
Whiteness, then – both its very essence and its pre-eminence – was often
reliant on 'that which cannot be scrutinized.'[37] The horrific violence
enacted on white bodies in several African American fictions about the
Great War, however, shows those bodies as 'reduced' to pure corporeality,
and therefore denuded of a claim to difference from a 'blackness' often
defined solely in terms of bodily appetites, capabilities and identity. In the
scene described above, exactly this kind of assertion of corporeal equality
takes place. Second, such scenes occurred in no-man's-land, a different kind
of space, one not oriented – as most US social space was – by nuanced codes
of racial etiquette, belonging, and potential transgression. Instead, as the
African American poet Walter E. Seward wryly remarked, it was a social
space indiscriminate in its violence:

> Bullets have no special people,
> No one especially they hate;
> And the Germans' large artillery
> Sure did not discriminate.[38]

In this way, and in several fictions of the time, no-man's-land became a space which was oddly liberating in its egalitarianism – even if what was equal was the chance of violent death. It allowed for an interracial contact and even intimacy which – whilst not actively being encouraged – was not prohibited in these life-and-death situations.

As in the scene in *There Is Confusion*, this intimacy often had overtones of homoeroticism: this can be seen in the embrace of Peter and Meriwether, and the shock of the stretcher-bearer when he finds them together. Their situation also makes literal what fears of miscegenation traded on as its highest metaphorical currency: the mixing of bloods (notably Peter is 'dabbling' in Meriwether's blood when the stretcher-bearer finds them). By the end of the novel, we realise that this tableau – and Meriwether's last words – are in fact indicative of a deeper truth binding the men together; it transpires that Peter's enslaved great-grandfather was actually the son of the patriarch of the white Bye family, and that consequently Peter and Meriwether are distantly related. Their homoerotic intimacy is therefore revalued as familial intimacy, or the erotic intimacy of their distant fore-bears; the tableau of the two characters covered in each other's blood is not therefore a caution about the mixing of racial 'blood', but a statement of its historical occurrence, vividly revealed by the extraordinary pressures of war. No-man's-land is therefore experienced as a space of revelation and truth, a stage where veneers of racial protocol, dissimulation and politeness are stripped away to reveal the essentials of national and familial identity. Such forms of identity are the source of the various types of 'confusion' which the novel considers, confusions made clearer by the revelatory and unprecedented space of no-man's-land.

Similar events take place in Victor Daly's 1932 novel *Not Only War*. Daly's foreword suggests that 'Not only War is Hell'; as well as war, 'There is yet another gaping, abysmal Hell into which some of us are actually born or unconsciously sucked . . . This other, is a purgatory for the mind, for the spirit, for the soul of men.'[39] As well as the stronger tone of pessimism, Daly's novel is distinguished from Fauset's by being more autobiographical. A first lieutenant in the 367th 'Buffaloes' regiment of the 92nd Division, a unit composed mostly of New York draftees, Daly won the Croix de Guerre for his battlefield service. He later worked as the business manager for the socialist magazine

The Messenger and, as Chad Williams observes, forcefully endorsed its editorial line on interracial working-class solidarity, its relaxed attitude to interracial marriage, and its policies of armed resistance to white provocation.[40]

Daly's brief novel uses a stock device of melodramatic war narratives – a device also apparent in Fauset's novel – of twinning characters from across a social divide who meet on the battlefield. His are two men from South Carolina; the first is patrician Robert 'Bob' Lee Casper, the only son of a plantation-owning family, trained at military school and 'faithful to his creed' of 'the Baptist Church, the supremacy of the white race and the righteousness of the Democratic Party'.[41] The other is Montie Jason, an African American college man studying in Spartanburg. Unlike earlier novels such as *There Is Confusion*, Walter White's *The Fire in the Flint* (1924) or Edward Christopher Williams's *The Letters of Davy Carr* (1925–6), *Not Only War* refuses to celebrate the Des Moines officer as a symbol for the progressive potential of a racial uplift spearheaded by 'race men' skilled in martial and civic leadership and combativity.[42] Instead, Montie comes up against the realities of the officer camp for African Americans: that the minimum age limit is 25, and that many places are allotted to non-commissioned officers from the peacetime army's African American regiments, rather than to college men. He enrols in the fabled 369th, the Harlem Hellfighters, but begins and ends the war as a private – in stark contrast to the lieutenantship which Bob Casper easily obtains.

The main way in which the characters are 'twinned', however, is in sexual terms. The two men are attracted to the same two women, first in the US and then in France: the African American Miriam Pinckney, who lives in the same county as Bob Casper and is an old flame of Montie from college; and the white Blanche Aubertin, a French woman, whose house Montie is billeted in. Bob had met Miriam by chance, and throughout the novel conducts a secret relationship with her; at one point Miriam reflects bitterly that it is an example of how 'Southern white men ... could only seek friendship with comely colored girls for one purpose – a social equality that existed after dark.'[43] In contrast to Bob's aggressive pursuit of Miriam, Montie is initially reluctant to befriend Blanche; through her persistence, however, he eventually begins to teach her English, and their friendship develops. This is rudely interrupted as Bob finds Montie billeted in Blanche's house and, incensed at this, has him court-martialled and busted down from sergeant to private. As well as white male hypocrisy over interracial sexual relations, the novel also dramatises the many conflicts which occurred over white French women's relationships with African American soldiers in service in France during the war. As the contemporary African

American historian Charles H. Williams bitterly noted, 'two-thirds of the difficulties experienced by the colored soldiers in France were due to American resentment of the attitude of the French people in receiving them on equal terms, and especially of the kindly disposition of the French women'.[44]

Magazines such as *The Crisis* stressed the warm welcome afforded by white civilians to African American soldiers; and more radical magazines such as *The Messenger* went further, such as in this impish poem by Robert L. Wolf entitled 'Les Noirs':

> 'Tres gentils – les noirs,'
>   So the French girl said;
> How the phrase did jar
>   My friend! Flushing red.
> 'We at home don't go
>   With those – colored men.'
> Quoth the French maid, 'Oh,
> Don't they like you, then?'[45]

Daly robustly defended the principle of interracial sexual freedom in the aftermath of the war, remarking in the letters pages of *The Messenger* in 1919 that 'over one thousand Negro stevedores intermarried with white French girls and I doubt if French honor suffered in any way for it'.[46] Many sections of the African American press were wary of venturing onto such territory, aware that couching African American political demands for equality in sexual terms was a favoured scare tactic of white supremacists, and thus risked being strategically counterproductive in the fight for improved civil rights across a broad range of issues. Yet Daly's bold approach asserted that personal and sexual freedom was indissociable from political and civic freedoms, that sexual desire existed both ways across the colour line, and that creeds of racial/sexual exclusivity were very prone to hypocrisy. Moreover, rather than demonising Bob as a sexual predator in his novel, it is noticeable how alike Daly makes his characters, how codes of social class give Miriam, Blanche, Montie and Bob a similar set of aesthetic, romantic and moral tastes which cut across race and nationality. Furthermore, if this class similarity exists across racial and national divides, then discovering that similitude is made easier by the new forms of mobility which surround the war. Bob's secret affair with Miriam is only made possible by using automobiles to get away from Spartanburg, and Montie only meets Blanche as a result of the mass mobilisation of American soldiers in Europe. The interracial, international codes of the middle class, and the ever-increasing mobility of that class are therefore shown as rendering codes of racial segregation hopelessly anachronistic.

This point is emphasised further in the novel's closing scenes, which again stage an interracial *rapprochement* in the deadly terrain of no-man's-land. The regiment of Bob and Montie is leading an assault on a heavily defended German position, and at the limit of the advance between the two opposing lines, Montie is forced to take cover. Initially, he plans to wait until dark before returning in safety to his own trenches. However, he discovers Bob, badly wounded from his part in an earlier wave of attack, and he tends to Bob's wounds as best he can. Bob, fainting intermittently through loss of blood from the horrific injury to his leg, recognises it is Montie – who quickly determines he will risk his own life by breaking cover to try and drag Bob back to his own lines to receive medical attention. 'God, but you're a prince,' whispers Bob, adding, 'war isn't the only hell that I've been through lately'.[47] As Montie drags Bob over the exposed sections of no-man's-land to safety, both are killed by a burst of machine-gun fire, and the novel abruptly finishes as 'two bodies slumped as one. They found them the next morning, face downward, their arms about each other, side by side.'[48]

This closing tableau, of two antagonists in war sharing a moment of intimacy at the moment of death, was a stock one in melodramatic war fiction and cinema. Similar scenes had been deployed in the two biggest US war movies to that point, D. W. Griffith's *The Birth of a Nation* (1915) and King Vidor's *The Big Parade* (1925). The former dramatised this intimacy occurring between a white Confederate and a white Union soldier; in the latter it was a white American and a white German soldier. (One of Griffith's First World War movies, *The Greatest Thing in Life* (1918) even had such a moment shared by two American soldiers, one black and one white.) Moreover, as previously noted, that intimacy occurring between black and white American soldiers was a tableau which African American writers regularly employed in their war fiction. Yet *Not Only War* is different from most of these, in that it does not merely construct the battlefield moment of interracial *rapprochement* along the liberal narrative of the previously racist white character realising the error of his ways. Instead, Bob realises that he too has been involved in the 'hell' of racial convention, that his whole life has not just been wrong, but personally and socially destructive – he has condemned the relationship with the woman he loves, Miriam, to secrecy and illicitness, and his source of wealth and social status is grounded in the horror of slavery.

Not Only War therefore provides a very different polemic than *There Is Confusion*, notably in its reluctance to endorse the potential for nation building amongst the African American middle class; it was dedicated to

'The Army of the disillusioned'.[49] This is partly because it refuses to view suffering shared by black and white Americans as productive of any kind of domestic social change, or of a broader understanding of US racial history. Unlike Fauset's novel, the lessons of no-man's-land will remain there: war is not so much a learning experience or a new platform for the resolution of intranational affairs as a meaningless carnage. The novel's abrupt closure reflects the impact of premature death: it breaks off the progress of character development and halts the resolution of the novel's key relationships; it is aesthetically unsatisfying because warfare is aesthetically unsatisfying. Moreover, whilst there is hope for interracial relationships in a class-based affinity which exists beyond race, they are so hemmed in by convention that they overwhelmingly conclude in disgrace and misunderstanding rather than reconciliation.

Daly's pessimism also reflects the growing ignominy heaped upon veterans in the early Depression years; in 1932, veterans had been dispersed at gunpoint by the US army from makeshift accommodation in Washington where they had been assembled in protest at the government's refusal to cash in their veterans' bonuses early.[50] Yet the ambivalence of his work, and the work of other African Americans writing about the war – which praises the virtues of martial heroism as a code for peacetime masculinity, and which suggests at least the potential for change in race relations spurred by the extraordinary social circumstances of war – established a broad legacy. In Second World War writing, Gwendolyn Brooks, Chester Himes, Ralph Ellison and William Gardner Smith drew on motifs which these earlier writers had deployed, and more recently Rita Dove and Toni Morrison have included First World War veterans in their work. In his 1940 autobiography *Dusk of Dawn*, W. E. B. Du Bois would remark that during the First World War he had not adequately grasped 'the full horror of war and its impotence as a method of social reform'.[51] Yet the reaction of African American writers to the war was far from impotent; it cast a distinctive stamp on the African American culture of the subsequent twenty years, and would inform future generations of African Americans writing about war.

NOTES

1 Langston Hughes, 'Income Tax', 1947. Reprinted in *The Best of Simple* (New York: Hill and Wang, 1961), 65.
2 See Joanna Bourke, *Dismembering the Male: Men's Bodies, Britain and the Great War* (London: Reaktion, 1996), 107–22.
3 Jessie Redmon Fauset, *There Is Confusion* (1924; Boston: Northeastern University Press, 1989), 269.

4 Modris Eksteins, 'The Cultural Legacy of the Great War', in Jay Winter (ed.), *The Great War and the Twentieth Century* (New Haven: Yale University Press, 2000), 343.

5 Richard Wright, *Twelve Million Black Voices: A Folk History of the Negro in the United States*, with photographs by Edwin Rosskam (1941; London: Lindsay Drummond, 1947), 88–9.

6 Alain Locke, 'The New Negro', in Alain Locke (ed.), *The New Negro* (1925; New York: Simon and Schuster, 1992), 6.

7 See, for example, James R. Grossman, *Land of Hope: Chicago, Black Southerners, and the Great Migration* (Chicago University Press, 1988); and Alferdteen Harrison (ed.), *Black Exodus: The Great Migration from the American South* (Jackson: University of Mississippi Press, 1991).

8 These arguments and some of the issues addressed here are developed at greater length in my monograph *The Great War and the Culture of the New Negro* (Gainesville: University Press of Florida, 2008).

9 Jack Foner, *Blacks and The Military in US History* (New York: Praeger, 1974), 111. The figures for how many African Americans served in the army varies between historians; Foner puts this at 380,000 (119); whereas at the other end of the scale Astor lists 404,000 (Gerald Astor, *The Right to Fight: A History of African Americans in the Military* (Novato: Presido Press, 1998), 110).

10 See Arthur E. Barbeau and Florette Henri, *The Unknown Soldiers: African American Troops in World War I* (New York: Da Capo Press, 1996), 56–69, 128–9.

11 See Mark Ellis, *Race, War and Surveillance: African Americans and the United States Government during World War I* (Bloomington: Indiana University Press, 2001), 31–47, and Barbeau and Henri, *The Unknown Soldiers*, 21–32.

12 Barbeau and Henri, *The Unknown Soldiers*, 42–3.

13 Claude McKay, *Home to Harlem* (1928; London: X-Press, 2000), 3.

14 Barbeau and Henri, *Unknown Soldiers*, 116–21; see also Richard Slotkin, *Lost Battalions: The Great War and the Crisis of American Nationality* (New York: Henry Holt, 2005).

15 Barbeau and Henri, *Unknown Soldiers*, 114–15.

16 *Ibid.*, 137–63; see also Chad Williams, 'Torchbearers of Democracy: The First World War and the Figure of the African American Soldier', unpublished PhD dissertation, Princeton University, 2004, 145–54.

17 William N. Colson, 'The Failure of the Ninety-Second Division', *The Messenger*, September 1919, 22.

18 Mark Van Wienen, *Partisans and Poets: The Political Work of Poetry in the Great War* (Cambridge University Press, 1997).

19 Roscoe C. Jamison, *Negro Soldiers ('These Truly are the Brave') and Other Poems*, 2nd edn (William F. Neil: Kansas City, 1918). No pagination.

20 Leslie Pinckney Hill, 'The Black Man's Bit', in his collection *The Wings of Oppression* (Boston: Stratford, 1921), 23–4.

21 Alice Dunbar-Nelson, *Mine Eyes Have Seen*, in *The Crisis*, April 1918, 273–4.

22 See Theodore Kornweibel, *Seeing Red: Federal Campaigns Against Black Militancy, 1919–1925* (Bloomington: Indiana University Press, 1998).

23 Andrea Razafkeriefo, 'Civilization', *The Crusader*, October 1921, 20. Reprinted in Robert A. Hill (ed.), *The Crusader: A Facsimile of the Periodical* (New York: Garland Press, 1987), 1,254.

24 For the best introduction to this topic, see David Levering Lewis, *W. E. B. Du Bois: Biography of a Race, 1868–1919* (New York: Henry Holt, 1993), 515–80.

25 W. E. B. Du Bois, 'The Battle of Europe', *The Crisis*, September 1916, 216–17. Reprinted in his selection *W. E. B. Du Bois: An ABC of Colour* (International Publishers: New York, 1969), 87–8.

26 Russ Castronovo, 'Beauty Along the Colour Line: Lynching, Aesthetics, and *The Crisis*', *PMLA* 121 (2006): 1,443–59, 1,443.

27 See David Levering Lewis, *When Harlem Was in Vogue* (Oxford University Press, 1981), 14–24; Barbeau and Henri, *The Unknown Soldiers*, 178–89.

28 Cited in Barbeau and Henri, *The Unknown Soldiers*, 174.

29 The most influential analysis of this type was James Weldon Johnson's in *Black Manhattan* (1930; New York: Da Capo Press, 1991); more recently Ann Douglas has downplayed the significance of the war in relation to the New Negro Renaissance in her *Terrible Honesty: Mongrel Manhattan in the 1920s* (London: Papermac, 1997), 88. For fuller discussion of this issue, see Whalan, *The Great War and the Culture of the New Negro*, 37–46.

30 Johnson, *Black Manhattan*, 276.

31 For detailed attention to these issues, see Whalan, *The Great War and the Culture of the New Negro*.

32 The phrase 'race man' refers to an African American man who, through his personal example and frequently his political engagement, furthers the cause of African American civil rights and prosperity. See Hazel Carby, *Race Men* (Cambridge, MA: Harvard University Press, 1998).

33 Fauset, *There Is Confusion*, 243.

34 *Ibid.*, 240.

35 *Ibid.*, 253.

36 George Hutchinson, 'Aftermath: African American Literary Responses to the Great War', in Flavia Brizio-Skov (ed.), *Reconstructing Societies in the Aftermath of War: Memory, Identity, and Reconciliation* (Boca Raton: Bordighera Press, 2004), 197.

37 Richard Dyer, *White* (London: Routledge, 1997), 23.

38 Walter E. Seward, 'Who Went Over the Top?' in his collection *Negroes' Call to the Colours and Soldiers' Camp-Life Poems* (Athens, GA: Knox Institute Press, 1919), 46.

39 Victor Daly, *Not Only War* (1932; New York: AMS Press, 1970), 7.

40 See Williams, *Torchbearers of Democracy*, 268–9.

41 Daly, *Not Only War*, 13.

42 Williams's novel, which appeared serially in the *Messenger* between 1925 and 1926, was republished as *When Washington Was in Vogue* (New York: HarperCollins, 2003).

43 Daly, *Not Only War*, 40.

44 Charles H. Williams, *Sidelights on Negro Soldiers* (Boston: B. J. Brimmer, 1923), 73.

45 Robert L. Wolf, 'Les Noirs', *The Messenger*, January 1923, 578.

46 Williams, *Torchbearers of Democracy*, 268.

47 Daly, *Not Only War*, 104.

48 *Ibid.*, 106.

49 *Ibid.*, 5.

50 See Irving Bernstein, *The Lean Years: A History of the American Worker 1920–1933* (Boston: Houghton Mifflin, 1960), 437–55.

51 W. E. B. Du Bois, *Dusk of Dawn: An Essay towards an Autobiography of a Race Concept* (New York: Harcourt-Brace, 1940), 255.

Afterword
Death and the afterlife:
Britain's colonies and dominions

Michèle Barrett

Jane Urquhart's remarkable novel *The Stone Carvers* (2002) imagines a young woman, of European wood-carving ancestry, travelling to Vimy in northern France from a village near Hamilton, Ontario. Disguised as a man, she obtains work on the Canadian monument and early one morning she steals into the workshop to carve the face of one of Walter Allward's allegorical figures in the image of her dead lover Eamonn. When Allward discovers her, he is angry that she has 'ruined' his torchbearer, explaining 'he had wanted this stone youth to remain allegorical, universal, wanted him to represent everyone's lost friend, everyone's lost child'. Allward, we are told, 'wanted the stone figure to be the 66,000 dead young men who had marched through his dreams when he had conceived the memorial'. But the face Klara was carving 'had developed a personal expression', it was 'becoming a portrait', and this had 'never been his intention'. Confronted by this determined young woman, Urquhart's fictional Walter Allward realises that she has 'allowed life' to enter his monument and relents: 'you can finish carving his face', he agrees.[1]

Klara Becker's desire to impose the face of one particular young man onto the body of Allward's universal young man can be seen as a metaphor for the philosophy of commemoration that prevailed on the Western Front, and in Europe generally, after the war. The Imperial War Graves Commission was attempting to bridge a gap between the universal and national on the one hand, and the personal and individual on the other. Headstones were to be of a standard size, let into the ground on beams that would keep them in perfect rows. Famously, there would be no distinction of military rank, and hence also no distinction of civil rank, or social class. On the body of the blank headstone would be carved the face of the individual – their name, their rank and regiment, their religion, perhaps some personal words from the family. Of these markers of the individual, the name was the most important, a fact that came into its own in the commemoration of those with no known grave – the missing. At Vimy Ridge, the 11,000 names of the missing, about a sixth of Canada's casualties, form an important element of the design and structure of the monument. For the fictional Klara Becker, too, the name itself is important. As she is being helped to chisel out Eamonn O'Sullivan's name, Allward tells her to 'let it go out of your heart and into the stone'.[2]

The principle of the individual name forming the basis for modern commemoration is held up as a mark of progress – publicly naming each private soldier or naval rating is democratic.[3] The Imperial War Graves Commission's strategy, led by its Vice-Chairman, General Sir Fabian Ware, was based on equality of treatment, which meant uniformity. Fabian Ware, in *The Immortal Heritage* (1937), stressed the general principle, and many early documents of the Imperial War Graves Commission also make this clear. For some while, however, the present Commonwealth War Graves Commission (the name was changed in 1960) has claimed that the principle of equality applies not only to military rank and social class, but also to issues of 'race and creed'. This may be true now, but certainly was not true after the First World War, and given what we know about the imperial context of that war, it would be very surprising if that had been the case.

Britain's self-governing 'dominions' offer examples of memorials on the Western Front, such as Canada's Vimy Ridge and South Africa's Delville Wood, where extensive naming occurred. Whether this is inclusive is a source of debate, since black Africans were until recently ignored at Delville Wood. The colonies were a different matter altogether. How different can be decisively clarified by a letter in the archives of the Imperial War Graves Commission, to be sent to the Governors of the Crown Colonies in 1921 by Winston Churchill, then Colonial Secretary. Churchill stressed the importance of 'equality of treatment for the graves of all' and advised that local administrations 'should not erect memorials of a different nature from those adopted by the Commission'. Churchill's letter makes clear this policy does not apply to colonial natives; they are not included in 'all'. In a separate paragraph, he unites these excluded people:

The erection of memorials to the memory of native troops, carriers, etc., depends upon local conditions. In ordinary circumstances the Commission would not erect individual headstones but a central memorial in some suitable locality to be selected by the Government concerned.[4]

Important differences emerged in how the dead were commemorated in European theatres of the war and elsewhere in the world; different parts of the empire were treated differently.

BRITAIN'S AFRICAN COLONIES: EXAMPLES OF
THE IMPERIAL WAR GRAVES COMMISSION'S POLICY

In 1922, the Imperial War Graves Commission was in discussion with the colonial authorities in Africa about how to deal with the casualties of the war there. It is estimated that 'upwards of 200,000' Africans died in the First World War, a figure including labourers as well as soldiers.[5] Estimating how many porters, carriers and soldiers died in the various campaigns in Africa has proved complex; Geoffrey Hodges suggested a figure of 'far above 100,000' African deaths in the East Africa campaign alone.[6] The files of the Imperial War Graves Commission contain notes of a meeting with the Governor of Tanganyika Territory in East Africa (now Tanzania). The Commission had been canvassing opinion as to whether native Africans who had died should be individually commemorated or not. The Governor was on the side of those who thought this would be a waste of public money:

He considered that the vast Carrier Corps Cemeteries at Dar es Salaam and elsewhere should be allowed to revert to nature as speedily as possible & did not care to contemplate the statistics of the native African lives lost in trying to overcome the transportation difficulties of the campaign in East Africa.[7]

Broadly speaking, the Commission accepted the view of the British colonial authorities that Africans had not reached 'the stage of civilisation' at which individual graves would be appreciated.[8] They decided to put up 'central memorials' in the towns, commemorating unnumbered and unnamed African lives lost. They differentiated sharply between the graves of whites or Europeans (including their German enemies), and those of natives. What they called 'white graves' have been maintained in perpetuity, often through exhumation and reburial in 'concentrated' cemeteries. Many identified graves of Africans were abandoned; in a move that Commission staff wryly referred to as 'sent Missing', the names were simply reallocated to memorials to the missing. Religion was important as well as race, and there is evidence of converted Christian Africans being treated differently from their pagan brethren.[9]

Several of these 'central memorials' were put up in Africa, perhaps the best-known being the one in Mombasa, Kenya (Figure 7). Situated at the southeastern end of Jomo Kenyatta Avenue, the memorial consists of fine bronze sculptures, by J. A. Stevenson, of four types of men who contributed to the East African campaign. They include *askari*, African soldiers, often in the King's African Rifles regiment (left and centre right); Arab riflemen, usually Yemenis or Hadramouts (centre left); and porters and carriers

7. African War Memorial at Mombasa, Kenya

PA-066815

8. Recruits from the File Hills Indian Colony in Saskatchewan with their parents before the departure of the 68th, Regina, Battalion for England

(right). I use the word 'type' advisedly, for the brief was specific in requiring typicality. In 1923 the sculptor sent to East Africa for exact copies of the men's uniforms and equipment, and J. N. Cormack, the Imperial War Graves Commission's Deputy Director of Works in East Africa, obtained clothing, headgear, belts, haversacks and water bottles, and had them all shipped to London for Stevenson. For the porters, apparently there was 'no proper or "fixed" equipment issued', and 'when on the march they seldom wore puttees or sandals but protected their feet with such makeshifts of grass, skin, etc. which they could obtain'.[10]

The 'central memorials' contain no names and no numbers of men killed. Many other troops, notably from the Indian Army, were commemorated 'numerically', which meant that lists of names existed on 'nominal rolls' and printed registers but it was decided not to put them on the memorial – instead an exact number of deaths was recorded alongside the name of the regiment or military unit concerned. With these African

memorials, however, what appears are general inscriptions. For the plinth
below, in several African languages as well as in English, were the specially
composed words of Rudyard Kipling: 'This is to the memory of the Arab
and Native African troops who fought; to the Carriers and Porters who were
the feet and hands of the army; and to all other men who served and died for
their King and country in Eastern Africa in the Great War, 1914–1918. If you
fight for your country, even if you die, your sons will remember your name.'
Kipling was a genius at the finely calibrated epigraph in tricky colonial
situations. He was perfectly aware that these men would need to be
remembered by their families, as neither the colonial authorities nor the
Imperial War Graves Commission would be giving their names an afterlife.

Similar memorials were erected in Nairobi and Dar es Salaam, and also in
western Africa, including one in Lagos (now dismantled). On the present-
day Commonwealth War Graves Commission website the figure for native
deaths in East Africa is put at 'almost 50,000' and it is stated that 'as no
complete record of their names exists, no names appear on the memorials'.[11]
There is undoubtedly no complete record today, but in the years following
the First World War the argument about inadequate records often functioned as a screen for discrimination. Taking the issues of 'race' and 'creed',
I will give some examples of systematic inequality of treatment in the work
of the Imperial War Graves Commission in Africa. Consider the following
policy ruling made at the IWGC on 24 November 1925, and stated by its
Principal Assistant Secretary, Lord Arthur Browne. It concerns cemetery
memorial registers for natives. Browne begins by adverting to Fabian Ware's
view that 'identical treatment' of British and native troops should be
accorded so far as 'circumstances permit'. From this he concludes that
registers should be compiled, which would include the names of native
soldiers, and also followers 'to the extent that satisfactory records may exist'.
Browne then sails confidently into the definition of a 'native', which for him
includes Indians, Egyptians, Arabs, and East, West and South Africans, 'but
not South African coloured people'. As we shall see, although he regarded
Indians as 'natives', he was far more sympathetic to Indian cultures and
religions than he was to African. Browne continues with a ruling on the
position of natives buried in cemeteries but not accorded an IWGC headstone: these names, he says, should be put in the registers of appropriate
memorials, but not in the registers of the cemeteries. He concludes: 'if we
were to include all the names of the latter class in the cemetery register
I think we should be unnecessarily drawing attention to the fact that we
have neglected to commemorate by a headstone'.[12] Earlier that year, in
discussing graves in Nyasaland (now Malawi), Browne's opinion was

recorded as being that 'in the case of Native African soldiers headstones should not be erected unless obliged to do so'.[13]

The purpose of Browne's policy becomes clear only when one appreciates that native graves in Africa were not usually maintained, that mostly they were not accorded a headstone, and that many of their known occupants were redefined as 'missing'. By and large Africans, whether soldiers or labourers, were not commemorated individually, and their graves were allowed to 'revert to nature'. These decisions were not entirely based on arguments about 'race', but were also about religion (or in War Graves Commission parlance, 'creed'). Some instances can be taken from a summary of decisions given by Browne in an internal memo in 1924. Regarding the policy of the Commission in East Africa, we hear that

at the 159th Management Committee Meeting the P.A.S. [Principal Assistant Secretary, i.e. Browne] stated that the usual policy of the Commission was not to erect headstones on Indians and Natives although identification of Natives might be known, but European Cape Boys would be commemorated.[14]

He further states that 'coloured South Africans are not reckoned as Natives. They are half castes and should be treated as European Christians and commemorated precisely as British soldiers.' Similarly, as regards West Indian Natives 'i.e. Negroes in West Indian Regiments', they were 'commemorated individually where buried in East Africa – Christians'. The general rule for African natives, however, was 'no individual commemoration'.[15]

Commission officials went to some lengths to administer these policy decisions. Clerk of Works Milner, overseeing the 'concentration' of graves into selected cemeteries in East Africa, engaged in a 'close scrutiny of the remains' that he found in a common grave at Salaita Hill. He identified the remains, by shape of skull and other anthropometric devices, to be those of 14 Europeans and 6 Indians.[16] On the same trip he found another common grave, near the railway station at Taveta. He reports that 'on 15th May 1923 I excavated the 11 graves at this place and gathered 11 remains who were undoubtedly not Europeans as the shape of the skulls, leg and arm bones, were different, also the teeth were in perfect condition.'[17] The image of Imperial War Graves Commission employees picking through human remains in order to 'race' them is unexpected and disturbing.

Religion was an important issue. Following the widespread practice among British travellers in Africa, the natives were regarded simply as 'pagans', as seen in the blunt memo that 'Director of Works on tour stated that Pagan Natives have no regard for graves, . . . and Graves would revert to Nature.'[18] In 1925 the Commission was working on the cemetery at Rufiji

River in East Africa, with Mr Cormack again in charge. Captain Miskin, the IWGC Registrar, wrote in June that year to the Director of Records, attempting to rescue two graves of Christians from the 'revert to nature' policy being applied to African natives: 'The burial book shows that Hospital Boy Zensuriguiza was a Roman Catholic, and 13050 Cape Boy William was evidently a Christian too. I think Major Cormack should be asked about those two cases, and whether their bodies could be found and removed to Morogoro' [cemetery].[19] The headstone decision was, on the ground, an evaluative one. Major Cormack would have been sympathetic to the request. In a 1922 report he had noted that among 'numerous other natives who died in the vicinity', only nine had been buried in the Christian cemetery, and he concluded, 'the inference I draw is, that they may be regarded as Christians and *worthy of commemoration* by the standard type of Headstone' [my italics]. [20]

By 1930, these policy decisions had become routinised. Arthur Browne, summarising the position for West Africa [Gold Coast (now Ghana), Nigeria and Sierra Leone], was able to state that

so far as I know nothing has occurred to alter the policy of the Commission under which all known European graves in West Africa will have headstones and all Natives (whether buried in known graves or not) will be commemorated on memorials.

He added that 'for statistical purposes I should imagine that the only course practicable for the great majority of West African natives is to count them as missing'. [21]

INDIAN CULTURAL MATTERS AND
THE MEMORIAL AT BASRA

In comparison with African native troops, the soldiers of the Indian Army were highly regarded by the men of the Imperial War Graves Commission. A perhaps unexpected side to Lord Arthur Browne emerges here in his knowledge of Indian cultural forms – it transpires that his father had been in the Bengal Civil Service. In September 1923 Arthur Browne explained to the Director of Works that 'the religion of natives of India can always be told from their names except perhaps in the case of some of the followers'; he even offered to get involved personally: 'if you will send me down names I will probably be able to say what they are', adding that 'Bhagwan Tikkum would be a Hindu'.[22] Earlier that year Browne had written to Sir Frederick Kenyon, the Director of the British Museum, for information on a point on which he had drawn a blank at the India Office – what religious emblem to use on the headstones of Indians buried in France, 'whose religion is given as "Animist"'. In the African context, such people would simply be 'pagans' (and there would be no headstones to worry about), but Browne takes a far more relativist stance here – 'as far as my experience goes Indian Animists appear to worship the spirits of the jungle, water, mountains, etc', he says chattily – and wonders if it might be best to put up a headstone without any religious emblem.[23] By the end of 1925, Browne was getting frustrated at the fact that the India Office was not willing to take responsibility for the spelling of Indian names, which he said 'does not absolve the Commission from doing their best to engrave inscriptions at which no one with a knowledge of India can reasonably cavil'.[24]

The Imperial War Graves Commission was aware that many mistakes had been made during the war in the disposition of dead Indian soldiers and followers. After the war a policy was worked out, attempting to reduce some of the damage (or, more accurately, the evidence of what had happened). The circumstances at Gallipoli, where many Indian soldiers died, led Lieutenant Colonel Hughes (the IWGC's Director of Works there) to discuss the matter with General Cox and determine a policy. One simple principle was that 'in the case where Hindoos and Moslems are mixed up together, and are unidentified, a decision should be made as to which shall be ignored'.[25] Similarly, 'where individual Moslems are buried in Christian Cemeteries, these graves should not be marked, or action taken'. The policy regarding Moslems was no exhumation: 'Mussulman graves should not be touched or bodies removed'. The policy for 'Hindoos' included Sikhs and Gurkhas, and was directed at redressing the proscribed burial of Hindu soldiers: 'where it is known *for certain* that Hindoos have been buried, their remains should be exhumed, burnt, and taken out to sea to be scattered on the water by Hindoo soldiers, under a Hindoo officer, or if a Hindoo regiment is returning to India, they should be given an opportunity to take the ashes back with them'. After that, a tablet was to be erected near where the remains were burnt, naming the soldiers who 'fell near this spot'.[26]

The major casualties of the Indian Army in the First World War occurred in Mesopotamia, and are commemorated there on the Basra Memorial. This was unveiled in the late 1920s, standing on the bank of the Shatt-al-Arab waterway. In the early 1990s it was removed, by Saddam Hussein, and re-erected in the desert near Nasiriyah. Invading British forces found it in 2003, and took great interest in finding their regimental comrades of the First World War (particularly of the Black Watch) and in helping to restore the dilapidated monument. Approximately 8,000 British soldiers were commemorated there, by name, in the usual way. But for the Indian soldiers, the Commission had eighty years earlier taken a decision that departed significantly from the principle of equality of treatment. A telegram sent on 4 August 1928 from the Commission to the Indian Army in Simla states the facts baldly: 'Basra Memorial. Total number of missing from Indian Army commemorated by name officers 665[,] numerically other ranks 33,222'.[27] Put plainly, the Indian casualties were differentiated by rank: the 665 Indian officers were commemorated individually by name, as were British casualties of all ranks, while the huge number of Indian 'other ranks' were recorded on the monument merely as the number of men killed from each military unit.

To take an example, consider the wording from a photograph of Panel 55 of the Basra Memorial, on which the deaths of men from the 36th Sikh Regiment are commemorated.[28] On the left at the top of this panel are the names of two British officers, Captain J. Grey and Captain A. D. Martin. Ranging to the right of them are six Indian officers, Subadars Gurmukh Singh, Harnam Singh, Jagat Singh and Jaimal Singh, and Jemadars Hakim Singh and Harnam Singh – and underneath is a line that reads 'AND 149 OTHER INDIAN SOLDIERS'. The pattern is repeated below for the two units of the Garhwal Rifles, the first naming one subadar (as spelt here) and 51 'other Indian soldiers' and the second naming two subadars and 65 'other Indian soldiers'. The journalist Fergal Keane, visiting the Basra Memorial in 2003, commented that the inscription to 'Subhadar Mahanga and 1,770 other Indian soldiers' was 'a sentence as sad as any I've read in war'.[29]

The names of the dead 36th Sikhs other ranks are not engraved on the memorial, but they are in the Register. Generally, cemeteries and memorials have a published register available to visitors in a box at the entrance, listing more particulars, including family details, than is possible to put on a memorial. Registers for the memorial at Basra were compiled in the usual way, so we can see the names of those men who were commemorated numerically: the first entry reads 'Amar Singh, Havr., [Havildar], 2645. 1st Feb, 1917. Son of Ram Singh, of Sherpur Gobind, Hoshiartpur, Punjab'.[30] But if one looks for the name of Singh, A. in the online Debt of Honour Register of the Commonwealth War Graves Commission, one will not find it. If you enter the name Singh – the common Sikh family name – in the CWGC database, for all forces, for the entire duration of the war, a total of 12 records appears, 6 of whom are on the Basra Memorial.[31] Captain Martin, on the other hand, is easily found, with his military and personal details, and is 'remembered with honour' and 'commemorated in perpetuity' by the CWGC. The 'certificate' that appears for printing shows an unusual image:

a display table containing two large books, a map and pictures of Iraq, some text and a caption reading (note the precise wording) 'The Rolls Of Honour held at the Commission's Head Office commemorating by name all the Commonwealth casualties who died in Iraq during the two World Wars'. Closer inspection of these Rolls, held in Maidenhead, reveals that the names of the Indian rank and file do indeed appear in them – the printed registers of the Basra Memorial rather than the memorial itself have been used as their basis.[32] The text indicates that it is difficult to go to Iraq at the moment and so the Commission has erected this memorial here.

Why are so few Singhs on the database?[33] Unlike the native Africans of the interwar period, these Singhs have not been deliberately 'sent missing' by the present Commonwealth War Graves Commission. Since the early 1990s the policy has been to 'correct the anomalies' of the past.[34] The original registers for the Basra Memorial adopted the usual practice, for the British names, of putting a surname or family name first, followed by the given name (mostly Christian names). For the Indian names, however, the order was reversed. Page 307 of the Basra register shows the switch from British to Indian casualties, reading WOODWARD, Lt Edward Seymer; WOODYATT, Capt NGR; WYNNE, Capt. Eric Ralph Lovall; WYNNE, 2nd Lt W, then ABDUL ALI, Follr [Follower]; ABDUL GHANI, Dvr [Driver]; ABDUL HAQ, Havr [Havildar]; ABDUL MAJID Follr.[35] It is not clear what the logic for this reversal was, although there may have been good reasons for it. Its consequences are, however, odd. The only way to find those men is to type the names in the wrong boxes. So, for example, the details of Ajab Singh will come up if you search for [Surname] Ajab, [Initial] S. Even the Indian officers whose names *were* actually engraved on the memorial are hard to find in the modern database. Then, there was discrimination by military rank (and no doubt also by social rank). Now, that discrimination has been, inadvertently we assume, reversed. It is easier to find an Indian follower or mule driver who only had one name recorded in the register, for example driver Anokhi. The CWGC database makes it unlikely that anyone searching for an ancestor who died in the pre-partition Indian Army in Mesopotamia would find the information sought. The Basra Memorial continues to pose the problem of how to present an appearance of equal treatment when differences of rank, race and creed have determined whether or not any given individual is commemorated. As Director of Records Chettle put it when handpicking the wording of an inscription at Mosul, 'it is the only method I can think of by which to avoid the difficulty that the British names will be recorded on the Basra memorial but not the Indian names'.[36] A certain casuistry is an element of the

Commission's impression management here. At the 143rd meeting of the
IWGC the Vice-Chairman, Fabian Ware, 'asked the meeting for sugges-
tions as to an inscription indicating that the names of those commemorated
were in the register' (but not on the memorial). After discussion, a proposal
was agreed: 'Mr Kipling suggested that a Persian word, which meant "The
Book of the Dead" might be inscribed on the Register Box, with the English
words "Their names are in the Book".'[37]

The decision taken about Basra was in line with other memorials in the
Middle East. In 1924, Arthur Browne had a discussion with General Cobbe
of the India Office about the memorial at Port Tewfik, on the Suez Canal.
Cobbe thought that 'the engraving of the names of all Indian soldiers would
have little interest', and that 'they would never be seen by the relatives'.[38]
(The policy was inconsistent: at Gallipoli, for instance, it was belatedly
realised that Indian names might be added to the Cape Helles memorial,
and they were.)[39] In line with its later thinking, the Commonwealth War
Graves Commission replaced the Port Tewfik memorial, when it was
destroyed in Israeli–Egyptian fighting in 1967, with a memorial near
Cairo on which the four thousand names in the registers were actually
engraved. It appears that the present-day Commission is intending, after the
war in Iraq, to do something similar.

VIMY RIDGE AND FIRST NATIONS CANADIANS

Perhaps the finest of the national memorials on the Western Front is Walter
Allward's Vimy Ridge: a successful collaboration between architecture and
sculpture, it is a modernist masterpiece. The memorial was the object of an
enormous pilgrimage when it was opened in 1936. The ninetieth anniversary of the battle of Vimy Ridge, 2007, was marked by the restoration of
Allward's magnificent memorial, and another pilgrimage from Canada. The
memorial's importance as a marker of 'monumental history' sits hand in
hand with its aesthetic modernism, exemplified in the soaring twin pylons,
representing France and Canada: the twin peoples of anglophone and
francophone Canada. Attention focuses repeatedly on the twin pylons, on
the figure of Canada mourning her fallen sons, and on the 11,000 or so
names of the missing carved into the base at the back. Less attention is paid
to the complex, sometimes troubling, allegorical figures, with names such as
Truth, Charity and Sacrifice. Laura Brandon has recovered their history,
material and iconographic. The allegorical meanings are in an explicitly
Christian register – they meditate the relation of individual and collective
suffering and redemption. These figures came to Allward in a dream, he

said, and dreamlike they remain. The easiest to grasp, and the one con-
stantly reproduced, is that usually entitled *Canada Mourning Her Fallen
Sons*, otherwise *Canada brooding over the graves of her valiant dead*, or
Canada 'Bereft'. This figure, modelled by a young Englishwoman in
Allward's London studio, had, he thought, 'shoulders wide enough to
carry the sorrows of dead sons'.[40] The resolutely Christian iconography –
faith, hope, charity, the winged angels of knowledge – are central to
Allward's original conception. What does this Christian view of the world
exclude? Vimy Ridge, with its twin pylons representing Canada and France,
replicates on a more minor scale the central exclusion of the South African
memorial at Delville Wood. There the twin races of the Anglos and the
Boers, represented in a statue of Castor and Pollux and 'expressing Anglo-
Africaner racial unity',[41] exclude all native Africans, an exclusion that the
present government of South Africa has recently done its best to correct at
the site. At Vimy Ridge the symbolically excluded group are the First
Nations Canadians.

Canadian historians such as Fred Gaffen and James Dempsey have
researched the involvement of First Nations Canadians in the First World
War,[42] and official publications such as *Native Soldiers: Foreign Battlefields*
have also recently drawn attention to this issue.[43] It is estimated that
approximately 4,000 First Nations men volunteered, and that approximately 400 were killed. Accounts of their participation in the war show
that these native men were disproportionately admired as snipers and as
despatch runners. Henry Norwest, with an outstanding sniper's tally of 115
officially observed hits and winner of the Military Medal and Bar, has been
described in the trope of an animal hunting stereotype: 'frequently in the
darkest hours of the night he actually penetrated the enemy lines, where he
waited and watched, finally making his kill at early dawn, and then returned
safely to his own lines'.[44] The most detailed account remains Duncan
Campbell Scott's long official 1919 essay on 'Canadian Indians and the
Great World War'; Scott was the Deputy Superintendent for Indian Affairs
in Ottawa.[45] There are also first-hand accounts, such as Mike Mountain
Horse's chapter on the war in his memoir *My People, the Bloods* (1979) and
the visual 'war deed' that he had made of his experiences.[46] Mountain Horse
was insistent that 'the fighting spirit of my tribe was not quenched through
reservation life', that the bravery of 'our warriors of old' was shown in the
numbers of them who volunteered to fight. But he asked himself, as he
listened one night to an enemy bomber over the lines in France: 'where is
the God that the white man taught the Indian to believe in? Why does He
allow this terrible destruction?'[47]

One image stands out as emblematic of the complex and powerful social, cultural and political relations in play: a photograph of First Nations recruits posed in uniform with their parents and tribal leaders (Figure 8).[48] It forms the cover image of a Veterans Affairs booklet entitled *Native Soldiers Foreign Battlefields* and was included in Scott's original essay. These men volunteered from the File Hills Colony in Saskatchewan, and the white man in the centre of the photograph is William M. Graham, an Indian Commissioner, who had set up the File Hills Colony in the period 1901–4. File Hills has been described as 'a model agricultural colony', made up of 'progressive young Indians [who] appreciate[d] their share in the advantages of civilization and were ready to fight for it when the test came'.[49] William Graham was an ambitious man and a key figure in selling off Indian land.[50] One of the heavy ironies of this period is the fact that the Indian land was sold for post-war veteran settler land schemes, for which the Indian veterans of the war were not usually eligible. Graham's personal memoir of his 'treaty days' contains a selection from the letters written to him by Indian soldiers who were fighting in France. Graham declares that these letters 'indicate the spirit of patriotism, loyalty and endurance that filled these boys and men from the reserves, these wards of the Government who went so willingly to war when they could so easily have remained at home'.[51] There is much in the letters to warrant Graham's judgement. But how could he select and print, in this context, the following from Harry Stonechild, in France?

Mr Graham, did you ever think for a moment and say: Are we White people witnessing the vanishing of a great race full of integrity and promise, and letting them come over here and be cleared off the map? If so, put a stop to it and have me claimed back to File Hills where I will make the best man you ever had in that Colony. Could it be possible, Mr Graham, I wonder?[52]

Some of those First Nations Canadians who were 'cleared off the map' in the First World War are recorded in the registers of the War Graves Commission and in the Canadian virtual war memorial. The name of Lieutenant Cameron Brant, who was killed in 1915, is 'commemorated in perpetuity' on the Menin Gate (at Ypres in Belgium). But the official commemorative coverage is very patchy. The roll of honour associated with the 'Six [First] Nations' on the Brantford war memorial lists 40 names, many of which are not in the CWGC database. After the war, the British Prince of Wales visited the town of Brantford, Ontario, to unveil a bronze tablet containing the names of the Six Nations soldiers who had made 'the supreme sacrifice in France'.[53] The tablet, donated to the Six

Nations, remains enigmatic; its present whereabouts are unknown and a photograph of the ceremony appears to be the only image of it.[54]

It is difficult to make many generalisations about this complex set of attitudes and practices. The contrast between how the native dead of Britain's African colonies and dead Indian soldiers were treated is a striking one. In the case of the colonies I have looked at in Africa, the Imperial War Graves Commission clearly did not apply any principle of equality of treatment. These instances provide the most egregious cases of an acknowledged 'policy' based on unequal treatment of 'whites' and 'natives'. Graves of Africans were simply abandoned, and left to 'revert to nature', and the names of those buried in them were not commemorated. This was the case even where adequate records existed. Similarly, African religious or cultural beliefs were attributed no value, and a sharp distinction was made between 'pagans', and those Africans who had adopted Christianity and were treated as honorary whites. (Ironically, according to one missionary in East Africa, many Africans jettisoned their Christian attachments and Western clothes, and reverted to their previous cultural identities, in order to avoid being pressed into military service.)[55]

The casualties of the Indian Army were treated with far greater respect. In many instances (though not all) in the aftermath of fighting in Africa, Indian soldiers were commemorated individually when native African soldiers were not. Officers of the Imperial War Graves Commission were notably more interested in, and respectful of, varying cultural and religious traditions with regard to the disposition of the bodies of Indian soldiers in many different locations around the world. In many cases, however, pragmatic solutions were found for errors made through haste or ignorance, or for whatever other reason, resulting in transgression of key precepts, such as the decision to commemorate on the Basra Memorial numerically, rather than engrave the names of, the 33,000 Indian 'other ranks' who died in Mesopotamia.

In both the African and Indian cases, the Imperial War Graves Commission was working in tandem with local colonial officials on the ground, or with the India Office and other authorities in London. The IWGC's formal commitment to equality, presented publicly through the views of its Vice-Chairman Fabian Ware, appeared liberal and progressive in relation to the attitudes evinced by the other players on these colonial scenes. The IWGC, founded in 1917, was unlikely to have been able, had it wanted in that colonial context, to mount any radical challenge to established attitudes and practices concerning native peoples.

The Canadian memorial at Vimy Ridge invites us to consider the cultural politics of a memorial holding a central place in the national affect of an erstwhile self-governed, white-settled 'dominion' of the British empire. Vimy Ridge poses questions, related to the insistently Christian content of its iconography, about who is included and who is excluded. Interestingly, at the end of the approach to the memorial is the site of the memorial to the Moroccan division, and around this, splintering away from the dominating presence of the Vimy memorial's white stone for a white Canada, there have accreted many other small and specific memorials of ethnic and national minorities. Beneath France's memorial 'Aux Morts de la Division Marocaine', itself a very modest affair currently situated at the exit of the Vimy Ridge car park, are small plaques paying tribute to others who died for France – 'volontaires Hellènes' [Greek volunteers], 'volontaires Juifs' [Jewish], 'volontaires Suédois' [Swedish], 'volontaires Armeniens' [Armenian], 'volontaires Tchècoslovaques' [Czechoslovak], 'volontaires étrangers' [generic foreigners] and to some of France's colonial troops, including the 4th and 7th Tirailleurs and the 8th Zouaves. These small tablets, which you have to stoop to read, create a commemorative melting pot of nationality, ethnicity and religion, at ground level, in the shadow of Walter Allward's imposing, soaring, modernist triumph.

As far as the Commonwealth War Graves Commission is concerned, their policy has been where possible to 'correct the anomalies' caused by the unequal treatment of the interwar period. At a cautious pace, new memorials are being constructed in which the names not engraved on memorials after the First World War but held in registers are being engraved. Indicative of the current commitment to equality, Director General Richard Kellaway sent me 'Let Us Die Like Brothers', a CD-ROM educational resource revisiting the tragedy of the sinking of the SS *Mendi* in 1917, in which more than 600 members of the South African Native Labour Corps died on their way to serve in France. Through the story of a Xhosa boy named Samuel, the presentation recalls the failure of the authorities to notify the bereaved families of their loss, and emphasises the poor treatment of these labourers at the time. Endorsed by the High Commissioner for South Africa in London, this Commonwealth War Graves Commission resource, we are told, 'redresses some of the imbalance' caused by lack of information available to young people about the sacrifices made by black people during the two world wars. The programme focuses at some length on the care taken by the Commission to reproduce correctly the names of the victims of the tragedy on its memorial at Hollybrook, near

Southampton. In line with the Commission's respect for the individual name of even the most humble casualty, the lists have been checked and some names have been recarved, in a recent restoration of the memorial. One piece of information not given is that when the SS *Mendi* sank, native casualties outside Europe were generally not commemorated by name (if at all). If that ship had sunk earlier on in its voyage from South Africa, those names would have joined those of the other Africans in the care of the Imperial War Graves Commission – and be lost for good. Perhaps, in silently 'correcting' inequalities rather than frankly admitting the exclusions of the past, the Commission is still concerned with projecting an *appearance* of equality.

NOTES

This research was assisted by a small research grant from the British Academy, for which I am grateful. Dr Tracey Loughran, of Cardiff University, acted as research assistant for part of the project: many thanks. This chapter is based on a talk given at Queen's University, Kingston (Ontario), and at the Post-Colonial Studies seminar at the Institute of English Studies, London University – my thanks to the respective organisers, Roberta Hamilton and Sumita Mukherjee. I would also like to thank Nadia Atia, Santanu Das and Gilly Furse.

1 Jane Urquhart, *The Stone Carvers* (London: Bloomsbury, 2002), 336–40.
2 Urquhart, *The Stone Carvers*, 377.
3 Thomas Laqueur suggests that the need to name all these names ('commemorative hypernominalism') arose because there was no agreement on what had been achieved. Thomas W. Laqueur, 'Memory and Naming in the Great War', in John R. Gillis (ed.), *Commemorations: The Politics of National Identity* (Princeton University Press, 1994), 150–67.
4 Commonwealth War Graves Commission Archive, Maidenhead, UK (hereafter CWGC Archive), File Reference WG5 (Catalogue number 221, Box 1001). The archive's catalogue was published in 1977, compiled by Alex King, and is available at the British Library (Manuscripts Room).
5 Hew Strachan, *The First World War*, vol. I *To Arms* (Oxford University Press, 2001), 497. See also Melvin Page, 'Black Men in a White Man's War', in M. Page (ed.), *Africa and the First World War*, (Basingstoke: Macmillan, 1987), 14.
6 Geoffrey Hodges, 'Military Labour in East Africa and its Impact on Kenya' in Page (ed.), *Africa and the First World War*, 148.
7 CWGC Archive, File WG122 Pt 2. The carriers' death rate was much higher than the death rate of African soldiers: Hodges puts it at over 20 per cent for Nigerian carriers (many of whom were drafted to East Africa), compared with an average death rate among the military of 7 per cent. Approximately half the deaths of carriers were from dysentery, caused by them being given the wrong food, which was not cooked properly. 'Military Labour', 143.
8 The original (1921) report to the IWGC from Major Evans in British East Africa asserted that 'most of the Natives who died are of a semi-savage nature and do

not attach any sentiment to marking the graves of their dead'; his report, including a proposal for central memorials in towns, formed the basis of the IWGC approach there (CWGC Archive, File WG122 Pt 1). In 1923 Lord Arthur Browne, writing to consult the Governor of Nigeria, explained the decision not to commemorate British East African natives individually: there was the problem of poor records, and 'also because it was realised that the stage of civilisation reached by most of the East African tribes was not such as would enable them to appreciate commemoration in this manner' (CWGC Archive File 243/1 Pt 1).

9 Detailed examples of all these steps, drawn from the CWGC archive, are set out in Michèle Barrett, 'Subalterns at War: First World War Colonial Forces and the Politics of the Imperial War Graves Commission', in *Interventions*, vol. 9 (3) 2007, 468–70.

10 CWGC Archive File WG 219/12, Letter sent by J. N. Cormack

11 Commonwealth War Graves Commission website, www.cwgc.org, accessed 19 August 2008.

12 CWGC Archive, File WG 290, 'Rulings'.

13 CWGC Archive, File WG 219/12.

14 *Ibid.*

15 *Ibid.*

16 Barrett, 'Subalterns at War', 467.

17 CWGC Archive, File WG 122/8/2.

18 CWGC Archive, File WG 219/12.

19 CWGC Archive, File WG 219/12/Pt1.

20 CWGC Archive, File WG 122/8/2.

21 CWGC Archive, File WG 243/1.

22 CWGC Archive File WG 1267 (27/9/1923).

23 CWGC Archive File WG 1267 (4/4/1923).

24 CWGC Archive File WG 219/16/1.

25 CWGC Archive, File WG 909/5.

26 *Ibid.*

27 CWGC Archive, File WG 219/19.

28 Photograph supplied by The War Graves Photographic Project, www.twgpp.org

29 Fergal Keane, 'Basra's "lost" imperial war grave' 20/9/2003. http://news.bbc.co.uk/1/hi/world/middle_east/3124828.stm (accessed 24 May 2009).

30 *Register of the Basra Memorial, Iraq* (London: Imperial War Graves Commission, 1930), 980 (consulted in the Department of Printed Books at the Imperial War Museum, London).

31 As at February 2009.

32 There are many Singhs in the online database but Singh is not recorded as a 'surname' there; to find them you must enter a common Sikh given name in the surname search box.

33 To make the new Rolls of Honour displayed at Maidenhead, the Commission has presumably digitised the registers of the memorial. It seems unlikely that they would type out or scan 33,000 names into the computer and not include

them on the Debt of Honour database. A look at the Basra Memorial's register, housed at the Imperial War Museum in London, showed that all but two of the 153 casualties from the 36th Sikhs carried the name Singh. Many thousands of those names are Singh.

34 Personal correspondence: letter 20 November 2007 to the author from Mr Richard Kellaway, Director-General of the CWGC – 'when names have been recorded in registers, there was the option to correct the anomalies. In 1995 my predecessor therefore took the decision that these inequalities should be corrected . . .'

35 *Register of the Basra Memorial, Iraq*, 307.

36 CWGC Archive, File WG 219/19 Pt 1 28/4/25.

37 CWGC Archive, File WG 219/19 Pt 2.

38 CWGC Archive, File WG 219/16/1, 7/3/1924.

39 CWGC Archive, File WG 219/16/1, 30/1/1925.

40 The maquette of 'Canada' is on permanent display at the Military Communications and Electronics Museum in Kingston, Ontario. See Laura Brandon, *Art or Memorial? The Forgotten History of Canada's War Art* (University of Calgary Press, 2006), 7–16; see also Laura Brandon, 'Making Memory: *Canvas of War* and the Vimy Sculptures', in Briton C. Busch (ed.), *Canada and the Great War: Western Front Association Papers* (Montreal & Kingston: McGill and Queen's University Press, 2003), 203–15.

41 Bill Nasson, *Springboks on the Somme: South Africa in the Great War 1914–1918* (Johannesburg: Penguin Books, 2007), 229.

42 Fred Gaffen, *Forgotten Soldiers* (Penticton, BC: Theytus Books, 1985); L. James Dempsey, *Warriors of the King: Prairie Indians in World War I* (Regina: Canadian Plains Research Centre, 1999).

43 Janice Summerby, *Native Soldiers: Foreign Battlefields* (Ottawa: Veterans Affairs Canada, 2005).

44 Dempsey, *Warriors*, 52

45 Duncan Campbell Scott, 'The Canadian Indians and the Great World War', in 'Various Authorities', *Canada in the Great World War* (Toronto: United Publishers of Canada Limited, 1919), vol. III, Appendix 1, 285–328.

46 Mike Mountain Horse, *My People The Bloods*, ed. Hugh A. Dempsey (Calgary: Glenbow-Alberta Institute and Blood Tribal Council, 1979). Mountain Horse's 'war deed', recording his First World War experiences in visual form on cow hide, is copyrighted to the Esplanade Museum, Medicine Hat, Canada, and reproduced in Dominiek Dendooven and Piet Chielens (eds.), *World War I: Five Continents in Flanders* (Ypres: Lannoo, 2008), 94.

47 Mountain Horse, *My People The Bloods*, 143, 144.

48 The image appeared in the fascinating exhibition 'Man–Culture–War' in 2008 at the In Flanders Fields Museum, Ypres, about the presence of troops from five continents in Ypres.

49 Scott, 'The Canadian Indians', 307–8.

50 See E. Brian Titley, 'The Ambitions of Commissioner Graham' in Titley, *A Narrow Vision: Duncan Campbell Scott and the Administration of Indian Affairs in Canada* (Vancouver: University of British Columbia Press, 1986).

51 William M. Graham, *Treaty Days: Reflections of an Indian Commissioner* (Calgary: Glenbow Musuem, 1991), 112.

52 *Ibid.*, 105.

53 F. Douglas Reville, *History of the County of Brant* (Brantford, Ontario: Brant Historical Society, 1920), 200–1. The Annual Report of the Department of Indian Affairs gives a little more detail, referring to 'a bronze tablet inscribed with the names of eighty-eight members of the Six Nations Indians who had given their lives ... headed by the names of Lieutenant Cameron D. Brant ... and Lieutenant J. D. Moses, an Indian Aviator, who died in a German prison camp' (Ottawa: Dominion of Canada Sessional Paper, No. 27, 1919), 7–8.

54 'The Prince of Wales at the Brant memorial', available through the website of the Brantford Public Library: http://Brantford.library.on.ca/genealogy/royalvisits.php#1919 (accessed 23 May 2009).

55 Elizabeth Knox, *Signal on the Mountain: The Gospel in Africa's Uplands before the First World War* (Brookvale NSW: Acorn Press, 1991), 205–6. 'The army needed porters. For this they preferred mission people to pagans ... The fear of being caught for war service made people revert to native dress, and burn their books ... The recruiting officers would come to a village on Sunday in order to catch the Christians easily.'

Index

Made in the USA
Columbia, SC
13 July 2018